HONOR'S VOICE

HONOR'S VOICE

❧

The Transformation of
Abraham Lincoln

DOUGLAS L. WILSON

Alfred A. Knopf / New York / 1998

THIS IS A BORZOI BOOK
PUBLISHED BY ALFRED A. KNOPF, INC.

Copyright © 1998 by Douglas L. Wilson
Maps copyright © 1998 by Alfred A. Knopf, Inc.
All rights reserved under International and Pan-American Copyright
Conventions. Published in the United States by Alfred A. Knopf, Inc.,
New York, and simultaneously in Canada by Random House of Canada
Limited, Toronto. Distributed by Random House, Inc., New York.

www.randomhouse.com

Library of Congress Cataloging-in-Publication Data
Wilson, Douglas L.
Honor's voice : the transformation of Abraham Lincoln / by
Douglas L. Wilson. — 1st ed.
p.   cm.
Includes bibliographical references and index.
ISBN 0-679-40788-x (alk. paper)
1. Lincoln, Abraham, 1809–1865—Political career before 1861.
2. Presidents—United States—Biography.   3. Illinois—Politics
and government—To 1865.   I. Title.
E457.35.W547   1998
973.7'092—dc21
[B]   97-37586   CIP

Manufactured in the United States of America
First Edition

For Sharon

Can Honor's voice provoke the silent dust . . . ?

– *Thomas Gray,*
"Elegy Written in a Country Churchyard"

Contents

HONOR'S VOICE

INTRODUCTION

WHEN ABRAHAM LINCOLN was nominated for the presidency in 1860, the leading Republican paper in Illinois, the *Chicago Press and Tribune*, assigned John L. Scripps, one of its principal editors, to write a brief campaign biography. While Lincoln duly cooperated by furnishing biographical information and answering questions, the candidate had one serious reservation. "The chief difficulty I had to encounter," Scripps wrote to Lincoln's law partner and biographer, William H. Herndon, "was to induce him to communicate the homely facts and incidents of his early life. He seemed to be painfully impressed with the extreme poverty of his early surroundings – the utter absence of all romantic and heroic elements." Knowing that there was electoral gold to be mined from Lincoln's humble beginnings, Scripps pressed his inquiries until, as he reported to Herndon, Lincoln finally protested: " 'Why Scripps' said he, on one occasion, 'it is a great piece of folly to attempt to make anything out of my early life. It can all be condensed into a single sentence, and that sentence you will find in Gray's Elegy:
"The short and simple annals of the poor."
That's my life, and that's all you or any one else can make of it.' "[1]

But if Lincoln did not think his early life could be idealized and did not welcome a romanticized version of it, his wishes were coolly ignored. His most influential campaign biographers, such as Scripps and William Dean Howells, made much of their candidate's bottom-rung beginnings, which served to accentuate his dramatic rise and make it appear all the more remarkable. Predictably, his detractors found ways to use this against him, as when the editor of an opposition newspaper in his former neighborhood rehearsed his youthful career in unflattering terms under the title of "A Romance of Reality."[2] But the successful prosecution of the Civil War and his assassination immediately thereafter would change all that. With his murder and subsequent martyrdom, Lincoln's ascension from poverty and obscurity to the highest office in the land was widely seen as miraculous, or something very near it, and his entire career became invested with symbolic meaning.

The romanticization of Lincoln's early life thus had its beginnings in the historical circumstances and romantic ethos of the nineteenth century, but it has persisted with great tenacity and continues to the present day. The sentimental excesses of this tradition brought about a strong reaction from professional historians earlier in this century, so that the central issue in Lincoln studies has become, according to James Hurt, "the conflict between romance and reality." As a result, "the goal of professional Lincoln historians has been to recover the real Lincoln of history as opposed to the mythic Lincoln of the popular imagination."[3] The practical effect of this has been that scholars and other students of Lincoln have virtually abandoned his early life as a field for serious investigation and have instead concentrated their efforts almost exclusively on his presidential years.

Lincoln's early life and the circumstances that brought about his emergence as a man of consequence have thus been little studied in recent years. Nonetheless, they still constitute an important part of the Lincoln story and, it can be argued, are in particular need of attention. The rough conditions in which Lincoln was raised and made his way as a young man are undeniable, but they are all too easily rationalized as what he rose above, rather than what stamped his character. It is, of course, the transcendent Lincoln that has been honored and admired, rather than the unsophisticated country bumpkin he once was. But passing too quickly over the process detracts from our understanding and appreciation of the product. To fully appreciate the historical phenomenon of Lincoln's rise from obscurity to greatness, we must come to terms with the process by which he emerged and distinguished himself. The romantic Lincoln of legend rose by dint of his moral superiority and commitment to higher and better things: he didn't swear, use tobacco, or drink; he read uplifting things, such as the Bible and Shakespeare; he aimed at higher goals than subsistence farming or manual labor, setting his sights on a profession and progressive politics.

Like the Lincoln of legend, the historical Lincoln did most of these things, more or less. But he did other things as well that tell us at least as much about his rise and even more about the road of his ascent, a road that was often rockier (and by turns swampier) than the legend allows. Though frequently played down or lost sight of in telling Lincoln's story, there were more difficulties to surmount than poverty and ignorance and more temptations than profanity and strong drink. That as a young man he was stronger and faster and readier with a joke or a story and better informed than those around him is well known. But that he also struggled with doubts and fears about who he was and what he could become, that he was sharply at odds with the prevailing religious beliefs of the time, or that as a young man he suffered from periods of deep depression and moments of suicidal desperation are only dimly a part of the picture, if we are aware of them at all.

This calls to mind something Lincoln himself reportedly once told his law partner, William H. Herndon. Deeply skeptical of the biographies of his day, Lincoln most objected, according to Herndon, to their tendency to magnify the subject's "perfections – if he had any – and [suppress] his imperfections." In so doing, Lincoln reportedly said, the effect was not only to flatter the subject but to "cheat posterity out of the truth. History is not history unless it is the truth."[4]

-❧-

THE TRUTH, particularly the whole truth, is a lofty and elusive ideal. The aims of this book are admittedly more modest. A primary aim is, by focusing on certain aspects of Abraham Lincoln's life between 1831 and 1842, to shed light on his rise from obscurity and his emergence as a man to be reckoned with. By almost any measure, Lincoln's fortunes during this eleven-year period fairly soared. From being an uneducated backwoods youth without property or family connections, he rose to a position of relative prominence. Whereas in 1831 he had been little more than a refugee from his father's farm, an unskilled laborer and store clerk in the tiny frontier village of New Salem, by 1842 he was a leading politician in the Illinois capital of Springfield and the partner of its foremost lawyer; he had married into an aristocratic family and was positioning himself for election a few years later to the United States Congress.

To present a full and complete account of all that happened to Abraham Lincoln during these eventful years is beyond the scope of this book. Instead, it attempts to explore certain themes and episodes in his early life that figure importantly in his successful rise: his self-education, his search for a vocation, his relations with women, his venture into politics, and his courtship and marriage. Further, it tries to explore these themes and shed what light it can primarily through the medium of reminiscent testimony.

This is a consideration that calls for special comment. One of the principal reservations of professionally trained historians concerning Abraham Lincoln's early life is that most of the evidence pertaining to it is of a highly questionable sort. The evidence that historians find most reliable – written or printed documents that are contemporary with the events in question – is, in this case, largely lacking. In the absence of reliable evidence, Lincoln biography for this period must be almost exclusively woven out of a more doubtful material: the recollections and anecdotes, reported long after the fact, of people who knew him.

Reminiscent tesimony is admittedly problematical. Not only is it often vague and ambiguous, it is notoriously subject to the aberrations of memory, the prejudices of the informant, the selective character of the reporting, and the subtle transformations that occur when a story is either resurrected from the depths of the past or recalled repeatedly over time. "The historian must use reminiscence," the great Lincoln scholar James G. Randall allowed, "but he must do so critically. Even close-up evidence is fallible. When it comes through the mists of many years some of it may be true, but a careful writer will check it with known facts. Contradictory reminiscences leave doubt as to what is to be believed; unsupported memories are in themselves insufficient as proof; statements induced under suggestion, or psychological stimulus, . . . call especially for careful appraisal."[5]

Randall was undoubtedly right. Given the well-known fallibility of human memory, even the most knowledgeable and well-meaning informant, testifying about what happened thirty years before, could easily be mistaken. Indeed, the existing reminiscences about Lincoln prove to be strewn with errors of fact. To cite a single example, there were two Black Hawk Wars: one in 1831, another in 1832. Some of those who had served with Lincoln and told anecdotes of their army life failed to remember correctly which of these two engagements they concerned. The documentary record and much other evidence, including Lincoln's own testimony, make it clear that he was involved only in 1832, so we know that the informants who remembered otherwise were in error. Here Randall's rule of checking reminiscence against "known facts" can be applied, and error or confusion can be avoided.

The problem is that a large proportion of the testimony about Lincoln's early life cannot be confirmed by "known facts," and consequently there is very little that qualifies, by Randall's standards, as reliable historical evidence. Most of our information about what happened to Lincoln between 1831 and 1842 comes from older informants testifying after his death in 1865, and they are often in disagreement. Many interesting and potentially significant recollections are entirely unsupported by other evidence. Much of the testimony collected by Herndon and Lincoln's secretary John G. Nicolay, for example, came in response to directed questions, many of which would qualify, in Randall's terms, as "suggestion, or psychological stimulus." In short, were we to follow a strict rule and put aside all testimony about Lincoln's early life that has a potential for error, there would be almost nothing left to work with. David Herbert Donald has recently observed that "if Randall's criteria were applied, almost nothing could be unquestionably proved about the first thirty years of Lincoln's life."[6] To approach this subject at all, we are compelled to forgo historical certainty and venture into the riskier realm of likelihood and possibility. This book is such an excursion.

~

A VERSE of the poem that Lincoln quoted to John L. Scripps, Thomas Gray's "Elegy Written in a Country Churchyard," poses the timeless question of whether human memorials of the dead can re-create their vitality or otherwise do justice to their lives and accomplishments.

> Can storied urn or animated bust
> > Back to its mansion call the fleeting breath?
> Can Honor's voice provoke the silent dust,
> > Or Flattery soothe the dull cold ear of Death?

While these lines, in context, are intended to indicate that honoring and flattering the dead cannot bring them back to life, the poem goes on, nonetheless, to affirm the value and importance of paying tribute. Honor and perhaps even flattery are thus vindicated as having a legitimate place in the process by which the living pay homage to the dead.

The legend that has arisen around Abraham Lincoln is compounded largely of flattering testimony about him, but it is important to bear in mind that this has been filtered out of a larger body of testimony whose aim is generally descriptive. That is, most personal testimony offered about Lincoln's early life was given not primarily to add praise to his name but simply to describe his actions and the impression he had made in the past. It is equally important to bear in mind that most of those who offered personal testimony about the early life of Abraham Lincoln were undoubtedly observing standards of propriety that pressured them to ignore or suppress incidents that would show the deceased, especially a martyred president, in an unfavorable light. Joshua F. Speed, a close personal friend and important source for this period, confessed to Herndon: "As my mind runs back to my long & intimate acquaintance with that great & good man – I endeavour to forget that which is not worth remembering and to treasure only that which is of value."[7] The result, of course, is a conscious emphasis on honorable, or at least unobjectionable, behavior, and the question naturally arises: is it possible to derive a balanced and accurate picture from such materials? The answer is: most assuredly not. Balance and accuracy, the perennial bywords of sound biography, are simply not achievable under these conditions. But neither does it follow that because these sources are biased, they can tell us nothing. The present study proceeds on the premise that even with its biases and omissions, Honor's voice can tell us a great deal, and sometimes tells us much more than it intended.

Another principal feature of this work has to do with its handling of the informant testimony. Most biographical studies, in the interest of readability and narrative flow, tend to paraphrase the primary source materials and present them to the reader mainly in a digested form. An attempt has been made in this book to present the themes and arguments as much as possible in the language and terms of the evidence itself. Continually investing the text with passages of raw, undigested testimony admittedly affects the flow and readability of the narrative and makes greater demands on the reader. But this procedure seems appropriate here for two reasons. First, because Lincoln's early life is the subject of a familiar and culturally powerful legend, it can easily drift free of its historical moorings. Keeping the pertinent testimony in the foreground helps one to stay in touch with the evidence on which any given incident or judgment about Lincoln is based. Second, a number of incidents and interpretations presented in this book differ significantly from those set forth in traditional Lincoln biography. In these circumstances, it has seemed important to be forthright in presenting the evidence on which the divergent accounts and interpretations are based. While this is no guarantee of historical accuracy or validity, it does make the basis of what is presented more readily apparent and the evidence itself more open to scrutiny.

Featuring the words and the voices of the informants on whom we are dependent for our ideas of what Lincoln did as a young man and what he was like carries its own dangers and risks. Since the evidence provided by these voices is often in conflict, we are constantly faced with the question of determining, in matters that cannot be confirmed by "known facts," which testimony to credit, which to regard with suspicion, or which to disregard altogether. Unfortunately, there is no easy answer. A leading American historian and Lincoln scholar, Don E. Fehrenbacher, has grappled with the vexing question of how to evaluate recollections of what Lincoln is supposed to have said on various occasions and warned that "there is no simple formula for judging the authenticity of recollected utterances" and that every such recollection "is a separate problem in historical method."[8] Indispensable as personal recollections are to our knowledge of history, there is no accepted formula for judging their accuracy.

A related problem is the informants' silence on certain subjects. Since most of the informants whose testimony has come down to us were reasonably friendly to Abraham Lincoln, it is safe to assume that they felt more or less constrained to say nothing for public consumption that might injure his reputation. Lincoln himself, in sending someone to his old friend William G. Greene for information about his early life, reportedly said: "He knows what not to tell you, which is more important than what he does tell you."[9] For just such reasons, the reader is further advised that a great many of the facts, judgments, and conclusions in this book are necessarily conditional – they depend for their validity on the relative authenticity and accuracy of the sources on which they are based.

The testimony about Lincoln's early life by those who claimed to know something about it is surprisingly extensive, and only a small portion of it is presented in evidence in the following pages. This means, of course, that the available evidence has been heavily winnowed and sifted for the most pertinent and telling testimony. Some recollections are offered more confidently than others, but all the testimony that is presented is presumed to have some evidentiary value. It seems appropriate in these circumstances to try to specify the criteria that were employed in selecting and assessing informant testimony. Insofar as they can be codified succinctly, the criteria may be said to be these:

- *Likelihood* – Is it likely that a reported event actually occurred or that a statement is true?

- *Preponderance of evidence* – Given conflicting accounts and alternative versions, where does the weight of the evidence lie?

- *Specificity* – Specific details and circumstances lend credence to what is recalled, though vagueness, being normal, is to be expected.

- *Reputation and reliability of informant* – Where positive, this represents a strong endorsement of an informant's testimony, and vice versa.

- *Known prejudices of the informant* – Prejudice is understood to affect both what is said and what is withheld.

- *Whether the informant was in a position to know what happened* – Firsthand testimony carries more weight, though hearsay from well-placed informants may be well informed and may be distinguished from mere gossip.

None of these criteria should be understood as definitive. Unlikely things do happen. Preponderant testimony can be mistaken. Specificity does not guarantee accuracy. Prejudiced informants can be right. And reputable informants, alas, can be wrong. It bears repeating that in the case of Lincoln's early life, one does not have the luxury of working with only the most reliable forms of evidence. We are compelled by the nature of the situation to find ways of working with what is at hand.

What does this mean in practical terms? For example, what can be made of the testimony about Lincoln in the Black Hawk War that includes the erroneous information that he served in 1831? The solution here is reasonably straightforward. Being wrong in one notoriously slippery particular – a date – hardly proves an informant generally unreliable or suggests that one should disregard the whole of his testimony. Unless there is good reason to doubt such informants' truthfulness or accuracy, what they say about army life and their experiences in the Black Hawk War should be accorded due weight, though like all reminiscence, it can scarcely be put down as a certainty.

Sometimes the context in which the testimony is given clearly regulates the degree of candor. David Davis, a longtime friend whom Lincoln had appointed to the Supreme Court, gave a memorial address on Lincoln a few months after his assassination. In his speech Davis presented a presumably truthful but wholly favorable and honorific picture of Lincoln as a lawyer. But later on, in interviews with Herndon, he felt free to mention a number of criticisms of Lincoln and some of his character flaws. In the speech, he emphasized how strong and effective Lincoln was in court when he knew that right and justice were on his side. In the interviews, he confirmed the view of many others that Lincoln could be a weak advocate for clients he believed to be in the wrong.[10] Testimony can thus sometimes appear to be in conflict when the discrepancies may actually reflect a difference in context and varying degrees of candor and confidentiality.

A more complex example might be that of Herndon's recollection, quoted above, of what Lincoln told him about biographies. What Lincoln is reported to have said in connection with a certain biography of Edmund Burke in 1856 is probably not verbatim, though few would doubt that it approximates something Lincoln actually said. Herndon knew Lincoln well and was in a position to be party to such a discussion, but some caveats are in order. First, we should note that Herndon himself despised biographies that ignored their subject's faults, that he flew in the face of convention when he vowed to avoid this pitfall in his own life of Lincoln, and that in citing Lincoln's reaction to the biography of Burke, Herndon was clearly enrolling Lincoln on his side.

Furthermore, readers who are not familiar with Herndon's tarnished reputation should be advised that he has long been in the doghouse of Lincoln scholarship. Herndon – for just such use of Lincoln to bolster his own views, for claiming credit for influencing Lincoln on important issues, for supposedly harping on certain themes and ignoring others, for intuitive psychologizing, and for getting certain things wrong about Lincoln's life – has for some time been widely regarded by serious students of Lincoln with deep suspicion. And because he solicited and preserved an extensive collection of letters and interviews about Lincoln, Herndon's informants and their testimony have been included in this aura of suspicion.

Nonetheless, Herndon has been found to be an honest and truthful informant, even by those who have faulted his methods and conclusions as a biographer. His own quite critical biographer wrote: "There is not, to the present writer's knowledge, a single letter or other manuscript of Herndon's that reveals a desire or willingness to tell an untruth about

Lincoln."[11] Because Herndon and his informant materials were so central to his subject, the Lincoln biographer Albert J. Beveridge said he took particular pains to investigate Herndon's reliability: "I have gone into his credibility as if I were trying a murder case." There was no doubt about his "entire truthfulness and trustworthiness generally," according to Beveridge. "When Herndon states a fact as a fact, you can depend upon it. It is only when he gets to analyzing the souls of others . . . that he is not to be relied upon."[12]

We thus have little reason to believe that Herndon was either inventing or seriously misrepresenting Lincoln in citing his opinion on biography. But recollections being what they are, one must be aware that Herndon could easily have gotten the date wrong or possibly even the subject of the biography. What we are left with then, as a usable biographical datum, is essentially the gist of Lincoln's opinion of flattering biographers and how they deceive their readers, an opinion that is, in fact, reflected in other testimony.[13]

The practical difficulty with such evidence comes when it runs counter to one's expectation or wish. Biographers of Lincoln, to say nothing of admiring readers, tend to accept unconfirmed revelations with equanimity, so long as these favor their subject or are compatible with their view of him. But both biographers and readers tend to balk hard at intimations or allegations that are unfavorable or otherwise incompatible with their views. As the renowned Lincoln scholar Paul M. Angle once noted, most students "have simply adopted those parts of [Herndon's biography] which harmonized with their own conceptions of Lincoln, and have branded as obviously untrue those statements which they preferred not to believe."[14] These same students tend to be very quick, in such cases, to make an issue of the unconfirmed nature of the evidence.

The danger of this all-too-human impulse is the creation of a double standard: one standard for favorable or unobjectionable testimony and another for its opposite. Herndon's testimony about the illegitimacy of Lincoln's mother, Nancy Hanks, is a case in point. In a letter to Ward Hill Lamon, Herndon recalled that "Lincoln openly and candidly and sincerely told me that his mother *was a bastard*." The circumstances, he wrote Lamon, were these:

> Lincoln & I had a case in the Menard Circuit Court *which required a discussion on hereditary qualities of mind – nature* &c. Lincolns mind was dwelling on his Case – Mine on Something Else. Lincoln all at once

Said – "Billy – I'll tell you something, but Keep it a secret while I live. My Mother was a bastard – was the daughter of a nobleman – So called of Virginia. My Mothers Mother poor and [credulous?] &c. and she was shamefully taken advantage of by the man. My Mother inherited his qualities and I hers. All that I am or hope ever to be I get from my Mother – good [*sic*] bless her. – Did you never notice that bastards are generally smarter – Shrewder & more intellectual than others? Is it because it is Stolen." This is a substantial statement made to me by Lincoln just on a hill overlooking Spring Creek on the road to Petersburg 2 1/2 miles west of this City about 1851, and about which there is nor can be any material mistake and in there last expression I have sometimes thought that Lincoln intended to include himself. I do not assert this to be so: it only seems So, by a loose [intendment?], made by me – a loose [impression?] made by me. The manner of Lincoln I never shall forget – nor what was said nor the place, whatever may become of time.[15]

Herndon's unconfirmed testimony, which appeared in his biography in another form, has met with strong resistance and has prompted several quixotic attempts to rescue Nancy Hanks from the supposed shame of illegitimacy.

But the testimony meets virtually all the cautionary criteria. Herndon was very certain about what he had been told; he was specific about the context and even the place; he was in a position to hear such testimony from Lincoln and capable of judging what he was told; it is extremely unlikely that Herndon would invent or misconstrue such a story; the preponderance of evidence on the issue of legitimacy, including Lincoln's other references to his mother and her family, clearly favors the truth of the story; and, perhaps most important of all, Herndon has been found by several careful investigators to be an honest and reliable informant when reporting his own experience.[16]

All Lincoln biography relies heavily on what Herndon wrote about the sayings and doings of his law partner. To reject his testimony in this instance merely because it has Lincoln admitting to an embarrassing family secret would be difficult to justify on objective grounds, which is why Angle concluded, "Herndon's account of Lincoln's belief in his mother's illegitimacy, one of the main points of controversy in the biography, must be accepted without qualification, for it comes as an unequivocal statement made directly by Lincoln to the author."[17]

This does not mean that Herndon could not be mistaken or misled. In the case of his recollection of Lincoln's remark about his mother's illegitimacy, for example, he was not entirely clear about when it happened and gave varying estimates of its date.[18] When having to make judgments or reconstruct what happened from the reports of others, Herndon was certainly fallible, and his reputation as a biographer has been damaged by his occasional failings in this regard. Perhaps no episode in Herndon's biography is more notorious than the wedding ceremony on January 1, 1841, at which the groom failed to appear. This account caused a great stir when it appeared because the defaulting bridegroom was Abraham Lincoln himself, and Lincoln's closest friends and relatives were certain that no such incident had ever taken place. Herndon thought his source for this story, the hostess of the wedding supper who was also the elder sister of the abandoned bride, was in a position to know what happened and, having repeated her story independently to his collaborator many years after she gave it to him, could not be mistaken about such a matter. In retrospect, we can see that while Elizabeth Edwards was in a position to know and was capable of judging intelligently, Herndon should have asked himself, among other things, whether it was more likely that everyone close to Lincoln (including himself) had totally forgotten so dramatic a chapter in Lincoln's life or that Elizabeth Edwards, who may have been thinking about another event, was confused.

Unfortunately, but perhaps inevitably, the people who supplied the information about Lincoln's early life from their recollections of what happened many years before were often in error – about dates, about people, and about events. If the testimony given by Herndon's informants is any indication, this would seem to be mostly a function of the fallibility of human memory, for clear instances of deliberate deception are exceedingly rare.[19] This alone should remind us that most recollections were probably prompted by something with at least a basis in reality, even if the informant's re-creation of it was fanciful or twisted or otherwise in error. But from the known presence of error, it would be senseless to conclude that nothing whatever can be made of this kind of testimony.

❧

THE DESIGN of this book has resulted in a highly focused and selective presentation. In concentrating on certain themes and episodes and in giving so much prominence to the primary source material, there is admittedly much in Lincoln's life during these eleven years that is left out of account. A comprehensive biography for this period would present a great many significant developments and details of which little or no mention has been made in these pages. In the same way and for much the same reasons, the narrative usually does not include a comparative discussion of the divergent findings and opinions of others. However necessary and appropriate this might be in works intended mainly for an academic audience, it would have made for another kind of book. Nor, to cite another constraint, is there anything like an adequate treatment of the historical contexts – local, regional, or national – in which the reported events transpire. These limitations on the scope of coverage are not, of course, cited as virtues but rather as the historiographical liabilities of choosing to focus on particular themes and episodes of a given period and to feature a particular body of evidence.

A word, in closing, about the opening chapter, "Wrestling with the Evidence." It represents, first and foremost, an attempt to illustrate the basic challenge that reminiscent testimony presents. The central event of this chapter, Lincoln's famous wrestling match with Jack Armstrong in 1831, was selected less for its biographical importance than for the example of its evidence. Because campaign biographies in 1860 had depicted this wrestling match as a significant event in Lincoln's early life and career, Herndon collected a great deal of testimony about it from the former residents of the New Salem area where it took place. When these are added to the other accounts of the match that appeared independently, the result is a very sizable body of testimony, but predictably, there is nothing like agreement among the witnesses, and the accounts of what actually took place differ dramatically. To sift and assess this discordant evidence for clues to the likeliest sequence of events and their possible biographical significance constitute the principal burden of the chapter. It concludes with a look at the way the match has been presented through the years in Lincoln biography. Both parts are intended to demonstrate a more general point that the book as a whole seeks to establish: that there are still significant refinements to be made in the familiar Lincoln story and that the available evidence about Lincoln's early life, problematical as it is, still has much to tell us.

NEW SALEM
(1831-37)

Chapter 1

❧❧❧

WRESTLING WITH
THE EVIDENCE

I
T ALL STARTED with John T. Stuart. Abraham Lincoln and
Stuart had first become acquainted as volunteers in the Black
Hawk War of 1832, where the well-educated Stuart had been
attracted by the conspicuous potential of his uncultivated companion in
arms. After the war, Stuart had made the younger Lincoln something
of a protégé, helping him get started in politics, showing him the ropes
during his first term in the Illinois state legislature, and loaning him
books with which to study law. When Lincoln acquired a license to
practice, Stuart took him in as a partner and soon thereafter entrusted
him with the management of the firm while Stuart was serving in Congress. Their relationship was to be made even closer by Lincoln's marriage a few years later to Stuart's cousin, Mary Todd.

When Lincoln was nominated for the presidency in 1860, a young
reporter sent out from Ohio to gather information for a campaign biography was directed to Stuart for information on the candidate's past.
Though Stuart and Lincoln had grown apart politically and their personal relations were not what they once had been, they had nonetheless
been closely associated for nearly thirty years, and the interviewer,
James Q. Howard, looked to Stuart for insight into Lincoln's phenomenal rise from obscurity to political prominence. Perhaps feeling awkward in this role (he was supporting someone else for president), Stuart
was somewhat guarded, and Howard's notes reflect a cautious reserve.
"There are no striking points in his history," Stuart said. "Growth was
steady, gradual and constant – L not so ready or ingenious as Douglas –

first impressions not so reliable – When he has time to reflect is a very safe Man."[1] But when Stuart recounted their earliest acquaintance in the Black Hawk War and their subsequent exploits as youthful political allies, he warmed to his subject. The episode he particularly called attention to was a wrestling match Lincoln had had soon after his arrival in the village of New Salem with the champion of the Clary's Grove boys, Jack Armstrong. About the significance of this colorful event, Stuart was emphatic: *This was the turning point in Lincoln's life.*[2]

The Clary's Grove boys, Stuart explained, were the regulators of the neighborhood and "took it upon themselves to try the mettle of every new comer and ascertain what sort of stuff he was made of." But Lincoln had proved an exceptional case, and it didn't take Armstrong long, according to Stuart, "to discover that he had got hold of the wrong customer, and when it was evident that Lincoln was getting the better of their champion, the whole band *pitched in* and gave Lincoln several blows which had no very salutary effect on the strength of his legs. Lincoln however took all this in perfect good humor, and by laughing and joking displayed such an excellent disposition that he at once won their hearts and was invited to become one of the company."[3]

Thus alerted to a colorful incident of potential significance, Howard sought out further testimony on Lincoln's wrestling match with Armstrong, but the two other informants who claimed to know something about it told somewhat different versions of the story. Royal ("Rial") Clary was probably not only an eyewitness but himself one of the Clary's Grove boys, and like many of the residents of the neighborhood, he was related to Armstrong (a nephew).[4] Clary told Howard: "Jack Armstrong legged Lincoln – Jack said before his death that he threw L but did not do it fairly – He won us by his bravery and boldness."[5] Unlike Stuart's account, Clary's asserts that Armstrong had actually thrown Lincoln, albeit unfairly, a charge that was repeated by Howard's other informant on the match, William G. Greene. Greene had worked alongside Lincoln as a store clerk about the time this incident occurred in 1831 and was undoubtedly another eyewitness. According to Greene, Lincoln chided those who bet against him and boasted of his prowess. "Said in contest with Jack Armstrong I am sorry that you bet the money, I do not believe that there is a man on earth that can throw *me now.* Jack after they had worked for a long time, caught him by leg and got better of him – [6] L said if they wanted to wrestle fair he was ready, but if they wanted to fight he would try that – Jack quailed – called it drawn."[7]

Back in Columbus, Ohio, Howard's interview notes were duly turned over to the writer retained by the publisher to compose the campaign biography, William Dean Howells. Obviously struck by the story of the wrestling match, Howells reconstructed his own version of what happened.

> When the encounter took place, the "Clary's Grove Boy" found that he had decidedly the worst half of the affair, and the bout would have ended in his ignominious defeat, had not all his fellow-boys come to his assistance. Lincoln then refused to continue the unequal struggle. He would wrestle with them fairly, or he would run a foot-race, or if any of them desired to fight, he generously offered to thrash that particular individual. He looked every word he said, and none of the Boys saw fit to accept his offer. Jack Armstrong was willing to call the match drawn; and Lincoln's fearless conduct had already won the hearts of his enemies. He was invited to become one of their company. His popularity was assured.[8]

While he modified Stuart's version of the story (in which the match ends with Lincoln's pummeling) and merged it with Greene's, Howells did not hesitate to draw the conclusion suggested by Stuart: that in giving Lincoln "a reputation for courage necessary in a new country" and gaining him a core of loyal and politically useful friends, his wrestling match with Armstrong "seems to have been one of the most significant incidents of his early life."[9]

&

ABRAHAM LINCOLN'S election to the presidency and his eventual elevation to the pantheon of American heroes have transformed his wrestling match with Jack Armstrong from a rowdy initiation rite in an obscure pioneer village into a notable historical event. If the outcome of the match truly was decisive for the twenty-two-year-old Lincoln and in some significant sense constituted a "turning point" in his life, then what really happened that day on the bluffs of the Sangamon River becomes a matter of biographical and historical interest, with the potential for affecting the way we understand Lincoln's basic character and his subsequent development. But taking this episode seriously as history and biography means seeking the answers, if answers there be, to certain questions. What exactly was the situation that Lincoln confronted? Being set upon by the Clary's Grove boys for getting the best of their champion? Being fouled by his opponent? Or both? And how did Lincoln respond? By refusing to take offense at being ganged up on, as Stuart had it? Or by defying his attackers and offering to fight them one at a time? These are very different circumstances, and while the end result with respect to winning over the Clary's Grove boys may have been the same, each of the responses suggests a distinctly different way of meeting adversity, if not a difference in basic outlook and personality. What, then, really happened, and what did Lincoln do?

To attempt to answer these questions is an especially difficult task, for here, as with almost every event in Abraham Lincoln's early life, the historian's prime sources of reliable information, contemporary documents, are entirely absent. Because the match between Lincoln and Armstrong was too obscure at the time to have been reported in a newspaper or referred to in any surviving letter, we are left with only one source of evidence as to its character and outcome: the testimony of those who professed to know something about it. Fortunately, a number of such accounts have come down to us, but less fortunately, they fail to agree and, in fact, differ even more widely than the three accounts collected by Howard in 1860.

It was Howells's campaign biography that first brought the match before the public and started the process by which it became one of the most memorable incidents in Lincoln biography and a cornerstone of the ensuing legend. But its appearance in print had another effect that concerns us here, which is that it put a particular version of the story into circulation among Lincoln's friends and former New Salem neighbors. Before the campaign life was published in 1860, the testimony about Lincoln's encounter with Armstrong could be classified, to use a legal distinction, as either firsthand or hearsay. In this case, either you were there at the time it happened and witnessed it yourself or you heard about it from someone else. Rial Clary and Bill Greene would seem to qualify as eyewitnesses, but John T. Stuart, a resident of Springfield, almost certainly was not present and must have had the story from others. After 1860, one must allow for the possibility that those who claimed to know something about the match may have been influenced by a third source – namely, Howells's campaign life or one of many succeeding biographies.

Because some of the notes that Howard took in interviewing Clary, Greene, and Stuart in 1860 survive, we are able to see that Howells's widely read description of the match is actually an amalgamation of the testimony Howard collected. Clary and Greene told Howard nothing about others' intervening in the match; this came only from Stuart, who in turn made no mention of Lincoln's being unfairly "legged." And Howells tactfully left out Greene's recollection that Lincoln had boasted of his powers and chided his friends for betting money against him.

Howard himself wrote a brief sketch of Lincoln's life and presented the wrestling match in a campaign publication that had far less exposure than that of Howells. Howard told essentially the same story, but while he drew heavily on Stuart's account, he differed from Howells in pointedly omitting Stuart's claim that the Clary's Grove boys interceded in the match.[10] Neither Howard nor Howells mentioned the bet, for they, after all, were writing for political effect and selected their evidence accordingly, just as subsequent biographers would use evidence selectively to bring out or reinforce their own conceptions of the man. This serves to remind us that even the best informants probably did no less.

Consider the account of James Short, who had been one of Lincoln's closest New Salem friends and who found a permanent place in Lincoln biography for an act of friendship in a time of misfortune. In one of his biographical statements, Lincoln wrote that his employment as deputy county surveyor during his New Salem years "procured bread, and kept soul and body together."[11] When his creditors seized most of his worldly goods and auctioned them off, Lincoln's former neighbors reported that Short purchased his surveying instruments and returned them so that the impoverished surveyor could continue to make a living.[12] In a letter to William H. Herndon in 1865, Short described the by then famous wrestling match:

> New Salem & the surrounding Country was settled by roughs and bullies, who were in the habit of winning all the money of strangers at cards, & then whipping them in the bargain. Offut in '31 made bet of 5$ that L could throw Jack Armstrong. Armstrong was a regular bully, was very stout, and tricky in wrestling. Lincoln was a scientific wrestler. They wrestled for a long time, withough either being able to throw the other, until Armstrong broke holds, caught L by the leg & floored him. L. took the matter in such good part, and laughed the matter off so pleasantly that he gained the good will of the roughs and was never disturbed by them.[13]

Short doesn't say that he was present, though he lived in the neighborhood of New Salem and may very well have been. Certainly he had heard this encounter talked about at the time by people who were present, and there is no reason to think that he was attempting to relate anything but what he believed had taken place. Short has a noticeably poorer opinion of Armstrong and his gang than Stuart, who described them benignly to Howard as "a band of rollicking, roystering fellows."[14] But Short's version of the way the match concluded – with Lincoln accepting his being unfairly thrown in good part – is very similar to that related by Stuart, with the notable exception of his saying nothing about the unsportsmanlike intervention of the Clary's Grove boys. Given the circumstances, Short's testimony casts doubt on this part of Stuart's version, for it seems reasonable to expect that if Short had known of the interference of men he considered bullies, he would not have failed to mention it.

Short's account raises a point not mentioned in those considered previously: the role of Denton Offutt. Offutt was the proprietor of the store Lincoln worked in and was said to have had a very high opinion of his chief clerk. They had met when Offutt engaged Lincoln and two of his relatives to help take a flatboat of goods to New Orleans, and Lincoln had proved himself an enterprising member of the crew. Offutt was described as "a trader and speculator and always had his eyes open to the main chance."[15] Short's characterization of him was similar to others Herndon collected: "a wild, harum-scarum kind of man."[16] A flamboyant frontier promoter who opened his store in hopes of New Salem's becoming an important trading center, Offutt is said to have skipped out on his creditors some months later, when his business failed.[17]

Two other accounts of the match by New Salem area residents have Offutt betting Bill Clary, a tavernkeeper, on the outcome of the match, and one of these makes the bet itself a key source of contention.[18] L. M. ("Nult") Greene, Bill's brother, told Herndon:

Armstrong after Struggling a while with but a prospect of throwing Mr Lincoln broke his holts & caught Mr Lincoln by the legs & they came to the ground. Clary claimed the money & said he would hav it or whip Offutt & Lincoln both Offutt was inclined to yield as there was a score or more of the Clarys Grove Boys against him & Mr Lincoln & my brother W. G. Greene But Lincoln said they had not won the money & they should not have it & although he was opposed to fighting if nothing else would do them he would fight Armstrong, Clary or any of the set So the money was drawn, and from that day forward the Clary Grove boys Were always his firm friends.[19]

Nult Greene's account may or may not have been firsthand, but like Short, he lived nearby and was intimate with many of those who were present, including his older brother, Bill. Nult's version of what happened has all the features of a tightly scripted one-act play, with not only a protagonist and antagonist but several characters involved in a central conflict, a conflict that produces a chain reaction of contention and recrimination. The wrestling match is here merely the catalyst for a more serious confrontation with Bill Clary, whose threat to have his money is ominously backed up by the Clary's Grove boys. Offutt is represented as being inclined toward the better part of valor, in dramatic contrast to a defiant Lincoln. If he had taken being thrown unfairly in good part, the act of courage that wins admiration is Lincoln's standing up to Bill Clary and anyone else who says he lost the match. Perhaps because of its dramatic complexity, Nult Greene's account has considerable appeal and is the kind of anecdote that is often described as having the "ring of truth." And so it has, but whether it is accurate, of course, is another question.

⁂

TO JUDGE WHAT is described in the accounts of Lincoln's wrestling match with Jack Armstrong and, through them, what actually happened, it is necessary to know something about the kind of contest that was involved. Contrary to what a modern reader might assume, this was not a fight. There was a lot of fighting on the frontier, some of it very rough. The most wide-open form of frontier fighting was almost without rules and featured eye gouging and ear biting as regular and expected tactics.

For the class of frontier men who liked to fight, the opponent did not need to be an enemy nor the provocation very great. A native of New Salem remembered an encounter that began after a party of revelers had mounted their horses and were about to return to their homes. "They were on their horses and trying to pull each other off when Little John Wiseman said to Greasy George Miller – 'George, you have torn my shirt.' 'Yes,' said George, 'and I can tear your hide too.' That was enough. They all got down and hitched their horses and formed a ring and the crowd all stopped to see fair play. The two combatants shook hands and then stepped back eight or ten feet and at the word 'go' rushed at each other." And while the combatants might be friends,

"Old Salem battles had no rules. They were strike, gouge, bite, kick, anyway to win."[20]

A somewhat more subdued form of combat was the fistfight. Sometimes the combatants actually had seconds who made formal arrangements as to time and place and assisted their champions by keeping an eye on the opponent's backers and seeing fair play. Lincoln once served as the second for a man who claimed to be a witness to the Armstrong wrestle, Henry Clark, who was "beautifully whipped" in a bloody fistfight by his opponent, Ben Wilcox. Buoyed by the victory of his champion, Wilcox's pint-sized second reportedly challenged Lincoln, saying, "Well Abe, my man has whipped yours, and I can whip you." Herndon's informant for this story reported: "Mr Lincoln agreed to fight provided [the other man] would 'chalk out his size on Mr Lincoln's person, and every blow struck outside of that mark should be counted foul.' "[21]

Lincoln had engaged in fistfights as a boy in Indiana, but by the time he reached New Salem at the age of twenty-two, he seems to have given up fighting, except as a last resort. When he visited his parents in eastern Illinois about this time, a relative recalled:

> Lincoln was a great wrestler – he returned home about 1831 from N. O from one of his trips, and his fame for this was wide Spread -. Danl Needham heard of it and Came to see Lincoln – Lincoln & Needham met at Wabash point in Coles Co. – and Needham challenged Lincoln – Lincoln accepted it, agreeing both to wrestle side holts. Lincoln threw Needham twice – Needham said – Lincoln "You have thrown me twice, but you can't whip me." Lincoln replied – Needham are you satisfied that I can throw you? If you are not and must be convinced through a thrashing I will do that too for your sake."[22]

Part of the reason for Lincoln's distaste for fighting, as the story about Ben Wilcox's second suggests, may have been his size, for he was larger at six feet four than almost anyone else, and fighting someone your own size was a standard rule of fairness, even on the frontier. But another important reason was surely his peaceable disposition. Once established and accepted in New Salem, Lincoln became an active peacemaker and is reported to have prevented and broken up many fights.[23]

But Lincoln did like to wrestle. Wrestling was not considered so much a form of combat as a test of strength and skill. It was a popular recreational sport that was engaged in by a broad spectrum of the population, particularly in what was then called the West. A generation earlier the West had included upstate New York, where frontier conditions resembled those of Lincoln's Illinois and where wrestling was a common form of recreation. After a barn raising, according to one settler, "almost invariably a ring was formed for wrestling, and frequently commenced with boys, the men looking on. The boy thrown, would bring in one to wrestle with the victor, and so on till all had wrestled, and the one was victor, who could keep the ring against all comers; so also with the men, who never expected to separate without a goodly number of wrestling matches."[24] Even the landed squire might try his hand with the local champions, which is how James Fenimore Cooper's father, the founder of Cooperstown, New York, came to offer one hundred acres of land to anyone who could throw him and promptly lost.[25]

Lincoln may have come by his love of wrestling naturally, for there were apparently noted wrestlers in his family. Usher Linder was born within a few days of Lincoln's birth and within a few miles of his birthplace. Growing up in the part of Kentucky that Lincoln's parents left when Lincoln was seven years old, Linder was well acquainted with Lincoln's relatives who stayed behind, including his charismatic uncle Mordecai. Linder reports that Lincoln once told him: "Linder, I have often said that Uncle Mord had run off with all the talents of the family."[26] One of Uncle Mord's most conspicuous talents was wrestling, and according to Linder, he was not the only one in Lincoln's family with such a reputation.

Wrestling was apparently not an exclusively male sport in early-nineteenth-century rural America. A history of American sports during this period reports the case of the wife of a famous New Hampshire wrestler who offered to oblige a stranger who had come to challenge her temporarily absent husband. Reluctant to put a woman on her back, he soon found himself on his own.[27] What makes this story of interest here is Linder's further testimony that Lincoln's mother was such a wrestler. "His mother, whose maiden name was Nancy Hanks," Linder wrote, "was said to be a very strong-minded woman, and one of the most athletic women in Kentucky. In a fair wrestle, she could throw most of the men who ever put her powers to the test. A reliable gentleman told me he heard the late Jack Thomas, clerk of the Grayson Court, say he had frequently wrestled with her, and she invariably laid him on his back."[28]

No other testimony has come to light confirming Nancy Hanks Lincoln's prowess as a wrestler, and Linder, who was not reporting her wrestling ability at first hand, is admittedly a witness whose fondness for a colorful story was thought to be stronger than his commitment to the truth. There is also the possibility that this anecdote was told with a wink or a double meaning, indirectly referring to the many stories current in Kentucky about Nancy Hanks's allegedly unchaste behavior. But it is worth noting that Herndon's impression, from questioning those who knew her, was that Nancy Hanks "cared nothing for forms, etiquette, customs,"[29] and by most accounts, Lincoln physically favored his mother, who was described by one who knew her as five feet ten and weighing as much as 130 to 140 pounds.[30] Lincoln's father was solidly built and very strong, but he was not tall, definitely not competitive, and was credited with no athletic prowess by those who knew him. His son's athletic abilities, on the other hand, were exceptional and may very well have come, along with his advantageous height and length of limb, from his mother.

James Short described Lincoln as "a scientific wrestler," which was not a casual term but one with a specific meaning. It referred to someone who wrestled according to prescribed rules and succeeded as much by skill, agility, and mastery of the standard holds and techniques as by main strength. Here it also serves to differentiate "wrestling" from the rough-and-ready activity preferred by the Clary's Grove boys and known as "scuffling." The account of Henry McHenry, Jack Armstrong's brother-in-law and another of the Clary's Grove boys, suggests that Lincoln stubbornly insisted upon wrestling. McHenry told Herndon: "I was present at the wrestle of Lincoln & Armstrong –: We tried to get Lincoln to tussel & scuffle with Armstrong. L refused – saying – I never tussled & scuffled & will not – don't like this wooling – & pulling –. Jack Armstrong was a powerful twister. At last we got them to wrestle: they took side holts."[31]

From the evidence available, it is not possible to specify in more than a general way the rules that governed Lincoln's match with Armstrong. There were many different styles of traditional wrestling, most of which came to America from England. "Tussle and scuffle" was apparently a version of what was known in England as the "loose" or "catch-as-catch-can" style of wrestling, in which the contestants begin by facing each other with their arms free and have a good deal of latitude in besting their opponent, including the use of the painful twisting in which Jack Armstrong apparently specialized.

The style of wrestling that Lincoln insisted on seems to have been a version of that favored in the North of England, where the opponents begin by taking certain agreed-upon holds. The object is to throw one's opponent, but here the rules are more restrictive. According to a historian of wrestling, "with the exception of kicking [the participants] are allowed to use every legitimate means to throw each other; but if either 'breaks his hold' – that is, leaves loose – he is accounted the loser, and if either man touches the ground with one knee only or any part of his body, though he may still retain his hold, he is not allowed to recover himself, but is counted beaten."[32] The wrestlers agree beforehand on how many falls constitute victory or defeat in the match. The initial holds assumed by the opponents could vary, but the reports of witnesses to this and other matches support the testimony of Lincoln's Springfield neighbor, James Gourley, that "his [Lincoln's] Specialty was side holds: he threw down all men."[33]

What was a side hold? The history of frontier wrestling remains to be written, and it is uncertain what hold this term referred to. One version of the side hold apparently involved gripping the belt of your opponent, which would explain the remark of one of Lincoln's comrades in the Black Hawk War: "While in the army he Kept a handkerchief tied round him very near all the time for wrestling purposes. . . ."[34] Whatever form the hold may have taken, the wrestler who was either thrown to the ground or broke his hold was the loser of the fall. Lincoln and Armstrong apparently struggled in this position for some time with neither gaining an advantage. This was not unusual for well-matched opponents in this style of wrestling, which many spectators considered dull and uneventful. According to a saying in the Lake District of England, where this style prevailed, "the only way to realise that something is happening in a Lakeland tournament is to enter as a competitor."[35]

To illustrate this style of wrestling further, a report exists that purports to feature Lincoln's own account, albeit at second hand, of his other famous wrestling match, which took place during the Black Hawk War. In 1904 Colonel Risdon Moore, a professor of mathematics at McKendree College, published his recollection of a conversation he had with Abraham Lincoln in 1860, in which the presidential candidate described his match with Lorenzo Dow Thompson, the champion of a St. Clair

County company that was contesting Lincoln's own company for the right to a particular campground at the rendezvous of volunteer militia near Beardstown. Moore remembered Lincoln's account as follows:

> Gentlemen, I felt of Mr. Thompson, the St. Clair champion, and told my boys I could throw him, and they could bet what they pleased. You see, I had never been thrown, or dusted, as the phrase then was, and, I believe, Thompson said the same to the St. Clair boys, that they might bet their bottom dollar that he could down me. You may think a wrestle, or "wrastle," as we called such contests of skill and strength, was a small matter, but I tell you the whole army was out to see it. We took holds, his choice first, a side hold. I then realized from his grip for the first time, that he was a powerful man and that I would have no easy job. The struggle was a severe one, but after many passes and efforts he threw me. My boys yelled out "a dog fall," which meant then a drawn battle, but I told my boys it was fair, and then said to Thompson, "now it's your turn to go down," as it was my hold then, Indian hug. We took our holds again and after the fiercest struggle of the kind I ever had, he threw me again, almost as easily at my hold as at his own. My men raised another protest, but I again told them it was a fair down. Why, gentlemen, that man could throw a grizzly bear.[36]

"Indian hug" was probably a western version of the standard hold in the North of England, where the contestants stand directly in front of each other, each one grasps his opponent with his arms around the other's body, and digs his chin into the other's shoulder at the collarbone. Additional testimony that Lincoln preferred the side hold suggests the possibility that Moore inadvertently reversed the favorite holds of the two wrestlers. This lively account is interesting for making clear the kind of wrestling Lincoln engaged in, but also for the candor with which Lincoln described his own misplaced confidence and subsequent defeat.

❧

IF QUESTIONS of how the match between Lincoln and Armstrong began, how it was conducted, and how it progressed are not crystal clear from the testimony, there is at least no serious disagreement among the witnesses about the early stages of the match. But what happened after the contestants had grappled evenly for some time is, as we have seen, much disputed. There is some indication that there were actually two falls in the match prior to the difficulty. In taking Bill Greene's statement about the match, James Q. Howard first wrote: "Lincoln threw

Armstrong first fall[,] dogfall second[.] A caught L by leg and got better of him." For whatever reason, Howard struck this out and substituted "Jack after they had worked for a long time, caught him by leg and got better of him."[37] Another indication comes from the judge in the famous murder trial many years later in which Lincoln gained an acquittal for Armstrong's son Duff. Herndon's notes on his interview with Judge Harriott read: "he Said that L told him that when he L Came to Salem that the Clary boys intended to whip L & run him off – can him &c – he threw Jack Armstrong."[38]

John T. Stuart claimed that when it became "evident that Lincoln was getting the better of their champion the whole band *pitched in* and gave Lincoln several blows which had no very salutary effect on the strength of his legs," something found in no other account. Stuart says nothing about Armstrong's breaking his hold, but with one exception, the informants closest to the action all refer to it. Rial Clary's testimony, cited earlier, even asserted that Jack himself admitted something of the kind before he died, only a few years prior to the interview.[39]

The exception was Henry McHenry, a relative by marriage and life-long friend of Armstrong's. He told Herndon about himself and his friends trying to get Lincoln to "tussle & scuffle" with Armstrong. "At last we got them to wrestle: they took side holts – we bet Knives – whiskey – &c. L at last picked up Armstrong – swing him around – couldn't throw him – set him down – Saying – Jack let's quit – I can't throw you – you can't throw me. Abe & Jack quit – were always good friends – Lincoln would have fought any or all of them if necessary."[40] For men locked in side holds, this may not have been as dramatic as it sounds, since picking an opponent up and swinging him around may only have meant raising him a few inches off the ground. Still, why Lincoln couldn't throw Armstrong if he could get him up in the air is somewhat puzzling. Whatever it means, it does little or nothing to undercut the testimony of the eight other informants who said positively that Armstrong broke his hold.[41]

If we may reasonably conclude from this clear preponderance of evidence that Armstrong did break his hold, the next question is: how did Lincoln respond? Everyone agrees that the ultimate result of the match was that Armstrong and the Clary's Grove boys became Lincoln's fast friends, but was it because he refused to get upset at being "legged," as some testified? Or because he defied Bill Clary and the gang when they either menaced him or tried to claim their bets on an illegal throw?

William H. Herndon, who collected and preserved most of the surviving testimony about the match, apparently accepted the version of
R. B. Rutledge, who had been a boy of twelve at the time and may have
been an eyewitness. Rutledge wrote to Herndon: "The match took
place in front of Offatt's store. All the men of the village and quite a
number from the surrounding country were assembled[.] Armstrong
was a man in the prime of life, square built, muscular and strong as an
ox. The contest began and Jack soon found so worthy an antagonist that
he 'broke his holt,' caught Abe by the leg, and would have brought him
to the ground, had not Mr Lincoln seized him by the throat and thrust
him at arms length from him."[42]

Although Herndon and his collaborator, Jesse W. Weik, seem to
have credited Rutledge's account of Lincoln's retaliation by seizing
Armstrong by the throat, none of the other informants mentions it. Not
even Rutledge's older brother, who claimed to have seen the match and
with whom Rutledge consulted before writing to Herndon, refers to
any retaliation on Lincoln's part. In his own letter to Herndon, John M.
Rutledge wrote: "Jack armstrong & Lincoln had a restle in New Salem
on the hill neare the mill no one Shoed foul play as I remember, but I
think Jack loosed his holts and caught Lincoln rather by the legs and
partly threw him I did not think it fairly done. thare was like to be a
fuss but was Setled, I notised Lincoln standing with his back against a
Store house neare by whare they wrestled and a crowd of men Standing
around him he Seamed to be undanted & fearless. if I remember rite
the bet was made by Offet though not Sure."[43]

This account is interestingly qualified and contains the kind of concrete detail that quickens belief. In his letters to Herndon, Rutledge
himself is so modest about his knowledge of Lincoln and so reluctant to
give evidence that his testimony fairly epitomizes the notion of the
"ring of truth." One of the noteworthy points in his testimony is the
suggestion that there may have been some disagreement about whether
what Armstrong did was "fairly done." Rutledge allows that he didn't
think it was, but at the same time he specifies that "no one Shoed foul
play as I remember." He leaves open the matter of whether Armstrong's
behavior was questionable or irregular, with the implication that others
may have seen it differently.

And so it would seem. It is quite striking that most of the informants
who mention Armstrong's breaking his hold pronounce no further

judgment in the matter. Henry Clark's laconic summary for Herndon is, in this respect, representative: "Saw Jack Armstrong & Lincoln once wrestle – Jack took the advantage of Lincoln – threw him – good humored."⁴⁴ Clark's meaning would seem to be that even though Armstrong "took advantage" of him, Lincoln was the kind of good-natured fellow who didn't let it bother him. A member of the Purkapile family, who claimed that Armstrong "made a kind of dive under those long legs of Lincoln's and tripped him up," allowed that "It wasn't fair, but the fellow claimed the stakes and his crowd backed him." Lincoln, he said, "wanted to try it over," but his opponent was unwilling.⁴⁵ Apart from Purkapile, Rial Clary and John M. Rutledge are the only ones who expressly say that they thought Armstrong's breaking his hold was something less than fair, and in only one account – that of R. B. Rutledge – is it implied that Lincoln reacted in protest to having been unfairly thrown.

If the informants tended to avoid saying that Armstrong was guilty of foul play, others actively disputed it. Not surprisingly, Jack's wife, Hannah, was one of these. She told Herndon: "Jack Armstrong and Lincoln never had a word: they did wrestle – no foul play – all in a good humor – commenced in fun and ended in sport."⁴⁶ And when Herndon asked the village schoolteacher, Mentor Graham, about this point, he got this response: "Says that no foul or ill play was shown to Lincoln in his wrestle with Jack Armstrong – That it was an ordeal through which all Comers had to pass."⁴⁷ Graham's testimony reminds us of something that everyone present, including Lincoln, understood about the match – namely, that this was a rite of passage; that as a newcomer Lincoln was being tested to see what he was made of.

In these circumstances there may be another good reason why Armstrong's breaking his hold and taking unfair advantage of Lincoln was not more harshly judged by the witnesses. Whether something in a wrestling match is unfair is not just a matter of rules but of judgment. In organized wrestling, what goes and what doesn't depend on the ruling of a designated referee, something that this match conspicuously lacked. Thus, in the minds of the spectators, for whom Lincoln was then merely an untried outsider and perhaps even a blowhard, fairness was a matter of individual judgment and not a fixed, judicial determination. If Armstrong, who was known to be "tricky in wrestling," livened up an initiation rite that had unraveled and was turning into a dull match by using a questionable maneuver, what else did one expect? What mattered most to them, and what they remembered as significant, was not so much Armstrong's behavior as Lincoln's. He had proved himself by managing to keep his composure and to handle the situation in such a way that he and Armstrong emerged not as enemies but as real friends.

This consideration would seem to have a bearing on a final question to be resolved: how Lincoln reacted to being thrown. If he became angry and retaliated against Armstrong, only R. B. Rutledge remembered or reported it. And this response implies that Lincoln lost his composure and, contrary to what was repeatedly noted, his good humor. What seems far more likely is that Lincoln was able to win over his new neighbors by taking the same view of Armstrong's legging him as they did, as a kind of undisguised but essentially nonmalicious irregularity, a rebellious gesture of impatience at the stifling restrictions of this style of wrestling on the part of a local favorite who much preferred to "tussle & scuffle."

But if we accept this explanation, how do we account for the unmistakable strain of testimony that suggests that Lincoln, in the words of Rial Clary, "won us by his bravery and boldness"? Bill Greene testified that Lincoln said defiantly that if "they wanted to wrestle fair he was ready, but if they wanted to fight he would try that." John M. Rutledge remembered Lincoln "with his back against a Store house neare by whare they wrestled and a crowd of men Standing around him he Seamed to be undanted & fearless." And R. B. Rutledge recalled as a result of Lincoln's being unfairly thrown, "there was every prospect of a general fight."

Clearly, a satisfactory explanation of what happened in the match must reconcile the testimony of Lincoln's taking his being "legged" in good humor with the reports of his fearlessly defiant behavior. The solution seems to lie with a consideration that can easily be lost sight of as incidental but that was all-important to many of those present: the betting on the outcome of the match. We know that betting was an important part of any such contest, and to say that the betting could strongly influence the disposition and demeanor of frontier spectators is clearly an understatement. As we have seen in the account of Lincoln's match with Thompson, the wrestler was in no small degree himself responsible for the kind of bets placed. It was one thing for Lincoln to accept being unfairly thrown by Armstrong without taking offense, but it was quite another for him to accept this as an out-and-out defeat, such that his employer and others who had backed him would lose their bets.

In 1886 a St. Louis reporter seeking interviews in the neighborhood of New Salem with people who had known Lincoln was referred to a seventy-eight-year-old man known as Uncle Johnny Potter, who gave him a version of Lincoln's wrestling match with Jack Armstrong. Like the Greenes and the Clarys, the Potters were closely related to the Armstrongs, and Uncle Johnny had been related to Jack through marriage (his brother had married Jack's sister). Besides the possibility of bias, conditions for the historical reliability of the testimony were hardly propitious. Fifty-five years had passed since the match had occurred, and with the passage of so much time, the likelihood was great that Uncle Johnny's memory would have faded. Just as great was the possibility that his recollections had become blurred by the many accounts already in circulation of what was now almost a legendary match. Nonetheless, Potter's account is very much his own and proves to be not only one of the most incisive, but one of the most revealing as well. It is given added interest in the reporter's story by coming at the request of Armstrong's own son.

"Uncle Johnny, tell him about the wrestling match with father," said a sturdy, middle-aged man, with a pleasant face. "You remember all about that."

The speaker was Jack Armstrong, the son of the famous Jack Armstrong, who was the champion in all athletic sports in this valley of the Sangamon fifty years ago.

"I remember it," said Uncle Johnny. "Your father was considered the best man in all this country for a scuffle. In a wrestle, shoulder and back holds, there was now and then a man he couldn't get away with. When Lincoln came to this country there was a crowd called the Clary Grove boys, who pretty much had their own way, and Jack Armstrong was the leader among them. Most every new man who came into the neighborhood had to be tried. Lincoln was pretty stout, and the boys made it up to see what there was in him. They got him to talking about wrestling one day, and he said he could throw any man around there. Bill Clary kept at Lincoln until he got him into a bet of $5. Then he put Jack Armstrong against him. They were pretty well matched, but Abe was a good deal taller, and could bend over Jack. They wrestled a good while, and I think Abe had thrown Jack two joints, and was likely to get him down. Clary, I expect, thought he was in danger of losing his money, for he called out: 'Throw him any way, Jack.' At that Jack loosed his back hold and grabbed Abe by the thigh, and threw him in a second. Abe got up pretty mad. He didn't say much, but he told somebody that if it ever came right he would give Bill Clary a good licking. You see, the hold Jack took was fair in a scuffle, but not in a wrestle, and they were wrestling. After that Abe was considered one of the Clary's Grove boys."[48]

Potter's description of the match appears to be a firsthand account, but what is even more important is that it exhibits a shrewd understanding of what happened and what was really at stake. In pointedly stressing the distinction between scuffling and wrestling, he puts Armstrong's performance in (from the local point of view) a proper perspective – what he did was fair in his accustomed style of scuffling, but not in a wrestle. And Potter gives the betting a suitably prominent place in the story. By indicating that Lincoln's anger was directed more at Bill Clary than at Jack Armstrong, Potter suggests how and why Lincoln was willing to tolerate Armstrong's almost predictable behavior, but not Clary's.

Potter's description of the match is perhaps even more vivid than a modern reader, whose idea of wrestling has been shaped by the predominance of the catch-as-catch-can style, would ordinarily realize. It is possible (and would make more sense) that the reporter misunderstood Potter when he described the progress of the match and that he was talking about "points" rather than "joints." In the older style of wrestling that Lincoln had insisted on, a fall was often defined as "three points down," meaning two shoulders and one hip (or vice versa) touching the ground. Two points down was close, but under these rules, it was counted a dog fall. If Potter actually said "They wrestled a good while, and I think Abe had thrown Jack two *points*, and was likely to get him down," his meaning quite possibly was that Lincoln had thrown Armstrong, perhaps repeatedly, for two points, and it was becoming evident that it was only a matter of time before Jack would be thrown for three points and lose the match.

It was at this juncture, according to Potter, that Clary, sensing the inevitable, decided to urge Jack to dump the upstart in defiance of the rules. In trying to win his bet by means of a foul, Clary proved himself one of the roughs and bullies described earlier by James Short, "who were in the habit of winning all the money of strangers at cards, & then whipping them in the bargain." But, as other accounts indicated, Lincoln could not be intimidated, and the man who contemplated giving

Bill Clary a good licking was obviously in no mood to forfeit his employer's or anybody else's bet, including his own.

What really happened in the match? We have considered the most pertinent testimony of all the known informants, and while they scarcely agree on the details, there is universal agreement on the final outcome: that Armstrong and the Clary's Grove boys became Lincoln's friends and admirers. But what was it they admired? His good-humored imperturbability or his "bravery and boldness"? The evidence suggests that it was probably both. There seems little doubt that Lincoln was "legged" by Armstrong, who violated the rules by breaking his hold in order to gain an advantage and throw Lincoln unfairly. But the weight of the evidence suggests that Lincoln accepted this in reasonably good part. With the exception of R. B. Rutledge, none of the informants says that Lincoln retaliated against Armstrong, whose inability to accept the constraints of scientific wrestling was apparently not considered a serious breach by most onlookers. Lincoln's reported anger and defiance would seem to have been directed not so much toward Armstrong as toward those who would construe his being illegally thrown as a defeat, a matter of some consequence because it entailed forfeiture of the bets placed on him. What saved the situation from degenerating into a "general fight" is not clear. R. B. Rutledge told Herndon that at this point his father, James Rutledge, "ran into the crowd and through the influence which he exerted over all parties, succeeded in quieting the disturbance and preventing a fight."[49] Certainly the testimony indicates that hostilities were prevented, but the prospect of a fight, which seems to have been quite real, serves to emphasize that Lincoln impressed the crowd by his willingness to meet that possibility. This willingness seems to have constituted the "bravery and boldness" by which Lincoln won the admiration of the crowd and thus successfully passed the test of his initiation.

❧

ABRAHAM LINCOLN'S assassination in 1865 inevitably prompted a series of biographies, in which the story of Lincoln's wrestling match with Jack Armstrong in 1831 was often retold. The version related in the most successful and widely read of the early books, Joshiah G. Holland's *The Life of Abraham Lincoln* (1866), seems to have been gleaned not from Howells's account in the campaign biography but directly from Howard's notes, which Holland apparently was able to consult. Though working with the same information, Holland painted a somewhat different picture from that of Howells five years earlier. The organization of the details and the similarities of language and phraseology leave little doubt that Holland's main source was Howard's interview with John T. Stuart, though he made one concession to the claims of Howard's other witnesses, Rial Clary and Bill Greene. "The bout was entered upon, but Armstrong soon discovered that he had met with more than his match. The 'Boys' were looking on, and, seeing that their champion was likely to get the worst of it, did after the manner of such irresponsible bands. They gathered around Lincoln, struck and disabled him, and then Armstrong, by 'legging' him, got him down."[50]

Holland's version of the climax of the match is just as selective and creative as Howells's, but with a different twist. Having the Clary's Grove boys pitch onto Lincoln when he seemed to be getting the best of it was indeed Stuart's idea of what happened, but having Armstrong foul Lincoln *after* his friends had disabled him is something unauthorized by the testimony and would appear to be Holland's attempt to reconcile the differences among the witnesses. Jack's legging Lincoln *before* the Clary's Grove boys joined in would remove the provocation and make little sense, so Holland apparently assumed it must have happened afterward. His description of Lincoln's reaction to this outrageous treatment is taken directly from Stuart: that Lincoln took it all in "perfect good humor" and thereby won the admiration of his tormentors. Particularly with the added insult of the fortuitous legging, this seems an incongruous result, an incongruity that even Holland has to acknowledge. "Strange as it may seem," he concludes, echoing Stuart, "this was the turning point, apparently, in Lincoln's life. . . ."[51]

Far and away the most substantial account of Lincoln's early life before the appearance of Herndon's biography later in the century was that of Ward Hill Lamon, who had purchased in 1869 copies of the letters and interviews Herndon had collected. Lamon farmed out the composition of his book, *The Life of Abraham Lincoln* (1872), to a ghost-writer, Chauncey F. Black, who drew upon Herndon's materials almost exclusively for his account of Lincoln's New Salem years. Black's reconstruction of the wrestling match is deliberately more dramatic and colorful than Howells's or Holland's and manages to combine the accounts of several of Herndon's informants into a reasonably coherent narrative.

It begins with Offutt and Bill Clary's bet and proceeds to Lincoln's objection to "tussle and scuffle," to the taking of side holds, and then to Henry McHenry's curious report of Lincoln picking Armstrong up off the ground without being able to throw him. Lincoln next offers Armstrong a draw, but Jack's friends, "being covetous of jackknives, whiskey, and 'smooth quarters,'" induce him to continue, after which he breaks his hold and throws his opponent unfairly. Lincoln's "righteous wrath [then] rose to the ascendent," and "the astonished spectators saw him take their great bully by the throat, and, holding him out at arm's-length, shake him like a child." When Bill Clary claims the stakes and the excited Clary's Grove boys threaten a general fight, Lincoln stands firm, as in Nult Greene's account, refusing to yield and offering to fight "Armstrong, Clary or any of the set."[52] Finally, James Rutledge steps in and preserves the peace.

Though consciously dramatized and embellished with melodramatic gestures, Black's account seems to represent a serious effort to combine a broad range of the testimony Herndon had collected and to reconcile some of the inconsistencies inherent in the evidence. Relying heavily on McHenry's testimony, which makes no mention of Lincoln's being legged, Black, like Holland, felt obligated to find a place for Armstrong's foul in his narrative. By not losing sight of the role of the betting, he presented a more plausible reaction by Lincoln than Holland did and a more believable outcome overall.

Isaac N. Arnold, a former congressman from Chicago and a friend of Lincoln's, wrote a eulogistic life of the martyred president that appeared in 1884. As becomes clear in his correspondence with Herndon, the pious Arnold felt it his duty to portray his friend in the best possible light and to avoid anything that smacked of the unsavory or the unseemly. It is thus no surprise that his account of the wrestling match, which was too famous by this time to leave out, spends little time with the actual incident and emphasizes the civilizing effect that Lincoln managed to exercise over a band of bullies. He makes no mention of betting and says Armstrong "resorted to foul play which roused Lincoln's indignation." After Lincoln takes Armstrong by the throat and shakes him, there is the predictable reaction on the part of Jack's friends, who are met by a defiant Lincoln. But at this point Arnold introduced a new element into the story. He has Armstrong resolve the impending crisis by stepping forth, shaking Lincoln's hand, and saying,

"Boys! Abe Lincoln is the best fellow that ever broke into this settlement. He shall be one of us."[53]

Whether Arnold got Armstrong's fight-saving pronouncement from an unidentified witness or inferred it from the outcome is not known, but the latter seems more likely. Arnold was certainly uncomfortable with the idea that Lincoln had anything in common with rowdies such as the Clary's Grove boys and could not quite bring himself to see Lincoln as one of them, as the text makes clear. The loyalty and support of Jack and his friends "belonged to Lincoln," according to Arnold, but he did not belong to them. "He treated them like men, and always brought out the best in them. They felt his moral and intellectual superiority, but they also felt that he did not despise them, and that he sympathized with them. In a certain sense he was one of them, but he was their ideal, their hero."[54] Needless to say, Arnold did not consider the match the turning point in Lincoln's life.

Lincoln's presidential secretaries, John G. Nicolay and John Hay, set out to write a definitive biography of their former chief, but they were hampered in their treatment of their subject's early life by the sensitivities of his son, Robert Todd Lincoln, who controlled access to their prime asset, Lincoln's papers. By informal agreement, Robert supported and abetted Nicolay and Hay's biographical efforts in return for a tacit oversight of what went into their text. Determined to keep his father's private life as much out of view as possible, he was particularly sensitive about revelations bearing on the crudeness and uncultivated environment in which his father had grown up. Under such constraints, Nicolay and Hay devoted only a small fraction of their sprawling ten-volume narrative to the events and developments of Lincoln's formative years.

Like Arnold, Robert Todd Lincoln was probably not comfortable with the wrestling match. Perhaps for this reason, Nicolay and Hay felt obliged to present it apologetically as an "ignoble scuffle." In their version, no mention is made of betting or even of Lincoln's being legged by Armstrong. When Lincoln is perceived as getting the best of their champion, the Clary's Grove boys descend on Lincoln in force, which only arouses his ire and his strength. "At this, as has been said of another hero, 'the spirit of Odin entered into him,' and putting forth his whole strength, he held the pride of Clary's Grove in his arms like a child, and almost choked the exuberant life out of him. For a moment a general fight seemed inevitable; but Lincoln, standing undismayed with his back to the wall, looked so formidable in his defiance that an honest admiration took the place of momentary fury, and his initiation was over."[55]

Whereas Arnold had rationalized the wrestling match as an opportunity for Lincoln to exercise moral leadership with the aberrant Clary's Grove boys, Nicolay and Hay returned to the perspective on the match first put forward by Stuart. Choosing their words carefully and avoiding Stuart's emphatic "turning point" thesis, they nonetheless underscored, even as they qualified, the event's significance. "This incident, trivial and vulgar as it may seem, was of great importance in Lincoln's life. His behavior in this ignoble scuffle did the work of years for him, in giving him the position he required in the community where his lot was cast. He became from that moment, in a certain sense, a personage, with a name and standing of his own."[56] Trivial and vulgar, but (in a certain sense) important.

Nicolay and Hay's biography ran serially in the *Century* magazine before it was published in book form in 1890, so that the wrestling episode actually appeared in 1887, two years before the publication of *Herndon's Life of Lincoln* (1889). Herndon's *Life*, written in collaboration with Jesse W. Weik, is in many respects the opposite of Nicolay and Hay's. Avoiding the personal and private life of their subject and skimming quickly over his early and middle years, Nicolay and Hay concerned themselves almost exclusively with Lincoln's public life and his presidency. Herndon's purpose from the beginning was to write what he described as a "subjective" or "inner life" of his great law partner.[57] When his correspondence and interviewing turned up so much unexpected and interesting material on Lincoln's early life, Herndon expanded the scope of his efforts and ended up producing a full-fledged account of Lincoln's prepresidential years, with only a few sketchy chapters on the presidency.

There can be little doubt that the resourceful Herndon, in his original researches in the 1860s, was concerned to get at the truth about the wrestling match. He took testimony from ten different informants on the matter, and as we have seen, he made special inquiry about the question of whether Armstrong had shown foul play. But somewhat surprisingly, when it came time to sort through the conflicting testimony and put forward an authoritative account, Herndon and his collaborator seem simply to have acquiesced in the treatment the match had already been given by previous biographers. "It is unnecessary to go into the details of the encounter," they wrote. "Everyone knows how it ended; how at last the tall and angular rail-splitter, enraged at the suspicion of foul tactics, and profiting by his height and the length of his arms, fairly lifted the great bully by the throat and shook him like a rag; how by this act he established himself solidly in the esteem of all New Salem, and secured the respectful admiration and friendship of the very man whom he had so thoroughly vanquished."[58]

Here Herndon and Weik were opting, in effect, to accept the common element in the accounts of the leading biographies since Holland – Lincoln's angry grasping of Armstrong by the throat – as the quintessential feature of the match. This is a circumstance overrun with ironies. In the first place, Herndon, who prided himself on taking more pains and being more courageous about the truth than other Lincoln biographers, was here merely going along with a dramatic and forceful image that his predecessors had winnowed out of the welter of testimony that appeared in Lamon's book but that he himself had collected. In so doing, Herndon was effectively endorsing R. B. Rutledge's unconfirmed testimony and ignoring what he, unlike his predecessors, had the means of determining was the likeliest import of the evidence.

This was no mere methodological lapse, for as a consequence, Herndon and his collaborator were inadvertently helping to perpetuate what is surely a false picture of their hero as a man who became so angry and so lost his composure that he committed the one act that was sternly forbidden in all such contests, the choke hold. This alone should count against the credibility of Rutledge's version, but Herndon and Weik seem here to have succumbed to the preference of biographers and apparently the public for a certain dramatic image of their martyred president, rather than present a reasoned estimate of the probable truth.

Where Holland, Arnold, and Nicolay and Hay did little in the way of original research for information on Lincoln's New Salem years and produced largely derivative accounts, Ida M. Tarbell, coming to the Lincoln field in the 1890s, went back to all the scenes of Lincoln's early life and searched diligently for additional testimony and new information. Yet she could do no better than repeat, in her turn-of-the-century biography, the by then standard story.

Neither could throw the other, and Armstrong, convinced of this, tried a "foul." Lincoln no sooner realized the game of his antagonist than, furious with indignation, he caught him by the throat and, holding him out at arm's length, "shook him like a child." Armstrong's friends rushed to his aid, and for a moment it looked as if Lincoln would be routed by sheer force of numbers. But he held his own so bravely that the "boys" in spite of their sympathies, were filled with admiration. What bade fair to be a general fight ended in a general handshake, even Jack Armstrong declaring that Lincoln was the "best fellow who ever broke into the camp."[59]

All the elements in Tarbell's account are familiar enough, though each successive writer apparently felt obliged to provide a slightly different twist. R. B. Rutledge originally told Herndon in 1866 that Armstrong caught Lincoln by the leg "and would have brought him to the ground, had not Mr Lincoln seized him by the throat and thrust him at arms length from him." When this report was first offered to the public in Lamon's biography in 1872, it was duly enhanced: "the astonished spectators saw him take their great bully by the throat, and, holding him out at arm's-length, shake him like a child." Lamon's ghostwriter, Black, was apparently responsible for adding the shaking, which was then taken up faithfully, though not slavishly, by succeeding biographers. Arnold wrote that Lincoln "shook him like a boy," and Hay, who was responsible for the early chapters of his and Nicolay's biography, wrote with a flourish that Lincoln "held the pride of Clary's Grove in his arms like a child, and almost choked the exuberant life out of him." Hay's flourish may have got the better of him, as the more one tries to picture what he describes, the more problematic it appears. Herndon and Weik had Lincoln, without any warrant from their own witnesses, shaking Armstrong "like a rag." Tarbell, as we have just seen, closed the circle by returning to the "child" introduced in Lamon's biography, where all the shaking began.

❧

IN THE TWENTIETH century the story of Lincoln's wrestling match languished for a time, as serious biographers like Lord Charnwood (1916) and Nathaniel W. Stephenson (1922) were content to pass over the incident as simply one in which Lincoln prevailed over the local champion. Neither Lord Charnwood nor Stephenson claimed to base his biography on new or original research, but one who did, William E. Barton, apparently found nothing to shed additional light on the wrestling match. In his *Life of Abraham Lincoln* (1925), Barton reworked the familiar elements of the story, so that after Armstrong committed his foul, Lincoln picked him up and "bodily threw him to the ground," thus both ending the match and solving the problem posed by Henry McHenry's original testimony, which seemed to hold that Lincoln could get Armstrong up in the air without being able to get him to the ground.[60]

Carl Sandburg's biography of Lincoln's early life, *The Prairie Years*, appeared in 1926, and though poetically rendered and fictionalized to some extent, it was based not only on the findings of its predecessors but on a considerable amount of original research as well. This is sharply evident in Sandburg's rendition of the match with Armstrong, for he introduces some altogether new elements, not found in previous biographies. Instead of taking their holds and grappling evenly for a time, as in previous accounts, he plotted a wholly different beginning for the match and introduced a startlingly new form of Armstrong's foul.

In Sandburg's version, Armstrong tried from the outset "to get in close on his man where he would have the advantage of his thick muscular strength. Lincoln held him off with long arms, wore down his strength, got him out of breath and out of temper. Armstrong then fouled by stamping on Lincoln's right foot and instep with his boot heel."[61] But having begun with a novel opening, Sandburg supplied the familiar elements soon enough:

> This exasperated Lincoln so that he lost his temper, lifted Armstrong up by the throat and off the ground, shook him like a rag, and then slammed him to a hard fall, flat on his back.
>
> As Armstrong lay on the ground, a champion in the dust of defeat, his gang from Clary's Grove started to swarm toward Lincoln, with hot Kentucky and Irish epithets on their lips. Lincoln stepped to where his back was against a wall, braced himself, and told the gang he was ready for 'em.
>
> Then Jack Armstrong broke through the front line of the gang, shook Lincoln's hand and told the gang Lincoln was "fair," had won the match, and, "He's the best feller that ever broke into this settlement."[62]

By now the reader can readily recognize the layered elements and most of their sources. Grasping Armstrong by the throat came ultimately from R. B. Rutledge, though shaking him was Black's idea, and shaking him like a "rag" was Herndon and Weik's. Slamming Armstrong on the ground was the recent contribution of Barton, and Jack's

pronouncing Lincoln the "best feller that ever broke into this settlement" was the legacy of Arnold. But what are we to make of Sandburg's
beginning for the match, with Armstrong trying in vain to get close
enough to Lincoln to take hold of him and Lincoln fending him off
with his long arms? And what about the foul? How could a painfully
stamped instep have been mistaken for an illegal "legging"? Where, in
short, did Sandburg get his information?

Surprising as it may seem, it came from an eyewitness. William G.
Greene, who claimed to have worked alongside Lincoln in Offutt's
store, later became known in the region as "Slicky Bill," and his treatment of the wrestling match may help explain why. When asked about
the match in 1860 by James Q. Howard, Greene, it will be recalled,
described it thus: "Jack after they had worked for a long time, caught
him by leg and got better of him. L said if they wanted to wrestle fair he
was ready, but if they wanted to fight he would try that – Jack quailed –
called it drawn." As we have seen, this brief account stands up quite well
when judged by the character and weight of the other testimony. But
Greene apparently did not stick to his story and later began to retail a
much more elaborate version.

In spite of giving Herndon extensive testimony on all manner of
incidents involving Abraham Lincoln's New Salem years, and in the
process conducting himself as something of a know-it-all where Lincoln was concerned, Greene seems not to have had anything to say
about the wrestling match with Armstrong. But when it became clear in
later years that the match was to have an important place in Lincoln
biography, Greene found his voice. In 1884 he gave a correspondent for
the *Chicago Tribune* this account: "Jack Armstrong, the biggest [of the
Clary's Grove boys], took him [Lincoln] in hand and tried to throw
him. He tried all sorts of tricks, got foul holds and inside leg hitches, all
in vain. Then Lincoln said that if they were for enemies, he was ready;
or friends, as it suited them. Big Jack Armstrong slapped him on the
back and said, 'Oh, we were only in fun.' "[63]

Between this interview and the time of his death ten years later,
Greene seems to have further expanded his revisionist version and even
to have written in an important part for himself. When Thomas P.
Reep compiled and published the oral traditions pertaining to Lincoln
and his New Salem neighbors, he reported at length what he and his
associates in the Old Salem League apparently considered the most
authoritative account of the wrestling match. In this account, Greene

is prominently featured as Lincoln's coach and adviser. "During the intervening time before the match, [Greene] advised him that, with his long arms and powerful shoulders, he would be able to keep Armstrong from getting close enough to him to make his tricks effective and in this way wear him out." Needless to say, Lincoln follows Greene's advice and frustrates Armstrong to such an extent that the Clary's Grove champion fouls Lincoln by driving his heel against Lincoln's instep. "Enraged by this act, and before Armstrong had time to recover from the forward thrust of his body, Lincoln heaved his great shoulders and flung his adversary backward over his head."[64] If Reep and his associates, many of whom had known Greene, were willing to credit him, it is hard to fault Sandburg for following suit, but the history of Greene's own testimony goes far to undermine the credibility of its later incarnations.

The extensive archive of letters and interviews about Abraham Lincoln collected by Herndon was not at the disposal of most later biographers, such as Tarbell, Barton, and Sandburg, much as they would have liked to consult it. But because of a friendship with Weik, who acquired possession of the archive after Herndon's death, Albert J. Beveridge was permitted the free use of this unique collection in preparing his 1928 biography of Lincoln. Though because of his death it was completed only through the year 1858, Beveridge's biography is easily the most detailed, and in many respects the most authoritative, account of Lincoln's prepresidential years to date. The massive collection of notes and materials he left behind shows that Beveridge went to extraordinary lengths to absorb and analyze not only Herndon's documents but an immense volume and variety of other material as well. In spite of this, he was unable to shed any light on the wrestling match with Armstrong. "Three or four accounts of the wrestling match between him and Lincoln agree only that it ended in such fashion as to win the friendship of Armstrong and the allegiance of his band. Probably the most accurate story of what took place is that of Rowan Herndon, an eye-witness, who says that after striving a long time without either man prevailing, Lincoln said: 'Jack, let's quit. I cant throw you – you cant throw me.' Armstrong agreed and the matter was ended in fun."[65]

Beveridge's text mistakenly attributes McHenry's remarks to Herndon's cousin, Rowan Herndon, but what is interesting here is that Beveridge saw through the popular but improbable story about the choke hold and abandoned it. He may well have settled on McHenry's account as the most likely because its conclusion – an agreed-upon draw and a handshake – sounds most like the ultimate result of the match.

The most highly regarded one-volume biography of Lincoln was for many years Benjamin P. Thomas's *Abraham Lincoln* (1952). Not only is Thomas's book gracefully written, but it carries the authority of a professionally trained historian who spent many years steeping himself in the details of Lincoln's life. While serving as executive secretary of the Abraham Lincoln Association in Springfield, Thomas was a principal contributor to *Lincoln Day by Day*, the authoritative compilation of the documented facts of Lincoln's life. Another measure of Thomas's scholarship is that his *Lincoln's New Salem* (1934), though a brief survey of its subject, is still unsurpassed after more than sixty years.

When he wrote *Lincoln's New Salem*, Thomas did not have access to the evidence concerning the wrestling match collected by Herndon, except as the witnesses' testimony had been quoted in other biographies, but he did have a document that he believed was very pertinent to what happened in the match. This was a copy of Howells's campaign biography that Lincoln had annotated for his friend Samuel C. Parks. In its margins Lincoln corrected a number of errors, but he made no correction of Howells's description of the wrestling match. Thomas pointedly noted that his account followed "that given by William Dean Howells."[66]

For his biography, Thomas might have consulted the accounts of Herndon's informants, for these had become available in the interim at the Library of Congress, but he seems to have largely ignored them. Here is the account of the match given in Thomas's *Abraham Lincoln*:

> The two men circled cautiously, came to grips, broke, pawed for a hold again. They closed, twisted, wrenched, and tugged. Lincoln gained the hold he wanted, and as they went down he flopped on top. Relentless pressure forced Armstrong's shoulders toward the ground; then his companions, unwilling to see their leader whipped, joined the scuffle. Lincoln freed himself and backed against a wall, voicing defiance as he offered to fight, race, or wrestle any or all of them singly. None saw fit to take him on, and Armstrong, appraising him admiringly, slouched forward to offer his hand.[67]

Here Thomas, like Beveridge, has wisely avoided the choke-hold story, but what is astonishing is how much he has introduced that is entirely new. Lincoln circling his opponent was, of course, part of Greene's revisionist version, but trying out holds, twisting and tugging until he got the hold he wanted, and throwing Armstrong and nearly pinning him – these are all new elements in the story, unauthorized by Howells or any other known source.

When we consider this account in the context of the actual testimony, it is hard to avoid the conclusion that in adding details that are apparently imaginary, Thomas permitted his narrative to drift away from the historical event. He depicted a style of wrestling that, as a historian of the sport relates, "is much the more amusing and intelligible to spectators, who are often immensely diverted by the antics of the men in manoeuvring for a hold."[68] But the most persistent element in the testimony of witnesses is that Armstrong "broke his hold," the logical implication of which is inescapable: that the contest was not a catch-as-catch-can match, in which the contestants begin by maneuvering for advantage, but one in which they begin by taking holds, the breaking of which is forbidden. Apparently to better dramatize Lincoln's gaining advantage over Armstrong, Thomas has Lincoln throw Armstrong and nearly succeed in pinning him to the ground, although nothing whatever is said about pinning in the testimony, and there is no reason to believe that anything but throwing the opponent was the object of the match.

～ð

THOUGH NOT the technical winner of the match, Abraham Lincoln came away with other prizes. He acquitted himself well in the eyes of the community at large. He made a friend of Armstrong and established himself as a favorite with the rough-and-ready crowd in the neighborhood of New Salem. Armstrong's friendship came to mean much, including a family with whom to lodge from time to time and someone, in Hannah Armstrong, to launder and mend his clothes. The goodwill of the Clary's Grove boys earned him the captainship of the local militia unit and a first taste of leadership when, some months later, he was summoned to duty in the Black Hawk War. In addition to being captain of their company, Lincoln distinguished himself by upholding their honor in the obligatory wrestling matches that enlivened the long and largely uneventful bivouacs of the volunteers. In these engagements his only defeat came, as we have seen, when he met a man, some said the only man, who could throw him: Lorenzo Dow Thompson of St. Clair County.⁶⁹ Like many another military engagement, the Black Hawk War became the breeding ground for public men in frontier Illinois, and it was here that Lincoln laid his claim to public service and became acquainted with many of the men with whom he would be associated politically and as a lawyer in succeeding years: John T. Stuart, John J. Hardin, Joseph Gillespie, Edward D. Baker, and William Butler.

But for all its salutary effect on his young career, it is hard to see Lincoln's wrestling match with Jack Armstrong as the "turning point" in his life. Had he previously been cowardly or unsure of himself or unable to cope with difficult situations and then, for the first time, "found himself" in the trying circumstances of the match, one might be justified in representing it as such. Frederick Douglass, by contrast, says in his *Narrative* that his wrestle with Covey, the slave breaker, which occurred about 1833, was "the turning-point in my career as a slave. It rekindled the few expiring embers of freedom, and revived within me a sense of my own manhood. It recalled the departed self-confidence, and inspired me again with a determination to be free."⁷⁰

But the qualities that sustained Lincoln in his wrestle with Armstrong – great physical strength, good humor, courage, and self-assurance – he seems to have had when he arrived in New Salem. And if these qualities were already firmly in place, they were bound to have asserted themselves in due time, so that the contest with Armstrong was little more than a fortunate occasion for putting them on public display. Had Stuart not mentioned it to Howard in such histrionic language, the match might well have remained one of many obscure and uncelebrated events in Lincoln's life.

But however incidental it may have been in Lincoln's own life, there is no denying that it was a providential event for his biographers. It afforded them a dramatic occasion for illustrating Lincoln's incipient character, for showing his personal qualities of fortitude and forbearance in action. Though the logic of biography would suggest that one first find out the facts and then form conceptions of a subject's character, it rarely works this way, and strong preconceptions are more often the rule. As a campaign biographer, Howells knew that he was going to include only details and incidents that showed his subject in a favorable light, not just as a person but as a presidential candidate.

Holland, writing shortly after Lincoln's assassination, was looking for incidents and explanations that would fit the character of a martyred leader whose strength, courage, and perseverance were thought to have saved his country. Arnold's preconceptions were such that he was bound to present a wrestling match with a ruffian as an opportunity for moral uplift.

As with biographers, so also with informants. It is difficult, for example, not to see Greene's reinterpretation of the match as a reflection of the character of Lincoln the war president, cannily maneuvering with his opponent, refusing to be unduly provoked or drawn into an unfavorable position, husbanding his great strength and then using it with devastating effect at the proper moment.

If it is inevitable that the events of the past should be colored by the preoccupations of the present, this should be all the more reason to be on guard against the distortions that can result in this process. Because Lincoln acquitted himself honorably and even nobly as president does not imply that all actions of his previous life were equally honorable and noble. This event must surely tell us something about his character, but it was, like every other young person's, a character in the making, in flux. The evidence suggests that Lincoln conducted himself well under trying circumstances, but had it revealed that he fouled Armstrong in return for being fouled, his actions as president would have been no less honorable or noble. No better proof of this could be cited than the preference of Lincoln's nineteenth-century biographers for just such an interpretation, for in seizing upon the unlikely story of Lincoln's retaliation against Armstrong with a choke hold, they inadvertently presented their hero as reacting to a minor foul by angrily retaliating with one that was life-threatening and strictly forbidden.

The evidence, however, suggests that Lincoln did no such thing. The prevalence of the unconfirmed choke hold in early Lincoln biography cannot be accounted for in terms of what the weight of the testimony tells us about the match and probably speaks more pointedly of what the biographers and their publics considered a fitting response to the provocations of a bully. Modern, professionally trained biographers are admittedly much less susceptible to such pitfalls than their nineteenth-century predecessors, but that they can encounter pitfalls of their own is evident in the example of Benjamin P. Thomas. By ignoring the actual testimony and embellishing Howells's account, which was itself a creative redaction, Thomas moved away from the historical event he was presenting and performed a biographical feat comparable to one for which Herndon was roundly taken to task. In his biography, having credited dubious testimony about an aborted wedding ceremony, Herndon conjured up a dramatic scene complete with a marriage license and bridal flowers that probably never existed. Both Thomas and Herndon were, of course, guilty of no more than trying to fill a blank spot in the picture with imaginative details. Thomas's error was no more fatal to his admirable biography than Herndon's was to his, but the aberrations of such notable biographers serve to emphasize the importance of not losing sight of the sources.

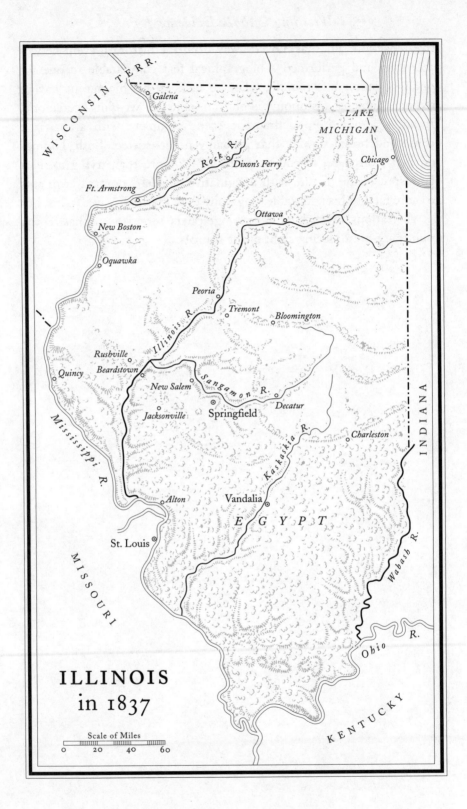

WISCONSIN TERR.

Galena

LAKE
MICHIGAN

Rock R.

Dixon's Ferry

Chicago

Ft. Armstrong

Ottawa

New Boston

Oquawka

Peoria

Tremont

Bloomington

Illinois R.

Rushville

Beardstown

New Salem

Sangamon R.

Decatur

Quincy

Jacksonville

Springfield

INDIANA

Charleston

Kaskaskia R.

Mississippi R.

Alton

Vandalia

E G Y P T

St. Louis

MISSOURI

Wabash R.

Ohio R.

ILLINOIS
in 1837

KENTUCKY

Scale of Miles

0   20   40   60

Chapter 2

❦

SELF-EDUCATION

What he has in the way of education, he has picked up.
— Lincoln, of himself

ABRAHAM LINCOLN ARRIVED at New Salem in 1831 at the age of twenty-two. He was, he said later, "a strange, friendless, uneducated, penniless boy, working on a flat boat – at ten dollars per month."[1] For the people of New Salem, he was a memorable sight. Henry Onstot recalled Lincoln's very first appearance in the area: "When he jumped off the boat bare headed, and bare footed with a coarse homespun shirt the Sleeves rolled up to his elbows and coarse homespun Pants. (Jeans or Linsey Woolsey) and these rolled up nearly to his knees, often combing his dark bushy hair with his fingers and being rather lank and tall [he] made a rather Singular grotesque appearance."[2] When the lanky stranger returned a few months later to work in New Salem, his unrolled pants attracted even more attention because, as everyone noticed, they were several inches too short. Even on the frontier, people judged by appearances, and the impression made by the young Abraham Lincoln was hardly favorable. William Butler, who later became a close friend, described him "as ruff a specimen of humanity as could be found."[3]

Even more memorable to the people of the New Salem neighborhood was the startling disparity between his unpromising appearance and the impression he made as soon as he began to talk. "When i first [met] him i thought him a Green horn," said Caleb Carman. "His Appearance was very od," but "after all this bad Apperance i Soon found [him] to be a very inteligent young man."[4] Carman was himself relatively unlettered and may have been all too readily impressed by someone who could recite Robert Burns and talk about books, politics, and the world's great men.⁵ But Carman's experience seems to have been typical: "after half hours Conversation with him i found Him no Green Horn."⁶ An educated physician who began a practice in New Salem about the time Lincoln arrived, Dr. Jason Duncan, concurred: "his external apperance was not prepossessing, but on cultivating an acquaintance with him [I] found some thing about the young man verry attractive evincing intellegence far beyond the generality of youth of his age and opportunities."⁷

In truth, the gawky and unkempt young man was a surprising speci-men of his time and place. In his dress and physical appearance he was every inch a bumpkin, a yokel, a slightly eccentric example of a recog-nizable type. Nothing would have been more typical than for a poor boy raised in the sparsely populated backwoods of southwestern Indiana, without means or worldly goods, to have drifted into flatboating or working as a hog drover, as Lincoln reportedly did.⁸ But it came as a revelation to the settlers of Sangamon County, Illinois, to find such a person strikingly articulate, exhibiting book learning and political acuity, and animated by a lively intelligence.

How, they were the first to wonder, had this come about? Abraham Lincoln's childhood education, conducted almost entirely by himself, with only a modicum of schooling, is one of the most familiar stories in American history. According to the legend, the young backwoods farm boy educated himself by a determined program of nightly reading after the day's work was done, systematically consuming all the books in the sparsely inhabited neighborhood where he grew up. His determination and youthful quest for enlightenment, the distinctive inner qualities that set him apart, have long been symbolized by the indelible image of the boy reading alone by firelight.

Legends, by their nature, are not so much factual accounts as sym-bolic embodiments or expressions of what the facts represent. America's attraction to the image of the boy reading alone by firelight is thus the tribute paid to the humble origins and noble attributes of a great national hero, but the Lincoln of history, insofar as can be determined from the testimony of those who knew him, proves in many respects worthy of the legend. Most of his Indiana friends and neighbors who were questioned by William H. Herndon, and William M. Thayer before him, remembered the young Lincoln as an ardent reader. His cousin John Hanks, who lived for a time with the Lincolns, called him "a Constant and voracious reader."⁹ His near neighbor and close friend David Turnham told Herndon, "We had but few books at that time and our opportunities were poor," but "what [Lincoln] read he read well and thoroughly – Never forgetting what he read."¹⁰ These same witnesses confirmed Lincoln's own testimony that he attended the primitive schools of the period only briefly and intermittently, and they further suggested that he eventually outstripped his teachers. "The Schools we went to taught Spelling – reading – writing and Ciphering to single rule of 3 – no further," reported one of his schoolmates. "Lincoln got ahead of his masters – Could do him no further good: he went to school no more."¹¹

To judge from the recollections of those who knew him, the books Lincoln read as a boy in Indiana seem to have been very few in number: the Bible, Aesop's *Fables*, Bunyan's *Pilgrim's Progress*, Defoe's *Robinson Crusoe*, *Sindbad the Sailor*, James Riley's *Narrative*, and biographies of Franklin and Washington.¹² This was typical popular reading fare of the time, and most of it is still familiar. Though no longer remembered, Riley's *Narrative* (1817) may have made a considerable impression, for he mentioned it to a campaign biographer in 1860.¹³ The book was a widely read account of the capture of a shipwrecked American captain and crew and their enslavement in North Africa at the hands of Arabs. Lincoln also made use of some standard textbooks of the time – Dilworth's *Spelling-book*, Pike's *Arithmetic*, Scott's *Lesson in Elocution* – and a family copy of Barclay's famous etymological *Dictionary*.¹⁴

It has sometimes been argued that there must have been something strangely propitious about this selection of titles to have constituted the preparation of so great a man. But the truth of the matter seems to be that these were simply the only books available, for one thing his Indiana friends and relatives agreed on was that Lincoln read "everything he could lay his hands on."¹⁵ Doubtless he read other books whose titles are lost to us, and he certainly read other things, such as pamphlets, magazines, and newspapers. Somewhere in his Indiana reading he acquired a strong attraction for poetry that never left him, possibly from the sampling of English poets in Murray's *Reader* and Scott's *Lessons* but also in the newspapers of the day, where poetry was often featured. It was probably exposure to these highly political newspapers that helped spark Lincoln's early interest in politics.¹⁶

His stepmother, who came into his life when he was ten years old and to whom he remained devoted, described for Herndon the young man's unusual commitment to his studies: "Abe read all the books he could lay his hands on – and when he came across a passage that Struck him he would write it down on boards if he had no paper & keep it there till he did get paper – then he would re-write it – look at it – repeat it – He had a copy book – a kind of scrap book in which he put down all things and this preserved them."[17] His stepmother's evident pride in Lincoln's educational efforts contrasted with his father's attitude, which was apparently less than approving. Herndon may have asked about a scene in William M. Thayer's *The Pioneer Boy and How He Became President* (1863), which depicted the young Lincoln resisting his father's command that he quit reading and go back to work. Sarah Bush Lincoln spoke protectively of her husband's behavior, which she tried to put in a positive light, telling Herndon: "As a usual thing Mr Lincoln never made Abe quit reading to do anything if he could avoid it. He would do it himself first. Mr. Lincoln could read a little & could scarcely write his name: hence he wanted, as he himself felt the uses & necessities of Education his boy Abraham to learn & he Encouraged him to do it in all ways he could."[18] But one senses a defensiveness in her description, particularly when she says that her husband never made the boy quit reading "if he could avoid it."

Lincoln's cousin Dennis Hanks, who lived with them, spotlighted the tension between Lincoln and his father in characterizing the boy's reading habits: "He was a Constant and I m[a]y Say Stubborn reader, his father having Sometimes to slash him for neglecting his work by reading." That this was a continuing problem rather than an isolated incident is further suggested by a saying of Thomas Lincoln that Dennis remembered in this connection. "Mr Lincoln – Abs father – often said [I] had to pull the old sow up to the trough – when speaking of Abes reading & how he got to it, then and now he had to pull her away."[19] In other words, he had to force his son to take up reading, but once the boy became a reader, only force could get him stopped.

Sarah Bush Lincoln's testimony laid great stress on her stepson's devotion to reading and study, but she also told things that are at odds with the picture presented by the time-honored legend. "He read diligently – studied in the day time – didn't after night much – went to bed Early – got up Early and then read – Eat his breakfast – go to work in the field with the men."[20] If he didn't read at night, what about the boy reading by firelight? Implicit in this image of nighttime reading is an understanding that daytime had to be given to farm work or other chores, but his stepmother's testimony that he rarely read at night suggests otherwise.[21]

Reading during the day raises the specter of the boy shirking his chores and stealing time from work for reading, something that is confirmed by Thayer's anecdote and by Dennis Hanks's recollection of Lincoln's father "slashing" him for neglecting his work by reading. There was difficulty between Lincoln and his father that, while probably quite important in his development, is hard to get at, for there are many clues but few concrete details.[22] Thomas Lincoln is reported to have told William G. Greene a few years after Lincoln left home, "I suppose that Abe is still fooling hisself with eddication. I tried to stop it, but he has got that fool idea in his head, and it can't be got out."[23] If Thomas Lincoln was as antagonistic to education as this suggests, we can be sure that the difficulty between them was serious. The symbolic boy reading by firelight has done his part and is at peace with his father; the actual boy was probably something of a rebel.

Not part of the popular image, for obvious reasons, is that Lincoln's studiousness, which he apparently indulged at the expense of his duties, was roundly judged by his contemporaries as an indication of his laziness. A neighbor and former employer, John Romine, told Herndon: "Abe was awful lazy: he worked for me – was always reading & thinking – used to get mad at him."[24] Dennis Hanks admitted, "Lincoln was lazy – a very lazy man – He was always reading – scribbling – writing – Ciphering – writing Poetry &c. &c."[25] That Lincoln did not like physical labor was apparently never disputed, for even his adoring stepmother admitted it. In this sense, judged by the standards of his contemporaries, he clearly *was* lazy, where laziness was regarded as something between a character fault and a cardinal sin.

But Sarah Bush Lincoln saw in the situation, at least retrospectively, something that the neighbors and even Dennis Hanks did not: that the young Lincoln, while lazy about farm work, had been industrious in another direction. She told Herndon that "he didn't like physical labor – was diligent for Knowledge – wished to Know & if pains & Labor would get it he was sure to get it."[26] Her daughter, Lincoln's stepsister, gave the situation another positive spin: "Abe was not Energetic Except in one thing – he was active & persistant in learning – read Everything he Could."[27] With historical hindsight, we have little trouble rationalizing Lincoln's youthful reading as a form of striving, as it surely was, but we miss an element in the equation if we fail to take into account the

construction his father and most others put on his dislike of farm work
and his appetite for reading. For them it was avoiding work; for him it
was a way of asserting his individuality and his aspirations.

While growing up in Indiana, the young Abraham Lincoln was, by
all indications, an inveterate reader or, as Dennis Hanks put it, "a Constant and I m[a]y Say Stubborn reader."[28] The more one looks at the
evidence behind the familiar legend, the more meaning Hanks's carefully chosen word "stubborn" seems to have. For Lincoln paid a price
for being a habitual reader as a boy in Indiana. Not only was he occasionally "slashed" by his father, but he was judged "lazy" by his friends
and neighbors. His persistence in these circumstances was, indeed, an
act of youthful stubbornness; it was carried on in defiance of the opinions of family and community. Looking back on these events in the
light of what happened subsequently, we can see that Lincoln was a
reader in his youthful days in Indiana, in part as a way of escaping farm
work, but more important, he was reading because he had decided very
early that he didn't want to be a farmer.

❧

MUCH OF THE MOTIVATION behind Lincoln's intensive effort at
self-education after he arrived at New Salem was surely compensatory.
Having largely missed out on formal schooling and living for the first
time among people who had had common schooling and occasionally
some form of higher education as well, the ambitious Lincoln was naturally concerned to catch up. Equally easy to understand is that an
unusually intelligent boy raised in the middle of nowhere would want
to acquire knowledge of the larger world around him, although neither
of these concerns was typical for people in his circumstances. Finally,
there was the plain fact that reading held a fascination for the young
Abraham Lincoln, for the evidence suggests clearly that he was attracted by the wit and pathos of poetry, the dramatic incidents and person-
alities of history, and the intellectual stimulation of new ideas and
philosophical perspectives.

Lincoln helped his parents move from Indiana to Macon County,
Illinois, in March 1830 and spent a year helping them get established.
During this time he "worked out" as a laborer, splitting fence rails and
breaking prairie. The following spring he struck out on his own and
landed in the raw but aspiring village of New Salem on the Sangamon
River. For the first several months he was employed, as we have seen, by

Denton Offutt, principally as a store clerk but also as manager of a milling operation. He was remembered by those who knew him then as a good worker and an obliging clerk, who occasionally took time out to socialize and participate in sports and athletic contests, in which he always excelled. In addition to the impression that he was surprisingly knowledgeable and well read, he quickly earned the reputation of a serious student.

By the time he arrived in New Salem, Lincoln's reading had clearly become more selective and more purposeful. His New Salem acquaintances did not frequently claim, as did the Indiana informants, that Lincoln read everything he could get his hands on. Their emphasis was on how often he was seen with a book in his hand and on the doggedness of his dedication to his studies. Robert B. Rutledge recalled:

> While clerking for Offatt as Post Master or in the pursuit of any avocation, An opportunity would offer, he would apply himself to his studies, if it was but five minutes time, would open his book, which he always kept at hand, & study, close it recite to himself, then entertain company or wait on a Customer in the Store or post office apparently without any interuption, When passing from business to boarding house for meals, he could usually be seen with his book under his arm, or open in his hand reading as he walked.[29]

Because Herndon was interested in how his former partner acquired his education, he purposely solicited testimony on the subject of his reading. That he tried to determine what Lincoln had read before he came to New Salem is evident from the questions he put to Caleb Carman, who had known Lincoln when he was building the flatboat for Offutt in Sangamontown, before he got to New Salem. The difficulty of eliciting such information is evident in Carman's reply: "I Recd your letter of the 5th Decb whishing to know if Lincoln quotied Shakespear in Sangamon Town it was in Sangamon Town & Newsalem the words I can not Recollect often in Conversation he would Refer to that Great man Shakespear allso Lord Byron as being a great man and Burns & of Burns Poems & Lord Nellson as being a Great Admarall & Naval Commander & Adams & Henry Clay Jackson George Washington was the Greatest of all of them & was his Great favorite."[30]

Lincoln's lounging and recreational hours in New Salem, when he was not employed in sports or telling stories, appear to have been devoted largely to reading, or so the witnesses remembered it. Mentor Graham said of his first sight of Lincoln: "he was lying on a trundle bed rocking a cradle with his foot – was almost covered with papers and books."[31] Russell Godbey, a farmer, remembered finding him astraddle a wood pile in New Salem reading a book,[32] and William G. Greene reported that on bringing some friends home from Illinois College expressly to meet Lincoln, he "was mortified to find that Abe was lying stretched out flat on his back on a cellar door reading a paper – I introduced him and he appeared so awkward and ruff, that I was afraid my college friends would be ashamed of him."[33] Asked to describe Lincoln's reading posture, one of his friends replied: "he was some times seting some times stading and some times on his Back and very [often] would walk Down to the River Reading when he would Return the same way."[34]

Reading is a solitary occupation, but Lincoln was known for his sociability and love of company. How these two modes were occasionally mixed is suggested by R. B. Rutledge's description of Lincoln walking in the village:

> have seen him reading, walking the streets, occasionally become absorbed with his book, would stop & stand for a few moments, then walk on, or pass from one house in the town to an other, or from one crowd or squad of men to an other, apparently seeking amusement with his book under his arm, when the company or amusement became dry or irksome, he would open his book & commune with it for a time, then return it to its usual resting place, and entertain his audience.[35]

Switching easily back and forth between reading and socializing suggests that Lincoln had a distinctive ability to focus his attention so as to manage competing attractions.

What did he read? The schoolmaster Mentor Graham said that "he devoted more time to reading the Scripture, books on science and comments on law and to the acquisition of Knowledge of men & things than any man I ever knew."[36] An interview with James Short, a trusted friend who saw much of Lincoln during his New Salem years, revealed:

> He used to read a great deal, improving every opportunity, by day and by night. S. never knew of his reading a novel. History and poetry & the newspapers constituted the most of his reading. Burns seemed to be his favorite. S. had a copy of "The American Military Biography" which he read a great deal. He read aloud very often; and frequently assumed a lounging position when reading. He read very thoroughly, and had a most wonderful memory. Would distinctly remember

almost every thing he read. Used to sit up late of nights reading, & would recommence in the morning when he got up.[37]

In New Salem, according to Rutledge, Lincoln "was ever ready with an appropriate response, to any vein of humor or eloquence when occasion required, have frequently heard him repeat pieces of prose & poetry." This and other testimony about his phenomenal memory suggests that learning was effortless, but Rutledge remembered a practice similar to that described by Lincoln's stepmother of Lincoln's commonplacing what he wanted to remember from his reading: "his practise was, when He wished to indelibly fix any thing he was reading or studying on his mind, to write it down, have known him to write whole pages of books he was reading."[38] Unfortunately, except for a few pages of a Sum Book he kept in Indiana while learning arithmetic, none of Lincoln's commonplace books is known to have survived.

Nor have any volumes from Lincoln's own New Salem library, except for the copy of Kirkham's *Grammar* that he reportedly gave to Ann Rutledge. He probably owned very few books, for not only was he poor and without means, but his lack of interest in material acquisitions extended to books, and he seems never to have owned many, even when he became reasonably well off later in life. Charles Maltby, a fellow clerk, referred to "his small collection of books [in which] he had secured the poetical works of Cowper, Gray, and Burns,"[39] but this is virtually the only reference to Lincoln's having a personal library in New Salem. Although this was a pioneer village and books were generally scarce, there were educated and reading people among the inhabitants, and books were much more plentiful than in the Indiana neighborhood where Lincoln had grown up. Herndon was told that some residents – such as the well-to-do Kentuckian, Bennett Abell, the justice of the peace, Bowling Green, and the merchants John McNamar and Isaac Chrisman – had appreciable book collections and that Lincoln "had axcess to any Books that was in and arond the town of Salem for all Knew that he was fond of Reading."[40] Not surprisingly, the prolific reading that Lincoln was reported doing in New Salem was largely from borrowed books.

Newspapers were an important part of Lincoln's New Salem reading. He had become, according to his stepmother, a "constant reader" of newspapers in his teens while living in Indiana, a practice he continued in Illinois. Dr. John Allen said that when Lincoln was appointed New

Salem's postmaster, he "Never saw a man better pleased." This, Allen said, "was because, as he said, he would then have access to all the News papers – never yet being able to get the half that he wanted before."[41] Except in the case of his vocational studies, it seems likely that Lincoln read newspapers, as R. B. Rutledge believed, "More than he did books."[42] Herndon's cousin, J. Rowan Herndon, who boarded Lincoln for a time and sold him half interest in a store, recalled: "as to the News Papers he Read all that Came to the Plase the Congreshinal Globe Acts of Congress Legislator and the Louisville Journal Sangamon Journal Stlouis Republickin and papers that Came to the offisce as he had full axcess to the offisce as to his Readng he spent the time Mostly of Knights in Reading history and Day tim News Papers for he generly Read for the By standers when the male Come which was weekly."[43]

This picture is instructive. Reading other people's newspapers surely gave him a broader perspective than merely reading his own favorites, the *Missouri Republican* and the *Louisville Journal,* and reading out loud to others probably served him in several ways. Reading aloud was the way he had learned, but he persisted in it, as he explained to Herndon years later, because he believed it made him more retentive by giving him the sound as well as the sight of the words.[44] It also gave him the opportunity to perform for his fellows, something that he liked to do from an early age. And it had the effect of making him a center of news and opinion and thus an integral part of public discussions. His newspaper reading remained so entrenched that Herndon, judging from what he knew of later years as well as what he learned from his informants, concluded: "Mr. Lincoln's education was almost entirely a newspaper one."[45] This was plainly an exaggeration, but to judge from the testimony, his opportunities, and the character of his serious interests in his maturity, it probably contained a large measure of truth.

⤙

THE INTENSITY with which Lincoln laid siege to certain subjects stamped itself indelibly on the memories of his New Salem acquaintances. The most diligently pursued studies were undoubtedly those related to vocational pursuits, most notably surveying and the law. But even his study of English grammar, the first subject he took up in earnest, was probably related to a recognition that he needed to come to terms with standard English in order to make a more presentable appearance in public. Therefore, the decision to study grammar is evidence that he was already considering a career in politics, the law, or both.

Lincoln had grown up a hoosier. The term has survived as a nickname for inhabitants of Indiana, because it was a state first settled by the tribe of poor white farmers from the southern uplands, like Lincoln's family, who were called hoosiers. Mostly from Kentucky and Tennessee, the hoosiers migrated in substantial numbers into the new states of Indiana, Illinois, and Missouri in the early years of the nineteenth century, speaking English with a distinctive vocabulary and twang. It would have been clear to any hoosier who was also an avid reader of books that the language he spoke was distinctly at variance from the English employed in print. This presented no practical barrier to farmers, artisans, or most tradesmen, but the inability to speak and write standard English served to limit the opportunities of those with higher aspirations, and Lincoln's decision to tackle English grammar is strong evidence that the young store clerk considered himself one of these.

The testimony about his study of grammar is comparatively abundant, though there is disagreement about such things as exactly when he took it up, what textbook he used, and who served as his mentor. The principal claimant to the last-named honor has usually been the village schoolmaster, Mentor Graham. Graham was an elderly man when Herndon interviewed him, and while Herndon believed him honest, he noted that he was "flighty – at times nearly non copus mentis."[46] When interviewed in 1860, Graham had laid the basis for a legend by telling James Q. Howard: "When L[incoln] was about 22 said he believed he must study Grammar – one [grammar book] could not be obtained in neighborhood – walked for 8 miles and borrowed Kirkhams old Grammar."[47] Five years later, after Lincoln's presidency and martyrdom, Graham had found a place in the story for himself. He told Herndon:

> Mr Lincoln spoke to me one day and Said "I had a notion of studing grammar." "I replied to him thus ["]If you Ever Expect to go before the public in any Capacity I think it the best thing you can do." He said to me "If I had a grammar I would Commence now." There was none in the village & I said to him – "I know of a grammar at one Vances about 6 miles" which I thought he could get –. He was then

at breakfast – ate – got up and went on foot to Vances & got the Book. He soon Came back & told me he had it. He then turned his immediate & almost undivided attention to English grammar."[48]

The details of this account – the conversation before breakfast, the name of the owner of the grammar, Lincoln's eagerness exemplified by the walk to fetch the book – all lend it an air of reality, and Graham's remark about going before the public seems to shed light on Lincoln's own motivation. Another detail, or the absence thereof, adds to the credibility of Graham's account: the fact that he had no grammar of his own to lend. For in spite of his lifelong service as a schoolmaster, there is reason to believe that Graham's own attainments were quite meager and that he was nothing like a learned man.[49]

This is undoubtedly one of the reasons William G. Greene immediately questioned Graham's claim to have taught Lincoln grammar. When Greene, who had clerked alongside Lincoln in Offutt's store, heard that Graham had made such a claim, he confronted him and reported to Herndon: "when I questioned him wher when & what school house he had to admit that it was on the street behind the Counter when at Diner &c &c." Greene insisted to Herndon that "Mr Lincoln had no Teacher after he came to New Salem that he was self Taught," and he also later claimed that it was he who had loaned Lincoln the grammar he used.[50]

At least three other acquaintances have reasonably credible claims to some role in Lincoln's study of English grammar, an episode that tells us more about Lincoln than his interest in mastering the past participle. "Lincoln was a hard student," according to Daniel Green Burner, who as a boy had known Lincoln in New Salem. "It seemed to me he was studying all the time for he always had a book around him and employed his spare time in reading. In the dry goods store he studied grammar, his teacher being a young man by the name of Charles Maltby, who was a good scholar."[51] Maltby, like Greene, claimed to have been a fellow clerk in Offutt's store and published a small book about his old companion, which offered a firsthand picture of Lincoln's daily activities.

The business in the store being mostly with country traders, was transacted between the hours of 9 A.M. and 3 P.M., giving several hours in the day in which one of the clerks could perform all the duties required in the store. It was on those occasions that Lincoln frequently would, for an hour at the close of the day, engage in ath-

letic sports, such as wrestling, jumping, pitching quoits or heavy
weights and similar exercises, diversions peculiar to and common to
that day and age. The store was usually closed at 7 P.M., when occasionally an evening would be spent with some family or young people
in the village, and those occasional visits or calls were seasons of
mutual pleasure and gratification. Lincoln's humorous fund of anecdotes and stories made him a welcome visitor at all times. The most
of the evenings, however, after closing the store, were, from 8 to 11
o'clock, employed by Lincoln in reading and study; a short time then
was spent in reviewing the reading of the evening, and then blankets
were spread upon the counter and the inmates retired to rest on their
hard couch, which prepared them for the labors and duties of the
coming day.[52]

This account was published more than fifty years after the fact and
may present a less than precise picture of life in Offutt's store, but
Maltby does remember and emphasize Lincoln's dedication as a reader.
"While he was attentive to business and to all the interests of his
employer, he gave his leisure hours to study and to the acquisition of
useful information. In studying Murray's Grammar he often remarked,
'that it was very dry reading, but that he would master the general principles,' which he did; but his correct mastery of the language was
acquired more from reading and writing than from study."[53] (This is an
interesting qualification, particularly Maltby's recollection that Lincoln
was working on his writing.) In spite of what Burner remembered and
the penchant for some of Lincoln's early friends to make the most of
their association with him, Maltby advanced no claim to have assisted
his fellow clerk in the study of grammar. In fact, he seemed to rule it
out: "He had no teachers, few books and no learned and intellectual
companions."[54]

One who might have qualified as an intellectual companion, Dr.
Jason Duncan, put forth a very modest claim to have assisted Lincoln.
"The winter following [Lincoln's arrival in New Salem]," he wrote
Herndon, "Abraham requested me to assist him in the study of English
Grammar, which I consented to do to the extent of my limited ability.
his application through the winter was assiduous, and untiring, his
intuitive faculties were Surprising. he seemed to master the construction of the english language and apply the rules for the same in a most
astonishing manner."[55] Duncan, Maltby, and Greene all agree that Lincoln studied and fairly mastered grammar during the first months in the
village while clerking for Offutt, roughly between July 1831 and April

1832, but Greene's brother, L. M. ("Nult") Greene, had a different recollection. "In the summer after he came home from the Black Hawk
War [late July 1832] he got possession of one of Kirkham's Grammars &
began studying it on the hill sides of old Salem I spent several days
giving him instruction in this manner. In fact all the instruction he ever
had in Grammar he rec'd from me as above indicated."[56]

As a candidate for president in 1860, Lincoln referred to his feat of
tackling English grammar on his own, which he says occurred "after he
was twentythree"[57] and which would place it no earlier than 1832.
Whether Lincoln studied grammar in 1831 or 1832 (Graham insisted on
1833) is probably a matter of no great importance, nor is the question of
whether he used Samuel Kirkham's textbook or Lindley Murray's.
Clearly the more important matter is that all the informants agree he
studied grammar fairly early in his New Salem years, that he studied
diligently and with marked success. The discrepancies in the testimony
are no more than one would expect from recollections at a remove of
thirty-five years or more, and in fact, the discrepancies in this case may
be more apparent than real. Lincoln may very well have begun his study
of grammar in the fall of 1831 using Murray's *English Grammar*, taken it
up again upon his return from the Black Hawk War with Kirkham's,
getting advice and assistance along the way from anyone he came upon
who seemed to know something about the subject.

A copy of Kirkham's that apparently was once in Lincoln's possession,
preserved and handed down in the Rutledge family, is now in the
Library of Congress, but it contains no evidence of having belonged to
John C. Vance and sheds no light on questions of chronology. What it
does serve to remind us is that learning formal English grammar from a
nineteenth-century textbook, without a qualified teacher, was a truly
daunting task, as anyone who picks up a copy of Kirkham's will readily
see. Just to take the first step, mastering the technical terminology,
was intimidating: "Grammar is divided into four parts; 1. Orthography,
2. Etymology, 3. Syntax, 4. Prosody." "Orthography," the first and by far
the briefest section, nonetheless is crowded with terms and definitions
that the student is required to learn by rote: terms such as "consonant,"
"diphthong," "triphthong," "primitive word," and "derivative word." The
student is also required to learn all the sounds of all twenty-six letters.

C sounds like a *k* before *a, o, u, r, l, t,* and at the end of syllables; as in
cart, cottage, curious, craft, tract, cloth; victim, flaccid. It has the sound

of *s* before *e, i*, and *y*; as in *centre, cigar, mercy*. *C* has the sound of *sh* when followed by a diphthong, and is preceded by the accent, either primary or secondary; as in *social, pronunciation*, &c.; and of *z* in *discern, sacrifice, sice, suffice*. It is mute in *arbuscle, czar, czarina, endict, victuals, muscle*.[58]

At the end of each section are the review questions. Because he had Greene read him these questions to test his comprehension, Lincoln as president playfully introduced him to some of his cabinet as the man who taught him grammar.[59] Some of the review questions Greene must have read are: "What are relative pronouns? – Repeat them. – From what words is the term *antecedent* derived? – What does antecedent mean? Are relatives varied on account of gender, person, or number? – To what are *who* and *which* applied? – To what is *that* applied? – Should *who* ever be applied to irrational beings or children?"[60]

For an understanding of Abraham Lincoln's formative years, there are a number of indicative points in the story of his studying English grammar. It shows his wish to improve his command of language, his willingness to tackle an excessively dry and daunting subject, and his diligence in pursuit of a goal. But perhaps the most salient point in the story is the apparent ease and dispatch with which he handled the subject. In 1860 Bill Greene told James Q. Howard: "2 or 3 mos. after he landed [in New Salem], said he would study grammar – good practical grammarian in three weeks – Said to me Bill if that is what they call a science I'll subdue another."[61] Although Greene no doubt overstates the matter, as he often does, the supporting evidence makes it reasonably clear that Lincoln's study of grammar had the effect of proving his intellectual mettle not only to his neighbors but to himself.

⁓

ONE OF THE THINGS that immediately struck those who met Lincoln at this time was the wit and verbal facility that seemed so surprising in an unprepossessing drifter. After his gawky appearance, his ability as a storyteller seems to have made the strongest initial impression, although Herndon had great difficulty getting his informants to repeat the stories. This was because, as Row Herndon told him, they were "on the vulger order."[62] Though there is not much to judge from, there is little doubt that the stories for which Lincoln soon became locally famous were mostly off-color. A. Y. Ellis, who kept a store in New

Salem for a time, recalled a storytelling session in connection with his first meeting with Lincoln in 1833 that probably captures something of the role storytelling played in men's social lives:

> he [Lincoln] was Setting on a Saw log taking to Jack and Rial Armstrong and a Man by the [name of] Hohammer. I shook hands with the Armstrongs & Hohamer and was conversing with them a few Moments when we was Joined by My old freind and former townsman George Warberton pritty tight as Usual and he Soon asked Me to tell the old story about Ben Johnson and Mrs Dales Blue Dye &c &c which I did. and then Jack Armstrong Said Lincoln tell Ellis the story about Govenor Tickner his city bread son & his Negro Bob Which he did with several others by Jacks Calling for them.[63]

Ellis's circumspect descriptions suggest that these stories were probably what we would now call "unedifying," were certainly not intended for mixed company, and would no doubt have been judged, by the standards of polite society, to be in decidedly bad taste. But this was not, of course, polite society. This was the culture of frontier farmers and merchants, in which this kind of storytelling not only was standard behavior but could be, as in Lincoln's case, an important aspect of one's social identity. The story of Ticknor and his city-bred son and his Negro Bob has probably been lost to us, but there is little doubt that one of the very things that made it entertaining for these men at New Salem was its calculated impropriety.

Lincoln was known all his adult life for his fondness for "improper" stories and his skill at telling them. The handful that have survived, all from later periods in his life, suggest a repertoire that dealt typically with such things as illicit sexuality, scatology, flatulence, physical handicaps, and ethnic stereotypes.[64] By one of the ironies of history, what would probably have given least offense in Lincoln's time – the racial and ethnic stereotypes – are considered most objectionable today.

Almost the only surviving Lincoln story that can be confidently assigned to his New Salem years was related by Row Herndon and probably was considered acceptable for mixed company. It concerned a preacher whose trousers were invaded by a lizard and who tried to discourage the lizard from ascending his leg by slapping at it, even as he continued to preach. The climax of the story features the reaction of a woman in the congregation when the preacher's attempts to get free of the lizard caused him to kick off his trousers and finally to disrobe completely. The off-color stories that Ellis repeated for Herndon seem to date from a later period,[65] but he said of those he heard Lincoln tell in his earliest political campaigns, "I remember them but Modesty and my Veneration for his Memory forbids me to relate."[66] This reticent testimony conceals, but it also tells us some important things: that Lincoln told "vulgar" stories on the stump that were worse than the ones Ellis did repeat, that it was not considered in keeping with a veneration for his memory to make them public, and that Ellis still remembered them after the passage of more than thirty years.

If it seems difficult to conceive of a great national hero and moral exemplar as being, from an early age, a notorious fountain of tasteless stories, one should bear in mind that while he was an exceptional person and not a typical hoosier, Lincoln was very much a creature of his environment and that these stories were the cultural staple of that time and place. Lincoln's mastery of this kind of storytelling endeared him to the men he came in contact with, the same men who were to be his future constituents and clients. Furthermore, it no doubt served as an aid to his eventual mastery of a more socially acceptable form of storytelling.

The straitlaced A. Y. Ellis, in writing to Herndon of these matters, called attention to the disparity between the great man that Lincoln became and his private demeanor as a teller of off-color stories. "I think Mr Lincoln Was Not as high minded as a man of his honor and Integrity ought to have been for instance Just think of his low flung, black guard story Many of them was redicilus as we both Know." But Ellis believed that Lincoln had come by this practice naturally and took note of his friend's capacity for change and growth: "It is Not Strange to Me that Mr L. Should have Such a Great passion For dirty Stories it was his Early training by the Hanks Boys his Cousins and after he left them he commenced a different train of thought and Studdie."[67]

~∂~

LINCOLN'S ABILITY as a storyteller, which was part of his early affinity for performing and public speaking, presumably led to his participation in a New Salem debating club or literary society. When he was a candidate for president in 1860, his old friend Dr. John Allen told James Q. Howard, "First speech L made in that region was at a country debating club which met in an old store house. Did pretty well – Used to walk 6 miles to attend another debating Society, and 'practice polemics,' as they said. These 'polemics' were equal some times to the best farces played in theatre. With but a rare exception Clubs were composed of men of no education whatever."[68] William G. Greene, when questioned by Herndon about this, flatly denied it: "We never had any *Debating* Society at New Salem."[69] But the weight of other testimony indicates that this was something he either didn't know about or didn't remember.

Dr. Jason Duncan remembered much the same thing as Dr. Allen: "The first time I ever heard him attempt to Speak in public, was at a polemic Society meeting in an underground room of a rude log cabin which Stood on the South hillside to the right of main street looking toward the river from the west. . . . I am inclined to the belief that in that cabin he uttered his maiden Speech."[70] R. B. Rutledge, who claimed that his father, James Rutledge, was founder and president of this "debating club," offered his own account of Lincoln's maiden speech:

> Both hands were thrust down deep in the pockets of his pantaloons. A perceptible smile at once lit up the faces of the audience for all anticipated the relation of some humorous story. But he opened up the discussion in splendid style to the infinite astonishment of his friends. As he warmed with his subject his hands would forsake his pockets and would enforce his ideas by awkward gestures; but would very soon seek their easy resting place. He pursued the question with reason and argument so pithy and forcible that all were amazed.[71]

No records of the New Salem club have survived, but Fern Nance Pond, who made a study of the literary clubs of the region, has drawn this general picture:

> The members subscribed to a Constitution and Bylaws, and held meetings once a month. One outstanding rule was that no member should use the name of the Supreme Being in debate. Any member failing to give attention to the speeches was fined from three to six and one-fourth cents; any one guilty of disorderly conduct was fined from one to six candles. Every member was required to perform in all the several departments, – debating, declaiming, composing, criticising, and lecturing. Some of the standing committees were: Commerce, Agriculture, Military Affairs, Navy, Morals, and Education. The purpose of the last committee was to "establish a library and a high school, and to report upon the current systems of quackery."[72]

One of the clubs in the New Salem neighborhood whose records do survive was that started by Thomas J. Nance, a well-educated and civic-minded Kentuckian who promoted education and schools in the area and later served with Lincoln in the Illinois legislature. It is possible that this was the other debating society referred to by Dr. Allen that Lincoln walked six miles to attend. Their discussions and topics of debate, as reported by Pond, appear to have been timely and spirited. "On three occasions, as shown by the records, the question of slavery was ardently debated. One popular subject was the straightening and clearing of the Sangamon River, and another, the building of a canal from Petersburg to Beardstown." These were questions that Lincoln, as a budding politician, would speak out on in the months and years ahead. So, for that matter, were most of the rest of the public issues that Pond lists as having been debated: "Should females be educated and have the right to vote?; should banks be abolished?; should people join temperance societies?; is it right to treat during political campaigns?; should a wife promise to obey her husband?; should Congress reduce the price of public lands?"[73]

Lincoln's participation in the literary clubs is not nearly so well known as his reading or his study of grammar, but it was surely an important part of his education. The clubs put him in touch with the cultural issues of the day, some of which had little or no currency among the poor farmers that constituted the majority of the populace, people of little education whose existence was almost wholly taken up with the providing for basic needs. As Jack Armstrong's wife, Hannah, told Herndon, "we didn't think about books – papers – We worked – had to to live."[74] The literary clubs were, for Lincoln, a much-needed supplement to the kinds of religious and political discourse that dominated the world he grew up in. Of no less significance was the opportunity for speaking in public, an all-important testing ground for learning the conventions of civility in argument, as well as the tactics of debate. Alongside the image of the boy reading (when he should have been working) we would do well to place one of the gawky young man on his feet before an expectant crowd, learning what to do with his hands.

-ᴔ-

FROM CHILDHOOD to the time of his death, Abraham Lincoln was attracted to poetry. Though none of his Indiana neighbors refers to it, his well-known fascination with Shakespeare may date from his boyhood, but it blossomed at New Salem. John McNamar, a prominent storekeeper during Lincoln's first year at New Salem, claimed to own copies of Shakespeare, Pope, and *Don Quixote* but didn't remember

Lincoln as being a fellow devotee of Shakespeare when he first knew him.[75] It seems certain that Lincoln's appetite and appreciation for Shakespeare were quickened by his acquaintance with a shadowy and intriguing figure, Jack Kelso, who arrived in New Salem about the time McNamar was leaving.[76] Herndon realized that the rare, almost unique literary friendship of Lincoln and Kelso was of great biographical interest, but in spite of many inquiries, he could find out little about Kelso. He was remembered primarily, if at all, as a hunter and fisherman, and a lazy one at that. So strong was this impression on Lincoln's friend James Short that he doubted that Kelso was "much of a literary man."[77] But Herndon's researches convinced him that "Kelso was an educated as well as a well read man – deeply & thoroughly read in Burns & Shakespeare."[78]

From unspecified traditional sources, the New Salem historian Thomas P. Reep put together a colorful picture of Kelso, whom he described as "one of those peculiar, impractical geniuses – well educated, a lover of nature, with the soul of a poet and all of a poet's impracticability, and who could 'recite Shakespeare and Burns by the hour.' " According to Reep's unnamed sources, Kelso was completely untypical for that time and place. "Kelso and his wife had no children. To make a living, he and his wife occasionally kept a boarder [Lincoln was reportedly one for a time], and Jack did odd jobs at which he was exceedingly handy. He did not seek and could not keep any steady employment. He loved to fish and to hunt and could catch fish when others failed and always had his smokehouse filled with venison when winter set in and a surplus of venison hams for sale."[79]

Hardin Bale, who had run the carding mill in New Salem, told Herndon that "Kelso and Lincoln were great friends – always together – always talking and arguing."[80] The most detailed account of their relationship in Herndon's surviving files is found in an interview with Caleb Carman, who told Herndon: "I Knew John A. Kelso: he was a School Master: well educated – loved Shakespear and fishing above all other thing. Abe loved Shakespear but not fishing – still Kelso would draw Abe: they used to sit on the bank of the river and quote Shakespear – criticise one an other. Kelso lives now as I understand in Mo. Kelso, if at himself is a good Shakesperian Schollar for a western man."[81]

In later years Lincoln would claim he had read and reread some of Shakespeare's plays "perhaps as frequently as any unprofessional reader,"[82] and he could recite long passages from memory. Not much is known about his affinity for Shakespeare during his New Salem years, except the recollection of some of his close friends that Shakespeare was one of his favorites. James Matheny told Herndon: "My opinion from what [I saw] of Lincoln is that he Knew Shakespear as well – probably better in New Salem than he did in Spfgd."[83] In later years Lincoln allowed that *Macbeth* was the play that fascinated him most – "I think nothing equals Macbeth"[84] – but Milton Hay, who knew him well shortly after he moved to Springfield, remembered that " 'King Lear' was his favorite in Shakespeare."[85] As with other texts and writers, what Lincoln liked he read and reread, a pattern that continued throughout his life. The literary base that he established in his formative years was thus not broad, but in its concentration on such texts as Shakespeare and the Bible, it was conspicuously rich, both in language and in thought.

His strong attraction to another poet may have been even more important in the development of his intellectual bent. The Indiana informants on Lincoln's reading do not mention the popular Scottish poet Robert Burns, but by the time Lincoln arrived in New Salem his strong partiality for Burns was very evident. This probably tells us what he had been reading the previous winter when confined in his father's cabin by the infamous "winter of the deep snow." Almost all of the testimony about his literary tastes in New Salem refers to his penchant for Burns, often specifying the poet as his favorite. Lincoln "was always reading Burns & Shakespeare," was the way William G. Greene recalled it in 1860. "Knew all of Burns by heart."[86] Charles Maltby wrote of that time: "It was usual for him, after reading and studying Murray or Blackstone for two or three hours, to take up Burns' poems, which he read much and admired greatly. He read with that hilarity which usually was so peculiar to him, some of the most humorous productions of that versatile poet."[87]

That Lincoln would have been acquainted with the life of his favorite poet is beyond doubt, and there was much in Burns's biography with which the young Lincoln could strongly identify. The son of a poor farmer, Burns rebelled against the life of unremitting physical labor and against the religion he had been brought up in. He had a talent for versemaking and satire. Though moody and prone to fits of depression, he loved humor, company, and fun, and he loved to recite and perform for his friends. Moreover, he always carried a book to read when not otherwise occupied.[88] The physical worlds Burns and Lincoln inhabited were not really so different. As McNamar observed to Herndon, " 'the Cotters Saturday Night' By Lincolns favorite Author would describe many a prarie Cabin here away in times past."[89]

The young Lincoln's attraction for Burns's poetry is not hard to understand. The poems are lyrical and witty, they often have a broad and biting humor that would have had great appeal, and when read aloud, they make for a lively performance. According to Milton Hay, Lincoln had mastered the Scots dialect in which Burns's most provocative and animated poems are written. "He could very nearly quote all of Burns' Poems from memory. I have frequently heard him quote the whole of 'Tam o'Shanter,' 'Holy Willie's Prayer' and large portions of the 'Cotter's Saturday Night' from memory only. He had acquired the Scotch accent, and could render Burns perfectly."[90] Lincoln's natural talents probably lent themselves to a ready grasp of dialect and inflection. McNamar, who had a literary bent of his own, recalled: "I remember Mr Lincoln's first miscellaneous Reading he got possesion of a Copy of Burns and repeated with great Glee 'Sic a wife as willy had I wudna Gie a button for her.' "[91]

"Tam o'Shanter" is Burns's comic masterpiece. Tam, the farmer who stays late in town to drink with his cronies while his sullen wife waits for him, "Nursing her wrath to keep it warm," had much in common with the Clary's Grove boys, and his drunken adventures on the way home were doubtless received by Lincoln's New Salem listeners as high comedy. Nor were they themselves immune to the fear of the supernatural that Burns plays on in the climactic scene, when Tam, drunkenly betraying his presence to a gathering of dancing warlocks and witches, is chased and barely escapes with his life. Lincoln is reported to have improvised a prank while in New Salem that sounds as though it were inspired by Burns's poem. As Row Herndon told it,

> there was a man that use to come to salem and get tight and stay untell dark he was fraid of Gosts and some one had to goe home with him well Lincoln Perswaded a fellow to take a Sheet and goe in the Rod and perform Gost he then Sent an other gost and the man and Lincoln started home the Gost made his appeerence and the man Became much fritend But the Second gost made hs appear[ance] and frightend the first Gost half to Deth that Broke the fellow from staying untell Dark anymore.[92]

If Herndon remembered this prank correctly, its careful choreo-graphy affords a rare insight into Lincoln's puckish sense of fun. He apparently set out not simply to frighten the man who is afraid to walk home after dark but to teach him a lesson. Going along with him put Lincoln in a position to direct the action as well as to enjoy the spectacle. What makes this story something more than an ordinary prank and shows a distinctive imagination at work is, of course, the second ghost. Scaring the toper by arranging a confrontation with the object of his fears is the straightforward stuff of which such pranks are predictably made; sending the second ghost to frighten the first shows real ingenuity.

⁊

IN HIS ATTRACTION for Burns, an important point of affinity for Lincoln was Burns's religious skepticism, which seems to have mirrored his own. "His mind was skeptical and hence his deep humanity & skeptical tinge of mind made him love Burns,"[93] wrote William G. Greene. This is presumably as close as Greene cared to get to the sensitive subject of Lincoln's "infidelity," and most New Salem informants say nothing about Lincoln's religious belief, or lack of it. Herndon's investigations persuaded him that "a good deal of religious skepticism existed at New Salem, and there were frequent discussions at the store and tavern, in which Lincoln took part."[94] Moreover, Herndon collected strong evidence of Lincoln's rejection of the basic tenets of Christianity at the time he left New Salem in 1837.[95] One of those who knew him well at that time, James Matheny, admitted to Herndon that Lincoln's skeptical views on Christianity and the Bible had "shocked" him, and added: "Lincoln used to quote Burns. Burns helped Lincoln to be an infidel as I think – at least he found in Burns a like thinker & feeler. Lincoln quoted Tam o'Shanter – "What send one to Heaven and ten to Hell all &c."[96]

The line that Matheny quoted (imperfectly) is not from "Tam o'Shanter" but from another poem of Burns that was said to be a favorite with Lincoln, "Holy Willie's Prayer." In fact, Matheny said of this poem "That it was L[incoln's] religion."[97] The poem has been called "the greatest of all Burns's satirical pieces"[98] and is based on an actual incident and a real person, a local church elder whose self-righteousness and hypocrisy Burns held up to scorn. The satiric note is struck in the

first stanza, which presents the Calvinistic doctrine of election – the
tenet that only a few are chosen by God for salvation – in caustic terms:

> O Thou, wha in the heavens dost dwell,
> Wha, as it pleases best thysel',
> Sends ane to heaven and ten to hell
>   A' for thy glory,
> And no for ony guid or ill
>   They've done afore thee!

The satire of "Holy Willie's Prayer" is predictably scathing in its treatment of what a critic has called "the moral absurdity of the speaker's
beliefs."[99] Because he considers himself one of the elect, Holy Willie
sees his own sins as worthy of forgiveness:

> O Lord! – yestreen, – thou kens – wi' Meg –
> Thy pardon I sincerely beg;
> O! may't ne'er be a livin' plague,
>   To my dishonor!
> An' I'll ne'er lift a lawless leg
>   Again upon her.

But Willie sees nothing amiss in urging damnation for his enemies,
ostensibly for their sinfulness but actually for making him a laughingstock and besting him in court.

> Lord in the day of vengeance try him;
> Lord, visit him wha did employ him,
> And pass not in thy mercy by them,
>   Nor hear their pray'r:
> But, for thy people's sake, destroy them,
>   And dinna spare!

The dramatic monologue in the form of an overheard prayer makes
for colorful theater, and there is reason to think that part of the fun for
Lincoln was that an effective rendering of it would have made many of
his Baptist neighbors squirm. Lincoln had been himself raised in a Baptist family, and while he seems to have resisted most of the religious
beliefs of his parents, he retained throughout life a fatalism that one
may believe was fostered in part by the Calvinist bent of his Baptist
upbringing.

—❧—

LINCOLN'S RELIGIOUS skepticism at New Salem, which some of his
latter-day admirers have found hard to accept, rests on a broader foun-

dation than his attraction to Burns. There is strong evidence of his familiarity in New Salem with the two authors whose names at that time were synonymous with religious skepticism, Thomas Paine and Constantin de Volney. Lincoln's friend, A. Y. Ellis, who was apparently quite orthodox, reported to Herndon: "I think he read some of Tom Pains Works as he frequently spoke of Pains Book Common Since he once asked Me if I had ever Read Volneys ruins he Said he had and supposed that I had by My calling my oldest son Volney, – though I had never read them and never wished to."[100] Other sources, which Herndon does not name, led him to specify more precisely the texts and something of the context of Lincoln's religious speculations: "In 1834, while still living in New Salem and before he became a lawyer, he was surrounded by a class of people exceedingly liberal in matters of religion. Volney's *Ruins* and *Payne's Age of Reason* passed from hand to hand, and furnished food for the evening's discussion in the tavern and village store. Lincoln read both of these books and thus assimilated them into his own being."[101]

The clarity of Paine's prose and the incisive lucidity of his rationalism made his writings popular with thoughtful readers of the day, particularly those inclined toward freethinking. His defiant deism was widely regarded as little more than atheism, which contributed greatly to his notoriety among conventional readers and to his appeal among nonconformists. *The Age of Reason,* despite early attempts to suppress it, was widely read from the time of its publication in the 1790s. Written in France during the Revolution as the church was being brought down, *The Age of Reason* was Paine's conscientious attempt to salvage a rational theology "lest in the general wreck of superstition, of false systems of government and false theology, we lose sight of morality, of humanity and of the theology that is true."[102]

Paine's religious creed is forthrightly stated at the outset: "I believe in one God, and no more; and I hope for happiness beyond this life. I believe in the equality of man; and I believe that religious duties consist in doing justice, loving mercy, and endeavoring to make our fellow creatures happy."[103] State churches are given short shrift: "All national institutions of churches, whether Jewish, Christian or Turkish, appear to me no other than human inventions, set up to terrify and enslave mankind, and monopolize power and profit."[104] Religion, for Paine, as for his friend and admirer Thomas Jefferson, was personal and private: "My own mind is my own church."[105] His emphasis on the primacy of mind and reason would be echoed later, as we shall see, in some of Lincoln's earliest printed speeches.

In the first part of *The Age of Reason*, Paine brings his talents as a practiced dissenter and controversialist to bear on the Bible. Under his relentlessly rational analysis, its claim to be divine revelation is found to be wanting in every respect.

> When also I am told that a woman called the Virgin Mary, said, or gave out, that she was with child without any cohabitation with a man, and that her betrothed husband, Joseph, said that an angel told him so, I have a right to believe them or not; such a circumstance required a much stronger evidence than their bare word for it; but we have not even this — for neither Joseph nor Mary wrote any such matter themselves; it is only reported by others that *they said so* — it is hearsay upon hearsay, and I do not choose to rest my belief upon such evidence.[106]

One may imagine the appeal that this would have for a skeptically minded young law student immersed in the rules of evidence, and Herndon heard testimony that convinced him that ridiculing the virgin birth and referring to Christ as a "bastard" were staples of the New Salem freethinkers with whom Lincoln was associated.[107]

For reasons that will presently become clear, it seems certain that he would have taken notice of another passage in the early pages of *The Age of Reason*, in which Paine uses a wry humor to drive home his point about the baselessness of biblical "mythology."

> The Christian Mythologists, after having confined Satan in a pit, were obliged to let him out again to bring on the sequel of the fable. He is then introduced into the Garden of Eden, in the shape of a snake or a serpent, and in that shape he enters into familiar conversation with Eve, who is no way surprised to hear a snake talk; and the issue of this *tête-à-tête* is that he persuades her to eat an apple, and the eating of that apple damns all mankind.[108]

Constantin de Volney's language and approach in his *Ruins* are very different. Written in a wistful, self-consciously poetic vein, Volney's *Ruins* is ostensibly a meditation on the fate of past civilizations, but its aim is similar to Paine's in presenting natural reason as an alternative belief system to the "arbitrary opinions" of the world's religions, which are, in the words of the preface, "not demonstrable and often absurd."[109] The book begins with the author contemplating the ruins of the great

Middle Eastern civilizations and reflecting on their meaning for the modern world.

> What Egypt and Syria had once possessed, I was gratified to find in modern Europe the departed splendor of Asia: but the charm of my revery was soon dissolved by a last term of comparison. Reflecting that such had once been the activity of the places I was then contemplating: Who knows, said I, but such may one day be the abandonment of our countries? . . . Who knows if some traveller, like myself, shall not one day sit on their silent ruins and weep in solitude over the ashes of their inhabitants, and the memory of their greatness."[110]

The questions the author is led to propound about the fate of mankind are taken up by an apparition, the Genius of History, who leads the author through a historical account of the development and ultimate corruption of human institutions. According to the apparition, "self love, the desire of happiness, aversion to pain, are the essential and primary laws imposed on man by NATURE herself," and these laws, "like those of motion in the physical world, are the simple and fruitful principle of whatever happens in the moral world."[111] But willfulness, personal weakness, and bad government eventually lead to the negation of these natural laws and the substitution of their opposites.

> Hence originated fatal doctrines, gloomy and misanthropic systems of religion, which painted the gods malignant and envious, like their despots. Man, to appease them, offered up the sacrifice of all his enjoyments: he environed himself in privations, and reversed the laws of nature. Conceiving his pleasures to be crimes, his sufferings expiations, he endeavoured to love pain, and to abjure the love of self; he persecuted his senses, hated his life; and a self-denying and antisocial morality plunged nations into the apathy of death.[112]

The fault for these disastrous developments is increasingly laid on religious cults and their leaders, and the book culminates in a grand symposium at which the conflicting and irreconcilable claims of the great religions are argued at length. The Muslims claim to have the true faith, only to have it come out that they themselves have bitter internal disagreements. The inability of the Catholics to agree with the Lutherans demonstrates that the same is true with the Christians. Other groups, such as the Zoroastrians, the Buddhists, the Hindus, and the Jews, take turns ridiculing one another's doctrines. One critique of Christianity that probably struck a meaningful note for Lincoln, who was giving serious thought to a law career, was this: "Where are the proofs, the witnesses of these pretended facts? Can we receive them without examining the evidence? The least action in a court of justice requires two witnesses; and we are ordered to believe all this on mere tradition or hearsay!"[113]

Like Paine in *The Age of Reason*, Volney attacks the Garden of Eden story as absurd and an offense against reason. "What! because a man and woman ate an apple six thousand years ago, all the human race are damned? and you call God just? What tyrant ever rendered children responsible for the faults of their fathers! What man can answer for another's actions: Is not this subversive of every idea of justice and reason?"[114] The criticisms of Paine and Volney struck a responsive chord in the young Lincoln, and this is nowhere better illustrated than in their castigation of the doctrine of eternal damnation. Though Lincoln was increasingly unwilling to discuss his religious views in later years, the apparent injustice of eternal damnation was one theological topic that he was said by friends to have addressed early and late. Isaac Cogdal, who claims to have discussed religion with Lincoln from 1834 to 1859, called him a universalist, one who believed in universal salvation. He told Herndon: "He could not believe that [God] created a world and that the result of that would be Eternal damnation &c."[115]

Mentor Graham recalled late in life that while living in New Salem, Lincoln had asked him what he thought about "the anger of the Lord" and then had shown him an essay he had written "on the subject of Christianity, and a defense of universal salvation." The essay began, Graham wrote, with "something respecting the God of the universe ever being excited, mad, or angry. . . . I remember well his argument. He took the passage, 'As in Adam all die, even so in Christ shall all be made alive,' and followed with the proposition that whatever the breach or injury of Adam's transgression to the human race was, which no doubt was very great, was made just and right by the atonement of Christ."[116] Whether by this Graham meant that Lincoln's purpose was to affirm not only universal salvation but the doctrine of atonement as well is not clear, but Lincoln's basing an essay on the theme of a God who becomes "excited, mad, or angry" suggests that it may have been prompted by Paine's story in *The Age of Reason* of how he first came to doubt Christian teachings. Hearing, as a boy of seven or eight, a sermon by a relative on "the subject of what is called *redemption by the death of the Son of God*," Paine says that he "revolted at the recollection of what I had heard, and thought to myself that it was making God Almighty act like a passionate man who killed His son when He could not revenge Himself in any other way."[117]

Graham recalled Lincoln's essay on universal salvation in a letter to B. F. Irwin, a longtime political friend of Lincoln's, who, in the midst of a controversy in 1874 about Lincoln's religious beliefs, was actively trying to gather testimony to refute Herndon and others on the question of Lincoln's "infidelity." Of particular concern was the charge that Lincoln had written a long essay against the claim of the Bible to be divine revelation and that the storekeeper Samuel Hill had snatched it from him and thrown it in the fire. Graham thought his own recollection refuted this story, but it clearly does not. There is little reason to doubt that Lincoln may have written an essay on what the Bible says about eternal damnation, but the evidence that he wrote another, more provocative one that Samuel Hill wanted destroyed is independent and very strong.

Herndon apparently first heard the story from Hardin Bale on his initial interviewing trip to Menard County, the locale of the vanished New Salem, in May 1865. Bale told him: "About the year 1834 A Lincoln wrote a work on infidelity, denying the divinity of the Scriptures and was persuaded by his friends – particularly by Saml [Hill] to burn it which was done."[118] Hill himself was dead, but Herndon promptly called on his son John, who told him the story, the substance of which Herndon put into a letter to Francis E. Abbot five years later:

> Lincoln and Hill were very friendly. Hill, I think, was a skeptic at that time. Lincoln, one day after the book was finished, read it to Mr. Hill – his good friend. Hill tried to persuade him not to make it public – not to publish it. Hill at that time saw in Mr. Lincoln a rising man, and wished him success. Lincoln refused to destroy it – said it should be published. Hill swore it should never see the light of day. He had an eye to Lincoln's popularity – his present and future success; and believing that, if the book were published, it would kill Lincoln forever, he snatched it from Lincoln's hand, when Lincoln was not expecting it, and ran it into an old-fashioned ten-plate [*sic*] stove, heated as hot as a furnace; and so Lincoln's book went up to the clouds in smoke.[119]

After hearing this story from John Hill in conversation, Herndon wrote a few days later to inquire further into the story, and Hill replied:

> Since my early childhood I remember to have heard it alluded to, hundreds of times by different old settlers. Of late years I have heard

less of it, as these old men have many of them passed away. I have a
better remembrance of it by my fathers connection with it. You know
that there are always some few things that strike into the minds of a
child at early age which time will never eradicate. This is one of the
circumstances from which I date my earliest remembrance. It could
not have been on account of Lincoln's position, as at the time I
knew no more as to who he was than I did of the inhabitants of the
Fejee Islands. When I heard of my father having morally compelled
Mr Lincoln to burn the book, on account of its infamy &c pointing
to Voltaire, Paine &c, the circumstance struck me so forcibly that I
have never heard the word infidelity, Paine or Voltaire, since, without
thinking of it. My mother was strictly religious, and before hearing of
this I had always thought my father to be averse to religion. I was so
surprised that I suppose it made the deeper impression. As to date I
do not know. It was in the winter time, as tradition says it was done
in fathers store, while there was fire in the stove, & that there it was
burned.[120]

Hill may have misremembered the story, but his letter is replete with
indications of authenticity: his father and others frequently retelling
the story; the effect on him of the words "infidelity," "Paine," and "Voltaire"; the fact that his father seemed to be uncharacteristically concerned about manifestations of irreligion.

John Hill's testimony is at second hand, and even if he remembered
the story accurately, he was neither present in the store nor part of the
New Salem network for local news. But Hardin Bale *was* part of the
network, and so was Isaac Cogdal, who told Herndon: "I do Know
that Mr Lincoln did write a letter, pamphlet – book or what not on the
faith as I understand he held – denying Special & miraculous [Reseta-
tion?] – Inspiration & Conception."[121] Herndon also had the story,
at least the part about the writing of such an essay, from Lincoln's
close friend James Matheny. When Herndon questioned Matheny,
who had not lived in New Salem, how he knew about the book,
he grudgingly admitted after much prodding, "I got it from Lincoln's
own mouth."[122] In an earlier interview Matheny put the matter into
an interesting political context: "In 1834 & 5, my father being a strong
Methodist – a Kind of minister and loving Lincoln with all his soul
hated to vote for him because he heard that Lincoln was an Infidel. Mr
Lincoln did write a pamphlet attacking the divinity of christ – Special
inspiration – Revelation &c – ."[123]

The kind of critique of the Bible Lincoln is described as making is
strongly reminiscent of Paine's assault on both the Old and New Testa-

ments in *The Age of Reason*. In the second part of his treatise, Paine quotes passage after passage to demonstrate that the Scriptures are inconsistent, ahistorical, self-contradictory, and falsely represented as to author and time of composition. "These writers may do well enough for Bible-makers," he writes, "but not for anything where truth and exactness is necessary."[124] His most shocking claim for readers of his time is surely that the Bible, in giving "an account of a young woman engaged to be married, and while under this engagement she is, to speak plain language, debauched by a ghost," is "blasphemously obscene."[125] His most frequent charge is that its claims, when weighed in the scale of reason, are absurd.

This coincides almost perfectly with the critique of the Bible in Lincoln's ill-fated manuscript that Herndon pieced together from his informants: "His argument was grounded on the internal mistakes of the Old and New Testaments, and on reason, and on the experiences and observations of men."[126] James Matheny told Herndon that when Lincoln first moved from New Salem to Springfield in 1837, he used to come into the clerk's office where Matheny worked and his young friends congregated, "pick up the Bible – read a passage – and then comment on it – show its falsity – and its follies on the grounds of *Reason* – would then show its own self-made & self uttered Contradictions and would in the End – finally ridicule it and as it were Scoff at it."[127]

Disagreement about religion was commonplace at this time and place and was, in fact, the principal cause of the seemingly endless proliferation of Protestant sects, whose partisans disputed virtually every point of Christian doctrine and vied with one another for adherents. In this welter of conflicting beliefs, with no established churches and no sect predominating, freethinkers like Lincoln and Samuel Hill were apparently able to entertain and discuss heretical ideas without completely alienating their more conventional neighbors. Parthena Nance, the young woman who married Hill midway through Lincoln's stay in New Salem and who presumably heard much about these discussions, reported that she once asked Lincoln: "Do you really believe there isn't any future state?" Lincoln, she says, replied: "Mrs. Hill, I'm afraid there isn't. It isn't a pleasant thing to think that when we die that is the last of us."[128]

⁓

THAT LINCOLN was a religious skeptic in New Salem has been doubted or denied by some biographers, but those who knew him best at this time rarely questioned it. His cousin Dennis Hanks and his step-mother both told Herndon that Lincoln did not profess religion while growing up in Indiana. There is little doubt that Lincoln read the Bible as a child and continued reading it in New Salem, as Mentor Graham and Row Herndon attest,[129] but the evidence that he prepared an essay ridiculing its claim to be divinely inspired suggests strongly that his motivation was something other than credence.

Herndon believed that at New Salem Lincoln had been thrown into the company of freethinking scoffers and skeptics: "They were on all occasions, when opportunity offered, debating the various questions of Christianity among themselves; they took their stand on common sense and on their own souls; and though their arguments were rude and rough, no man could overthrow their homely logic."[130] It is noteworthy that in making the case in 1874 for Lincoln's being a Christian, a promi-nent Springfield minister, Rev. James Reed, confined himself expressly to Lincoln's later years and pointedly did not question the reports of his earlier skepticism.[131] Walter B. Stevens, a St. Louis reporter who inter-viewed people in Menard County in the 1880s and 1890s, heard the sto-ries relating to Lincoln's infidelity and concluded: "All of the time that he was living the life of the [New Salem] neighborhood he was reading, studying and thinking. This thinking was along original lines. It was speculative. It showed the mental activity of the young man. That is the most that should be said of it."[132]

Stevens was here putting the best face he could on Lincoln's career as a religious skeptic and critic of the Scriptures, which he clearly believed did Lincoln little credit and might be expected to detract from his stature. Such were the pressures of public piety and Victorian conven-tion that even Herndon, when first asked about Lincoln's religious beliefs in May 1865 by the biographer, Josiah G. Holland, had an-swered: "the less said the better."[133] If he meant that a frank presenta-tion of Lincoln's skepticism would make Lincoln few friends and his biographer many enemies, the public reaction to Ward Hill Lamon's book in 1872, based on Herndon's own research, proved him all too right. By the time he published his own biography of Lincoln in 1889, Herndon was so battle-scarred from skirmishing about Lincoln's reli-gious beliefs that he announced, "I do not intend now to reopen the discussion or to answer the many persons who have risen up and asked to measure swords with me."[134]

In constituting perhaps the most philosophical activity Lincoln engaged in during his New Salem years, his skeptical religious studies and speculations were a significant and revealing aspect of his self-education. Because such heterodox views did not seriously affect popularity or viability as a political candidate in New Salem, he could pursue a course of intellectual inquiry that challenged some of the most deeply held beliefs of his time and place. In a predominantly religious culture in a highly romantic and sentimental age, Lincoln's intellectual efforts, like his politics, were against the grain, taking the form of resistance to the pressures of conformity and pointing him in the direction of skepticism and rationality. In embracing Burns, Paine, and Volney, Lincoln was casting his lot with the rationalism of the Enlightenment and the skeptical spirit of the eighteenth century. As he was to indicate in many ways in the years ahead, he thought of himself as committed to the cause of reason.

❧✦❧

Chapter 3

FINDING A VOCATION

I WAS RAISED to farm work," wrote Abraham Lincoln, "which I continued till I was twenty two,"[1] but when he reached that age and left his father's house for good in the spring of 1831, farm work ceased to figure in his vocational thinking. His first ventures away from home in Indiana had been related to work on the nearby Ohio River. William H. Herndon collected evidence that Lincoln, before leaving Indiana, had worked along the Ohio on different occasions as a ferryman, as a woodcutter, as a laborer on the Portland Canal around the falls at Louisville, and that in 1828 he had made a trip down the Ohio and Mississippi rivers to New Orleans as a hired hand on a flatboat. One of his Indiana neighbors told Herndon that Lincoln had come to him the next year seeking a "recommendation to some boat," presumably a steamboat. When the neighbor, William Wood, objected that he was not yet twenty-one, Lincoln reportedly replied: "I Know that, but I want a start."[2]

During the winter of 1830–31, the "winter of the deep snow," while living in his father's new cabin in Macon County, Illinois, Lincoln and his cousin John Hanks had been sought out as flatboatmen by Denton Offutt. Described as "a trader and speculator,"[3] Offutt proposed to take a boatload of Illinois farm produce to market in New Orleans. Hanks told Herndon: "Offutt Came to my house in Feb'y 1831, and wanted to hire me to run a flat boat for him – Saying that he had heard that I was quite a flat boatman in Ky: he wanted me to go badly. I went & saw Abe & Jno Johnson – Abes Step brother – introduced Offutt to them.

We made an Engagement with Offutt at 50 per day and $60 to make the trip to N Orleans."[4] The boatmen canoed down the Sangamon in early March and rendezvoused with their employer at Springfield, but because Offutt had been unable to acquire a suitable flatboat for the purpose, Lincoln and his mates hired out to build one at Sangamon-town, a small settlement on the Sangamon River, seven miles north of Springfield. When the boat, which, according to John Hanks, was "80 feet long and 18 feet wide,"[5] got hung up on the Rutledge-Cameron milldam, the residents of nearby New Salem got their first look at Abraham Lincoln.[6] Those who saw him resourcefully get the boat over the dam seem to have formed a favorable impression, but Jason Duncan reported that when Lincoln first ran for office a year later, he was still known to some outlying residents living away from the village merely as "the man who went to Orleans on a hog boat for Offett."[7]

Soon after his return from New Orleans, Lincoln was hired to perform another feat of boatsmanship, colorfully recounted for Herndon by an old New Salem acquaintance, John McNamar: "there was a Dr Nelson came to the place with a Roman Catholic wife whom he married in Cincinnati whether whether from Religion or the want of it they did not live very hapily together Nelson built a small flat Boat and Started for Texas Lincoln piloted them out of the Sangamon the river was very full overflowing its Banks They Lost the river as I heard Mr Lincoln relate and ran about three miles out in the Prairie."[8] In fact, the lower Sangamon was notoriously difficult to navigate, not only because it was too shoal for larger boats and heavily obstructed by overhanging trees and driftwood but by virtue of its incessant twisting and turning — about 150 miles of river, by one account, to cover the distance of 45 miles to its mouth near Beardstown.[9] So meandering and serpentine was this stretch of the Sangamon that Abraham Lincoln once joked to his friend Mark Delahay that in traveling by boat downriver, he had camped at the same place three nights in a row.[10]

John Hanks told Herndon that Lincoln's first public speech, delivered in the summer of 1830, had been on the navigation of the Sangamon River.[11] When Lincoln decided to run for the legislature in the spring of 1832, he included in the public announcement of his candidacy a statement concerning the improvement of navigation on the Sangamon as "an object much better suited to our infant resources" than the "heart appalling" cost of building a railroad for the same purpose. "From my peculiar circumstances," wrote Lincoln, "it is probable that for the last

twelve months I have given as particular attention to the stage of the
water in this river, as any other person in the country."[12] Having established his credentials as a knowledgeable riverman, he went on to propose a specific plan for improving navigation on the Sangamon through
the clearing and straightening of the channel.

Denton Offutt was known as a man who "always had his eyes open
to the main chance."[13] Just how lucrative the navigation of the Sangamon might become was apparently not lost on him, if a story heard by
Lincoln's friend Coleman Smoot was true. Smoot told Herndon:

> Offitt Seemed to think that with Lincoln as Pilot or Captain there
> was no such thing as fail in the navigation of the Sangamon While
> building his flat Boat he determined on their Return from down the
> River to build a Steam boat for the Sangamon his friends Remon-
> strated with him on account of the lowness of the River for a large
> part of the Season and frozen over for months Offitt Said he
> intended to build it with Rollers underneath so that when it come to
> a Sand Bar it would Roll Right over and Runners underneath for to
> Run on the ice for when Lincoln Was Captain By thunder She would
> have to go.[14]

Offutt may have been something of a confidence man, but like other
young Kentuckians who came to Illinois to make their fortune, he was
on the lookout for what the people in an undeveloped country wanted
or needed.[15] The importance of access to river transportation was
demonstrated shortly after Lincoln's announcement of his candidacy
when a group of Springfield entrepreneurs engaged to bring the *Talisman*, a steamboat from Cincinnati said to be of 120 tons,[16] up the Sangamon to Bogue's mill, near Springfield. With the help of many
ax-wielding volunteers (Lincoln among them) removing obstructions,
the *Talisman* was able to make its way slowly up the river, past New
Salem, and all the way to Bogue's mill on high water, much to the
delight of all inhabitants of the valley. But when falling water forced an
early and discouragingly difficult return, with Lincoln hired to assist the
pilot, Row Herndon,[17] steamboat traffic on the Sangamon was virtually
at an end.

～

HAD THE SANGAMON proved more pliable and the *Talisman*'s venture
a success, Abraham Lincoln's early life would surely have been much
different. In the first place, the store and the mill of his employer would

have greatly benefited, and the influx of people and business would have brought a measure of activity and prosperity that would have brightened Lincoln's prospects and opened up new opportunities. Had the river assumed a new and critical role in the life of the community, Lincoln's status as an experienced riverman would possibly have made for a difference in his vocational plans, at least in the short run. But the *Talisman* enterprise was a bust, and far from reaping benefits, Abraham Lincoln was one of the losers, for he had gone surety for some of Bogue's speculations, and according to Charles Maltby, he had also invested with Maltby in a warehouse on the river (possibly Offutt's old store) in expectation of profiting from future steamboat business.[18]

No sooner had the *Talisman* been disposed of than Lincoln's attention was almost immediately claimed by the frontier disturbance that came to be known as the second Black Hawk War. The timing of this distraction proved fortunate for Lincoln. In a biographical statement written in the third person he noted that "Offutt's business was failing – had almost failed – when the Black-Hawk war of 1832 – broke out. A[braham] joined a volunteer company, and to his own surprize, was elected captain of it. He says he has not since had any success in life which gave him so much satisfaction."[19]

Lincoln served as captain until his company was mustered out after a month in the field, but he reenlisted as a private and eventually served a total of about three months. Though most of his service consisted of desultory marching from one outpost to another, never seeing battle, Lincoln distinguished himself with his New Salem neighbors by proving equal to the difficult task of commanding unruly volunteers and by defending the honor of their company (and winning most of their wagers) by wrestling. Moreover, he made contact with many of the men who were or would become influential leaders in Illinois, both in politics and at the bar. Perhaps most important of all, he fell in with and succeeded in impressing a young lawyer from Springfield, John T. Stuart.[20] Stuart was a well-connected and well-educated Kentuckian, a graduate of Centre College at Danville, who had come out to Illinois to practice law and enter politics. Different as they were in many respects, Stuart was attracted to Lincoln from the outset.

> I first met Lincoln at Beardstown, Ill. [Stuart recalled], the place of rendezvous for several companies of which L had been elected captain of one and I of another. I was a few days after elected Major of the battallion. Lincoln was exceedingly popular while in the service

on account of being so good natured, genial, upright, and on account of being able to tell a Story better and more of them, than any man in the batallion.

He was popular on account of his physical strength. Wrestling took place almost every day in which contests Lincoln had but one equal. He made a good officer.[21]

With Lincoln, Stuart reenlisted as a private when first mustered out, and the two were finally discharged together in Wisconsin. Making the long trip back to Sangamon County together, sharing Stuart's horse (Lincoln's having been stolen about the time of their discharge), they arrived in mid-July, less than two weeks before elections. Both were candidates for seats in the lower house of the Illinois legislature, and Stuart, who was up for reelection, was able to observe his new friend's political debut at first hand. "Lincoln in this race, although he was defeated, acquired a reputation for candor and honesty, as well as for ability in speech-making. He made friends everywhere he went – he ran on the square – and thereby acquired the respect and confidence of everybody."[22]

⟶

WHEN HE HAD announced his candidacy the previous March, Lincoln had concluded his public statement with a somewhat wistful, if wordy, sentiment: "My case is thrown exclusively upon the independent voters in this county, and if elected they will have conferred a favor upon me, for which I shall be unremitting in my labors to compensate. But if the good people in their wisdom shall see fit to keep me in the background, I have been too familiar with disappointment to be very much cha-grined."[23] Lincoln's brief speech at Pappsville was reported to have con-cluded with the same thought, but sharply conflated: "if Ellected I will bee thankful if beeting I can do as I have bin doing worke for a living."[24]

If this quotation is reasonably accurate, there are at least two things it may suggest. First, Lincoln was making a wry joke about politicians not having to work. Second, it may well reflect Lincoln's preoccupation with his lack of prospects – not only for election to the legislature but for finding, after the election was over, a suitable way to earn a living. Describing this juncture in his life, Lincoln wrote of himself: "He was now without means and out of business, but was anxious to remain with his friends who had treated him with so much generosity, especially as he had nothing elsewhere to go to. He studied what he should do –

thought of learning the black-smith trade – thought of trying to study law – rather thought he could not succeed at that without a better education."[25]

This is the only indication that Lincoln seriously considered black-smithing as an occupation, and at least one person who knew him well in New Salem insisted "he never intended to learn the black smith trade: this story I know to be a humbug."[26] But Lincoln was physically well suited to the trade, which typically required great size and strength, and this may suggest that he had seriously asked himself what a person with his physical assets might be good for. In Indiana, according to his cousin Dennis Hanks, the local blacksmith, John Baldwin, had been "Abes pertickler friend,"[27] and the August election occurred soon after the arrival in New Salem of Lincoln's literary friend, Jack Kelso, whose brother-in-law, Joshua Miller, became the village blacksmith. These associations may have put the idea of blacksmithing in Lincoln's head, but nothing seems to have come of it.

Like the fortuitous outbreak of the Black Hawk War, which rescued him from Offutt's failing enterprises, another timely event now intervened. The autobiographical statement quoted above continues: "Before long, strangely enough, a man offered to sell and did sell, to A. and another as poor as himself, an old stock of goods, upon credit."[28] The man who offered to sell on credit was Row Herndon, whose part Lincoln had taken in a fight at Pappsville in July.[29] Row and his brother James owned a stock of goods that they had bought earlier in the year from E. C. Blankenship, and James had already sold his half of the business to William Berry when Row decided, after the election, to sell out to Lincoln.[30] Although without funds, he was able to acquire half interest in a store simply by signing a promissory note.

The store proved a luckless venture that Lincoln would regret. Not only did it not succeed, but it dragged him further and further into debt. "They opened as merchants [Lincoln's third-person account continues] and he says that was *the* store. Of course they did nothing but get deeper and deeper in debt."[31] The details of Lincoln's storekeeping are far from clear, and the complicated indebtedness that resulted is still being unraveled.[32] His partner, Berry, was two years younger than he was and without experience.[33] It seems certain that they soon bought another stock of goods from James Rutledge and Henry Sinco, and yet another a few months later, when Reuben Radford's store was vandalized by the Clary's Grove boys and Radford impulsively sold out to

William Greene. Greene promptly disposed of his prize to Lincoln and Berry at a handsome profit in January 1833, though he had to give his own note to Radford, who was unwilling to take Lincoln's and Berry's. When the ill-fated store, in Lincoln's famous phrase, "winked out," and Berry died, Greene found himself enmeshed in the tangle of legal obligations that clung to Lincoln for several years and that Greene said the two friends referred to as the "*National* debt."[34]

In what may have been a last-ditch effort to rescue the store from bankruptcy, Berry applied for a license to sell liquor by the drink in March 1833, an event that laid the basis for a later controversy about Lincoln's storekeeping. In the first debate with Lincoln in 1858, Stephen A. Douglas described their early acquaintance: "We were both comparatively boys, and both struggling with poverty in a strange land. I was a school-teacher in the town of Winchester, and he a flourishing grocery-keeper in the town of Salem . . . but I believe that Lincoln was always more successful in business than I, for his business enabled him to get into the Legislature."[35] Lincoln replied: "The Judge is wofully at fault about his early friend Lincoln being a 'grocery keeper.' I don't know as it would be a great sin, if I had been, but he is mistaken. Lincoln never kept a grocery anywhere in the world."[36]

While Herndon knew that his law partner's statement was technically true, since a "grocery" in the strictest sense was a groggery or saloon, he recognized that Lincoln's reputation for truthfulness was jeopardized by so flat a denial, and he questioned former residents of New Salem about it. The answers were mixed. "Old Mrs Potter affirms that Lincoln did sell Liquors in a grosery," wrote George Spears. "I can't Say whether he did or not at that time I had no idia of his ever being President therefore I did not notice his course as close as I should of had."[37] In the 1890s Ida M. Tarbell collected the testimony of several of Lincoln's New Salem contemporaries who remembered that Berry & Lincoln did sell whiskey.[38] Others were sure that Lincoln, who was widely known in New Salem as a nondrinker, had not been party to Berry's scheme. James Davis was particularly emphatic:

> [Lincoln and Berry's] Store was a mixed one – dry goods, a few, groceries such as Sugar Salt &c – and whiskey – solely Kept for their Customers – or to sell by the Gallon – quart or pint – not otherwise – . . . . Lincoln & Berry broke – Berry subsequently Kept a doggery – a whiskey saloon, as I do [k]now or did – Am a democrat –

never agreed in politics with Abe: he was an honest man. Give the devil his due: he never sold whiskey by the dram in New Salem. I was in town every week for years – Know I think, all about it – I always drank my drams & drank at Berry's often – ought to Know – [39]

Though Lincoln's storekeeping has been immortalized in legend, it lasted only a brief period of time and was a dismal failure. His subsequent lack of interest in business and entrepreneurship lends weight to indications that Berry, not Lincoln, was the prime mover in the business and that Lincoln had withdrawn as an active participant by the spring of 1833. With the demise of his storekeeping venture, he was faced with the need to earn money, not just to pay off his indebtedness but simply to live. Fortunately, living in the New Salem area did not cost much, and Lincoln required little more than the price of room and board. When he first came in 1831, he is reported to have slept in Offutt's store and boarded with one of the town's founders, Rev. John Cameron. One of Cameron's daughters remembered that this cost him only a dollar per week.[40] This was confirmed by the testimony of Parthena Hill, who told Herndon: "Board was about $1.00 – $1.50 – washing about $1.00 – $1.25 per month – didn't cost much to live, I assure you."[41]

Where Lincoln lodged and boarded subsequently in New Salem is not always clear, though it is evident from the testimony of former residents that during his first three years there he stayed with a good many families. When he returned from the Black Hawk War in the summer of 1832, he may have resided in James Rutledge's tavern, but after the election in August he apparently moved in with Rowan Herndon, who wrote: "he Come to my house to Board soon after his Return from the army he most always had one of my Childern around with him During his stay at my house my family Became much atached to him he was always at home wherever he went."[42]

When Lincoln left Row Herndon's is not known, but Mrs. Herndon was shot to death in their cabin when Row's hunting rifle went off in January 1833, and Row left the village soon after.[43] This tragic incident almost certainly guided the memory of Mrs. Herndon's brother, Mentor Graham, when he specified to Lincoln's law partner, "In the month of Feby A D 1833 Mr Lincoln Came & lived with me. and Continued with me about Six months."[44] Lincoln was thus probably living with Graham as he extricated himself from involvement with Berry and the store and when he was unexpectedly appointed postmaster of the village in May.[45]

Thomas P. Reep, who gathered and reported traditional Lincoln stories from former residents and their descendants, wrote of this period: "Lincoln being out of employment, except the job of postmaster, was unable to live from the income, and sought odd jobs, made rails, looked after the mill, helped at the sawmill, harvested hay and grain and even helped out on occasions in other stores, particularly that of Samuel Hill. He earned barely enough for subsistence."[46] It was at this juncture, when, as Reep says, "his affairs were reaching their lowest ebb," that Lincoln experienced another unexpected windfall. He wrote in his third-person autobiography: "The Surveyor of Sangamon offered to depute to A[braham] that portion of his work which was within his part of the county. He accepted, procured a compass and chain, studied Flint, and Gibson a little, and went at it. This procured bread, and kept body and soul together."[47]

Because Lincoln apparently took up the study of surveying while living with Graham, and undoubtedly conferred with the schoolmaster about the difficulties of this technical subject, some thought that Graham had taken another pupil. And by the time Lincoln had become a martyred president, Graham thought so himself. Though he had neglected to mention it when interviewed in 1860, after the assassination Graham told anyone who would listen that he had been Lincoln's teacher. "I taught him the rules of surveying," he boasted to William H. Herndon. "I do not think that Mr Lincoln was any thing of arithmetic – Especially so of geometry & trigemonetry before he came to my house, and I think I may say he was my schollar & I was his teacher."[48] While it would appear to be true that Lincoln had little knowledge of geometry when he tackled surveying, the same was probably true for Graham.

Some of Graham's friends and former students, such as Henry McHenry and R. B. Rutledge, thought the schoolmaster deserved considerable credit for Lincoln's education, but the redoubtable William G. Greene disputed Graham's claim to have been Lincoln's teacher. "I have seen Graham since I recd. your letter," he wrote Herndon, "he still persists that he taught him but when I questioned him wher when & what school house he had to admit that it was on the street behind the Counter when at Diner &c &c."[49]

Greene had told James Q. Howard in 1860 that Lincoln studied surveying when a clerk for Offutt in 1831. After mastering English grammar, according to Greene, Lincoln "said to me Bill if that is what they call a science I'll subdue another — Asked about authors on Surveying told him Stuart's was good — borrowed it — Said he, If I thought the law was as easy as these, I would commence it — wanted to get hold of something that was knotty."[50] Greene told Herndon that the book Lincoln borrowed belonged to himself, but this seemed doubtful to others, and Greene's claim to have been Lincoln's adviser is weakened, as David C. Mearns pointed out, by the fact that "no Stuart ever wrote a textbook on surveying."[51]

But Lincoln's own testimony on the matter is that he taught himself, just as he had taught himself "ciphering" in Indiana and later would work his way through the first six books of Euclid. He may even have looked into surveying in Indiana, since Herndon came across a copy of Gibson's manual with several Lincoln signatures, plus that of Ben Romine, one of his Indiana neighbors.[52] For Lincoln had a mathematical bent, whereas his alleged teacher, Mentor Graham, apparently did not. John Hill, whose father had been the successful storekeeper in New Salem, told Ida Tarbell that Graham was an example of the old-timers who exaggerated matters "to give importance to themselves." Graham, in fact, had "practically no education & little natural ability." About Graham's mathematical acumen the college-educated Hill was quite specific: "As School Commissioner of Menard Co, about 1863 or 1864, I examined Mentor Graham under the law, in order to give him certificate to teach, (without which he could not) and had to refuse to give him certificate of qualification, except 4th grade which was for a special school under local permit, and teaches below *fractions* in arithmatic."[53]

By the summer of 1833 Lincoln had apparently left Graham's residence northwest of New Salem and moved into the village. He there became acquainted with a new storekeeper in town, A. Y. Ellis. In "the Summer and fall of 1833," Ellis told Herndon, "I went to New Salem with a stock of goods belonging to Mr N A Garland now of Springfield I then became I may say intimately acquainted with [Lincoln] We boarded at the Same log Tavern Kept by Henry Onstott and afterwards by Mr Nelson Ally During my stay their he was not engaged in any particular business, but I think he was preparing himself of Surveying."[54]

Robert Gibson's popular manual *The Theory and Practice of Surveying; Containing All the Instructions Requisite for the Skilful Practice of*

This Art begins not with surveying but with mathematics. It opens with a section on "Decimal Fractions" and goes on to logarithms, plane geometry, and trigonometry, with an essay on "Mathematical Drawing Instruments" along the way. Complete with theorems, problems, and definitions of terms, the first 133 pages constitute a short course in mathematics, carefully aimed at the needs of the land surveyor. Lincoln had the reputation of being able to remember everything he read, which may explain why, in later life, he was able to make effective metaphorical use of a section on "Axioms or self-evident Truths."[55]

Part II of Gibson's manual is the "Practical Surveyor's Guide," beginning with a section on "The Chain" and showing how to survey by various means, including with the chain only. The sighting device and direction finder that Lincoln's contemporaries knew as a compass is referred to by Gibson as a circumferentor. It measures angles by indicating the number of degrees the sighted object is from the heading of the needle. Two things – establishing the size of the angles and the precise lengths of the boundaries – are designated as the keys to accurate fieldwork. Part III covers the aspect of surveying that may have been most demanding for one with no training in mathematics, "Mensuration of Areas, or the various methods of calculating the superficial content of any field." A story handed down in Mentor Graham's family tells of sessions lasting long into the night in which Lincoln and Graham labored to arrive at the correct number of acres in a surveyed field. Graham's daughter told Herndon: "My father & Lincoln would sit till midnight Calculating, unless Mother would drive them out to get wood for Cooking or for Sunday."[56]

By contrast with Gibson's hefty manual, the other surveying book mentioned by Lincoln was pocket-size. Abel Flint's *A System of Geometry and Trigonometry: Together with a Treatise on Surveying* also begins with mathematics, but its discussions are highly abbreviated and succinct: "Geometry" (thirteen pages), "Trigonometry" (thirteen pages), and "Surveying" (forty-one pages), plus various appendixes and mathematical tables. Gibson's is a more substantial treatise and surely the better book for reading and study, but Flint's portability may have recommended it to Lincoln as a good book to carry into the field.

Lincoln does not seem to have begun surveying until late in the year, for his first recorded survey is dated January 6, 1834.[57] With the land in the neighborhood being taken up at a rapid rate, there was steady work for the deputy county surveyor whenever he was ready to begin, and the rate of pay established by law constituted an attractive wage, particularly for someone in debt.[58] Given the technical and exacting nature of the work and Lincoln's subsequent reputation as a trusted surveyor, his long period of study may reflect his unwillingness to take the field until he thoroughly understood proper surveying techniques. But it may also reflect the need to earn money to acquire the necessary tools of the trade, which were, minimally, a surveyor's compass, a jacob's staff, a flag staff, a chain, and a horse. He may at first have tried to get along without the horse, for a friend told Herndon: "In his surveying jobs & trips he needed a horse – told him so – He said he didn't need one – was somewhat of a *'hoss'* himself."[59]

Once launched, Lincoln's career as a surveyor was a decided success. One of his early political associates, Robert L. Wilson, explained: "Mr Lincoln had the monoply of finding the lines, and when any dispute arose among the Settlers, Mr Lincolns Compass and chain always settled the matter satisfactorily. He was a good woods man. at home in the dense forest."[60] The densely wooded area that alternated with broad stretches of open prairie presented a formidable problem for the surveyor, whose job it was to run true lines and make exact measurements in country that was often thick with trees and thorny underbrush. Elizabeth Abell remembered: "[Lincoln] stayed at our house on the bluff when he was surveying all those Hills between us and Petersburg our oldest boy carryed the Chain for him when Lincoln would come in at night all ragged and scratch up with the Bryers he would laugh over it and say that was a poore mans lot I told him to get me a Buck skin and I would fix him so the Bryers would not scratch him he done so and I Foxd, his pants for him."[61] If Mrs. Abell "foxed" his pants with skins, she was apparently not the only one. Russell Godbey was one of Lincoln's first clients, and he told Herndon: "Lincoln surveyed the first piece of land I Ever owned or Ever had Surveyed. He Stopt with me all one night after Surveying. I Sold two Excellent well dressed buck skins. He – Abe wanted them to fox his Surveyer's pants. to prevent thorns – briars – bushes & vines from cutting them – &c –. Mrs. [Hannah] Armstrong did the foxing and Sowing."[62]

Surveying paid well enough, and it took Lincoln to all parts of the surrounding country and enabled him to get widely acquainted. One of his surveying stories that illustrate this also contains a rather pungent example of his grosser hoosier stories. Lincoln told his friend John Weber how, when summoned to survey a parcel in a remote part of the county for a man reputed to be a stingy miser, he quickly discovered that the man was instead very friendly and hospitable. After a good dinner and an evening of agreeable conversation and storytelling, Lincoln told the man about his false reputation in New Salem and said:

> the facts show that we were very much mistaken, and I am happy to acknowledge that I have been agreeably disappointed, Well, said the Pennsylvanian, as you have done me the honor to give me an account of the first opinion formed by you of me, it is no more than right that I should now report my first opinion of you, and then Said when I first heard of you, I heard that you had been a Candidate for the Legislature, Consequently I had come to the Conclusion that on your arrival here I would see a smart looking man.[63]

On hearing this story, Weber protested to Lincoln that the Pennsylvanian's reply was "very ungenerous, inasmuch as your remarks Concerning him were highly complimentary," unless, of course, it "was only intended for the amusement of the moment." "No, No, said Mr Lincoln. He meant all he said, for it was before I was washed," and he then told Weber the following story.

> When I was a little boy, I lived in the State of Kentucky, where drunkeness was very comon on election days, At an election, said he, in a village near where I lived, on a day when the weather was inclement and the roads exceedingly muddy, a toper named Bill got brutally drunk and staggered down a narrow alley where he layed himself down in the mud, and remained there until the dusk of the evening, at which time he recovered from his stupor, Finding himself very muddy, immediately started for a pump (a public watering place on the street) to wash himself. On his way to the pump another man was leaning over a horse post, this, Bill mistook for the pump and at once took hold of the arm of the man for the handle, the use of which set the occupant of the post to throwing up, Bill believing all was right put both hands under and gave himself a thorough washing, He then made his way to the grocery for something to drink, On entering the door one of his comrades exclaimed in a tone of surprise, Why Bill, what in the world is the matter Bill said in reply, I G—d you ought to have seen me before I was washed.[64]

As a surveyor in an area being newly settled, Lincoln was called upon to lay out new towns, as speculators vied with one another to locate the likeliest places for new settlements. "New towns were laid out in every direction," Thomas Ford wrote of this period in his history of Illinois (1854). "The number of towns multiplied so rapidly that it was waggishly remarked by many people that the whole country was likely to be laid out into towns; and that no land would be left for farming purposes."[65] Most of these ventures produced only "paper towns," surveyed blocks and lots that never sold. At least one of the towns laid out by Lincoln, Huron, was just such a speculative town, being located on the Sangamon River at a point projected as the terminus of a canal to Beardstown.[66] Lincoln had no money to invest, as did many of the prominent citizens of Springfield, but he entered a forty-seven-acre parcel of swampland nearby.[67] Nothing came of this venture, but his having platted the neighboring towns of Petersburg and Bath became a point of ingratiation years later for the returning surveyor-politician who had platted them.

Ironically, the most detailed recollection of Lincoln's platting a town site came from Peter Van Bergen, the man whose debt-collection suit eventually caused Lincoln's surveying equipment to be put up for auction.

> Mr. Lincoln was a good surveyor I employed him to go with me and lay out a town [New Boston] on the Mississippi River. [Elijah] Iles had loaned some people some money and they couldn't pay it, and he took an 80 acres of Land – and Iles thought it might be a good thing to lay out a town on it, and said he would give me a share in it if I would attend to having it surveyed &c. . . . We traveled over there on horseback – found stopping places on the road – stayed there about a week, and Lincoln surveyed and laid out the town site – he did it all himself, without help from anybody except chainmen &c. and also made a plat of it.[68]

Lincoln's willingness to perform for Van Bergen a few months after being sued by him probably indicates the routine and nonvindictive character of this means of debt collection, though Van Bergen refused to discuss this suit when questioned about it by John G. Nicolay in 1875. Van Bergen's suit threatened to put Lincoln out of business by attaching his horse and surveying equipment but apparently posed no obstacle to their doing business as client and surveyor.

In addition to farms and town sites, Lincoln reportedly laid out a racetrack near New Salem for an eccentric early settler and racehorse fancier, Thomas Watkins.[69] He also seems to have done a fair business in wood lots. Central Illinois, where Sangamon County is situated, was then a landscape of alternating prairie and woodlands. Lincoln's friend Robert L. Wilson explained: "At the early period the Settlers made it a point to Secure choice lots of timber land, to go with their prairie land, often not entering the prairie part of the farm until it had been under cultivation long enough to make the money of the land to enter it. But the timber lots had to be surveyed for the purpose of entering them, but also to protect from trespass by cutting."[70] In other words, you could preempt farmland by farming it, but unclaimed standing timber was what whalers call a loose fish.

All reports indicate that Lincoln's work as a surveyor was highly regarded. Henry McHenry described for Herndon an occasion when Lincoln's ability was put to the test. McHenry's neighbors could not agree on the location of the intersecting lines of the government survey known as a corner.

> We agreed to send for Lincoln & to abide by his decision as surveyor & judge: he came down with Compass – flag staff – Chain &c and stopped with me 3 or 4 days and surveyed the whole section. When the disputed corner arrived at by actual survey, Lincoln then stuck down his staff and said – "Gentlemen – here *is* the Corner." We then went to work and dug down in the ground – & found about 6 or 8 inches of the original stake, sharpened & cut with an axe and at the bottom a piece of charcoal, put there by Rector – who surveyed the whole County –.[71]

-๑-

IN HIS 1860 autobiographical statement, Lincoln reported that after returning from the Black Hawk War in the summer of 1832, he had "thought of trying to study law – rather thought he could not succeed at that without a better education"[72] and that he did not take up the study of the law in earnest until two years later. But he had shown considerable interest in the law in Indiana, where his relatives said that "he was also in the habit of attending Law Suits before a neighboring Justice" when he was seventeen or eighteen. "He attended to several suits before this Squire for his Neighbors & in most of which he was Successful."[73] Many of those who knew him at New Salem testified that he was reading lawbooks soon after he arrived. "He Commenced reading law in 1832 & 3," Hardin Bale remembered, "– read in the mornings & Evenings – would play at varis games – jumping – running – hopping telling stories & cracking jokes. When his associates would return in the Evening to their various homes he would go to his reading & in the morning he would read till his associates would Come back the next day."[74] Lincoln clearly was informing himself on the law to some extent during this period, for he was drawing up legal documents for his neighbors, some of which still survive. A. Y. Ellis, writing of the summer and fall of 1833, when he first knew Lincoln at New Salem, said: "I remember he had an old form Book from which he used in writing Deeds, Wills & Letters when desired to do so by his friends and neighbours."[75]

And he did more than write deeds and wills out of a form book. Bill Greene recalled: "After [losing his first election in 1832] he read law – studied surveying – read the newspapers, wrote deeds – Contracts and general business & official man for the whole Community, never charging one cent for his time & trouble." Greene testified that Lincoln, as he had apparently done in Indiana, "would and frequently did, as we say Pettifog before Justice of the Peace in and about the County."[76]

The justice of the peace nearest New Salem was an amiable giant named Bowling Green. Weighing upward of 250 pounds, Squire Green was a native of North Carolina, a veteran of the War of 1812, and was related to many of the early settlers in the New Salem area.[77] By all accounts, Lincoln and Green became very close friends. A. Y. Ellis told Herndon that Bowling Green was to the young Lincoln "his allmost Second Father Mr Green Used to Say that Lincoln Was a Man after his own heart and I think Myself he was Mr Lincoln Used to say that he owed more to Mr Green for his advancement than any other Man."[78]

It was before Bowling Green's court that Lincoln began to try out his talents as an advocate. Jason Duncan, who came to New Salem at about the same time as Lincoln and boarded for a time at Green's, remembered Lincoln's amateur pleadings: "As there were no Attorneys nearer than Springfield his services were sometimes sought in suits, at law. and he frequently consented to appear before Esq Bowling Greens' court, to argue cases. but never charged his clients any fees so far as I Knew, the only lawbook which Mr Lincoln had in his possession was the first Old revised code of Illinois. from this he drew all his legal Knowledge."[79]

Duncan, who was practicing medicine in the village, conveyed a vivid picture of the large middle-aged farmer holding court in his cabin, listening with growing admiration to the arguments of the young Lincoln. "The manner in which he used to force his law arguments upon Esqr Bowling Green was both amusing and instructive, so laconic often as to produce a spasmatic shaking of the very fat sides of the old law functionary of New Salem Bowling Green permitted him to speak at first more for amusement than any thing else. but in a short time was led to pay great respect to his powers of mind in a forensic point of view."[80]

The degree to which Lincoln and Bowling Green shared the same wry sense of humor and love of fun is neatly illustrated by a story told by Row Herndon at the expense of the man for whom the neighboring town of Petersburg was named. Lincoln, he recalled, "was once whilst Living in salem Clled on By one peter Lukins to Prove his Carector and standing as to the velidity of his oath the Atturny said Please state what you know as to the Carector of Mr Lukins as for truth & varasity well said Lincoln he is Called Lying Peat Lukins But said the Lawer would you Beleave him on oath he turned Round and said ask Esquirer Geen he has taken his testimony under oath Many times Green was asked the Qustion and ancerd i Never Beleave any thing he say unless some Body elce Swares the same thing."[81]

The testimony of witnesses suggests that Lincoln appeared many times in Green's court and that the exceptional abilities as an advocate that became manifest later were amply foreshadowed and appreciated there. The contrast of the tall, youthful pleader and the obese Justice of the Peace stuck in Dr. Duncan's imagination. "I often imagine him Standing Six feet and upward pointing his long bony finger at Old Bowling Green who was presiding in his Court Capacity with great dignity, with [*illegible*] shirt and breeches on the latter supported by one tow linnen suspender over his shoulder, an enormously fat man weighing I should think not far from 300 lbs given to mirth as generally fat men are."[82]

A man who knew Lincoln in New Salem and carried chain for him as a surveyor, James McGrady Rutledge, wrote at the age of eighty-four a memoir that contains a vivid account of Lincoln's amateur pleading before another justice of the peace.

> One day there was a law suit to be tride. We was surveying that day. I was chain carer, Lincoln said less go to the law suit, so we went, it was a suit of damage brought by a young lady against a young man for refusing to marry her, her name was Sarah, his name was Samuel, the young lady was disgraced. The suit was tride before Mr. Berry. There was a man by the name of Dickeson in this end of the country, he boarded at Mr. Berry's understood some law, so the father of the young man got Dickeson to help him in the suit as the young man was not 21 years old. Edwards was the step father of the young lady. Edwards got Lincoln to help him. So Lincoln defended the lady. Lincoln had his surveying suit on. He maid a

comparison of the 2, he cald the young man a white dress, the young
lady a glass bottle, he said you could soil the dress, it could be made
to look well again, but strik a blow at the bottle and it was gon. Now,
he said who struck the blow, it was this young man. This was the first
case he ever tride. He got $100 dollars damage for the lady. The
father of the young man said it took 2 of his best horses he had to pay
for it, then he said it was good as 80 acres of land.[83]

There is reason to think that Lincoln's experiences in the courts of
the justices of the peace were formative and that he carried their lessons
with him throughout life. This is exemplified by the testimony of his
early political associate, Robert L. Wilson, who recounted for Herndon
a visit to Lincoln at the White House:

> I was with him one day in his office; parties were coming in, and
> doing business with him; he would send a card to the Department
> with which the business was being transacted. I remarked to him this
> reminds me of the office of the Justice of the Peace. Yes, says he, but
> it is hardly as respectable; he then went on to say that when he first
> commenced doing the duties, he was entirely ignorant not only of the
> duties, but of the manner of doing the business, he said he was like
> the Justice of the Peace, who would often speak of the first case he
> had ever tried, and called it, his "great first case least understood."[84]

-&

DABBLING IN the law, clerking in Samuel Hill's store off and on, acting as postmaster, surveying, doing odd jobs, but always having time
to read and socialize and tell stories, surely suited the young Lincoln very well, but it did not strike everyone as a pattern of industry.
Parthena Hill, who observed Lincoln in and around her husband's
store, the gathering point for political talk and socializing, told a
reporter years later: "I could generally see Mr. Lincoln about when I
looked out. He didn't do much. His living and his clothes cost little. He
liked company, and would talk to everybody, and entertain them and
himself." Her tactful conclusion: "I don't think Mr. Lincoln was over-
industrious."[85] Stephen T. Logan, who became Lincoln's law partner
several years later in Springfield, lacked Mrs. Hill's vantage point, but
from the county grapevine he formed a similar impression: "I knew
nothing then about his avocation or calling at New Salem. The impression that I had at the time was that he was a sort of loafer down there."[86]
But Lincoln was hardly a loafer. Growing up among people who

worked with their hands and who equated industry with physical labor, he apparently decided very early that he wanted something else – or something more. His cousin, Dennis F. Hanks, testified: "One thing is true of him – always was up to 1830 when our intimacy ended, because he went to Sangamon & I went to Coles Co.: he was ambitious & determined & when he attempted to Excel by man or boy his whole soul & his Energies were bent on doing it."[87] It seems clear that Lincoln had been entertaining the hope of becoming a lawyer for some time, perhaps for several years, before finally committing himself to the effort.

The testimony regarding Lincoln's studying law at New Salem is abundant. According to his autobiographical statement, his decision to study law in earnest came at the time of his first successful campaign for a seat in the Illinois legislature in the summer of 1834, but this does not preclude earlier exploratory reading in law, about which there is considerable testimony. William Greene claimed that Lincoln read lawbooks while clerking for Offutt, soon after his arrival in New Salem in 1831.[88] Isaac Cogdal said Lincoln studied law in 1832.[89] And two witnesses who left New Salem in 1833, Row Herndon and Jason Duncan, both remember Lincoln reading lawbooks.[90]

Like several others, Herndon and Duncan remember that one of the lawbooks Lincoln read early in his New Salem years was Blackstone.[91] Sir William Blackstone's *Commentaries on the Laws of England* (1765) was the most famous legal treatise of its time. It was originally delivered as a series of lectures at Oxford, and its ambitious aim was to put forward a coherent and comprehensive account of a notoriously unruly subject, the law as it had evolved historically in England. Though it was highly praised for its lucidity and graceful literary style, its vocabulary and intellectual presuppositions, to say nothing of its massive bulk, are still imposing for the uninitiated and must have been truly formidable for a self-educated frontiersman, whose only aid was a pocket dictionary. This may have been a principal reason Lincoln at first feared that "he could not succeed at [the law] without a better education."[92]

But Lincoln apparently took heart after gaining election to the legislature in August 1834 and being encouraged by another successful candidate, his friend and fellow Whig, John T. Stuart. Lincoln later wrote: "During the canvass, in a private conversation [Stuart] encouraged A[braham to] study law. After the election he borrowed books of Stuart, took them home with him, and went at it in good earnest. He studied with nobody."[93]

The last remark would appear to have a special meaning. Initially it indicates that Lincoln did not have the benefit, enjoyed by most law students of his day, of serving an apprenticeship with an established lawyer. But the copious testimony of his New Salem neighbors gives this blunt statement additional significance. Unlike Springfield, which attracted well-educated, propertied, and professional people, New Salem and environs were mainly settled by a relatively poor class of farmers, merchants, and tradesmen. There were no lawyers and, except for a few physicians, no professionally trained persons of any kind. The reputation of Lincoln's neighbors was that they were "rough," a term that probably relates to background as well as behavior, Lincoln being no exception. In these circumstances, his decision to study law was somewhat anomalous, and the spectacle of the young Lincoln, "barefooted seated in the shade of a tree,"[94] plowing through a treatise such as Blackstone, was for the residents of New Salem a bizarre sight. Russell Godbey's reaction captures the feeling: "the first time I Ever Saw him with a law book in his hands he was Sitting astraddle of Jake Bails wood pile in New Salem – Said to him – 'Abe – what are you Studying' 'Studying law' – replied Abe. 'Great God Almighty – ' Said Godbey."[95]

Lincoln as a law student was little less of an anomaly to more sophisticated observers. Stuart's partner H. E. Dummer, a graduate of Bowdoin College and Harvard Law School, recalled: "Lincoln used to come to our office in Spfgd and borrow books – don't Know whether he walked or rode: he was an uncouth looking lad – did not say much – what he did say he said it strongly – Sharply."[96] Studying an esoteric subject like the law alone, with no one to assist him, was clearly for the young Lincoln an act of self-definition. His friends, whose idea of fun was to "plague" somebody, offered little support. In fact, Henry McHenry's recollection suggests it may have been something like the opposite: "[Lincoln] Read law in 1832 or 3 – walked to Springfield for books – borrow them of Jno. T. Stuart – This is true – first Lincoln Said So – and others who saw him do it said so and I Know we plagued Lincoln for it and he never denied it."[97] It is a telling circumstance that walking twenty miles to borrow books, which would find such favor in the Lincoln legend, was something that he apparently did almost on the sly and for which he could expect to be "plagued" by his friends.

Reading books and reciting poetry had been part of Lincoln's New

Salem persona from the beginning, and he gave his neighbors the impression that he absorbed knowledge and information with particular ease. But his encounter with the law in 1834 was apparently different. "He never appeared to be a hard student as he seamed to Master his studies with little effort, until he commenced the study of Law," wrote R. B. Rutledge. "In that he became wholly engrossed." Rutledge noted something else about the usually sociable Lincoln: "I think he never avoided men until he commenced the study of Law."[98]

As a candidate for the presidency in 1860, Lincoln responded to a query from a young man asking "the best mode of obtaining a thorough knowledge of the law." Speaking from his own experience, Lincoln replied: "The mode is very simple, though laborious and tedious. It is only to get the books, and read, and study them carefully. Begin with Blackstone's Commentaries, and after reading it carefully through, say twice, take up Chitty's Pleading, Greenleaf's Evidence, & Story's Equity &c. in succession. Work, work, work, is the main thing."[99] The testimony of Lincoln's neighbors and acquaintances at New Salem leaves little doubt that a relentless schedule of "work, work, work" was his own formula for coming to terms with the law.

Lincoln's determined attack on the law coincided with two major developments in his life: his first term in the legislature and his courtship of Ann Rutledge. "He still mixed in the surveying to pay board and clothing bills," he wrote in his third-person autobiography. "When the Legislature met, the law books were dropped, but were taken up again at the end of the session."[100] To complicate matters, soon after the end of his first session his surveying instruments were attached and sold at auction.[101] In the succeeding months, during the summer of 1835, Ann Rutledge, to whom Lincoln was engaged, became desperately ill with fever. It is this combination of stressful circumstances, rather than any single one of them, that almost certainly accounts for the reports that Lincoln's law studies affected his health. McHenry, for example, told William H. Herndon: "he read so much – was so studious – took so little physical exercise – was so laborious in his studies that he became Emaciated & his best friends were afraid that he would craze himself – make himself derange from his habits of study which were incessant."[102]

The first year of his serious study of the law, which had begun following the election of August 1834, closed with the death of Ann Rutledge on August 25, 1835. Lincoln's grief and distraction at her death were reportedly so extreme as to attract attention. Some, like Mentor Graham, apprehended that the situation was complicated: "he was studious – so much so that he somewhat injured his health and Constitution. The Continued thought & study of the man Caused – with the death of one whom he dearly & sincerely loved, a momentary – only partial & momentary derangement."[103] Graham is here soft-pedaling one of the things about Lincoln's New Salem experience that were virtually unknown in Springfield and that Herndon was startled to discover: his temporary mental derangement following the death of Ann Rutledge. Interestingly enough, his law studies were seen as both the cause and effect of his aberrant condition. "Some thought it was [caused by] an increased application to his *Law studies*," according to McHenry, whereas Isaac Cogdal seemed to picture the intensification of his legal studies as an effect of his grief: "He was then [at the time of his derangement] reading Blackstone – read hard – day & night – terribly hard."[104]

If Cogdal was right, Lincoln's tenacious dedication to his law studies may have helped see him through the deep, and some thought possibly suicidal, depression that overtook him at the death of Ann Rutledge, an episode discussed later. However it may be, the documentary record of his activities in the succeeding months bears out his own testimony that he maintained himself largely by surveying when not attending the legislature and further shows that he took, in March 1836, the first formal step toward being certified to practice seven months later.[105]

Lincoln's admission to the Springfield bar after two years of solitary, if intermittent, study was apparently the fulfillment of a long-standing ambition to become a practitioner of the law, an ambition that he had despaired of as impracticable as little as three years earlier. With almost no formal education, no Latin, no apprenticeship or legal training, he had labored assiduously for the chance to compete for his livelihood against men who possessed all three. His mastery of the subject was by no means complete or even very great. He astounded no one with his legal knowledge, and his second partner, who knew the law well, thought his preparation weak. What was remarkable was that he had found a vocation largely on the strength of his appetite for reading and intellectual effort. His success before the justice of the peace court and on the stump had perhaps given him confidence in his abilities as an advocate, but if he had shipwrecked on Blackstone, it might have been a different story. His father thought his penchant for reading was the young man's weakness and is reported to have said about this time, "if Abe don't fool away all his time on his books, he may make something yet."[106] But this was almost certainly one of the reasons Lincoln left home and rarely returned.

Chapter 4

✣

WOMEN

T HE CONSENSUS of Lincoln's relatives and neighbors in
Indiana, where he lived from ages seven to twenty-one, was
that he was not much attracted to girls. His stepmother, for
example, told William H. Herndon, "He was not very fond of girls as
he seemed to me."[1] His male contemporaries volunteered a similar
verdict. Joseph C. Richardson said that Abe "never seemed to care for
the girls," and David Turnham, a close neighbor and friend, said flatly
that "Abe Lincoln – was not fond of the Girls."[2] Anna Caroline Gentry,
who was a schoolmate and one of the most eligible girls in the neighborhood, liked Lincoln but allowed that he "did not go much with the
girls – didn't like crowds – didn't like girls much – too frivalous &c."[3]

This was pretty much the reputation reported from his first years
at New Salem, where he went to live when he was twenty-two. His
good friend James Short, himself something of a ladies' man, told
N. W. Branson: "He didn't go to see the girls much. He didn't appear
bashful, but it seemed as if he cared but little for them. Wasn't apt to
take liberties with them, but would some times. He always liked lively,
jovial company, where there was plenty of fun & no drunkenness, and
would just as lieve the company were all men as to have it a mixture of
the sexes."[4]

This last consideration should probably be emphasized, for it accords
with virtually all the testimony about the youthful Lincoln's social talents. He had, from an early age, the inclination and ability to take
center stage in social situations, to engage his peers in games and feats

of strength and entertain them with jokes and stories. But girls did not compete with boys in athletic contests, and most of his stories would probably not have been considered suitable for a mixed audience. Without being particularly bashful, he preferred male company. A. Y. Ellis told Herndon:

> He also used to assist Me in the Store on busy days, but he allways disliked to wait on the Ladies he prefered trading with the Men & Boys as he used to Say. . . . I also remember that Mr Lincoln was in those days a Verry shy Man of Ladies – On one occasion while we boarded at this Tavern there came a family Containing an old Lady her Son and Three stilish Daughters from the State of Virginia and stoped their for 2 or 3 weeks and during theer stay I do not remember of Mr Lincoln Ever eating at the Same table when they did. I then thought it was on account of his awkward appearance and his wareing apparel.[5]

Ellis's explanation of his friend's avoidance of women on this last occasion may have had more to do with the "stilish" character of the company, but Lincoln's consciousness of his homeliness and unprepossessing attire was acute and probably affected his social relations with women generally.

Older women were apparently an exception. Mentor Graham's daughter, Elizabeth Herndon Bell, told Herndon: "Lincoln loved my Mother and would frequently ask her for her advice on different questions – Such as love – prudence of movements &c – girls – &c. &c."[6] That a young man not especially interested in the company of girls should discuss them with an older woman may be an indicative clue, or it may simply reflect what Bell, a toddler at the time, surmised on her own in later years. John Q. Spears remembered that Lincoln had a special relationship with his remarkable grandmother: "I Knew Mr. Lincoln from the time I was 4 years old – he used to Come out to my grand Mothers – the Doct – who was taken by the Indians in Tennessee – and liberated at Detroit – Mr. Lincoln used to talk to her instead of talking to Men: She was an intellectual woman. L said that if she had an Education she would have been Equal to any woman – Grand Mother and Mrs. Wm Green, among the women, were the first to bring Lincoln out to public view or notice."[7] Though Spears's last claim is questionable, it serves to suggest that older women may have been among the first to see that there was more to the newcomer than funny stories and athletic prowess.

Married women might provide Lincoln with congenial company outside the arena of courtship, but it was not without consequences. The testimony collected by William H. Herndon indicates that Lincoln paid the inevitable price exacted for such activity. "He used to worry – tire himself down at Study & work at Salem – ," said Caleb Carman, "would retire to Armstrongs – Shorts – Grahams & other places to get recruited –"[8] Jack Armstrong had early become one of Lincoln's close friends, but he was still Jack Armstrong. His rough love of fun, the hallmark of his personality, was unleavened by delicacy or anything like refinement, as evidenced by the running joke he made out of Lincoln's friendship with his wife Hannah. According to one of Herndon's informants, James Taylor, "Jack Armstrong used to plague Abe a great deal a bout his – Abe's son, which he had by Mrs Armstrong; it was a joke – plagued Abe terribly – ."[9] An echo of this byplay survives in Hannah's own testimony to Herndon about a visit she made to see President-elect Lincoln in Springfield. "A few days before Mr Lincoln left for Washington I went to see him – was a widow – the boys got up a story on me that I went to get to sleep with Abe &c – . I replied to the Joke that it was not every woman who had the good fortune & high honor of sleeping with a President. This stopt the sport – cut it short."[10]

If it seems likely that the cuckolding made sport of by Armstrong was purely imaginary, New Salem gossip could be more ambiguous. Row Herndon told his cousin that women "all liked [Lincoln] and [he] liked then as well." This was presumably from his own observation, as Lincoln had lived with him for several months. But Row could not resist a more titillating intimation: "after i left there i am told that he Borded with Benett able the fart. ing Law of Nult Green i think that Mrs able Could aid you Considerabe she has a dauter that is thought to Be Lincolns Child thay favor very much."[11]

Elizabeth Abell, the woman whose daughter had the misfortune to resemble Abraham Lincoln, was, in the words of Row Herndon, "a very smart woman Well educated and was of a Bigg & Welthy family in Ky."[12] William Butler confirmed this estimate in an interview with John G. Nicolay: "Mrs. Able was a cultivated woman – very superior to the common run of women about here. Able, who was from Kentucky, had married her rich, and had got broken down there, and in consequence had come out here."[13] Butler, another Kentuckian who had known Lincoln very early and became a close friend, thought that Lincoln had become acquainted with the Abells through their near neighbor Bowling Green and that this had led to their friendship. "He boarded with Mrs. Able — she washed for him and he generally lived there in a sort of home intimacy." Whether Butler is hinting at the rumor passed on by Row Herndon is not clear, but his main point about Elizabeth Abell had to do with her influence on Lincoln. "And my opinion is it was from Mrs. Able he first got his ideas of a higher plane of life — that it was she who gave him the notion that he might improve himself by reading &c."[14]

Elizabeth Abell was somewhat older than Lincoln and undoubtedly very fond of him. In a letter to Herndon, she described the young Lincoln she knew in discreetly admiring terms: "I never heard him use a profain word drink a drop of spirits or chew tobacco in my life and he was neither eccentric or visionary, he was very sensitive and backward nothing rash about him and certainly he was the best natured man I ever got acquainted with."[15] That Lincoln was "sensitive" was apparent in small ways, his marked solicitude for children and animals, for example. What Mrs. Abell meant by "backward" was perhaps his modesty and lack of self-presumption, a keen awareness of such liabilities as his poverty, homeliness, and lack of education. These are sides of Abe Lincoln that his male peers were much less aware of, if their testimony is any indication, suggesting that the older married women whose company he sought played an important role in his quest for identity and self-definition.

◆

ABOUT A YOUNG bachelor in a small community, there was bound to be sexual gossip and speculation. That so little found its way into the testimony collected by W. H. Herndon in the years following the assassination is no doubt largely explained by Lincoln's recent martyrdom and elevation to something akin to sainthood; that there is any at all, particularly in view of the Victorian restraint observed by the witnesses as a matter of propriety, is not a little surprising.

In the course of seeking information about Lincoln's friend Jason Duncan, Herndon elicited an unexpected piece of testimony from Bill Greene's younger brother, Gaines: "Says he knew Jason Duncan in or about New Salem about the year 1835 – 6: he was a physician — Knew Lincoln well ie Duncan did. D & Lincoln were great friends — Duncan married a Miss Burner — Jane: They live in Canton Fulton. Duncan's wife had a child — father uncertain — supposed to be Duncan's — or Lincoln's L. advised Duncan to leave and Marry."[16] Herndon lost little time in asking Bill Greene himself about this provocative charge. He replied: "I Know Jason Duncan well – Knew his wife – Miss Nancy Burner – well – was a good [clean?] girl – Duncan was quite a good physician – practiced in New Salem – This acquaintance with Duncan & wife in 1833 – possibly in 1832 – though not probable. Lincoln Knew the girl – Knew me – used to laugh at me – and at her – Lincoln never touched her in his life. This I Know – no man Ever touched her – . Lincoln & I urged Duncan to Mary her & go off."[17]

Herndon then reinterviewed Gaines Greene and asked particularly about his suggestion that Lincoln may have been the father of Nancy Burner's child. He responded: "I really do not Know who was the father of Miss____ Child – Mrs. Jason Duncan." But he proceeded to stir the pot nonetheless. "Bill Green & Lincoln used to run the machine. They have Said in my presence that she was a handsome woman – had not much Sense – had Strong passions – weak will – Strong desire to please & gratify friends – was a good woman. L & Green persuaded Jason Duncan to marry her and move off."[18] Greene's expression "run the machine" usually meant something like "called the shots," and in this situation may have meant "did as they pleased." In any event, Greene all but says his brother and Lincoln took sexual advantage of Nancy Burner.

Bringing his brother Bill into the picture effectively widened the pool of candidates for the fatherhood of Mrs. Duncan's child, but in conjunction with another piece of testimony Herndon collected, it served at the same time to narrow the circle of suspicion. John McNamar volunteered a story about Bill Greene that almost certainly revolved around the future Dr. and Mrs. Jason Duncan.

there was a little incident occured of which Bill Green was the Hero which may be worth relating as Lincoln enjoyed it Hugely, we the youngsters had attended a night meeting in Mass at Harrisons On starting home a young Doctor who had Set up a shop in old salem not unlike perhaps "Romeo's Apothecary" and remarkable for the frequent use of the word "Modes opperandi" he cut out Bill that is took his gal from him Bill Trudged along in Silence some time Either meditating on his sins or "Nursing his wrath to keep it warm" at length he came along side of his "Bright particular" who with the doctor was Leading the column and Began to plead his lost cause with the fair one The Girls in the rear began to hurry up to hear, After many arguments that Seemed unavailing Bill finaly put in a clincher Saying you Know we have done things that we ought not if we are going to seperate – The Girls wilted and fell Back in the rear.[19]

Greene, according to one of John Cameron's daughters, was known as "one of the beaux of the neighborhood – and there were none too many to go around."[20] But even with the shortage of "beaux," Lincoln seems to have held himself apart. "However strange it may appear," wrote New Salem historian Thomas P. Reep, "there had never been any suspicion or suggestion of a love affair between Lincoln and any of the Cameron girls [where he boarded] or any other of the young ladies at New Salem up to this time."[21]

–❧

EVENTUALLY Abraham Lincoln fell in love. William H. Herndon learned of this love affair from a wide variety of informants in the year following Lincoln's death, but he so sensationalized it in a public lecture in 1866 and so offended Lincoln's family and the public's sensibilities that the story itself eventually came into disrepute. In a landmark study, the Lincoln scholar John Y. Simon has traced the public career of the Ann Rutledge story from its first appearance in Herndon's lecture and has shown that by mingling evidence with speculation, by embellishing the story of Lincoln's derangement, and by tastelessly offending Lincoln's family, Herndon "grossly mishandled a major incident in the Lincoln story," from which "neither Herndon's reputation nor that of Ann Rutledge ever recovered."[22] The situation was further aggravated in the first half of the twentieth century, when such leading Lincoln scholars as Paul M. Angle and James G. Randall declared the evidence on which the story was based to be insubstantial, being nondocumentary, inconsistent, coaxed from the witnesses by leading questions, and after the fact.[23] As a result, the principal thing that most present-day students have been taught about Lincoln's love affair with Ann Rutledge is that it is largely a myth.

But the character and weight of the evidence ultimately show that this view is very much mistaken. A series of recent studies, culminating in John E. Walsh's full-length investigation, have demonstrated that the testimony relating to Lincoln's love affair with Ann Rutledge was not induced or fabricated by Herndon, that it came from the same sources as other information accorded credence, and that it is not only basically consistent but fairly overwhelming. In these circumstances, the prohibition that has prevailed for so long against the love affair in Lincoln biography must be lifted.[24]

Ann Rutledge was the daughter of one of the founders of New Salem, James Rutledge, and was eighteen years old when Abraham Lincoln arrived in 1831. Accounted the prettiest girl in the village, she had already had, by this time, a number of suitors. Some descriptions of her, like that of William G. Greene, seem extravagant: "This young lady was a woman of Exquisite beauty, but her intellect was quick – Sharp – deep & philosophic as well as brilliant. She had a gentle & kind heart as an angl – full of love – kindness – sympathy. She was beloved by evry body and evry boody respected and lovd her – so sweet & angelic was she. Her Character was more than good: it was positively noted throughout the County."[25] Other descriptions, such as James Short's, are more moderate: "Miss R was a good looking, smart, lively girl, a good house keeper, with a moderate education, and without any of the so called accomplishments."[26] But there was wide agreement that Ann Rutledge was bright, attractive, kindly, and well liked.

Lincoln seems to have admired the young woman who combined these qualities from an early date. Jason Duncan, who came to New Salem at the same time as Lincoln, wrote Herndon: "he [Lincoln] was verry reserved toward the opposite sex. while I lived and boarded in the same place with him, do not recollect of his ever paying his addresses to any young lady though I Know he had great partialities for Miss Ann Rutlege, but at that time there was an insurmountable barrier in the way of his ambition."[27] Duncan, who left New Salem in 1833,[28] is describing the state of affairs he knew at first hand and is referring to Ann's engagement to a man named John McNeil, which must have occurred within a few months of Lincoln's arrival. According to her family, she had been courted by both partners of the mercantile firm of Hill and McNeil, not knowing that the latter's name was really McNamar. Her brother Robert told Herndon: "Samuel Hill first courted Ann, she declined his proposition to marry, after which, McNamar paid his addresses, Resulting in an engagement to marry."[29]

The neighborhood tradition reported by Thomas P. Reep was that Hill, an irascible and impetuous man, was so angry at his partner's successful suit that he wrote him an abusive letter demanding that he either buy him out or sell out to him at the inventory price.[30] McNamar, a native of New York who had assumed the name of McNeil in coming West to recoup his family's fortune, sold out and announced his intention of returning to New York to bring his family to Illinois.[31] He apparently left about the time Abraham Lincoln was returning from the Black Hawk War in July 1832 and did not come back for three years.[32] "In the mean time," Ann's brother Robert told Herndon, "Mr Lincoln paid his addresses to Ann, continued his visits and attentions regularly and those resulted in an engagement to marry, conditional to an honorable release from the contract with McNamar. There is no kind of doubt as to the existence of this engagement David Rutledge [Ann's older brother] urged Ann to consummate it, but she refused until such time as she could see McNamar – inform him of the change in her feelings, and seek an honorable release."[33]

In legend, Ann is always the tavernkeeper's daughter and Lincoln the love-struck boarder, and while they probably became acquainted when he was staying at the tavern during his first year in the village, she was promised to another at that time, and her courtship with Lincoln was actually carried on at least two years later. By this time she was living on a farm with her family in the Sandridge neighborhood, several miles north of New Salem. Almost no details of this courtship have come down to us, and a large part of the reason surely has to do with the unusual circumstances just described. As far as her friends and neighbors were aware, Ann was publicly engaged to John McNeil, or McNamar, and very few outside the family knew differently. James Short, who lived near the Rutledge family at Sandridge, told Herndon: "Mr L. came over to see me & them every day or two. I did not know of any engagement or tender passages between Mr L and Miss R at the time; but after her death, which happened in 34 or 35, he seemed to be so much affected and greived so hardly that I then supposed there must have been something of the kind."[34] Here Short is acknowledging that he knew Lincoln visited the Rutledge farm every few days but didn't realize at the time that there was a courtship in progress. Though a majority of Herndon's two dozen informants giving testimony about the Ann Rutledge affair affirmed the existence of an engagement between Lincoln and Ann, most of them, like Short, probably learned about it after the fact.

Ann's reluctance to become publicly engaged to Lincoln while still betrothed to another man suggested to Herndon (and many others since) that perhaps she and Lincoln were never actually engaged. But her family, whose spokesman was Ann's brother Robert, insisted otherwise: "after McNamar left Menard Co. to visit his parents and during his prolonged absence, Mr Lincoln courted Ann, resulting in a second engagement, not conditional as my language would seem to indicate but absolute, She however in the conversation referred to by me, between her & David Rutledge urged the propriety of seeing McNamar, inform him of the change in her feelings & seek an honorable releas, before consumating the engagement with Mr L. by Marriage."[35] In other words, Ann felt justified in becoming engaged to Lincoln but thought, contrary to her brother David, that she owed McNamar an explanation before actually being married.

The engagement was most likely agreed to sometime in the first half of 1835, after state assemblyman Abraham Lincoln had returned in February from his first session in the legislature. The marriage was to take place, according to Ann's brother, "on the completion of the s[t]udy of law," which Lincoln had then been seriously pursuing since August 1834. Robert told Herndon that his understanding about the engagement had been corroborated by James McGrady Rutledge, "a cousin about her age & who was in her confidence." McGrady Rutledge had even more specific information: "Ann told me once in coming from a Camp Meeting on Rock creek, that engagements made too far a hed sometimes failed, that one had failed, (meaning her engagement with McNamar) Ann gave me to understand, that as soon as certain studies were completed she and Lincoln would be married.' "[36] "Certain studies" may well have included Ann's as well as Lincoln's, for there is evidence in one of her brother David's letters that she had "a notion of comeing to school" at the female academy in Jacksonville.[37]

But these bright prospects were not to be realized. The summer of 1835 was unusually hot, and the Illinois country became a breeding ground for disease. A medical thesis written the following year by a resident of Springfield spells it out:

Spring and summer of 1835 was the hottest ever known in Illinois: from the first of March to the middle of July it rained almost every day, and the whole country was literally covered with water. When the rain ceased, the weather became excessively hot and continued so until sometime in August. About the 10th of August, the people began to get sick – lasted until October 1st – a number terminated fatally. Twelve practicing physicians in Springfield [population fifteen hundred] were continually engaged almost day and night.[38]

It was in these conditions that Ann Rutledge was stricken with what may have been typhoid but which her family knew only as brain fever. Whatever it was, it proved to be fatal.

The agony of Ann's last illness may well have been magnified by emotional turmoil. Herndon's biography seems to have taken a page from romantic fiction in raising this possibility: "But the ghost of another love would often rise unbidden before her. Within her bosom raged the conflict which finally undermined her health."[39] The idea that Ann's illness was somehow related to anxiety and guilt over her two engagements, however, was not original with Herndon but came from his informants. Mrs. Hardin Bale, one of the first people to talk to Herndon about Ann Rutledge, had said in a follow-up interview that Ann had "died as it were of grief."[40] Parthena Hill was a new bride at the time of Ann's illness and repeated what her husband, Samuel (not a disinterested observer), had said: "Mr Hill told me that Anns Sickness was Caused by her Complications – 2 Engagements – She – Ann did not hear of McNamar for a year or more – at last got a letter from McNamar telling her to be ready they having been engaged &c to be married."[41] In a letter to her son many years later, Parthena added an interesting detail: "Anne got a letter from him [McNamar] just before she took sick. Saying, *be ready* – he would buy furniture in Cincinnati and wanted to be married as soon as he got here, and go to house keeping."[42] Ann's worst fear may well have been the specter of McNeil/McNamar arriving expectantly with his family and a wagonful of wedding presents. And if a suddenly realized nightmare cannot induce typhoid, it can probably make its onset more debilitating and more difficult to bear. On August 25, after an illness of some weeks, Ann died.

❧

ABRAHAM LINCOLN's reported reaction to Ann Rutledge's death is what most disturbed some modern critics of this story, and the reason is easily seen. A man who was world-famous for his fortitude in the face of adversity and for his extraordinary self-control was said on this occasion to have become quite unhinged by grief. "The effect upon Mr Lincoln's mind was terrible," according to the spokesman for Ann's family; "he became plunged in despair, and many of his friends feared that reason would desert her throne. His extraordinary emotions were regarded as strong evidence of the existence of the tenderest relations between himself and the deceased."[43] This concise summary accurately reflects what local residents came to believe and to remember about the aftermath of Ann's death, some of whom used words like "crazy" and "insanity" to describe Lincoln's condition.[44] Such provocative language and such uncharacteristic behavior are what prompted the skeptical Lincoln scholar Paul M. Angle to label this "the 'disastrous effect' legend."[45]

But however much the incident may have resembled an operatic rendition of ordinary grief, the evidence of Lincoln's excessive or extraordinary bereavement at Ann Rutledge's death is massive and relatively unmixed. Of Herndon's informants on this affair, eighteen affirmed this aspect of the story, the remaining six offering no opinion. None of the witnesses denied it. Their differences had to do with the severity of Lincoln's grief, some claiming that he became temporarily deranged, others that his friends feared for his sanity, and still others simply that he took Ann's death very hard. While some of the testimony is admittedly hearsay, much of it is too specific or too particular or comes from too knowledgeable a source to be discounted or explained away.

We have already seen that James Short claimed to have become aware of Lincoln's attachment to Ann only after he saw the extent of his grief at her death. John Jones also lived in the Sandridge area, and his testimony suggests that he made a similar deduction: "As to the relation existing between Mr. Lincoln and Ann Rutledge, I have every reason to believe that it was of the tenderest character, as I Know of my own Knowledge that he made regular visits to her. – During her last illness he visited her sick chamber and on his return stopped at my house. It was very evident that he was much distressed. I was not surprised when it was rumored subsequently that his reason was in danger."[46]

Henry McHenry drew a graphic picture of Lincoln's behavior but, as we have seen, allowed that there was room for interpretation with regard to its cause:

> As to the condition of Lincoln's Mind after the death of Miss R. after that Event he seemed quite *changed*, he seemed *Retired*, & loved *Solitude*, he seemed wraped in *profound thought, indifferent*, to transpiring Events, had but Little to say, but would take his gun and wander off in the woods by him self, away from the association of even those he most esteemed, this gloom seemed to deepen for some time, so as to give anxiety to his friends in regard to his mind, But various opinions obtained as to the Cause of his change, some thought it was an

increased application to his *Law studies,* Others that it was deep
anguish of *Soul* (as he was all soul) over the Loss of Miss R.

But none of the informants testified that Lincoln's distraction at the
time of Ann's death was caused solely by his studies, and McHenry left
no doubt about his own view: "My opinion is, & was, that it was from
the latter cause."[47]

William G. Greene usually presented himself as fully informed about
what happened in Lincoln's New Salem, and his testimony about the
aftermath of Ann's death is no exception: "Lincoln went & saw her
during her sickness – just before her death. Mr Lincolns friends after
this sudden death of one whom his soul & heart dearly & lovd were
Compelled to keep watch and ward over Mr Lincoln, he being from the
sudden shock somewhat temporarily deranged. We watched during
storms – fogs – damp gloomy weather Mr Lincoln for fear of an accident. He said 'I can never be reconcile[d] to have the snow – rains &
storms to beat on her grave.' "[48] Greene was admittedly something of a
know-it-all, whose testimony sometimes has a suspiciously florid or
flamboyant cast. But in the case of Lincoln's supposed melodramatic
remark about Ann's grave, which in isolation might raise suspicion,
there is notable confirmation.

Elizabeth Abell, who testified to some understanding of Lincoln's
"sensitive" nature, claimed to know little about his courtship of Ann
Rutledge, but she offered Herndon some personal testimony that left
little doubt about the effect of Ann's death: "the Courtship between
him and Miss Rutledge I can say but little this much I do know he was
staying with us at the time of her death it was a great shock to him and
I never seen a man mourn for a companion more than he did for her he
made a remark one day when it was raining that he could not bare the
idea of its raining on her Grave that was the time the community said
he was crazy he was not crazy but he was very disponding a long
time."[49] Casting doubt on or qualifying the allegations of craziness,
Mrs. Abell affirms Lincoln's emotional fixation on Ann's grave.

If Elizabeth Abell didn't regard Lincoln's despondency as dangerous
or threatening, others who were close to Lincoln clearly did. Greene's
testimony about having to watch and ward over Lincoln is supported by
that of several others. Mentor Graham, who claimed to have heard
about the engagement from both Lincoln and Ann, told Herndon: "He

Lincoln told me that he felt like Committing Suicide often. . . ."⁵⁰
Samuel Hill, mentioned as one of those who interceded in the interest
of Lincoln's safety, was dead by the time of Herndon's investigations,
but his son John informed Herndon of it and spelled it out explicitly for
Ida Tarbell many years later: "He [Lincoln] was fearfuly wrought up on
her death – My Father had to lock him up & keep guard over him for
some two weeks I think, for fear he might Commit Suicide – The
whole village engaged in trying to quiet him & reconcile him to the
loss."⁵¹ Apparently Lincoln's father-figure, Bowling Green, eventually
entered the picture decisively on Lincoln's behalf, as described for
Herndon's father-in-law by Green's widow: "Mrs Bolin Green Says
that Mr Lincoln was a regular suitor of Miss Ann Rutledge for between
two & 3 years next up to August 1835 in which month Miss Rutledge
died after a short ilness that Lincoln took her death verry hard so much
so that some thought his mind would become impared & in fear of
it . . . her husband Bolin Green went to Salem after Lincoln brought
him to his house and kept him a week or two & succeeded in cheering
him Lincoln up though he was quite molencoly for months."⁵²

The most arresting testimony about the effect of Ann Rutledge's
death on the young Abraham Lincoln (as well as the most disputed)
purports to have come from Lincoln himself. Isaac Cogdal was a long-
standing personal and political friend of Lincoln's, a fellow Whig from
Democratic Menard County, whose friendship went back to the earliest
New Salem days and who Herndon attests was sufficiently intimate
with Lincoln to discuss religious questions with him in his law office.⁵³
His visits to the law office were probably more than social, for Cogdal's
biographer says that "after Mr. Lincoln became a prominent lawyer, he
advised Mr. Cogdal to study law under his instruction, which he did."⁵⁴
Cogdal told Herndon that he once asked Lincoln about the Ann Rutledge affair and got a candid reply. Herndon's notes on this remarkable
interview read as follows:

> He [Lincoln] became acquainted with Miss Ann Rutledge in 1831 – 2,
> & 3: he courted her – and after he was Elected Presdt. he said to me
> one day – "Ike Call at my office in the State house about an hour by
> sun down. The Company will then all be gone" –
>   Cogdale went according to request & Sure Enough the Company
> dropt off one by one – his, Ls, Clerk included.
>   "I want to enquire about old times and old acquaintances" Said

Lincoln. He then said – "When we lived in Salem there were the Greens, Potters Armstrongs – & Rutledges. These folks have got scattered all over the world – some are dead. Where are Rutledges – Greens – &c."

"After we had spoken over old times – persons – Circumstances – in which he showed wonderful memory I then dare to ask him this question –

Abe is it true that you fell in love with & courted Ann Rutledge" Said Cogdale. Lincoln said, "it is true – true indeed I did. I have loved the name of Rutledge to this day. I have Kept my mind on their movements ever since & love them dearly" – said L

Abe – Is it true – Said Cogdale, that you ran a little wild about the matter:

I did really – I run off the track: it was my first. I loved the woman dearly & sacredly: she was a handsome girl – would have made a good loving wife – was natural & quite intellectual, though not highly Educated – I did honestly – & truly love the girl & think often – often of her now.[55]

Cogdal's testimony has been challenged by knowledgeable Lincoln authorities, principally because it has Lincoln discussing painfully personal matters, about which he was notoriously reserved. To James G. Randall, Cogdal's testimony "seems artificial and made to order. It was given out after Lincoln's death; it presents him in an unlikely role; it puts in his mouth uncharacteristic sayings."[56] But Randall and others who have objected to this testimony underestimate the length and character of Cogdal's association with Lincoln, and they neglect the context. Cogdal told Herndon that as president-elect Lincoln had invited him to his office in the statehouse to talk about old times and had asked him pointedly about the Rutledges and other New Salem families. Cogdal's interview reads: "After we had spoken over old times . . . I then dare to ask him this question – " at which point he relates his question and Lincoln's answer. Herndon, in taking down the interview, realized how critical the context was to the credibility of such an answer. He apparently queried Cogdal about the way in which his question was introduced into the conversation and recorded his response in the margin: "May I now in turn ask you a question Lincoln said Cogdall. Most assuredly. I will answer your question if a fair one with all my heart. then it was that he answered – as follows."[57]

As close friends of Lincoln, Cogdal and Herndon well knew that he did not customarily express himself on such intimate subjects. The wording of both of Cogdal's descriptions of the moment – "I then dare

to ask him" and "May I now in turn ask you a question Lincoln" –
together with the remembered heartiness of Lincoln's reply indicates
Cogdal's awareness of the rare opportunity that had been given him to
confront the reserved Lincoln on the subject of Ann Rutledge. Herndon's marginal addendum shows that he, too, was very much aware of
how pertinent the context was to crediting the extraordinary candor of
Lincoln's response. In his answer Lincoln not only admitted to having
been deeply in love with Ann Rutledge but also acknowledged, when
pressed by Cogdal, that he "run off the track" at her death.

Though Herndon had already heard the story many times before, the
last thing Cogdal remembered Lincoln's saying on that occasion contained something entirely new that seems to have made a particular
impression on Herndon: "I did honestly – & truly love the girl & think
often – often of her now." Herndon apparently took this to mean that
Lincoln was haunted by the memory of Ann Rutledge and that since he
couldn't get her out of his mind, he must have remained obsessed by her
all his life. In his 1866 lecture he offended Lincoln's family and almost
everyone else by suggesting that Lincoln thereafter never truly loved
another woman.

Herndon's wild surmise is the kind of speculation that has tarnished his reputation as a biographer. Linking his partner's well-known
attachment to the poem "O why should the spirit of mortal be proud!"
to the death of Ann Rutledge, he thought he had discovered in this
buried episode from Lincoln's early years the source of his lifelong melancholy. Moreover, Herndon was encouraged in this belief by many of
Lincoln's friends, to whom he sent copies of the lecture requesting reactions. One of these was Joshua F. Speed, who had been Lincoln's
closest friend and confidant after moving to Springfield. "I thank you
for your last lecture," he wrote Herndon. "It is all new to me – But so
true to my appreciation of Lincolns character that independant of my
knowledge of you I would almost swear to it."[58] So true did this explanation ring to Speed that he connected it to another episode of mental
stress that happened some five years later. "Lincoln wrote a letter (a
long one which he read to me) to Dr Drake of Cincinnatti discriptive of
his case. Its date would be in Decer 40 or early in January 41. – I think
that he must have informed Dr D of his early love for Miss Rutledge –
as there was a part of the letter which he would not read."

Though Herndon was probably wrong about the connection
between the poem and the death of Ann Rutledge (Lincoln's obsession

with the poem seems to have begun some ten years later[59]) and certainly lacked sufficient proof for making this misfortune the emotional crux of Lincoln's life, the evidence that he gathered shows that the reaction was nonetheless a very dramatic and revealing development. Something unusual happened to Abraham Lincoln when his attractive young fiancée died. He did more than grieve; he lost his composure and his emotional balance. His behavior was such that it alarmed his closest friends, who, in the absence of any immediate family, felt called upon to intervene for his own safety. While there were many previous signs of the young Lincoln's tenderness and sensitivity, his deportment in the wake of Ann's death is the first known indication of serious emotional vulnerability.

THOUGH IT IS impossible to specify precisely what caused Lincoln's severe mental distress, it seems reasonable to speculate that it was more than the death of his fiancée. As his neighbors observed, he had been hard at his legal studies and was showing the effects of fatigue and over-work. It would have been unusual if Ann's death did not bring back memories of earlier losses: that of his own "angel mother"[60] when he was nine years old and the death, in childbirth, of his only sister, Sarah, when he was eighteen. Both of these deaths, like Ann's, had come sud-denly and unexpectedly. Now, being away from his family and out on his own, he had no relatives to console him, and in the close quarters of a small community, he was in the position of having to bear his loss almost in public. Moreover, the magnitude of this loss for Lincoln per-sonally was something that most of the community, being unaware of the engagement, could not properly appreciate. This had to make his grieving appear all the more outlandish and excessive in the eyes of his neighbors, thereby making his emotional burden all the more difficult to bear.

There may well have been other factors. Even before he left home, Lincoln had been trying hard to raise himself from his inherited station in life and to improve his standing in the world. His incessant reading and study present the most conspicuous example, but part of this effort seems to have been a conscious program of reform. In Indiana he apparently was no more abstemious with regard to alcohol than the next person, but by the time he turned up in New Salem he was a near teeto-taler.[61] Nor had he been averse to bare-knuckled brawling in Indiana, where he was described by Herndon's informants as once breaking into a formally arranged fistfight and challenging all comers by waving a whiskey bottle over his head and swearing that "he was the big buck at the lick."[62] As we have seen, by the time he reached New Salem a few years later, he had all but given up fighting and was known as a peacemaker.

It seems possible and perhaps even likely that the sudden death of Ann Rutledge took on a symbolic significance for Lincoln. At the time of her death he was beginning to experience a measure of success. Even though he had as yet no profession and was considerably in debt, he had achieved popularity and had won election to the state legislature, and in spite of being poor and funny-looking, he had gained the hand of the most sought-after girl in the neighborhood. Her sudden and unexpected death may have presented itself as symbolic of the collapse of his aspirations generally and of the ultimate futility of his efforts. To a confirmed fatalist, which Lincoln seems to have been from his earliest days, this sudden and tragic loss may well have appeared a sign that his scheme to raise himself, in effect to shape and even to control events, was nothing but foolish vanity, a clear instance of the pride that goeth before a fall. Only a failure of this magnitude would apparently explain a dramatic reaction that suggested to those closest to him the possibility of suicide.

Lincoln's many friends at New Salem took an active interest in his plight, and with their help he eventually recovered. But the possibility of suicide in the testimony of his friends recalls a story told by one of Lincoln's political associates, Robert L. Wilson. Wilson was from the neighboring community of Athens and was, along with Lincoln, one of the "Long Nine," the ticket of tall Whigs from Sangamon County elected to the legislature about a year later. After describing for Herndon his close relations with Lincoln during this period, Wilson said that while still living in New Salem, Lincoln "told me that although he appeared to enjoy life rapturously, Still he was the victim of terrible melancholly. He Sought company, and indulged in fun and hilarity without restraint, or Stint as to time Still when by himself, he told me that he was so overcome with mental depression, that he never dare carry a knife in his pocket, And as long as I was intimately acquainted with him, previous to his commencement of the practice of the law, he never carried a pocket knife."[63]

It is difficult to know how seriously to take the suicidal implications of Wilson's story, the pocketknife hardly being a notorious means of self-destruction. Nonetheless, Wilson is a credible informant, and his testimony is the earliest evidence of something that would later become a commonplace with Lincoln's closest friends: that he habitually masked a deep-seated melancholy with a show of fun and frivolity.[64] What the detail of the pocketknife may suggest is that Lincoln was keeping himself constantly aware of the consequences of yielding to his recurrent depression and was already devising deliberate strategies to cope with his mental condition. Not carrying a pocketknife, something that virtually everyone else did and that Lincoln would do later, may have functioned more as a temporary reminder that it was possible to resist depression and regain emotional equilibrium than as a way of avoiding self-inflicted injury.

⁃ꜿ

HERNDON'S THEORY that the death of Ann Rutledge was the cause of Lincoln's lifelong melancholy may have had great appeal in the nineteenth century, but it now appears simplistic and hopelessly overdrawn. Nonetheless, the developments surrounding Ann's death did bring into biographical view for the first time something that would thereafter be a universally attested part of Lincoln's personality and emotional makeup: a marked susceptibility to melancholy.

But life, in the fall of 1835, went on. Devastating as the experience of bereavement had been, Lincoln eventually got his debilitating depression under control and went back to his law studies. In December he returned to his seat in the legislature, where he took an increasingly active part. He entered energetically into a scheme to promote a navigable canal along the Sangamon River that would effectively connect his home region with Beardstown on the Illinois River, working in the legislature to get a charter for a development company and even buying some shares in it himself. When he returned from the legislature in January, he went back to surveying, completing a plat of Petersburg, which some of his neighbors were already promoting as the seat of a new county. By summer he had laid out the prospective towns of Huron and Albany, the first of which was located at what was to be the terminus of the Beardstown canal.

It may have been on one of these surveying excursions that the basis was laid for a story that James Short passed on to Herndon, telling him he could "have the benefit of [the story] . . . even if your readers cannot." Lincoln, according to Short, used to tell this story on himself:

> Once, when Mr L was surveying, he was put to bed in the same room with two girls, the head of his bed being next to the foot of the girls' bed. In the night he commenced tickling the feet of one of the girls with his fingers. As she seemed to enjoy it as much as he did he then tickled a little higher up; and as he would tickle higher the girl would shove down lower and the higher he tickled the lower she moved. Mr L would tell the story with evident enjoyment. He never told how the thing ended.[65]

The story, whose authenticity as a Lincoln yarn we have little reason to doubt, represents a sexual encounter as essentially playful, certainly not as straightforward seduction, much less as romance. In this strictly male-audience story, the focus is not on the conclusion, which is left deliberately vague, but on the unexpected response of the woman, who consciously encourages the young surveyor and apparently seeks a more and more "dangerous" sexual involvement. From his conduct in New Salem, it seems clear that Lincoln did not want to be known as a pursuer or seducer of women, as his friends Short and Bill Greene to some extent were. But he was nonetheless, according to Herndon and others, a man with strong sexual drives, and most outlets for these drives, such as seduction and prostitution, involved moral transgressions. We have virtually no evidence of Lincoln's sexual experience up to this time, but one of the attractions of marriage to Ann Rutledge for the twenty-six-year-old Lincoln had surely been the prospect of finding an honorable outlet for his appetites.

Herndon apparently asked many of his New Salem informants if Lincoln had been involved with "bad women," and the answer, not surprisingly, was universally negative.[66] Herndon had a reason for asking. Lincoln had once told him about an incident with a woman in Beardstown in which he thought he had contracted syphilis. Herndon wrote the following account of the matter to his collaborator, Jesse W. Weik, nearly two years after their biography appeared. "When I was in Greencastle in '87 I said to you that Lincoln had, *when a mere boy*, the syphilis and now let me Explain the Matter in full which I have never done before. About the year 1835 – 6 Mr. Lincoln went to Beardstown and during a devilish passion had Connection with a girl and Caught the disease."[67]

Herndon is not clear about whether he got the date of the incident from Lincoln or fixed the date himself on the basis of his own researches, but the Beardstown location would fit the period under discussion very well. As indicated earlier, in the months following Ann's death Lincoln became deeply involved in the promotion of the Beardstown canal, helping to gain a charter for the developer, investing in it himself, platting a town at its terminus, and even purchasing forty-seven acres of government land nearby. The chief promoter of this venture was the Beardstown entrepreneur Francis Arenz, a fellow Whig who had published Lincoln's political pieces in his newspaper,[68] and it is a virtual certainty that Lincoln would have been in Beardstown to confer with Arenz during this period. Coming some months after the death of Ann Rutledge and some months before his courtship of Mary Owens, the period of involvement in the Beardstown canal would be a likely time for this incident to have taken place.

But did it, indeed, take place? Though Herndon was considered a truthful person, and the scholars who have investigated his veracity are agreed that what he testifies to of his own knowledge is reliable, this story has been widely treated as an exception. In fact, this letter has been cited as evidence of Herndon's malice toward Lincoln, of his recklessness or disregard for the truth, or as the height of irresponsibility in a friend and biographer. But these charges do nothing like justice to what Herndon actually said (quoted above) or the context in which he said it. Herndon told Weik that he wrote a note to himself about what Lincoln told him in a little memorandum book, which he unwisely loaned to Ward Hill Lamon.[69] Lamon never returned the little book, and Herndon worried that it might turn up after his own death and inadvertently give rise to the false notion that Lincoln had been unfaithful to his wife as a married man. "I now wish & for years have wished that the note was blotted out or burned to ashes. I write this to you fearing that at some future time the note – a loose thing as to date, place and circumstances, will Come to light and be misunderstood. Lincoln was a man of terribly strong passions, but was true as steel to his wife during his whole marriage life: his honor, as Judge Davis, has said saved many a woman & it is most Emphatically true as I Know." Writing a few months before his death, Herndon told Weik, "I write this to you to Explain the whole matter for the future if it should become necessary to do so. I deeply regret my part of the affair in Every particular."[70] In these circumstances, it hardly seems appropriate to accuse Herndon of bad faith, of planting a discreditable story, or, worse, of making the whole thing up.

Lincoln's confessing to Herndon that he contracted syphilis as a result of a misadventure in Beardstown doesn't necessarily mean he actually had the disease. As others have shown, fear of syphilis was common in the nineteenth century, and the aspiring and self-reforming young Abraham Lincoln, the ex-flatboatman and hog drover trying to gain respectability, would seem a prime candidate for just such a fear.[71] Another consideration is that if he thought he might have this highly communicable disease, it would almost certainly affect his attitude toward sexual contact with other women and, more particularly, toward the prospect of marriage. In this respect, his well-documented courtship of Mary Owens beginning in the fall of 1836 would seem to count against the likelihood that he thought at the time he had syphilis. But the details of that courtship, which are unusually revealing of Lincoln's behavior and state of mind, could also suggest something like the opposite.

HERNDON LEARNED of Lincoln's romantic involvement with Mary Owens early in his investigations and eventually collected several accounts from former New Salem residents. This perfectly parallels his discovery of the Ann Rutledge story, but there was an important difference. Mary Owens was still alive, and Herndon not only received testimony from former neighbors and from relatives who had talked the matter over with her recently but actually corresponded with her himself. And after persistent pleading, he persuaded the lady, now Mrs. Mary Vineyard of Weston, Missouri, to allow him to copy the letters Lincoln had sent her during their courtship.

L. M. ("Nult") Greene, who had married the daughter of Mary's sister Elizabeth Abell, described the general circumstances for Herndon:

> Miss Owens came to Ills in Oct 1833 on a visit of about 4 weeks During this visit Mr Lincoln became acquainted with her but not intimately as I think. Then she came to Ills again on the day of the Presidential 1836 I was at the Election & saw her pass through New Salem She remained in the neighborhood till April 1838 – She was *tall* & portly weighed in 1836 about 180 lbs at this time she was 29 or 30 years of age – had large blue eyes with the finest trimmings I ever

saw She was jovial social loved wit & humor – had a liberal English education & was considered wealthy.[72]

Nult Greene's brother Gaines gave Herndon additional details about their cousin and her family:

> Mr Owens [Mary's father] was a Kentuckian – rich & well Edu-
> cated – married the 2d time – his wife – the 2d one & Miss Owens
> didn't agree. Miss Owens Came to Ills as Early as 1836 – or 7 – lived
> with her Sister, Mrs Able – It was at Mrs Ables that Miss Owens &
> Mr Lincoln Saw Each other – Miss Owens was about 24 or 5 ys of
> age in 1837 – She is 5 feet – 7 in high[t] – Strong nervous & muscular
> woman – has dark blue Eyes – dark brown hair – flesh light colored
> and weighed 160 pounds.[73]

About Mary Owens's age in 1836 it is possible to be more precise: she was just four months older than Abraham Lincoln, or twenty-eight.[74] About her size, a matter of some significance in the story, there are varying estimates, all suggesting that she was, as Mrs. Hardin Bale said, "over ordinary size in height & weight of a standard woman."[75] There was also wide agreement with the opinion of another cousin, Mentor Graham, that "She was a very intellectual woman – well educated."[76] In fact, more than one informant testified, as Gaines Greene did, that Mary Owens was "decidedly the most intellectual woman I Ever Knew."[77] This keenness of intellect was several times cited by witnesses making comparisons between Mary Owens and Ann Rutledge. Caleb Carman, for example, told Herndon: "Miss Owen[s] was a handsome woman – a fine looking woman – was Sharp – Shrewd and intellectual, I assure you Miss Rutledge was a pretty woman – good natured – kind – wasn't as smart as Miss Owens by a heap."[78]

Carman may have been boarding Lincoln at the time he took up with Mary Owens, for he reported: "He [Lincoln] went to see & Courted Miss Owens about 1835 – or – 1836 She was frequently at my house & Abe would gallant her down to Abels about 2 M down the River. It is said that she came all the way from Ky to get Lincoln. This I know nothing about."[79] But if Carman claimed to know nothing about these circumstances, there were others who did. Parthena Hill refused to talk about the matter when first approached by Herndon's father-in-law because the lady was still alive, but many years later she told Walter B. Stevens:

> Mary came from Kentucky to visit her sister, Betsy Ables, who was
> Bennett Ables' wife. They lived near Salem, and Lincoln was at Ben-

nett Ables' a good deal, and Betsy, who was a great talker, and sometimes said more than she ought, perhaps had told Lincoln she was
going to bring her sister up from Kentucky to marry him. When
Mary arrived Lincoln told some one he was intimate with that he
supposed Mrs. Ables' sister had come up to catch him, but he'd show
her a thing or two. This friend of Lincoln's was also a great friend of
the Ables family, and it wasn't long until Mary heard just what Lincoln had said. Then she said she would teach him a lesson, and she
did, too.[80]

This may be hearsay, but Parthena Hill had attended the private
school established by Mary Owens's father in Green County, Kentucky,
and presumably was well acquainted with her.[81] Mary Owens's son furnished Jesse W. Weik with an account that apparently represented his
family's understanding of what happened, an account that must reflect
what his mother told him. "Lincoln had boasted, so it has been said,
that he would marry Miss Owens if she came a second time to Illinois, a
report of which had come to her hearing. She left her Kentucky home
with a predetermination to show him, if she met him, that she was not
to be caught simply by the asking."[82] If Mary Owens had such an idea,
only her sister Elizabeth could have given it to her.

That there was some idea of a match associated with Mary Owens's
visit and that her sister, Elizabeth Abell, was involved in it is attested in
Lincoln's own account of the matter. Without naming names, he wrote
a strangely personal letter to the wife of his fellow legislator Orville H.
Browning, whom he had met in Vandalia in December 1836. Browning
explained to John G. Nicolay: "At that time Lincoln had seen but very
little of what might be called society and was very awkward, and very
much embarrassed in the presence of ladies. Mrs. Browning very soon
discovered his great merits, and treated him with a certain frank cordiality which put Lincoln entirely at his ease. On this account he
became very much attached to her. He used to come to our room, and
spend his evenings with Mrs. Browning."[83]

Here is what Lincoln wrote to his married confidante, Eliza
Browning:

It was, then, in the autumn of 1836, that a married lady of my
acquaintance, and who was a great friend of mine, being about to pay
a visit to her father and other relatives residing in Kentucky, proposed
to me, that on her return she would bring a sister of hers with her,
upon condition that I would engage to become her brother-in-law
with all convenient dispatch. I, of course, accepted the proposal; for

you know I could not have done otherwise, had I really been averse to it; but privately between you and me, I was most confoundedly well pleased with the project. I had seen the said sister some three years before, thought her inteligent and agreeable, and saw no good objection to plodding life through hand in hand with her.[84]

But when he saw her, he tells Mrs. Browning, he was astonished and chagrined. "I knew she was over-size, but she now appeared a fair match for Falstaff." She put him in mind of his mother "from her want of teeth, weather-beaten appearance in general, and from a kind of notion that ran in my head, that nothing could have commenced at the size of infancy, and reached her present bulk in less than thirtyfive or forty years. . . . But what could I do? I had told her sister that I would take her for better or for worse; and I made a point of honor and conscience in all things, to stick to my word, especially if others had been induced to act on it, which in this case, I doubted not they had, for I was now fairly convinced, that no other man on earth would have her, and hence the conclusion that they were bent on holding me to my bargain."[85]

This letter was written partly as entertainment, as its April 1 date suggests, but passages like the one just cited – in which convoluted issues of impulse and honor, of holding oneself to a bad bargain while at the same time being held to it by others, are apparently being sorted out even as they are being presented – offer rare glimpses of Lincoln's mind at work. It is perhaps precisely because this letter is cast in a mildly satiric, self-deprecating format – fictional so far as the recipient knows – that Lincoln can reveal so much about the real difficulties this episode has caused him.

The letter went on to tell how he made up his mind to make the best of it, to see the young woman in question as his prospective wife and to focus his attention on her good qualities. "I also tried to convince myself, that the mind was much more to be valued than the person; and in this, she was not inferior, as I could discover, to any with whom I had been acquainted."[86] But the letter says nothing about the two incidents that were remembered as points of contention between its writer and Mary Owens by their New Salem neighbors. The first, an incident in which Mrs. Bowling Green and her large baby were involved, was described somewhat cryptically by Bill Greene: "she [Mary Owens] and Lincoln disagreed a bout carrying a Neighbors child when on some ramble (or in other words what was true politeness) neither would *yield* a hairs breadth."[87] Herndon later queried Mrs. Vineyard herself about it, and her reply indicated that the story had been much exaggerated. "We [Lincoln and Mary] never had any hard feelings towards each other that I knew of. On one occasion did I say to Mr. L— that I did not believe he would make a kind husband, because he did not tender his services to Mrs. Green in helping of her carry her babe."[88]

The second incident involved a meeting that was supposed to have taken place upon Lincoln's returning from a long surveying trip. Bowling Green's widow, Nancy, who remembered that Lincoln had gone to see Mary Owens, recalled such an incident but thought it had happened on Mary's earlier visit before the death of Ann Rutledge.[89] Gaines Greene visited his cousin at her home in Missouri in 1866 and reported to Herndon: "I had heard a great deal about Lincoln's & her Courtship – was determined to have it & dragged it out by degrees."[90] The rather full account that follows presumably represents what Gaines dragged out of his cousin, and interestingly enough, it contains both incidents.

> Lincoln had gone to Havana to Survey Some land – had been gone about 3 Weeks – One of Ables boys went up to get the mail – Lincoln had just got back: he asked the little boy if Miss Owens was at Mr Ables: the boy replied – yes: Tell her – Said Lincoln that I'll be down to see her in a few minutes". Able lived about 1 M north of Salem. The boy told Miss Owens this – Miss Owens had that Evening determined to go Mentor Graham's her Cousin: She thought a moment and Said to herself if I can draw Lincoln up there to Grahams it will all be right: they had had a difficulty about Mrs Bolin Greens boy before this – The difficulty arose in this way – Miss Owens & Mrs Bolin Green were going to Ables from Bolin Greens. Lincoln Came along just at that time – Mrs B. Green said they were going to Ables, and asked Lincoln to go along. Mrs B. G's child was along – it was a great big fat child – heavy & crossly disposed – Mrs. B G. had to Carry her own child up – L & Miss Owens walking behind – Lincoln did not appear to notice the old lady's struggles and when they all had got up to the house – Say 100 ft & pretty Steep. Miss Owens Said to Lincoln – laughingly – You would not make a good husband Abe: they Sat on the fence & one word brought on an other, till a Split or breach Ensued – It was with an Eye to this quarrel that Miss Owens wished to test L love That if he came to Grahams it was all right. She wanted to make L bend. Lincoln according to promise went down to Ables and asked if Miss Owens was in: Mrs Able replied that She had gone to Grahams, about 1 1/2 M from Ables – due south west – : Lincoln Said – "Didn't She

Know I was Coming". Mrs Able Said – "No." One of the children Said – "Yes Ma – She did for I heard one of the children – the boy Saml who went to the P. O told her So." Lincoln Sat a Short time – went to Salem to his office – place of business – bording house and didnt go to Graham's. The fat was now in the fire.[91]

Gaines Greene believed that the real difficulty here was something that did not appear on the surface – namely, Lincoln's belief that he was being put in his place by someone who regarded herself as his superior because of her wealth. "Lincoln thought that as he was Extremely poor and Miss Owens very rich that it was a fling on him on that account. This was at that time Abes tender spot. Abe was mistaken in his guesses for wealth Cut no figure in Miss Owens Eyes – Miss Owens regretted her Course – Abe would not bend and Miss Owens wouldn't: She Said if She had it to do over again She would play her Cards differently. She went back to Ky about 1838 – did not Court any one for Several years."[92]

Lincoln correctly discerned that he was being deliberately tested, and Mary Owens apparently later regretted this gesture, either as an unnecessary humiliation or simply as a miscalculation. Gaines Greene's testimony dramatizes what would appear to be the dynamics and peculiar tensions of the relationship, but what is misleading here is the implication that the incident ended the courtship, which is clearly not the case. This incident took place while Lincoln was still living in New Salem, and his own letters show that the courtship continued after he moved to Springfield in 1837. In fact, since Lincoln effectively gave up surveying soon after Mary Owens arrived, the story may represent their first, rather than their final, difficulty.

Lincoln's letters to Mary Owens are nothing if not revealing. The first catches his despondent mood after eight days of illness and inactivity at Vandalia, waiting for the new statehouse to be made usable so that the legislature can begin business. "I have been sick ever since my arrival here, or I should have written sooner. It is but little difference, however, as I have verry little even yet to write. And more, the longer I can avoid the mortification of looking in the Post Office for your letter and not finding it, the better. You see I am mad about that *old letter* yet. I dont like verry well to risk you again. I'll try you once more any how."[93] No information has come to light about "that *old letter*," and except for the implication that sending Mary a letter will hasten the period of disappointment (heightened dramatically to "mortification") that will ensue until she replies, one can only suppose that there has been some sort of discontent on Lincoln's part in the past about their correspondence.

Lincoln's earliest surviving letter to Mary Owens came at the beginning of what was to prove one of the most eventful and memorable sessions in his legislative career, and also one of the longest. Returning to New Salem in March, Lincoln and Mary could have had very little time together because of his court appearances in Springfield, where he moved on April 15, 1837, to assume a law partnership with John T. Stuart. Lincoln described for Mary, in his next surviving letter, his feelings of loneliness and of being out of place in Springfield, of being conscious of not knowing how to behave himself. But what he said of their prospective life together, which they had apparently been discussing, is forbidding almost beyond belief:

> I am afraid you would not be satisfied. There is a great deal of flourishing about in carriages here, which it would be your doom to see without shareing in it. You would have to be poor without means of hiding your poverty. Do you believe you could bear that patiently? Whatever woman may cast her lot with mine, should any ever do so, it is my intention to do all in my power to make her happy and contented; and there is nothing I can immagine, that would make me more unhappy than to fail in the effort.[94]

Poverty, ignominy, failure, unhappiness. The message here is relentlessly dour, but at least it is straightforward. The balance of the paragraph, in which there is at least a pretense of encouragement, is simply dizzying in its reversals:

> I know I should be much happier with you than the way I am, provided I saw no signs of discontent in you. What you have said to me may have been in jest, or I may have misunderstood it. If so, then let it be forgotten; if otherwise, I much wish you would think seriously before you decide. For my part I have already decided. What I have said I will most positively abide by, provided you wish it. My opinion is that you had better not do it. You have not been accustomed to hardship, and it may be more sever than you now immagine. I know you are capable of thinking correctly on any subject; and if you deliberate maturely upon this, before you decide, then I am willing to abide your decision.[95]

Mary's sister, Elizabeth Abell, described this letter from memory for Herndon thirty years later:

when Mr Lincoln was paying his respects to my sister he lived in old
Salem but in the mean time he remooved to Springfield after he had
been there some little time he wrote my Sister a letter and in it he
told her the subject they had been talking uppon he wanted her to
consider and reconsider it that he was poore and there was a great
deal of splashing and dashing in Buggys here and she would have to
be a silent looker on and not a percipitant but he said I rather have
you then any woman living it stoped at that, what man on earth
would have done such a thing but Abraham Lincoln he was two
honest a man for this world.[96]

Mrs. Abell's characterization probably combines the letter of May 3
with the one Lincoln sent a few months later on August 16, but it also
gives some indication of the way the letters may have been received by
Mary.

According to his confidential letter to Mrs. Browning nearly a year
later, Lincoln, at this stage of the affair, had given himself over to planning "how I might procrastinate the evil day for a time, which I really
dreaded as much – perhaps more, than an irishman does the halter."[97]
The letter just quoted, which is so notable for its constantly turning
back on itself, might be seen as part of such a strategy, but its successor,
written only three months later, seems more bent on forcing matters to
a head. Lincoln wrote to explain his feelings toward Mary, in spite of
having seen her that very day. Only an extensive extract can do justice to
the torturous course of Lincoln's pleading:

> I want in all cases to do right, and most particularly so, in all cases
> with women. I want, at this particular time, more than any thing else,
> to do right with you, and if I *knew* it would be doing right, as I rather
> suspect it would, to let you alone, I would do it. And for the purpose
> of making the matter as plain as possible, I now say, that you can now
> drop the subject, dismiss your thoughts (if you ever had any) from me
> forever, and leave this letter unanswered, without calling forth one
> accusing murmur from me. And I will even go further, and say, that if
> it will add any thing to your comfort, or peace of mind, to do so, it is
> my sincere wish that you should. Do not understand by this, that I
> wish to cut your acquaintance. I mean no such thing. What I do wish
> is, that our further acquaintance shall depend upon yourself. If such
> further acquaintance would contribute nothing to your happiness, I
> am sure it would not to mine. If you feel yourself in any degree bound
> to me, I am now willing to release you, provided you wish it; while,
> on the other hand, I am willing, and even anxious to bind you faster,
> if I can be convinced that it will, in any considerable degree, add
> to your happiness. This, indeed, is the whole question with me.

Nothing would make me more miserable than to believe you miserable – nothing more happy, than to know you are.[98]

The text of this pleading, insofar as there is one, is that the happiness of the suitor should count for nothing and that of the lady be considered all. But the subtext would seem to be that the suitor is, in fact, in a state of acute misery and wishes the pursued to take mercy on him and end it, one way or the other. Consult your own happiness, but please take my misery into account. It is difficult not to read this letter as an agonized plea for a decision, but Mary, who must have recognized as much, apparently would not rise to the bait. Lincoln's letter to Mrs. Browning makes no mention of such a stage in the proceedings, but it does frankly acknowledge the step that he was forced to take when the strategy represented by this last letter availed him nothing: he had to propose. "After I had delayed the matter as long as I thought I could in honor do, which by the way had brought me round into the last fall [1837], I concluded I might as well bring it to a consumation without further delay; and so I mustered my resolution, and made the proposal to her direct; but, shocking to relate, she answered, No."[99] He repeated the offer several times, but with the same mortifying result.

This experience is described for his confidante in the letter's quasi-jocular format and in self-deprecating terms, and we have the testimony of Browning that he and his wife took it in this spirit. "The letter was written in a droll and amusing vein, and both Mrs. Browning and myself laughed very heartily over it. We knew that Mr. Lincoln was fond of his jokes, and we supposed that the whole letter was sheer invention from beginning to end."[100] But one's perspective in recognizing the story as authentic transforms the description of the effect of the refusal, and indeed of the whole affair, into a revealing exercise in self-examination and self-disclosure. "My vanity was deeply wounded by the reflection, that I had so long been too stupid to discover her intentions, and at the same time never doubting that I understood them perfectly; and also, that she whom I had taught myself to believe no body else would ever have, had actually rejected me with all my fancied greatness; and to cap the whole, I then, for the first time, began to suspect that I was really a little in love with her."[101]

What Lincoln castigates himself for, on two or three different counts, is a failure of intelligence, which, since he lacked means and physical appeal, is supposed to be his strong suit. Basic stupidity and naiveté are compounded by a failure of self-knowledge, for he represents himself as so absorbed in his own machinations that he failed to observe a ripening affection for Mary. "Others have been made fools of by the girls; but this can never be with truth said of me. I most emphatically, in this instance, made a fool of myself." It is a mark of Lincoln's distinctive character that he can amuse his friends by making himself out the fool in an April Fool letter, and at the same time and by the same act painfully acknowledge his own shortcomings and defeats. The man who felt awkward and ill at ease in the society of women, and who was sensitive about the slights of the well educated and the well-to-do, can hardly have shaken off very readily the humiliation of this unqualified rejection.

Herndon's investigations provide some glimpses of how the courtship appeared from Mary Owens's perspective and why, presumably, the rejection was forthcoming. Mary told Herndon that while they had never had any hard feelings, she did chide Lincoln about his lack of concern for Mrs. Bowling Green, as we have seen. And she gave Herndon one further example how she thought him "lacking in smaller atentions."

> There was a company of us going to Uncle Billy Greens [she wrote], Mr. L. was riding with me, and we had a very bad branch to cross, the other gentlemen were very officious in seeing that their partners got over safely; we were behind, he riding in never looking back to see how I got along; when I rode up beside him, I remarked, you are a nice fellow; I suppose you did not care whether my neck was broken or not. He laughingly replied, (I suppose by way of compliment) that he knew I was plenty smart to take care of myself.[102]

Mary also told Herndon how she remembered explaining Lincoln's deficiencies to her sister, Elizabeth Abell, who was promoting the match.

> I think I did on one occasion say to my sister, who was very anxious for us to be married, that I thought Mr. Lincoln was deficient in those little links which make up the great chain of womans happiness, at least it was so in my case; not that I believed it proceeded from a lack of goodness of heart, but his training had been different from mine, hence there was not that congeniality which would have otherwise existed. From his own showing [in his letters] you perceive that his heart and hand were at my disposal, and I suppose my feelings were not sufficiently enlisted to have the matter consumated.[103]

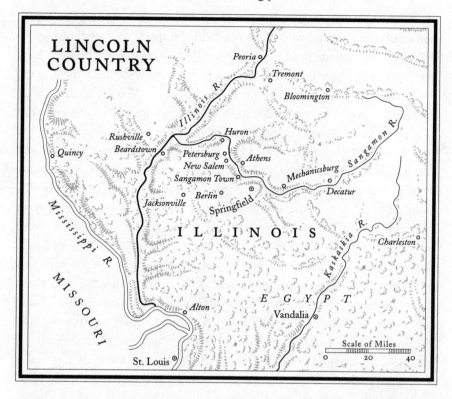

On at least two occasions – the incidents of Mrs. Green's baby and the ride across the "bad branch" – Mary Owens had made it clear to Lincoln in what respects "his training had been different" from her own. But what object was he pursuing? If it was to make himself unattractive as a mate and thus avoid marriage to a woman who was "a fair match for Falstaff," it is no surprise that he should be judged and found wanting. But if his letter to Eliza Browning can be taken as a guide, this was not his purpose. Instead, he had concluded that it was not honorable to evade the match and so had determined to reconcile himself to it. His letters to Mary, however, suggest that if he had indeed decided to accept a life sentence, he was still hoping, after several months of courtship, for a continuance, or even a quashed indictment. Being honor bound to Mrs. Abell, the matchmaker, seems weak enough, but if honor was still the motivating force, it was apparently not the only one at work, for other factors are prominently on display in those letters. The "comic" conclusion of the Browning letter, where he pictures himself as forcing his own hand in proposing marriage and being deeply "mortified" by his rejection, masks his final humiliation by admitting it.

He has lost by winning; surmounting obstacles and making good on his honorable determination that he must offer himself, he is refused.

There can be little doubt that the pain of rejection for Abraham Lincoln was real, regardless of how mixed his motives might have been. And they certainly seem to have been mixed. Mary Owens, as an unusually intelligent, well-educated woman, whose father was rich and in a position to assist an indigent son-in-law, would have been what Lincoln's contemporaries would have called a good catch. She was admittedly heavy, but she was highly intelligent, fair of face, and apparently possessed admirable "trimmings." He may have feared initially, as he confessed to Mrs. Browning, that she had designs on him or felt that she occasionally put on superior airs, but the letters from Springfield in 1837 suggest that her greatest liability, for Lincoln, was her lack of demonstrative feelings and commitment toward him. Or could the perplexing arguments and attitudes expressed in all these letters represent vacillation from a different or additional cause? Here the specter of Lincoln's syphilophobia presents itself as a possibility. While it does not appear to be a necessary piece in the puzzle, if we accept Herndon's date for the encounter at Beardstown, it remains a strong possibility.

After refusing Abraham Lincoln's repeated proposals, Mary Owens returned to Kentucky in early 1838. She wrote Herndon: "The last message I ever received from him [Lincoln] was about a year after we parted in Illinois. Mrs. Able visited Ky. and he said to her in Springfield, Tell your Sister, that I think she was a great fool, because she did not stay here and marry me.

"Characteristic of the man."[104]

-❧-

WHAT DID Mary Owens mean? She was not an inexperienced schoolgirl; by the standards of her time she qualified at age twenty-nine as an "old maid."[105] She was accounted on all sides an unusually discerning woman, and she had the benefit of a long look at her suitor. She was not blind to his virtues. She recognized, as her sister did, Lincoln's unusual sensitivity. "In many things he was sensitive almost to a fault," she told Herndon, and added, "In many things we were congenial spirits."[106] To some it probably seemed that she had concluded she could not dominate the stubbornly independent young man, who insisted on being taken on his own terms. Her cousin Nult Greene, for example, allowed that "She was a very superior woman but like some other pretty women (God bless them) she loved Power & conquest."[107] But her own testimony indicates convincingly that she had decided that she and Abraham Lincoln were too different, that his "training" had left him unresponsive to the expectations of hers. Having taken his measure, then, what in the incident of Lincoln's message did she see as "characteristic of the man"?

It could hardly have been a quality of boastfulness or immodesty, of which neither she nor anyone else complained. More likely it was that Lincoln, after a year's time to sort out what had happened between them, still didn't understand. He was sensitive to things like the suffering of fellow creatures and to points of honor, but he was curiously insensitive to the little things that mattered very much to Mary Owens. It was perhaps typical that he sent her a message that could be taken as lighthearted and jocular, but how could he still think or say that Mary had made a mistake? He was the one who had ignored all the red flags and had doggedly pressed an unpromising courtship to a proposal; she was the one who had seen what was wrong and what needed to be done. And he was calling her a fool. Characteristic of the man.

Chapter 5

BREAKING INTO
POLITICS

LTHOUGH HE HAD SEEN no actual combat in the Black
Hawk War, when Abraham Lincoln returned in late July 1832,
he plunged headlong into a political campaign in which the
fighting was unavoidable. He had only about ten days to campaign
before the election in early August, but he needed no prearranged
schedule, for candidates of that time and place appeared at any public
event that drew a crowd. James and Row Herndon believed that Lincoln's maiden appearance was at a public auction in a little place called
Pappsville, and James thought he could recite Lincoln's first campaign
speech almost verbatim.[1] Both Row and James remembered that Lincoln interrupted his speaking debut to intercede in a fight. Row said
that he was in the process of whipping one Jesse Dodson when
Dodson's friends "atempte to Sow foul Play and Mr Lincoln Pachd in
and threw them about Like Boys."[2] His brother, James, said he "Saw
Lincoln Catch a man by the nape of the neck and a— of the breeches
and toss him 10 or 12 feet, easily."[3] Far from putting the political newcomer in a bad light, Lincoln's decisive intervention, as Row Herndon
declared, "made him many friends."[4]

Because of his legendary reputation as a speaker and storyteller, it is
easy to underestimate the importance of the young Lincoln's other
resources as a frontier campaigner. Perhaps the most serviceable of
these was his supreme confidence in his own physical abilities; he could
not be intimidated. At six feet four inches in height and weighing 180
pounds, he was, by every account, extraordinarily strong. He could lift

weights that were beyond the capacity of others; he could throw heavy
objects, such as cannonballs, farther than his fellows; he was surpass-
ingly fast afoot; and he could easily outjump all competitors for distance. These were feats that were much admired by the men who
constituted the electorate in Sangamon County in the 1830s, and they
helped lay the groundwork for Lincoln's success on the hustings.

The fighting at political meetings was more or less expected and was
apparently something of a natural extension of the kind of rough-and-
tumble social life these pioneers brought with them. Stephen T. Logan
recalled: "In addition to the speeches at the Court House they used to
have a good many fights at the groceries [saloons]. Two gangs of
country bullies used to meet here and fight one another. One was from
Lick Creek, and the other from Spring Creek. I had seen a good deal of
that sort of thing in Kentucky, and was somewhat used to it, but a
stranger would have considered this a pretty hard country, I suppose."[5]
In his history of Illinois, Thomas Ford pictured the fighting as a logical
consequence of the way frontier campaigns were typically conducted.
"The stump speeches being over, then commenced the drinking of
liquor, and long before night a large portion of the voters would be
drunk and staggering about town, cursing, swearing, hallooing, yelling,
huzzaing for their favorite candidates, throwing their arms up and
around, threatening to fight, and fighting."[6]

But the twenty-three-year-old Lincoln could do more than handle
himself in a fight. At the courthouse in Springfield, when all the candidates spoke to the assembled crowd in turn, he caught the attention of
Logan, also a newcomer and a well-educated lawyer whose talents and
training were soon to make him a leader of the Springfield bar. "I never
saw Lincoln until he came up here to make a speech. . . . He was a very
tall and gawky and rough looking fellow then – his pantaloons didn't
meet his shoes by six inches."[7] The recollections of his friends suggest
that Lincoln capitalized on his untoward appearance. He is supposed to
have said in one of his speeches: "i have Been told that some of my
opponents have said that it was a disgrase to the County of sangamon
to have such a Looking man as i am stuck up for the Legislator now i
thought this was a free Cuntry that is the Reason that i adress you to
Day had i have Known to the Contrary i should Knot have Consented
to Run."[8] Another friend remembered his giving the theme a different
twist: "Gentlemen I have just returned from the Campaign My personal appearance is rather shabby & dark. I am almost as red as those

men I have been chasing through the prairies & forests on the Rivers of Illinois."⁹ But like many others, Logan was impressed by the performance of this unprepossessing candidate, reporting years later that Lincoln had attacked Senator Thomas Hart Benton's theory of gold circulation and "made a very sensible speech."¹⁰

Though he commanded an astonishing 98 percent of the vote in his own precinct, Lincoln was little known elsewhere in the county. Jason Duncan, one of his supporters in this race, wrote: "So little was Known of Mr Lincoln by the inhabitants of Sangamon at the time he first became a candidate for the legislature that when a few miles out of town in my rides [I] would be asked who Abraham was[.] they had never heard of such a man."¹¹ When the election was held on August 6, Lincoln managed to finish no higher than eighth (the top four being elected). But brief as his ten-day campaign had been, he had clearly made a strong impression. John T. Stuart acknowledged that "Lincoln in this race, although he was defeated, acquired a reputation for candor and honesty, as well as for ability in speech-making. He made friends everywhere he went – he ran on the square – and thereby acquired the respect and confidence of everybody."¹²

⁂

LINCOLN HAD undoubtedly been thinking about entering politics for some time before announcing for the state legislature in the spring of 1832. Accounts of his childhood in Indiana indicate that he practiced stump speaking at an early age. His interest in politics was probably quickened by reading the highly political newspapers of the time, and he seems to have acquired an appreciation for the crosscurrents of politics from a storekeeper he worked for, William Jones. Lincoln's backcountry neighbors in Indiana were almost entirely Jackson men, but the young Lincoln, reportedly following Jones's example, resisted. Possibly at the time of the 1828 election he began to line up with the anti-Jackson forces and soon pronounced himself a follower of Henry Clay.¹³

In 1830 Lincoln moved from Indiana with his family and resided for a year in Macon County, apparently "working out" when not helping establish his father's new farm. One of the few surviving stories about this year of Lincoln's early life comes from William Butler, who described an encounter between the famous circuit-riding preacher and politician, Peter Cartwright, who was out campaigning, and an unprepossessing young farmhand who was driving a team of oxen, breaking prairie on Butler's farm. The farmhand, of course, was Abraham Lincoln, and the cause of the encounter was politics. Cartwright, according to Butler, "laid down his doctrines in a way which undoubtedly seemed to Lincoln a little too dogmatical. A discussion soon arose between him and Cartwright, and my first special attention was attracted to Lincoln by the way in which he met the great preacher in his arguments, and the extensive acquaintance he showed with the politics of the State – in fact he quite beat him in the argument."[14]

Or so it seemed in retrospect. But confirmation of sorts is found in another incident remembered from that same summer concerning a speech Lincoln gave at a political gathering. Not surprisingly, the two eyewitnesses to this performance gave, many years later, very different accounts of the event. Lincoln's cousin, John Hanks, recalled:

> After Abrm got to Decatur – rather to Macon – My Co – a man by the name of Posey Came into our neighborhood and made a Speech: it was a bad one and I Said Abe could beat it. I turned down a box or Keg and Abe made his Speech. The other man was a Candidate – Abe wasn't. Abe beat him to death – his subject being the navigation of the Sangamon River. The man after the Speech was through took Abe aside and asked him where he had learned So much and what he did so well. Abe Explained, Stating his manner & method of reading and what he had read: the man Encouraged Lincoln to persevere.[15]

The other eyewitness, George Close, made no mention of Hanks's role in the proceedings or the subject of the speech but remembered certain other details: "Gen. W. L. D. Ewing and a man named Posey were candidates for legislature in 1829 – came to Decatur to make speeches – As Posey did not treat we persuaded L to get up and abuse him – said he would if I would not laugh at him – was frightened but got warmed up and made the best Speech of the day – Did not abuse Posey but spoke well of both men – pictured out the future of Ill. When he got through Ewing said 'he was a bright one.' "[16] This was the way Close remembered it in 1860, but after Lincoln's death he apparently told Andrew Goodpasture that the issue in dispute that caused Lincoln to take the platform was whether Illinois should become a slave state. This seems a clear example of how subsequent events can flavor recollections.

Though the date that Close gave in 1860 must be in error, Posey and Ewing were running for the legislature in the summer of 1830, and it is likely that it was their meeting that Lincoln addressed. While not a campaign speech in his own behalf, it was offered in a political context and apparently was effectively presented and well received. His New Salem friend, William G. Greene, says Lincoln himself spoke of this early effort. "His first Stump Speech ever made I have heard him say was in Macon Co in reply to two Men by the Names of a Mr Posey & Ewing this was no Political Speech but an *Experementer* in 1830 or 31 that was before I knew him all I know of that effort I learned from Mr Lincoln I have often heard him regret that he had no copy of it as it was Extempo."[17]

Lincoln left home for good in the spring of 1831 and within a year had announced, at age twenty-three, his candidacy for political office. In framing the public announcement he had printed in the Springfield newspaper, he no doubt remembered the warm reception his remarks on the navigation of the Sangamon River had received, for this topic took up much of his announcement, "To the People of Sangamo County." Opening the subject of the need for a reliable means of transportation, Lincoln glanced at the "heart appalling" cost of railroads before turning to the far more affordable improvement of the Sangamon. Because he was a flatboatman and the operator of a mill on the river, Lincoln claimed, "it is probable that for the last twelve months I have given as particular attention to the stage of the water in this river, as any other person in the country."[18] Clearing the Sangamon of "drifted timber" and straightening its tortuously meandering channel, Lincoln allowed, would provide a practicable solution.

It went without saying that this happy solution would particularly benefit the citizens of northern Sangamon County, especially those living in or near communities (like New Salem) that were located on the river and in a position to profit from its traffic. There is little doubt that this issue, so roundly treated in Lincoln's announcement, went with the territory and was not merely the brainchild of the candidate. In the absence of sharply partisan issues, the wise political aspirant presented himself as the champion of what people already wanted. "I do not think there was any party Politics hereabout in those days," one New Salem resident remembered, "candidates for Election [based] their Claims upon Local Hobeys."[19] Making the Sangamon navigable was such a hobby, and though he lost this first election, Lincoln did not abandon the issue. Nor was this the only hobby in the New Salem area.

The fact that Lincoln got "nearly every vote in his own precinct" was, according to John T. Stuart, mainly due to his personal popularity – though not entirely so – for remember this was a bitter fight between the Jackson and Clay men, and there were a great many Jackson men down there.

The complete explanation is found in the fact that the New Salem people were already then interested in a project for getting themselves set apart into a new County (afterwards Menard Co.) and Lincoln being their local candidate they expected to make him instrumental in bringing this about.[20]

Stuart here identified three factors that worked to Lincoln's advantage in the next election in 1834: his personal popularity, the bitter opposition between the known Clay and Jackson men, and the wish to have the New Salem region set apart as a new county.

Lincoln's personal popularity is everywhere evident in the testimony of those who knew him. He was considered friendly, sociable, good-natured, surprisingly well spoken, and a natural leader. Asked why Lincoln was regarded as a good candidate for political office at this time, William Butler replied: ". . . the prominence given him by his captancy in the Black Hawk War – because he was a good fellow – because he told good stories, and remembered good jokes – because he was genial, kind, sympathetic, open-hearted – because when he was asked a question and gave an answer it was always characteristic, brief, pointed, *à propos,* out of the common way and manner, and yet exactly suited to the time place and thing."[21]

A measure of Lincoln's popularity was the willingness of people who disagreed with his political and religious views to vote for him. Russell Godbey told Herndon: "I voted for him in 1834 against my political Creed & principles He was Elected. Snodgrass told me not to vote for him – because Abe was a Deist – &c – I did vote for him nonetheless – and never regretted it."[22] Lincoln's heterodox religious views were apparently well known at the time and surely bothered many voters. Though it is something most informants did not discuss, presumably because it would reflect unfavorably on Lincoln, James Matheny recalled that Lincoln's religious views were a problem for his supporters in those years:

In 1834 & 5, my father being a strong Methodist – a Kind of minister and loving Lincoln with all his soul hated to vote for him because he heard that Lincoln was an Infidel. Mr Lincoln did write a pamphlet attacking the divinity of christ – Special inspiration – Revelation &c –. All these things were talked about in 1835 – 6. & 7 – were talked of discussed &c in the Lincoln-Cartwright Congress race in 1846 –

Many Religious – Christian whigs hated to vote for Lincoln on that account – had to argue the question &c. with them.[23]

A number of things suggest that in the year following Lincoln's first run for political office, the Jackson forces, sailing under the flag of the Democratic party, were making overtures to this popular young hoosier from New Salem. Being the dominant party, both in the region and in the state, they controlled most of the offices, and it is hardly an accident that Abraham Lincoln was offered two political appointments in 1833: the deputy surveyorship for northern Sangamon County and the postmastership of New Salem. Neither, of course, required the exercise of partisanship, being merely the spoils of office and not overtly connected to political principles or policy. The postmastership, Lincoln later wrote, was "too insignificant, to make his politics an objection,"[24] but the offer of the surveyor's post gave him pause. Because it was more than slightly remunerative, he reportedly took the precaution of gaining the express assurance of the chief surveyor, John Calhoun, that no compromise of his political principles was expected.[25] Much has been made of Lincoln's career as postmaster, but the deputy surveyorship, as Lincoln himself put it, "procured bread, and kept body and soul together."[26]

These overtures by the Democrats become more important when seen in the context of the time. John T. Stuart told Herndon that "from 1830 up to 1837 the tendency in Illinois was for every man of ambition to turn Democrite – Ford[,] Forquer – Cartwright. There was a fear that the Yankees about 1832 to 1837 imigrating to Ills would be whig – but when they got here were no more than democrats."[27] Meanwhile, the Democrats of the New Salem area were apparently drumming up support for their champion across the county. According to Stephen T. Logan, "they told their democratic brethren in the other parts of the county that they must help elect Lincoln, or else they wouldn't support the other democratic candidates."[28] Perhaps in response, the Democrats proposed an accommodation, whereby they would drop two of their candidates and support Lincoln. John T. Stuart vividly recalled Lincoln's reaction:

> I remember we were out at Danleys on Clear Lake. They had a shooting match there. The country people met to shoot for a beef (the candidates as was the custom were expected to pay for the beef.) and we were there electioneering.
> Lincoln came to me and told me that the Jackson men had been to him and proposed to him that they would drop two of their men and

take him up and vote for him for the purpose of beating me. Lincoln acted fairly and honorably about it by coming and submitting the proposition to me.

From my experience in the former race in 1832 I had great confidence in my strength – perhaps too much as I was a young man – but I told L. to go and tell them he would take their votes – that I would risk it – and I believe he did so.

I and my friends knowing their tactics, then concentrated our fight against one of their men – it was Quinton – and in this way we beat Quinton and elected Lincoln and myself.[29]

What the trade-off for the Democrats was to be is not apparent, but it is likely that it was Lincoln's support for things he was already committed to, such as the division of Sangamon County. More than fifty years later, John Potter remembered: "When Abe ran for the legislature, the time he was elected, Ned Potter and Hugh Armstrong had a pledge from him that he would try to get us cut off and made into a new county."[30] Samuel Hill, New Salem's leading merchant, was apparently also active in this effort, for his son told Ida M. Tarbell, "Have often heard my Father say (he was a democrat) that he & many others united whig & democrat & got Mr Lincoln nominated & Elected on the County dividing question."[31] It is also likely that Lincoln was already committed to the promotion of a canal to improve navigation on the Sangamon River. Herndon told Ward Hill Lamon that Lincoln's "intense popularity in Menard County in 1834" was related to *"a local reason:* he advocated a canal from the Sangamon river some few miles below Petersburg down the bluffs – being lower there than near the Illinois river, to Beardstown – thus putting New Salem & Beardstown in nearer Contact."[32]

The campaign gave Lincoln the opportunity to stump the entire county and prove his mettle. Tradition has it that he was accompanied in his travels by the Clary's Grove boys, who were said to have "followed Lincoln over the country in his campaign in 1834, standing always ready to fight his battles for him, – ready to resent with their fists any abuse or slighting remarks about their idol."[33] That Lincoln needed anyone to fight his battles for him or that these men would desert their farms in midsummer whenever and wherever he spoke may be disputed, but they undoubtedly were a visual and vocal presence at his public appearances closer to home, and so would have constituted a notable deterrence to heckling and harassment of the candidate.

Robert L. Wilson, whose recollections of this period are unusually

vivid and valuable, first met Lincoln about the time of the 1834 campaign and described him thus:

> Mr Lincoln, a[t] this time, was about twenty four or five years old.
> Six feet a[n]d four inches high in his Stockings. Some Stoop Shoul-
> dered. his legs were long, feet large; arms long, longer than any man I
> ever knew, when standing Straiht, and letting his arms fall down his
> Sides, the points of his fingers would touch a point lower on his legs
> by nearly three inches than was usual with other persons. I was pres-
> ent when a number of persons measured the length of thire arms on
> thire legs, as here Stated, with that result. his arms were unusually
> long for his hight, and the droop of his Shoulders also producd that
> result.

Wilson accompanied his description of Lincoln's physical build and
posture with an early glimpse of the now-famous physiognomy:

> His eyes were a bluish brown, his face was long and very angular,
> when at ease had nothing in his appearance that was marked or
> Striking, but when enlivened in conversation or engaged in telling, or
> hearing some mirth-inspiring Story, his countenance would brighten
> up the expression woul[d] light up not in a flash. but rapidly the
> mucles of his face would begin to contract. Several wrinkles would
> diverge from the inner corners of his eyes, and extend down and diag-
> onally across his nose, his eyes would Sparkle, all terminating in an
> unrestrained Laugh in which every one present willing or unwilling
> were compelled to take part.[34]

One of the few stories that can be traced to the 1834 campaign points
to both the initial doubts that observers may have had about this political newcomer and the particular qualities that overcame their misgivings and made him successful. Row Herndon had boarded Lincoln for
several months in New Salem before moving away, and he described
his experience in introducing the candidate to the people of his new
neighborhood.

> he Came to my house near iland Grove During harvest there was
> some 30 men in the field he got his Diner and went out to the field
> where the men ware at wort i gave him & entroduction and the Boys
> said that they Could Not vote for a man unless he Could make a
> hand well Said he Boys if that is all i am shure of your votes he took
> hold of the Cradle Led the way all the Round with Perfect ease the
> Boys was satisfide and i dont think he Lost a vote in the Croud – the
> next Day was speaking at Burlin he went from my house with Doct
> Barrett the man that had asked me whoe this man Lincoln was; i

told him that he was a Canidate for the Legislator he lafed and said
Cant the party Raise No Beter Materials than that   i said goe
tomorrow and here all Before you pronounce judgement   when he
Come Back i said Dock what say you Now   why sir he is a perfect
take in he Knows more than all of them Put to gether [35]

Whether in the harvest field appealing to farmhands by demonstrating his facility with a cradled scythe or in town appealing to the educated classes by his surprising speaking ability and grasp of political
issues, Lincoln was apparently a resounding success, and he won election handily.

-◆-

APPEALING TO the voters of his district in the garb of a poor work-
ingman was one thing, but making a respectable appearance at the state
capital was another. Though already considerably in debt, Lincoln had
no alternative but to borrow money to buy suitable clothes for the
opening of the legislative session in December 1834. The man he
approached for a loan, Coleman Smoot, recalled the occasion for
Herndon many years later. "After he was Elected to the legislature he
came to my house one day in Company with Hugh Armstrong Says he
Smoot did you vote for me I told him I did Well Says he You must
loan me money to buy Suitable Clothing for I want to make a decent
appearance in the Legislature I then loaned him two hundred Dollars
which he Returned to me according to promise."[36] Hugh Armstrong
was one of those who, according to John Potter's testimony, were supporting Lincoln in return for his pledge to support a new county. This
may suggest that the loan, which Armstrong came to see about, was an
implicit part of the Democrats' strategy to woo Lincoln to their party.

The legislature met in Vandalia, a temporary state capital by law,
with aspirations to permanence. Lincoln and his fellow legislators from
Sangamon County made the ninety-five-mile journey by stagecoach,
traveling through the distinctive landscape that gave Illinois its early
identity as the Prairie State. One who came to this region about this
time remembered: "*Then* the population was sparse, the settlements
being near the timber, and around the prairie, no one dreaming that
those vast prairies would ever be entered, but that they would be held by
the Government, and used perpetually as grazing fields for their
stock."[37] If there were few settlements, what the traveler did see were
many immigrants from neighboring states moving in. "These came

with long trains of wagons covered with white sheets, filled with women and children, beds, bedding, and light furniture, all bound westward. The movers were of all grades and classes of society, from the cultivated ladies and gentlemen with ample means to the poor man who owns not more than his clothes, and who chopped wood and did work in the camp and drove the oxen as compensation for the privilege of moving with the train."[38] The combination of inviting open country and steady immigration suggested a state that held great promise of prosperity.

"There were but few houses in Vandalia then," John T. Stuart recalled. He and Lincoln roomed together in an upstairs room of a large frame house with other legislators.

> The members were very much thrown together and learned to know each other very well. We had a very pleasant time. The whole country was entirely new and there were but few accommodations to be had. I remember that one of the objections that were urged against keeping the seat of government at Vandalia was that they did not feed us on anything but prairie chickens and venison. A piece of fat pork was a luxury in those days – we had such a longing for something civilized.[39]

The descriptions of Lincoln in the Illinois General Assembly all date from thirty or forty years after the fact, and most deal with his activities in later terms. But the few that relate to his initial term point to interesting details. Jesse K. Dubois, for example, remembered that new suit that Lincoln wore. "He was then dressed in a very respectable looking suit of jeans – it was practically carrying out the protective idea of wearing home manufactures – Henry Clay once went to Congress in a suit of jeans, and it had become a sort of Whig dress."[40] If he had taken a loan arranged or backed by his Democratic supporters, Lincoln was apparently careful to buy an unmistakably Whig suit.

John T. Stuart was tall, handsome, and able. Two years older than Lincoln, he was the son of a college professor. Trained in the law, he came to Springfield in 1828 and became one of its earliest and most successful lawyers. Lincoln and Stuart had met in the summer of 1832 during the Black Hawk War, where Stuart had been taken with Lincoln's winning ways and had encouraged him in his political ambitions. In one of his autobiographical statements, Lincoln says that it was during the campaign of 1834 that Stuart "in a private conversation . . . encouraged A. [to] study law" and loaned him books for this purpose.[41]

As a one-term veteran of the legislature and an acknowledged leader of the anti-Jackson minority, Stuart inevitably became Lincoln's mentor.

In this context an unnoticed bit of testimony by Stuart is interesting, if not surprising. William H. Herndon recorded it as follows: "Mr Stuart Says that Lincoln during the sessions of the Leg in 1834 – & 36 he frequently traded Lincoln off: he was the author of no special or general act – had no organizing power – When he learned in 1838 & 40 more of the tricks &c of men he refused to be Sold. *He never had a price.*"[42] The idea of one of the most decisive and upright figures in American history permitting his vote to be traded away by someone else seems, in hindsight, hardly credible, but this compact summary of what Stuart told Herndon yields, in context, an entirely believable story.

Parties in 1834 were based largely on national questions, so that party loyalty was not a factor in most local issues. Almost the only means of gaining votes for your bill in the Illinois legislature (such as dividing a county) was by trading your own vote on a bill being promoted by another legislator. A few years later, David Davis wrote his father back East, "Legislation in our Western States is generally based upon barter, trade & intrigue – 'You vote for my measure & I will vote for yours.'" John J. Hardin, who joined Lincoln in the Illinois House of Representatives in 1836, reported in his hometown paper that "members often support measures that they would not otherwise vote for, to obtain another member's vote for a friend."[43] That the experienced Stuart, in making a deal, should know when it was possible to sweeten it with his protégé Lincoln's vote makes perfect sense. This is especially understandable in a statement intended to summarize Lincoln's progress as a legislator and to suggest that later on he became too experienced and independent for such liberties. The overriding point, which Herndon was careful to mark by underlining it, was that Lincoln, from first to last, could not be bribed.

Stuart has left an account that gives some idea of how trades were made and how, by combining forces, legislators could accommodate each other. Sidney Breese, who roomed across the hall from Stuart and Lincoln, was promoting a railroad that "was to be built by pledging the credit of the State . . . Lincoln and I made a trade with Breese to the effect that we would help pass his railroad bill if he would help us secure the appointment of the Canal Comrs. by the Governor. Breese's R R. bill came up one morning and was defeated. Then we made this arrangement with him and went back after dinner, got the question

reconsidered and passed his bill. In that way we secured the appointment of the three R R Comrs. by the Governor."[44] John G. Nicolay,
who took this interview with Stuart, noted parenthetically: "Stuart must
have done the trading." And so he probably did, but there seems no
reason to doubt that Lincoln was there at his elbow, learning how it was
done.

Learning the ropes from Stuart, whose tactics earned him the name
"Jerry Sly," Lincoln did little to distinguish himself in his first session in
the Illinois General Assembly, but he did manage to present "the peti-
tions of sundry citizens of the counties of Sangamon, Morgan and
Tazewell, praying the organization of a new county out of said counties
&c."[45] And in a specially called session in 1835, he sponsored an act to
incorporate the Beardstown and Sangamon Canal Company.[46] These
efforts, of course, were aimed at the special interests of his backers in
northern Sangamon County and helped assure his reelection in 1836. It
was in this election and the subsequent session of the legislature that
Abraham Lincoln began to make his mark as a legislator and political
leader.

⤴

LINCOLN ANNOUNCED his candidacy with a sprightly letter in the
Sangamo Journal:

New Salem, June 13, 1836.

To the Editor of the Journal:
    In your paper of last Saturday, I see a communication over the sig-
nature of "Many Voters," in which the candidates who are announced
in the Journal, are called upon to "show their hands." Agreed. Here's
mine!
    I go for all sharing the privileges of the government, who assist in
bearing its burthens. Consequently I go for admitting all whites to
the right of suffrage, who pay taxes or bear arms, (by no means
excluding females.)
    If elected, I shall consider the whole people of Sangamon my con-
stituents, as well those that oppose, as those that support me.
    While acting as their representative, I shall be governed by their
will, on all subjects upon which I have the means of knowing what
their will is; and upon all others, I shall do what my own judgment
teaches me will best advance their interests. Whether elected or not, I
go for distributing the proceeds of the sales of the public lands to the
several states, to enable our state, in common with others, to dig

canals and construct rail roads, without borrowing money and paying interest on it.

If alive on the first Monday in November, I shall vote for Hugh L. White for President. Very respectfully,

A. Lincoln[47]

The difference between this almost casual declaration and the labored announcement, "To the People of Sangamon County," he had published in the same paper four years earlier is a measure of the distance Lincoln had come as a politician. The earlier document had begun: "Fellow-Citizens: Having become a candidate for the honorable office of one of your representatives in the next General Assembly of this state, in accordance with an established custom, and the principles of true republicanisn, it becomes my duty to make known to you – the people whom I propose to represent – my sentiments with regard to local affairs."[48]

The contrast in tone is obvious, but so is the approach to issues. In the earlier declaration, Lincoln began by talking of the need for internal improvements, only to disparage canals and railroads as too expensive: "there is always the heart appalling shock accompanying the account of its cost, which forces us to shrink from our pleasing anticipations." Instead, he proposed a comparatively modest scheme to clear the Sangamon River for navigation. By 1836, with the movement for state-financed canals and railroads gathering momentum, the candidate was ready to urge a distribution of federal revenues to the states to cover the "heart appalling" costs that these projects entailed, a "pleasing anticipation" that could not be accomplished by any action of the state legislature.

The 1836 letter proves upon examination to be a much more shrewd performance than its breezy and apparently artless surface would indicate. Its lighthearted introduction, its deceptive brevity, its openhanded gestures, and its informal tone all work to produce a certain desired effect, one that clearly transcends the issues. Gone is the earnest talk about "local affairs" and practical solutions. Except for the parenthetical nod in the direction of women's suffrage, which is perhaps not in earnest, the letter contains nothing that would distinguish its writer from most other candidates and instead aims at creating an impression of friendly self-confidence. Almost as a footnote, apparently because he believes he must declare himself on the most controversial national

issue – the successor to Andrew Jackson as president – Lincoln states
his preference but gives it a somewhat humorous twist: "If alive on
the first Monday in November, I shall vote for Hugh L. White for
President."

The campaign in the summer of 1836, perhaps because it was the year
of an important presidential election, was boisterous and eventful.
Robert L. Wilson remembered its inception:

> The campaign commenced about six weeks before the election,
> which under the old Constitution was held on the first monday of
> August. Appointments being made and published in the Sangamo
> Journal and the State Register, the organs of the Parties then. We
> traveled on horseback from one grove to another – the praries then
> were entirely unoccupied – The Speaking would begin in the fore-
> noon, the candidates Speaking alternately until all who could Speak
> had his turn, generally consuming the whole afternoon. The discus-
> sions were upon National and State questions, prominant among
> which were the Subject of a National Bank, and the Tariff, and a
> general System of internal improvement, by the State and
> the finishing the Illinois and Michigan Canal, then in progress of
> construction. – [49]

In these meetings, Wilson recalled, "Mr Lincoln took a leading part,
espouseing the Whig side of all those questions, manifesting Skill and
tact in offensive and defensive debates, presenting his arguments with
great force and ability, and boldly attacking the questions and positions
taken by opposing Candidates."[50]

James Gourley, whose acquaintance with Lincoln began at this
period, remembered some colorful episodes in this campaign involving
Lincoln. One is reminiscent of his maiden appearance at Pappsville in
1832: "I heard Lincoln make a Speech in Mechanicsburg Sangamon Co
in 1836. Jno Neal had a fight at the time – the roughs got on him and
Lincoln jumped in and Saw fair play."[51] Gourley also remembered that
"the questions discussed were internal improvements – whig principles"
and that Lincoln "peeled" one of his opponents in debate.

"Peeled" is the equivalent of the more familiar "skinned," which is
what Gourley remembered Lincoln's doing to another opponent, Dick
Quinton, at Springfield. The excitement grew so intense at this courthouse meeting that according to Gourley, Lincoln's fellow candidate
and future brother-in-law, Ninian W. Edwards, "drew a pistol on
Achilles Morris."[52]

This may have been the same occasion described by Robert L. Wilson, himself a candidate, at which Lincoln dramatically put on display his powers as a peacemaker.

> The Saturday preceding the election [Wilson wrote Herndon] the Candidates were addressing the People in the Court House in Springfield. Dr Earley one of the Candidates on the Democratic Side made some charge that N. W. Edwards one of the Whig Candidates deemed untrue, climbed on a table so as to be seen by Dr Early and evey one in the house, and at the top of his voice told Early that the charge was false. The excitement that followed was intense, so much so, that fighting men [believed] that a duel must Settle the difficulty.[53]

Lincoln, who was scheduled to speak next, mounted the podium and "took up the subject in dispute and handled fairly, and with such ability, that every one was astonished, and pleased. So that difficulty ended there."[54] Wilson believed that one of the reasons Lincoln was able to subdue this boisterous and unruly crowd was his voice: "he spooke in that tenor intonation of voice that ultimately settled down into that clear Shrill monotone Style of Speaking, that enabled his audience, however large, to hear distictly the lowest Sound of his voice."

If Abraham Lincoln had shown an affinity for stump speaking at an early age and demonstrated real ability in previous elections, it was in this campaign that he proved he could hold his own with the best stump speakers in the state. This came about when Lincoln was unexpectedly challenged, late in the campaign, by one of the most experienced and highly regarded political speakers of the time, George Forquer. At least one account suggests that this occurred at the same meeting described above, when Lincoln "poured oil on troubled waters and, first quieting his auditors, launched into one of the most eloquent and convincing speeches he ever made, carrying the crowd with him almost to a man."[55] Whether or not it was the same occasion, the encounter with Forquer was vividly etched in the memory of Lincoln's friend Joshua F. Speed, who wrote out the following account for Herndon:

> I remember that [Lincoln's] speech was a very able one, using with great power and originality all the arguments then used to sustain the principles of the Whig party, as against its great rival the Democratic party of that day – The speech produced a profound impression – The Crowd was with him –
> The Candidates in opposition and the party opposed to him felt it – Depression on one side & exultation on the other was evident –

Mr George Forquer an old Citizen, a man of recognized prominence & ability as a lawyer was present – Forquer had been a whig –
one of the Champions of the party – But had then recently joined the
Democratic party and Almost simultaneous with his change – had
been appointed Register of the land office – which office he then
held –

Just about that time Mr F had Completed a neat frame house –
the best house then in the village of Springfield and upon it had
erected a lightning rod – the only one in the place and the first one
Mr Lincoln had evr observed – He afterwards told me that seeing
Forquers lightning rod had led him to the study of the properties of
electricity & the utility of the rod as a Conductor –

At the Conclusion of Lincolns speech the Crowd was about dis-
persing when Forquer rose and asked to be heard –

He commenced by saying that this young man would have to be
taken down and was sorry that the task devolved upon him – He then
proceeded to answer Linclns speech in a style which while it was able
and fair – in his whole manner asserted & claimed superiority –

Lincoln stood near him and watched him during the whole of his
Speech –

When Forquer Concluded he took the stand again – I have heard
him often since – in Court and before the people – but never saw him
appear so well as upon that occasion – He replied to Mr F with great
dignity and force – But I shall never forget the conclusion of that
speech –

Turning to Mr F. he said that he had Commenced his speech by
announcing that this young man would have to be taken down –

Turning then to the Crowd he said it is for you, not for me to say
whether I am up or down.

The gentleman has alluded to my being a young man – I am older
in years than I am in the tricks and trades of politicians – I desire to
live – and I disire place and distinction as a politician – but I would
rather die now than like the gentleman live to see the day that I
would have to erect a lightning rod to protect a guilty Concience
from an offended God.[56]

The reply to Forquer is notable in showing not only Lincoln's readiness in debate but his temperament and adaptability. When attacked
personally and unexpectedly by Forquer, who was not even a candidate,
he did not lose his composure, as Ninian W. Edwards had with Dr.
Early and Achilles Morris, nor did he respond with a merciless "skinning," which he had apparently used successfully against Quinton and
the unnamed opponent at Mechanicsburg. Instead, he patiently listened to what Forquer had to say, responded to his points with dignity,

and then decisively nailed him for his condescension, using Forquer's political trimming and the lightning rod to devastating advantage. It was the kind of performance that makes a deep impression on an audience and, as a consequence, makes reputations.

-*∂*-

IN THE MEMORABLE legislative session that followed, Lincoln took his place as a leader. Stuart was no longer a member of the legislature, having tried unsuccessfully for a seat in Congress. As Jesse K. Dubois remembered it, "Lincoln didn't take much prominence in the first session of the legislature in 1834. Stuart at that time quite overshadowed him. Stuart had been there the session before – besides he had been practising law, and generally had more experience than Lincoln. But the next session Lincoln was very prominent. He had by that time become the acknowledged leader of the Whigs in the House. Stuart had gone out and left him a clear field."[57]

The two great issues of this legendary session were the internal improvements program and the relocation of the state capital. Thomas Ford, who was himself an Illinois politician during this period, wrote in his history of Illinois that the delegation from Sangamon County, the famous "Long Nine," had irresponsibly connived to trade away their votes on the one to assure victory for Springfield on the other. "Amongst them were some dexterous jugglers and managers in politics, whose whole object was to obtain the seat of government for Springfield. This delegation from the beginning of the session threw itself as a unit in support of or opposition to every local measure of interest, but never without a bargain for votes in return on the seat of government question."[58] Questions have been raised as to whether the voting records actually bear out so clear a pattern of block voting, but what *is* clear is that the acknowledged leader of the "dexterous jugglers" was Abraham Lincoln.

About the dedication of the comparatively large Sangamon County delegation to capture the state capital for Springfield, there can scarcely be any dispute. Nor can there be much doubt that they employed, as charged, the legislator's principal tool – trading votes – to achieve their objective. And Lincoln was clearly at the head of this vigorous and sustained – and ultimately successful – effort. The judicious Stephen T. Logan, for example, told John G. Nicolay: "He (L.) was at the head of the project to remove the seat of government here [i.e., to Springfield];

it was entirely entrusted to him to manage. The members were all elected that session upon one ticket. But they all looked to Lincoln as the head."[59] The logic of these circumstances is that Lincoln must have been not merely a logroller but, in the eyes of his peers, the chief logroller, the coordinating manager in charge of all logrolling in the Springfield endeavor.

Because Abraham Lincoln is generally regarded as having been a person of integrity, the charge of logrolling has disturbed some of his admirers, but it should be noted that no wrongdoing or corruption is implied. The worst that can be said is that Lincoln may have voted for and helped to put over patently bad or otherwise inadvisable measures, purely for the sake of securing the state capital for Springfield. What proved to be the most disastrous measure passed in this session was the wildly ambitious scheme for a system of internal improvements. In hindsight, this system of roads, canals, and railroads, to be financed by state bonds in the mind-boggling amount of ten million dollars, was hopelessly beyond the means of an undeveloped and impecunious state, with no realistic chance of success. But the outlook of pioneers is necessarily upbeat, and the optimistic proponents of progress and prosperity carried all before them. "No scheme was so extravagant as not to appear plausible to some," wrote Ford. "The most wild calculations were made of the advantages of a system of internal improvements; of the resources of the State to meet all expenditures; and of our final ability to pay all indebtedness without taxation. Mere possibilities appeared highly probable; and probability wore the livery of certainty itself."[60]

Not everyone was taken in by the scheme. One of the stalwarts of the Whig faction, John J. Hardin, stood firm against it and, in the words of one of his fellow legislators, "predicted its fate with an accuracy that looks to me now almost like prophecy."[61] Stephen T. Logan recalled many years later that he confronted Lincoln about it at the time: "I was in Vandalia that winter and had a talk with Lincoln there. I remember that I took him to task for voting for the Internal Improvement scheme. He seemed to acquiesce in the correctness of my views as I presented them to him. But he said he couldn't help himself—he had to vote for it in order to secure the removal here of the seat of government."[62] Lincoln may well have had some private misgivings about the internal improvements venture, but all outward indications are that he, like most of his fellow legislators, was strongly in favor of it. That he was forced to vote for internal improvements to secure the state capital for

Springfield, as Logan remembers his saying, makes little sense in view of its overwhelming popularity and may have been simply a lame excuse to placate Logan.

Prime evidence of Lincoln's hopes for the internal improvements system comes from his friend, Joshua F. Speed. He told Herndon that Lincoln had said, "in reference to Internal improvements & the best interest and advancement of this State, that his highest ambition was to become the De Witt Clinton of Ills."[63] Clinton had earned an enormous celebrity during the previous decades as a promoter of public improvements in New York State, most notably the famous Erie Canal. If Speed remembered this correctly, it suggests that the glowing prospects of the internal improvements program served to focus Lincoln's aspirations and give him a tangible model for the fame and public esteem he might achieve. In the same interview, Speed offered details that suggest why Lincoln was in some ways ill equipped to bring about public projects involving large sums of money. Herndon's notes on this interview read: "Lincoln made a great Speech in 1837. or 8 – on internal improvements – Money – given him in 1837 or 8 – $200 – Spent 75c – paid back. $199.25 Saying I didnt Know how to Spend it. This money was given him to sustain & Maintain the Internal improvement policy as well as himself as its defender &c –."[64] If true, this story shows that Lincoln's conspicuous lack of cupidity simply unfitted him for certain kinds of political promotion and maneuvering. Many another politician would have thought it good politics and consistent with the wishes of the donor to spread such money around in the interest of making friends for the cause – in this case, the internal improvements system, where millions of dollars of state expenditures were in the offing.

By contrast, some of Lincoln's allies knew how to spread money around to help achieve their ends. The "Long Nine," so named because they were all tall men, and all Whigs but one, were assisted in their efforts to secure the capital for Sangamon by a number of Springfield citizens sent down to Vandalia as lobbyists. One of these, Peter Van Bergen, gave Nicolay some account of his activities: "Stuart, Logan, Iles & I went down to Vandalia the winter the seat of Govt was changed. I helped a great deal to drum up the members when it came to a vote. We had votes enough to carry our project, but they were not always on hand – would be off taking a drink &c – I used to go after them to the saloons &c. I spent about $1000 in treating &c."[65]

William Butler remembered it somewhat differently. "I was sent down to Vandalia to work in the interest of Springfield. Van Bergen was also sent down there with me – though he did no good – but to hear him tell it he did it all." Butler also remembered something about Lincoln's strengths and his limitations. "Lincoln and Linder were the two principal men we relied on in the Legislature to make speeches for us. John T. Stuart was the man we depended upon in caucus. Lincoln was not worth a cent in caucus."[66] This suggests that the caucus was not limited to elected members but that, in the case of planning strategy for acquiring the capital, it not only included the lobbyists but counted on the skills of one of them, Stuart, for leadership. That Lincoln should yield the stage to his mentor in such a situation seems readily understandable, though it apparently appeared like something short of competence to Butler.

Butler may have misremembered the role of Usher F. Linder, who, though an orator of consequence, is not known to have been an ally of the "Long Nine."[67] Linder wrote many years later about his first encounter with Abraham Lincoln in the 1836 session of the Illinois legislature. Lincoln, he said, "did not give promise of being the first man in Illinois, as he afterwards became. He made a good many speeches in the legislature, mostly on local subjects. A close observer, however, could not fail to see that the tall, six footer, with his homely logic, clothed in the language of the humbler classes, had the stuff in him to make a man of mark."[68] Linder did not remain in the legislature long, being elected attorney general before his first session was out, but he did cross swords with Lincoln on the floor of the House more than once. Lincoln's response to Linder's attack on the State Bank in January 1837 is notable for being the first speech of Lincoln's for which we have a complete transcript.[69] An examination of the speech shows that the hallmarks of his mature political debating style are already there: good-natured humor, self-deprecation, mock deference to the superiority of his opponent, bold strokes, close analysis, and skewering his adversary on a previous statement. While it is hardly a memorable speech in its own right, the record of Lincoln's performance shows that he could very effectively make the transition from the style appropriate to the stump to one more suited to the legislative forum.

Besides his well-attested strengths as a speaker, Lincoln had other assets. People liked him. From boyhood he had cultivated the goodwill of both elders and peers, and this habitual behavior served him well. Jesse K. Dubois, another member, bore witness to Lincoln's particular appeal for him. "As an illustration of his authority he made Webb and me vote for his scheme to move the seat of government to Springfield. We belonged to the southern end of the State. We defended our vote before our constituents by saying that necessity would ultimately force the seat of government to a central position. But in reality we gave the vote to Lincoln because we liked him and because we wanted to oblige our friend, and because we recognized his authority as our leader."[70]

Dubois's testimony on this point contains details that may shed light on how this country boy with winning ways was learning to put his assets to work as a politician.

> I think I never saw him stumped but once. That was on the passage of the legislation about removing the seat of government. Webb, Wilson and myself roomed together in 1836. Wilson, Blankenship, Gov. Duncan and John Taylor had entered a great lot of land, and laid out the town of Illiopolis, and were engaged in an effort to get the seat of government moved there. From our being such constant companions, Wilson had every right to suppose that Webb and I were his friends in that measure.
>
> Lincoln came to my room one evening and told me that he was whipped – that his career was ended – that he had traded off everything he could dispose of, and still had not got strength enough to locate the seat of government at Springfield – "and yet" said he "I cant go home without passing that bill. My folks expect that of me, and that I cant do – and I am finished forever."
>
> I said to him "well Lincoln, there is but one thing for you to do."
>
> "Well," said he "tell me how that is to be done."
>
> I said to him "first pass the bill to move the seat of government, and Springfield, Jacksonville, Peoria, and every other town that expects to get the seat of government will vote for that bill, Vandalia alone excepted. Then pass a joint resolution, locating the seat of government, and for beginning a suitable building so as to have it ready by the time provided in the Constitution for moving it."
>
> "By jings" said he "I reckon that will do it." And he had a bill ready that night, and we passed it. When we went into joint session the other fellows saw the trap, but it was too late. We carried the measure for Springfield, and old Wilson wouldn't speak to Webb or me for a week afterward.[71]

Dubois apparently believed that this story showed how he had handed a beaten and despairing Lincoln the key to a seemingly insoluble problem, but a critical look at the anecdote as told points to a different meaning. Dubois's interpretation of what happened rests on the very dubious assumption that Lincoln and his cohorts in caucus had not thought of the obvious parliamentary tactic he proposed: first to pass a resolution to build a new capital, which proponents of all competing towns would support. What seems far more likely is that Lincoln's mission in coming to their room was to draw Dubois and Webb into his "dilemma" so as to assure their support in a move that was bound to be opposed by their roommate, William Wilson.[72]

Another Wilson, who was a member of the Sangamon delegation and an eyewitness to Lincoln's comportment in the capital fight, paints a very different picture. "In these dark hours, when our Bill to all appearance was beyond resuscitation, and all our opponents were jubilant over our defeat, and when friends could see no hope, Mr Lincoln never for one moment despaired, but collect[ed] his Colleagues to his room for consultation, his practical common Sense, his thorough knowledge of human nature then, made him an overmatch for his compeers and for any man that I have ever known."[73] Neither picture may be completely accurate, and both may well depict someone playing a carefully crafted role, but what seems clear is that in spite of their attachment to their roommate, Dubois and Webb had been dexterously primed to vote Lincoln's way.

Governor Ford, whose history of Illinois is replete with descriptions of the machinations of the legislators and politicians of this period, would have called this a clear case of being "greased and swallowed." "A man was 'greased' when he was won over to the purposes of another by a feigned show of friendship and condescension; and he was 'swallowed' when he was made to act to suit the purposes of 'the intrigue,' whatever it might be. Sometimes the act of lubrication by which a man was fitted to be 'swallowed' was supposed to be performed with 'soft soap.' "[74] Dubois believed that Lincoln's despair was real and that he himself had suggested the expedient that turned the future president's fortunes around, but it seems more likely that he was instead a obliging victim of Lincoln's soft soap.

~∂~

A FEW DAYS before the legislative session for 1836–37 ended on March 6, Lincoln and his Sangamon County colleague, Dan Stone, presented a protest on the floor of the House that has become famous, but the context that shaped its meaning has been lost sight of. Although the joint protest states forthrightly that the protesters "believe that the institution of slavery is founded on both injustice and bad policy," it was almost certainly not an attempt to put them on record as two lonely voices crying out in the wilderness against the evils of slavery. The crux of the matter was apparently something else, even though, unfortunately, it is not possible to say with precision what that something else was.

Lincoln and Stone, as part of a tiny minority, had voted against a resolution in January 1837 that disapproved of "abolition societies, and of the doctrines promulgated by them" and proclaimed that "the right of property in slaves, is sacred to the slave-holding States by the Federal Constitution, and that they cannot be deprived of that right without their consent."[75] The meager record of the debate on the resolution makes it impossible to determine exactly what their objections were, but their protest makes it clear that they did not disagree with the leading propositions, quoted above, having to do with abolitionists and the property rights of slaveholders. A defeated amendment offered by Lincoln suggests that his opposition may have been tied to a side issue, having to do with whether and how the United States Congress might deal with slavery in the District of Columbia.

As proponents of the Springfield capital, Lincoln and Stone could not risk antagonizing their fellow legislators by protesting at the time of the debate, but neither could they permit their vote on the abolitionist resolution to be used against them by future antagonists, for to appear to side with abolitionists in Sangamon County in 1837 was simply political suicide. Sangamon was populated mostly by Kentuckians and immigrants from other slave states, and while a great many of these disliked slavery, they had no use for abolitionists, who seemed to them to be offensive agitators who presumed to claim divine authority for their views, who meddled publicly in the private affairs of others, and who set themselves above the Constitution. The overwhelming majority in Illinois agreed with Lincoln and Stone that where slavery was concerned, "the promulgation of abolition doctrines tends rather to increase than to abate its evils."[76]

The expedient chosen by Lincoln and Stone to protect themselves from future attack was shrewdly simple and effective. They prepared a statement of protest that, at the very end of the session, could be placed on the record without comment or debate. Their statement began: "Resolutions upon the subject of domestic slavery having passed both

branches of the General Assembly at its present session, the under-
signed hereby protest against the passage of the same." They then stated
their views in three concise propositions:

> They believe that the institution of slavery is founded on both
> injustice and bad policy; but that the promulgation of abolition doc-
> trines tends rather to increase than to abate its evils.
> They believe that the Congress of the United States has no power,
> under the constitution, to interfere with the institution of slavery in
> the different States.
> They believe that the Congress of the United States has the power,
> under the constitution, to abolish slavery in the District of Columbia;
> but that the power ought not to be exercised unless at the request of
> the people of the District.

This done, they concluded by stating: "The difference between these
opinions and those contained in the said resolutions, is their reason for
entering this protest."[77] Such an expedient had the effect of putting on
record the exact wording that they would have preferred for the anti-
abolitionist resolution, plus anything else they might care to slip in. The
consideration that takes on such importance in hindsight – their objection, twenty-four years before the Civil War, to slavery as an benighted
institution "founded on both injustice and bad policy" – was no doubt
an important one, for Lincoln hated slavery all his life. But putting their
demurrer to slavery on the record had little practical significance at that
time and place, whereas making clear that they, too, were opposed to
abolitionists was a pressing political necessity.

❧

AT THE END of the session, Lincoln and the "Long Nine" went home
in triumph. They had secured the seat of government for their county
and were duly feted at Springfield and elsewhere for a job well done.
The tone of these tributes suggests that the great victory was very much
regarded as a group effort and that much was owed to Springfield's
political allies in other parts of the state. Lincoln, while recognized as
an important participant, was not singled out for special praise. But his
signal value to the cause was confirmed that summer, when, during a
special session of the legislature, a strong effort was made to reverse the
decision and retain the capital for Vandalia.

For this purpose Vandalia arranged the election of one of the most
imposing orators and popular statesmen of the day, General W. L. D.

Ewing. Attacking the Sangamon County delegation in harsh terms, the former U.S. senator is alleged to have declared: "The arrogance of Springfield, its presumption in claiming the seat of government, was not to be endured." As Usher Linder recalled it more than thirty years later, Ewing charged that the bill to move the capital had been passed by "chicanery and trickery; that the Springfield delegation had sold out to the internal improvement men, and had promised their support to every measure that would gain them a vote to the law removing the seat of government."[78]

Though Ewing was a formidable opponent who was likely to challenge anyone offering him personal abuse, Lincoln impressed everyone by refusing to be intimidated. Linder says that Lincoln "retorted upon Ewing with great severity; denouncing his insinuations imputing corruption to him and his colleagues, and paying back with usury all that Ewing had said."[79] Ewing's initial response, according to Linder, was imperious disdain. "Gentlemen, have you no other champion than this coarse and vulgar fellow to bring into the lists against me? Do you suppose I will condescend to break a lance with your low and obscure colleague?"[80] But Lincoln persisted and attacked his opponent vigorously when "everybody thought and believed that he was digging his own grave; for it was known that Ewing would not quietly pocket any insinuations that would degrade him personally."[81] Somehow, Ewing's feelings were placated and "personal difficulties" were avoided, but Lincoln had carried the day.

Lincoln's brave and effective response to Ewing did more than help preserve the seat of government for Springfield; it exposed a further dimension of his abilities and earned him a new measure of respect. Linder, like many others, had seen him in action before, but as he remarked in his autobiography, "this was the first time that I began to conceive a very high opinion of the talent and personal courage of Abraham Lincoln."[82]

SPRINGFIELD
(1837-42)

Chapter 6

SPRINGFIELD

LINCOLN'S RETURN from Vandalia in March 1837 should have
been a bright moment in his career, full of promise and expectation. He had proved himself an effective leader in the legislature, he was moving to a town he had just helped make the capital of
Illinois, and he was about to begin a new career as the law partner of the
rising political star, John T. Stuart. But if the recollection of his friend
William Butler is accurate, Lincoln left Vandalia in a mood of deep
despondency.

> I was at Vandalia the last winter he spent there. Lincoln, myself, and
> two others traveled home together on horseback, after the fashion of
> those times. We stopped over night down here at Henderson's Point,
> and all slept on the floor. We were tired, and the rest slept pretty
> well. But I noticed from the first that Lincoln was uneasy, turning
> over and thinking, and studying, so much so that he kept me awake.
> At last I said to him, "Lincoln what is the matter with you?"
> "Well," said he "I will tell you. All the rest of you have something
> to look forward to, and all are glad to get home, and will have some-
> thing to do when you get there. But it isn't so with me. I am going
> home, Butler, without a thing in the world. I have drawn all my pay I
> got at Vandalia and have spent it all. I am in debt – I am owing Van
> Bergen, and he has levied on my horse and my compass, and I have
> nothing to pay the debt with, and no way to make any money. I dont
> know what to do."[1]

Poverty was not the issue, for Lincoln seems to have been quite content to live a simple life of very few material wants and possessions. The

issue was debt. Thanks to his ill-starred storekeeping venture – and perhaps other investments, such as his horse and surveying instruments – Lincoln owed money, the interest on which continued to grow, and he apparently felt discouraged and inadequate to the task of coping with it. Even the prospect of working with a successful attorney like Stuart failed to relieve the anxiety he felt because of his debt.

Butler's recollection of Lincoln's despondent mood and sense of inadequacy is confirmed by the memories of the man who was to become his closest Springfield friend, Joshua F. Speed. Speed was a wellborn Kentuckian who had come to Illinois in 1835. When Lincoln arrived in Springfield, as Speed told it, "I was a merchant at Springfield, and kept a large country store, embracing dry goods, groceries, hardware, books, medicines, bed-clothes, matresses, in fact every thing that the country needed."² Speed wrote that after moving his meager belongings from New Salem to Springfield, Lincoln came to Speed's store to buy "furnishings" for a bed. When Speed figured the cost at seventeen dollars, Lincoln allowed mournfully that he might not make enough in his "experiment" as a lawyer to pay Speed in a reasonable time.

> The tone of his voice was so melancholy [Speed wrote] that I felt for
> him. I looked up at him, and I thought then, as I think now, that I
> never saw so gloomy, and melancholy a face. I said to him; "The con-
> traction of so small a debt, seems to affect you so deeply, I think I can
> suggest a plan by which you will be able to attain your end, without
> incurring any debt. I have a very large room, and a very large double-
> bed in it; which you are perfectly welcome to share with me if you
> choose." "Where is your room?" asked he. "Upstairs" said I, pointing
> to the stairs leading from the store to my room. Without saying a
> word, he took his saddle-bags on his arm, went up stairs, set them
> down on the floor, came down again, and with a face beaming with
> pleasure and smiles exclaimed "Well Speed I'm moved."³

There is little reason to doubt that both William Butler and Joshua Speed came to Lincoln's aid at this period of his life, though their recollections are not entirely compatible. Butler's account of their arrival in Springfield from Vandalia, given to John G. Nicolay in 1875, is particularly colorful:

> When he went to get his horse they told him he had been taken
> down to my house. He came down there and asked where I had put
> his horse. I told I him I had sold him. He was greatly astonished.

"What in the world did you do that for?" he asked. "Why you couldn't sell him for Van Bergen had levied on him."

He then went back to get his saddlebags, and they told him they had been taken down to my house. So he came down and asked where they were. I said to him "I have had them brought down here, and have had your clothes taken out and washed. Now I want you to come down here, and board here and make my house your home."

You know he was always careless about his clothes. In all the time he stayed at my house, he never bought a hat or a pair of socks, or a coat. Whenever he needed them, my wife went and bought them for him, and put them in the drawer where he would find them.

When I told him that he couldn't have his clothes, that they were in the wash he seemed very much mortified. He said he had to go down home to New Salem. I told him that he might take my horse and ride him down there. I also told him that there were his saddle-bags, and that there was a clean shirt in them.

He took the saddlebags and went and got the horse, and rode down to New Salem, and stayed there about a week. Then he came back and put up the horse, and stayed right along at my house for about eight years.[4]

Since Lincoln married five and a half years later, Butler's "eight years" is clearly an exaggeration. And while Lincoln probably boarded with the Butlers most of the time and availed himself of Mrs. Butler's laundry services, there is good evidence that he slept a good part of the time at Speed's. That Butler took Lincoln in hand, however, and did much to relieve his anxieties seems clear enough. His claim in the same interview to have secretly paid Lincoln's outstanding debts, though unconfirmed, is further testimony to the extraordinary appeal Lincoln exercised over his friends. Strong and independent as he surely was in many ways, Lincoln's move from New Salem to Springfield shows that he owed a substantial part of his early success to his natural ability to attract the assistance of others.

⤙

LINCOLN'S MORBID misgivings about his chances may be hard to fathom when seen in the light of his legendary career, but Speed's account helps us put Lincoln's doubts in perspective:

In the spring of 1837 he took his license as a lawyer. Then began with him the real battle of life. Leaving the field of his youthful sports, pleasures, and pains, where he was the leading man, he came to a bar then considered the best in the State, and perhaps as good as any in the West. He entered with diffidence upon his new career, coming in contact with [Stephen T.] Logan and Cyrus Walker, older than he and men of renown, John J. Hardin, E. D. Baker, Douglas, and Browning, all near his own age. They were all educated men, in the ordinary acceptation of the word. They had read many books, and studied law, many of them with able lawyers.[5]

If he was understandably apprehensive about his ability to compete in the courtroom with these men, Lincoln plunged into his first major legal dispute with little hesitation. In this case Lincoln was apparently confident that he could gain his ends – justice for his client *and* solid remuneration for himself and his associates – with the skills he had been developing as a stump speaker and politician, for he proceeded to wade into his adversary in the same way he attacked his political opponents. But the incident turned into a debacle, and Lincoln learned a hard, if valuable, lesson.

In a book that attempts to draw its substance from the voices of witnesses and participants, this episode constitutes an anomalous exception, but the conspicuous silence surrounding it perhaps tells a story of its own. That no pertinent testimony has been forthcoming – that the hundreds of statements collected by Herndon, for example, should contain no reference to Lincoln's highly public joust with James Adams in 1837 – may simply indicate that the episode had been largely forgotten, but it may also reflect the reluctance of the informants to call attention to Lincoln's inglorious performance. Besides the published protests of Adams himself, virtually the only relevant voice that can be recaptured is strident, narrowly partisan, and increasingly abusive: an unflattering voice that belonged to Abraham Lincoln.

Lincoln's involvement in the case may have begun in a manner more true to the lawyer of legend, by seeing the opportunity to help a cheated widow retrieve her rightful property. Among his first clients after taking up residence in Springfield were Mary Anderson and her son, Richard, whose husband and father, Joseph Anderson, was supposed to have died owning a ten-acre parcel of land just north of Springfield. Title to the parcel was registered to Anderson's former attorney, James Adams, and Lincoln was asked to help the Andersons get it back. In examining the county records and Adams's deed, Lincoln thought he found evidence of a forgery and thus a fraudulent transfer of title. That he was on to something promising in the way of a legal case is evidenced by his successful enlistment of Stephen T. Logan, the leader of the Springfield bar, and a contract with the Andersons that called for the lawyers to receive half the land if they won and nothing at all if they were unsuccessful.[6]

Though Adams was an attorney of long standing, he was not in the same league as Stephen T. Logan and Cyrus Walker, and he had the unenviable distinction of having defended the accused in the first murder trial in Springfield's history in 1826. In spite of the fact that frontier juries were notoriously reluctant to convict in murder cases, Adams's defense was ineffective, and his client was hanged. In the course of the ensuing dispute, Lincoln referred to this incident with unbridled sarcasm: "Now, let it be remembered that when he first came to this country, he attempted to impose himself upon the community as a *lawyer*, and actually carried the attempt so far, as to induce a man who was under a charge of murder to intrust the defence of his life in his hands, and finally took his money and got him hanged."[7] Adams's lack of distinction as a lawyer may have emboldened Lincoln, especially with the likes of Logan and Stuart to back him up, but he was clearly convinced that there was something fishy about Adams's claim to ownership and the title deed itself.

Strong as Lincoln's conviction that Adams had illegally acquired title to his client's land may have been, it almost immediately became entangled in a political consideration, the fact that Adams was the Democratic candidate for an office being sought by Lincoln's close friend and political ally, Dr. Anson G. Henry. A politically motivated attack on Henry's role as commissioner of the new state capitol building, which Lincoln believed had been written by Adams, appeared in the Democratic newspaper, the *Illinois Republican*, about the time the campaign opened in June, coinciding with the filing of a suit by Lincoln and his associates in behalf of the heirs of Joseph Anderson. The *Republican*'s attack prompted a series of letters on Adams in the Whig paper, the *Sangamo Journal*, by someone signing himself as "Sampson's Ghost," who almost certainly was Abraham Lincoln.[8]

The idea behind the pseudonym, Sampson's Ghost, was quite pointed: Adams was a candidate for probate justice of the peace, an office dealing with the disposition of the property of the deceased, and a man named Sampson had been the previous owner of the Springfield property Adams was living on. "Before he assails the conduct of other men," the Ghost observed in the first letter, "he should take a retrospective view of his own conduct – official as well as private. He must know that his own house stands upon disputed ground."⁹ This insinuation of Adams's wrongdoing with respect to Sampson (and by implication his unfitness for an office dealing with the property of deceased persons) is a persistent theme in all six letters, but it was apparently without substance. Adams's reply showed that he knew how the game should be played: "If any person wishes to know the tenor [tenure] of the property on which I reside, it is a leasehold tenement of record, open to all persons, and when Sampson's heirs call for possession of their property, and cannot obtain it by reason that it is legally withheld, it will be early enough to commence complaining of injury."¹⁰ In other words, there had been no complaint of injury, only scurrilous insinuation, and Adams didn't intend to deny charges not directly made. Lincoln's strategy was apparently like that of another president's fictitious candidate for sheriff, who falsely accused his opponent of performing unnatural acts with chickens, while admitting privately that his real aim was to force his hapless adversary to stand up in public and deny it.

Of course, Lincoln had his own personal reasons for inventing Sampson's Ghost, and he brought them out in the open in his final letter, calling the Anderson case "another subject which the People wish to understand."¹¹ But in the course of the six letters he excoriated Adams for a variety of offenses, some of which Lincoln patently committed himself – such as writing under a pseudonym. When Adams, in one of his responses, denied writing the attack on Henry, Lincoln pointed out accusingly that Adams did not deny another of his accusations. This kind of unwarranted inference was neatly exposed by Lincoln himself in a later communication: "These logical gentlemen cannot sustain their argument only by assuming that I *did* say *negatively* every thing that I *did not* say affirmatively; and upon the same assumption, we may expect to find the General, if a little harder pressed for argument, saying that I said Talbott came to our office with his head downwards, not that I actually said so, but because I omitted to say he came feet downward."¹²

The Sampson's Ghost letters became increasingly slanderous and abusive as the August election date approached, but the most blatantly demagogic suggestion was that Adams, who proudly claimed the rank of general, was a traitor. Seizing upon Adams's boast that he had endured "sufferings and losses while in the United States service during the late war," Lincoln asked: "But what were the causes of his losses and why did he suffer? Was it while he was acting in defense of his country, or was it from any improper connection with the British in the war referred to?"[13] Following this with the disclaimer "This is a matter of which I know nothing" unwittingly serves to make the slur upon Adams's patriotism appear more reckless and underhanded. In a succeeding letter, Lincoln managed to compound this insult by perversely claiming that the matter was one of Adams's own red herrings.

> I am told Gen. Adams has proved most satisfactorily by affidavits that he was not a tory in the last war. The pains he has taken to clear up this matter, will show that there might be grounds for suspicion, particularly as he was formerly a violent advocate of the Hartford Convention candidate for Presidency.
>
> But I am at a loss to understand what connexion Gen. Adams' toryism, or support of a tory candidate for the Presidency, has with the property belonging to Sampson's heirs, and now in the possession of Gen. Adams. I have asked him to explain the manner in which he came into possession of Sampson's property. You answer that you are not a tory![14]

By the time the last communication from Sampson's Ghost appeared about a week before the election, the author of the pseudonymous weekly badgering of Adams with baseless charges had succeeded in alienating most of his audience, thereby helping to destroy his friend Henry's chances for election. If Lincoln had any awareness of this, it is nowhere evident in the final letter, which concludes: "My labors have now nearly ceased. I have only sought to promote inquiry. All I ASK – all I WISH is that TRUTH SHOULD PREVAIL. And before I am charged as a slanderer, I wish all the evidence in the case be fairly freely and fully examined."[15] But as the readers were certainly aware, Sampson's Ghost had presented no real evidence, only personal smear and innuendo.

Adams's signed weekly replies to Lincoln's unsigned weekly attacks had kept the dispute somewhat in balance, but Lincoln set out to make sure he got the last word by issuing a handbill two days before the election.[16] Issuing handbills as a way of making a timely political point was then an established practice. John T. Stuart said of his campaigning in the 1830s, "I used to be out making speeches and electioneering all day – and came home almost every night to issue a new handbill against some new charge or attack on me."[17] But issuing a handbill just before an election, when the accused had no time for an adequate reply, was a dirty trick, one that had been played on Lincoln and Stuart in the previous election by someone signing himself "Truth Teller." What Lincoln thought of such a tactic is made plain in the handbill he had hurriedly issued in response: "It is impossible to make a lengthy answer at this late hour. All I have to say is that the author is a *liar* and a *scoundrel*, and that if he will avow the authorship to me, I promise to give his proboscis a good wringing."[18]

Lincoln's handbill of August 5 is devoted exclusively to what he described as the "facts" of the Anderson case, which he claimed to present "without comment," but his timing and method of presentation point unmistakably to a political motive. In addition to doing damage to Adams at the polls, Lincoln clearly had an even more self-serving objective in mind. Having himself started a public controversy that was followed by newspapers all over the state, he hoped to use it as a venue in which to try his legal case before the public. Both of these gambits proved to be serious miscalculations. In the first instance, Dr. Henry was so badly beaten, particularly in areas where Lincoln hoped to have some influence, that the conclusion that the Sampson Ghost letters had hurt him was inescapable.[19] That much was plain immediately. As a student of the affair has observed, "if the result of the 1837 election was any measure of his persuasive skills, Lincoln failed miserably."[20] Lincoln continued to trade statements with Adams in the newspapers after the election, wrangling intemperately about the Anderson case over his own name and pseudonymously,[21] but he was beating a dead horse. And in spite of the fact that the *Sangamo Journal* made public in November that Adams had previously jumped bail in New York on a charge of forgery in a land transaction, Lincoln's lawsuit went nowhere. It was still hanging fire when Adams died six years later, and the ten-acre parcel eventually went to Adams's heirs, not those of Joseph Anderson.

It seems clear in retrospect that Lincoln's handling of the Adams affair was unfortunate in every respect but one. By abusing Adams with insinuations and slippery arguments, by trying to make political capital of his suspicions about Adams's malfeasance, and by attempting to try his client's case in public, Lincoln had defeated himself at every turn. The last may have been the slowest lesson to emerge, and the most painful, for it would take time to see that it says little for a young lawyer's professional acuity to sound off in public about having the goods on someone but finally to be unable to bring him to trial and make it stick. Learning this sour lesson was surely the one respect in which the Adams affair served Lincoln well.

⁓

IN ADDITION to debt and apprehensions about succeeding as a lawyer, Lincoln was then contending, as we have seen, with a love affair that had gotten out of hand. This circumstance probably heightened his sense of awkwardness and inadequacy in polite society, where his background and training left him almost completely in the dark. A few weeks after arriving in Springfield, Lincoln wrote back to Mary Owens in New Salem, "I am quite as lonesome here as [I] ever was anywhere in my life." He also complained that women avoided talking to him and that he himself avoided going to church "because I am conscious I should not know how to behave myself." Springfield, he observed, was a "busy wilderness."[22]

Lincoln had readily gained a secure social position in New Salem, but the people who mattered and who set the standard in Springfield were of an altogether different sort. Though still a raw village of about fifteen hundred people, Springfield had an elite social circle whose members were characterized by education and refinement. These were people, who, for the most part, had come from well-fixed families in Kentucky. Raised in an atmosphere of courtesy and breeding, they considered themselves above the mob, as in many ways they undoubtedly were. Most would probably have preferred to stay in Kentucky, but they had come to the prairies of Illinois to get ahead, to take advantage of cheap land, to set up as investors and merchants, to get in on the ground floor of government, and generally to seize such opportunities as a new country presented. Joshua Speed belonged to this privileged cadre of Kentuckians, being a member of a prominent Louisville family who had come to Illinois in 1835 to try his hand at storekeeping.

Because most of this group were Whigs and were politically active, they knew Abraham Lincoln as a remarkable country politician, but this did not of itself make him socially acceptable. Certainly he appears to have doubted his ability to move easily among them, as evidenced by his letter to Mary Owens and his doubts about his survival as a lawyer. For someone without connections or credentials, who looked and dressed awkwardly and spoke with a hoosier accent, his misgivings about not fitting in were hardly misplaced. Asked to explain years later how

Lincoln could have been excluded from the social excursions of this company, one of its members confessed: "Well in the light of subsequent events it sounds queer enough, but the fact is that we considered ourselves a 'tony' crowd, and that Lincoln, although an extremely clever and well-liked fellow, was hardly up to our standard of gentility."[23] Lincoln's letter to Mary Owens shows that he was keenly aware of being outside this circle, reporting that "there is a great deal of flourishing about in carriages here, which it would be your doom to see without shareing in it."[24]

As Lincoln knew too well, the key to acceptance in the genteel circle for a bachelor was the ability to get on with women, which happened to be his weakest suit. Orville H. Browning first met him about this time and recalled that "Lincoln had seen but very little of what might be called society and was very awkward, and very much embarrassed in the presence of ladies."[25] The hub of Springfield's elite society was the home of Ninian W. and Elizabeth Todd Edwards on "quality hill," at the edge of town, but Lincoln at first either avoided it or was not invited. Frances Todd, a younger sister of Elizabeth Edwards's, was living there at the time and reported that she heard Lincoln's name mentioned frequently by her brother-in-law. Finally she told him: " 'You are always talking of this Mr. Lincoln. I wish you would bring him down some time and let me see him.' So Mr. Edwards had him come down, and that is the way I met him. Yes, he took me out once or twice, but he was not much for society. He would go where they took him, but he was never very much for company. I don't think he could be called bashful. He was never embarrassed; that I saw, and he seemed to enjoy ladies company. But he did not go much, as some of the other young men did."[26]

Another eligible young woman who was introduced to Lincoln was Martinette Hardin, the sister of his fellow Whig legislator John J. Hardin.

> I was on a visit to my brother, Col. H., of Springfield, when I first met Mr. Lincoln. He was so tall the first time I stood beside him I noticed that I only came above his elbow, and so awkward I was always sorry for him. He did not seem to know what to say in the company of women; I think I never heard him say anything then that he would claim as original. He always prefaced his remarks with: "I read a little thing the other day," or "some one told me," and

then he would relate some anecdote or quote some saying that was appropriate.[27]

Lincoln's picture of himself as uncomfortable in the presence of Springfield's women is confirmed by this recollection and again by Elizabeth Edwards's description of his early behavior at her social gatherings. She told Herndon: "L. Could not hold a lengthy Conversation with a lady – was not sufficiently Educated & intelligent in the female line to do so."[28] At New Salem, though he preferred the company of men, Lincoln apparently knew how to talk to women at a social occasion. A story remembered by Riley Potter has Lincoln helping out at a party by filling plates, causing a girl named Liddy to protest: "Well, Mr. Lincoln, I didn't want a cartload." When Lincoln came around again and Liddy asked for a second helping, he announced loudly: "All right, Miss Liddy, back up your cart and I'll fill it again."[29] Lincoln did not have to be told that this kind of banter would not do for a Springfield lady.

What it comes down to, perhaps, is that Lincoln was simply ill at ease in polite society. Unaccustomed to its proprieties, he probably found the prescribed forms and manners an awkward fit, if not downright difficult and burdensome, for someone with his temperament and social background. The arts of ingratiation that Lincoln had learned and depended on were geared toward an exclusively male audience and were therefore useless. To make a suitable impression in this circle, a young man was expected to be formal and gracious, complimentary and deferential, witty if possible, and tastefully flirtatious when the occasion allowed. One gets a sense of the courtliness of which Lincoln was capable in the expression he is reported to have used when calling on Anna C. Rodney, a young woman of the Edwards circle. He asked the person answering the door, "Is Miss Rodney handy?"[30]

During much of his first year in Springfield, Lincoln was apparently attempting to wiggle out of his courtship with Mary Owens, in spite of the fact that he finally had to propose sometime late in the year to bring it to a resolution. Somehow it suits the picture we have of him at this time of confusion and uncertainty that he found himself regretting her refusal and thinking that he may have been in love with her after all. It is certainly evident that he didn't know clearly what he wanted, and this is reflected in his lame efforts at socializing with the

women of Springfield's upper crust. If he wanted to be accepted, he
didn't seem able to adopt the necessary behavior. Speed believed that
part of Lincoln's distinctiveness was that he was incapable of playing a
role. "He could act no part but his own. He copied no one either in
manner or style."[31]

Late in his life William H. Herndon confided to a correspondent
that "Lincoln had a strong if not a terrible passion for women: he could
hardly keep his hands off from women and yet much to his credit he
lived a pure and virtuous life while married."[32] But scarcely a hint of
this person ever appears in accounts of Lincoln's several courtships or
his relations with other young women to whom he may have been
attracted. This is not surprising given the inhibitions that could be
expected to govern most Victorian informants on such a subject, particularly where the reputation of a great national hero was at stake.
Silence may just as easily indicate a lack of substance as discretion, but
at least for Herndon, referring to Lincoln's strong sexual attractions was
a way of emphasizing his honorable restraint.

While it is true that he was speaking of Lincoln's fidelity to his marriage vow, the honorable restraint that Herndon refers to seems to have
been present in Lincoln's bachelor years, and it may have been related
to his feelings about seduction, a subject that seems to have offended his
sense of justice. Though extramarital sex was considered immoral for
both sexes, women who yielded to temptations were judged more
harshly and stood to lose much more than their male partners if discovered. It is a measure of Lincoln's discomfort with this sort of double
standard that sometime during this same period he composed a poem
for his male companions with the theme that no woman ever fell alone.

> Whatever Spiteful fools may Say –.
> Each jealous, ranting yelper –
> No woman ever *played* the *whore*
> Unless She had a man to help her.[33]

More than his lighthearted advocacy of women's suffrage, we may see
here Lincoln's sympathy with the plight of women and the pronounced
sense of injustice it could evoke in him, but it is not an outright con-
demnation of extramarital or professional sex.

Herndon once described for the young man who was to become his
collaborator some circumstances from this phase of Lincoln's life. "Lincoln came to this city in 1837 and from that time to 1843–44 he and
Speed were quite familiar, to go no further, with the women. I cannot

tell you what I know, especially in ink. Speed was a lady's man in a good and true sense. Lincoln only went to see a few women of the first class, women of sense. Fools ridiculed him; he was on this point tender-footed."[34] This is far from a clear picture, but it is obvious what Herndon is hinting at: that Lincoln and his friend Speed, during their early bachelor days, were involved with women in ways that could not be written about, while Lincoln's encounters with fashionable women were few and painful.

After they had worked together for several years on their Lincoln biography, Herndon offered his collaborator an anecdote that presumably enlarges on the earlier hint.

> Mr. Speed told me this story of Lincoln. Speed about 1839–40 was keeping a pretty woman in this City and Lincoln desirous to have *a little* said to Speed – "Speed, do you know where I can get *some*; and in reply Speed said – "Yes, I do, & if you will wait a moment or so I'll send you to the place with a note. You cant get *it* without a note or by my appearance". Speed wrote the note and Lincoln took it and went to see the girl – handed her the note after a short "how do you do &c.", Lincoln told his business and the girl, after some protestations, agreed to satisfy him. Things went on right – Lincoln and the girl stript off and went to bed. Before any thing was done Lincoln said to the girl – "How much do you charge." "Five dollars, Mr. Lincoln." Mr. Lincoln said – "I've only got \$3." Well said the girl – "I'll trust you, Mr. Lincoln, for \$2. Lincoln thought a moment or so and said – "I do not wish to go on credit – I'm poor & I don't know where my next dollar will come from and I cannot afford to Cheat you." Lincoln after some words of encouragement from the girl got up out of bed, – buttoned up his pants and offered the girl the \$3.00, which she would not take, saying – Mr. Lincoln – "You are the most Conscientious man I ever saw."[35]

This story sounds so much like a deliberate parody of the Honest Abe Lincoln legend that most writers have refused to take it seriously, but this "preposterous story," as one writer has called it, has a credible basis and merits consideration.[36] Herndon himself was aware of how doubtful this hilarious story appears at first glance, for he took the trouble to explain how it had gotten out and to assure Jesse Weik that he regarded it as reliable: "Speed had occasion to go and see the girl in a few days, and she told him just what was said and done between herself & Lincoln and Speed told me the story and I have no doubt of its truthfulness."[37]

Herndon and Speed both are decidedly friendly witnesses where

Lincoln is concerned, and this is clearly an insider's story, not intended for the public or for those who would use it against him. Since it would be unthinkable to include it in their biography, Herndon appears to have had no other motive in telling his collaborator this story than that he regarded it as true, and perhaps with the suggestion that it captured their hero in an embarrassing but highly revealing situation. Indeed, it exemplifies what Herndon could only hint at in his earlier letter: that Lincoln was awkward with women and that unlike his friend Speed, who was an accomplished ladies' man, even Lincoln's attempts at a more businesslike relationship were plagued by anxiety and irresolution.

In fact, the story accords very well with the picture of Lincoln's behavior in other accounts of the period. He was obviously unsure of himself with young women of the class he aspired to, and this may have led him to seek other outlets for his sexual appetites. That he should ask his close friend Speed for help appears logical, particularly if Speed had already made provision for the satisfaction of his own appetites. That Lincoln should underestimate what such an assignation would cost seems almost inevitable, considering his relative inexperience and un-worldliness, not to mention his conspicuous lack of a keen fiscal sense. Finally, his panicky decision to bail out at the mention of credit may be comic, but it can hardly be said to be out of character. At Speed's store he was as reluctant to get into his own bed on credit as he was with Speed's mistress.

But was the young Abraham Lincoln capable of consorting with a prostitute? Herndon, who knew him well, thought he was, and there are other indications that point in the same direction. We have seen that Lincoln told Herndon that he thought he contracted syphilis from a woman, presumably a prostitute, in Beardstown in the 1830s. John T. Stuart told Herndon that he and Lincoln, while staying in Galena, Illinois, during the Black Hawk War in the summer of 1832, "went to the hoar houses." His qualification – that "All went purely for fun – devilment – nothing Else"[38] – is open to the suspicion, at least, of being perfunctory, and the demurrer itself can be read as deliberately ambiguous, the kind of lawyer's denial that actually denies nothing.

It might be argued that for a young man aspiring to raise his social status, Lincoln would, if only as a practical matter, avoid such situations, just as he avoided fighting, drinking, and the use of tobacco. But visiting prostitutes was not strictly identified with lower-class behavior,

as the examples of Speed and Stuart would suggest. It is, in fact, possible to see in Lincoln's debacle with Speed's mistress a kind of inadver-
tent social climbing, like frequenting a fashionable restaurant without
realizing how expensive the food is until presented with a menu.

৵

WHERE LINCOLN *was* sure of himself was with the younger people
of the town. Known in New Salem for his way with children, Lincoln
endeared himself to the youth of Springfield as well. In the 1890s, Ida
Tarbell took notes on the recollection of a woman who grew up in
Springfield about this time. "She remembers Mr L. as a little girl. He
once she & her sister were going away for a trip for the first time alone.
The dray did not come for their trunks and they thought they were
going to be left – stood at gate crying. Mr L. came along & said Why
girls Whats the matter? They told him – How large a trunk is it? They
took told him & he said 'Dont you cry any more' picked it up and carried it off 3 blocks on his shoulders to depot." This was not an isolated
act of kindness. Tarbell's notes continue: "He used to take all the children of the neighborhood to circus. First time Mrs E. heard Ole Bull.
Mr L. took her."[39]

It is not surprising that he was popular with the young men of the
town, who admired his readiness with a funny story and his conspicuous ability in athletics. James Gourley, who later became a neighbor of
the Lincolns, especially remembered the latter.

> I Know when Lincoln Came to this City – in 1837 – probably in May
> 1836. We played the old fashioned town ball [an early version of base-
> ball] – jumped – ran – fought & danced. Lincoln played town ball –
> he hopped well – in 3 hops he would go 40.2 on a dead level. He was
> a great wrestler – wrestled in the black Hawk war: his mode –
> method – or way – his Specialty was Side holds: he threw down all
> men. Lincoln was a good player – could catch a ball: he would Strip
> and go at it – do it well–.[40]

Milton Hay, who later became a leading Springfield attorney,
remembered Lincoln as a regular source of fun and stories. "Matheny
was deputy clerk under Butler. Jim and I with other boys had been
cronies – we were in the habit of running about together as boys do
nights and Sundays, and we made the Clerks office a sort of headquarters. . . . Lincoln would often drop in on us. I remember the general
impression I have that it was always a great treat when Lincoln got

amongst us – we would always be sure to have some of those stories of his for which he had already got a reputation."[41]

James H. Matheny, the young deputy clerk mentioned above, was the son of the county clerk and knew Lincoln well in the early Springfield years. Nine years younger than Lincoln, he was invited a few years later to be one of the groomsmen at Lincoln's wedding. He told Herndon a great many things about the Lincoln of these years, recalling the poems he recited, the topics of his conversations, and the impression he made on people. Not surprisingly, the first thing he stressed was Lincoln's humor, that "the People would flock to hear him – loving jokes – humor &c –." "When he first came among us his wit & humor boiled over."[42] Like Hay, he remembered those sessions in the clerk's office and, in particular, Lincoln's shocking views on religion. "Stuart & Lincoln's office was in what is called *the Hoffman* row on North 5th Street near the public Square. Stuart & Lincoln's office was in the same building as the Clerk's office & *on the same floor*. Lincoln would Come into the clerk's office where I and some young men – Evan Butler – Newton Francis – & others were writing or staying; & would bring the Bible with him – read a Chapter – argue against it."[43]

Matheny's friends all were several years younger than Lincoln, and it is possible that his purpose was mainly to shock their tender sensibilities. According to Matheny, Lincoln would "pick up the Bible – read a passage – and then Comment on it – show its falsity – and its follies on the grounds of *Reason* – would then show its own self made & self uttered Contradictions and would in the End – finally ridicule it and as it were Scoff at it."[44] If Lincoln's harangues were partly aimed at scandalizing the young men in the clerk's office, it worked on Matheny, who told Herndon, "Sometimes Lincoln bordered on absolute Atheism: he went far that way & often shocked me. I was then a young man & believed what my good Mother told me."[45] But Lincoln's attacks on Christian orthodoxy were not confined to Matheny and his friends, for his law partner Stuart told Herndon they had the same effect on him. "Lincoln went further against Christian beliefs – & doctrines & principles than any man I ever heard: he shocked me."[46]

These frank declarations, which Lincoln seems to have indulged in freely at New Salem, must have caused repercussions in Springfield, for during the James Adams affair, Adams tried to score against his adversary by fanning rumors that Lincoln was a "deist."[47] And Matheny reported that his own father, "a Kind of minister and loving Lincoln with all his soul hated to vote for him because he heard that Lincoln was an Infidel."[48] Though at first "Lincoln was Enthusiastic in his infidelity," Matheny recalled, "as he grew older he grew more discrete – didn't talk much before Strangers about his religion."[49] That he probably reined in his "enthusiasm" on this subject fairly early in his Springfield years is suggested by Herndon's surprised reaction at hearing Matheny say Lincoln "scoffed" at Christian beliefs. Working in Speed's store and sharing the upstairs bedroom, Herndon had been much in Lincoln's company in 1838 and 1839, and testimony that Lincoln openly scoffed at Christianity seems to have been news to him.

As we have seen here and in a previous chapter, Lincoln, while not an atheist, was so strongly critical of orthodox Christian beliefs that he sometimes looked like one to his more conventional friends. Rejecting the divinity of Christ, the infallibility of the Scriptures, and an afterlife, he was indeed something of a deist in the tradition of Jefferson, Volney, and Paine. But whereas these three were all decidedly upbeat about the prospects of a less superstitious and more rational world, Lincoln's outlook remained fatalistic. Although he was ambitious to rise in the world and make his presence felt, his ingrained fatalism suggested that man could accomplish only what was fated to happen.

⤜

IF LINCOLN'S FIRST year in Springfield found him having to cope with anxiety over his indebtedness, apprehension about his prospects as a lawyer, feelings of social ineptitude and lack of acceptance, there was at least one more thing that must have given him serious concern: his recurring bouts with depression. Lincoln's melancholy eventually became the most conspicuous part of his demeanor and personality, and all his friends would remark on it. Admiring biographers who questioned that this trait could be so pronounced in one so attached to jokes and humorous stories were soon disabused of their doubts by knowledgeable authorities. Jesse W. Weik, for example, could not believe that Lincoln's gloomy sadness could have been so prominent and all-pervasive as it had been portrayed, so he sought out, in the 1880s, some of Lincoln's closest associates, who all confirmed it.[50] Herndon vividly fixed this image in the public imagination when he wrote that Lincoln "was a sad-looking man; his melancholy dripped from him as he walked."[51]

Precisely when Lincoln's melancholy began to plague him is difficult to say, but it does not seem to have become generally apparent to others until he moved to Springfield.[52] He had had the blues, and he had experienced something like a mental breakdown in the wake of Ann Rutledge's death, but none of his New Salem associates described him as a habitually sad or gloomy man. Although he was troubled and anxious and also very lonely when he first arrived in Springfield in April 1837, these feelings would seem to belong as much to the situation as to his emotional makeup, if not more. But sometime before this, if Robert L. Wilson's memory was accurate, he had confessed as a secret his "terrible melancholy," a condition that he disguised by appearing "to enjoy life rapturously."[53] Possibly about the time he moved to Springfield, he ceased to mask it, and his melancholy began to be part of his persona.

James H. Matheny's opinion was "that Mr Lincoln's sadness – melancholy – despair, grew on him" and that he "grew more. more abstracted – Contemplative – &c. as he grew older."[54] Herndon, who took Matheny's statement, agreed. In its advanced stages, in the 1850s, the mental abstraction that all his friends noticed took the form of trance-like states, in which Lincoln would lose complete touch with his surroundings. Most of the testimony on Lincoln's melancholy from his close friends and acquaintances relates to this later period, not to his early Springfield days. But even at this time his behavior still struck an observer like Matheny as odd. The man who entertained him and his young friends with stories and merriment could often be found not far away in his own office in a very different frame of mind. Herndon noted: "Mr [Matheny] remembers L's old office up stairs above the Court Room – a small dirty bed – one buffalo robe – a chair and a bench – L would lounge in it all day reading – 'abstracting' – 'glooming' &&c – Curious Man."[55]

Joshua F. Speed remembered Lincoln's characteristic mood as one of sadness that could readily brighten, and that this quality was an aspect of his uniqueness. "Generally he was a very sad man, and his countenance indicated it. But when he warmed up all sadness vanished, his face was radiant and glowing, and almost gave expression to his thoughts before his tongue could utter them."[56]

It is impossible to say how much of Lincoln's developing melancholy was attributable to his physical or psychological makeup, how much to his early losses, and how much was philosophical, reflecting the distinctive turn of his active mind. John T. Stuart characterized Lincoln's condition in terms that were strangely physiological. "Lincoln is – was a kind of vegetable," he told Herndon, "that the pores of his flesh acted as an appropriate organ for such Evacuations &c."[57] This apparently meant that Lincoln's temperament was traceable to the inactivity of his bowels, and Stuart went so far as to recommend blue mass – a popular laxative – when his old friend assumed the presidency.[58]

Herndon brooded over the source of Lincoln's melancholy for years. Though he seriously proposed in his 1866 lecture that the ill-fated love affair with Ann Rutledge might have been the precipitant cause, he generally inclined toward the notion that it was basically constitutional.

> As to the cause of this morbid condition, my idea has always been that it was occult and could not be explained by any course of observation and reasoning. It was ingrained, and being ingrained could not be reduced to rule or the cause assigned. It was necessarily hereditary, but whether it came down from a long line of ancestors and far back or was simply the saddened face of Nancy Hanks cannot well be determined. At any rate, it was part of his nature and could no more be shaken off than he could part with his brains.[59]

But Herndon also connected it, apparently at his partner's own suggestion, to Lincoln's growing sense of personal foreboding. "He always had a conviction more or less of ruin," Herndon wrote to Ward Hill Lamon. "This Sprang from his physical organization, as I think, & yet it grew in him all his life – so he told me – often spoke of it to me in my office & on the Circuit when we travelled together."[60] Several times, according to Herndon, Lincoln told him ominously, "Billy, I feel as if I shall meet with some terrible end."[61] Such conversations would come later, but during his first year in Springfield, as Lincoln coped with anxieties and difficulties that were essentially transient, that admitted of solution, he was having to wrestle with a deeper and more abiding anxiety, a persistent sadness whose source and meaning he constantly sought to fathom. Where others could appeal to a religious faith for hope and comfort in the contemplation of death, Lincoln's fatalistic deism, with no expectation of an afterlife, seems to have left him with a palpable sense of dread and staring into the abyss. As he had told Parthena Hill back in New Salem, "It isn't a pleasant thing to think that when we die that is the last of us."[62]

A poem he read and admired about this time offers a glimpse of how this nihilistic vision may have been stamped on his imagination. Lincoln was attracted to poetry from an early age, both as an enthusiastic reader and as a writer of verses. In New Salem he was remembered for his reading and recitation of poetry, particularly of Shakespeare and Burns. When he came to Springfield, he became an avid reader of the great Romantic poet Lord Byron. Joshua Speed told Herndon "I do not think he had ever read much of Byron previous to my accquaintance with him – He was a great admirer of some of Byrons poetry – Childe Harolde the Bride of Abydos Mazppa & some of his fugitive pieces."[63]

Byron's poetry enjoyed a tremendous vogue in the years when Lincoln was coming of age, and the romanticized story of his life, like that of Burns, was widely known. His autobiographical poem, *Childe Harold's Pilgrimage,* had made Byron an instant celebrity in 1812, when the first half of the poem appeared, and the character and philosophical musings of Childe Harold soon became world-famous. The brooding melancholy and restless probing of experience that characterized *Childe Harold* – and much of the rest of Byron's poetry – probably suited Lincoln's darker moods, and though its aristocratic, dissipated, and world-weary hero had little in common with Lincoln in other ways, his melancholy was a galvanizing point of contact. An early stanza in the first canto recalls what Lincoln told Robert Wilson about his own secret sadness:

> Yet oft-times in his maddest mirthful mood
> Strange pangs would flash along Childe Harold's brow,
> As if the Memory of some deadly feud
> Or disappointed passion lurked below:
> But this none knew, nor haply cared to know;
> For his was not that open, artless soul
> That feels relief by bidding sorrow flow,
> Nor sought he friend to counsel or condole,
> Whate'er this grief mote be, which he could not control.[64]

One of the "fugitive pieces" that James H. Matheny remembered as one of Lincoln's favorites was a poem titled "Darkness."[65] The poem is a tour de force, presenting graphically a horrific vision of the end of human life. It begins:

> I had a dream, which was not all a dream.
> The bright sun was extinguished, and the stars
> Did wander darkling in the eternal space,
> Rayless, and pathless, and the icy Earth
> Swung blind and blackening in the moonless air. . . .

The effect of the disappearance of the sun on humankind is the subject of most of the rest of the poem. The event is all-consuming: "men forgot their passions in the dread / Of this their desolation; and all hearts / Were chilled into a selfish prayer for light. . . ." To create light, they burn everything, including their own houses. People become distracted, go mad, then begin to make war on each other:

> . . . a meal was bought
> With blood, and each sate sullenly apart
> Gorging himself in gloom: no Love was left;
> All earth was but one thought – and that was Death,
> Immediate and inglorious. . . .

Even the dogs assail their masters, a point that is given emphasis by the description of one faithful dog, which guards his master's corpse against all encroachments and dies licking his hand. Two final survivors meet by the dying embers of an altar, only to discover in their last moment that they are sworn enemies. Finally, everything is lifeless.

> The World was void,
> The populous and the powerful was a lump,
> Seasonless, herbless, treeless, manless, lifeless –
> A lump of death – a chaos of hard clay.
> The rivers, lakes, and ocean all stood still,
> And nothing stirred within their silent depths;
> Ships sailorless lay rotting on the sea,
> And their masts fell down piecemeal: as they dropped
> They slept on the abyss without a surge –
> The waves were dead; the tides were in their grave,
> The Moon, their mistress, had expired before;
> The winds were withered in the stagnant air,
> And the clouds perished; Darkness had no need
> Of aid from them – She was the Universe.[66]

In later life Abraham Lincoln made no secret of his own belief in the significance of dreams as portents of the future. Byron's poem "The Dream," written at the same time as "Darkness" and appearing next to it in editions of his poetry, was also reported to be another Lincoln favorite. It contains this Byronic reflection on madness and melancholy:

> And this the world calls frenzy; but the wise
> Have a far deeper madness – and the glance
> Of melancholy is a fearful gift;
> What is it but the telescope of truth?
> Which strips the distance of its fantasies,
> And brings life near in utter nakedness,
> Making cold reality too real![67]

Whether the young Abraham Lincoln embraced the notion that his deepening melancholy was "a fearful gift" or a "telescope of truth" is not known, but one can be reasonably sure that Byron's phrases caught his attention.

What seems to have made a lasting impression was the poem's opening meditation on the duality of consciousness created by sleep and waking and what this duality represents. Ward Hill Lamon, who became acquainted with Lincoln in later years and was closely associated with him during the presidency, remembered Lincoln's attraction for the opening lines of "The Dream": "The natural bent of Mr. Lincoln's mind, aided by early associations, inclined him to read books which tended to strengthen his early convictions on occult subjects. Byron's 'Dream' was a favorite poem, and I have often heard him repeat the following lines: –

> "Sleep hath its own world,
> A boundary between the things misnamed
> Death and existence: Sleep hath its own world
> And a wide realm of wild reality.
> And dreams in their development have breath,
> And tears and tortures, and the touch of joy;
> They leave a weight upon our waking thoughts,
> They take a weight from off our waking toils,
> They do divide our being."[68]

Later in life, his receptiveness to dreams and presentiments would become evident and a provocative part of the Lincoln legend. If the Lincoln of the late 1830s took seriously Byron's proposition that dreams "divide our being," the lines that follow this passage in the opening of "The Dream" are of particular interest:

> they become
> A portion of ourselves as of our time,
> And look like heralds of Eternity;
> They pass like spirits of the past, – they speak
> Like Sibyls of the future; they have power –
> The tyranny of pleasure and of pain;
> They make us what we were not – what they will,
> And shake us with the vision that's gone by,
> The dread of vanished shadows –[69]

The power of dreams that is affirmed so forcefully here underscores the importance of the submerged half of one's being and also serves to dramatize the idea expressed in the opening words of the poem, "Our life is twofold." If Lincoln's inner life at this juncture was beginning to deepen, as seems likely, his fixation on Byron's lines about the duality of life is all the more pertinent and revealing.

From his arrival in Springfield in 1837, and possibly sometime before, Lincoln's divided nature began to make itself evident. His melancholy became more visible and presumably more pronounced, but he continued to be a conspicuous source of hilarity and conviviality among his acquaintances. Herndon told his collaborator "that Mr. L. had a double consciousness, a double life. . . . In one moment he was in a state of abstraction and then quickly in another state when he was social, talkative, and a communicative fellow."[70] With the exception of Speed, Lincoln seems to have become increasingly less open and less intimate with his friends and more and more reserved in personal matters. That these developments should coincide with his attraction for Byron is hardly surprising, for part of the appeal of Byron's poetry is its alternation of dark, brooding, melancholic moods and stinging and sometimes hilarious satire. Byronic heroes often suffer guilt from a secret past or plumb the depths of a nameless despair, but at the same time (and frequently in the same poem) the poet's impulse toward rollicking humor and wickedly funny personal invective is irrepressible.

⸺⸺

LINCOLN'S TRANSITION from New Salem to Springfield was obviously more than a change of location. It entailed a challenge to his developing sense of identity. He had established a viable niche for himself at New Salem, where he was not only accepted but regarded as something of a remarkable young man. But there was no future for a lawyer there, or for anyone else, for that matter, as the village began to falter and empty itself out. He could have followed most of the other inhabitants to the emerging town of Petersburg, two miles away, but the prospects were clearly brighter for a budding lawyer and rising politician in the new capital city of Springfield, even if the social and professional hurdles were more daunting.

His situation with Mary Owens, the girl he thought he could marry, may be regarded as what Kenneth Burke would call a "representative anecdote" of his situation. His attraction for Mary was riddled with doubts and misgivings, and these apparently soon got the upper hand. He wasn't sure that she was pretty enough, or that she didn't look down on him, or that he wanted to marry her, or that he could make her happy, but he thought he was somehow honor bound to propose marriage. Her refusal caught him by surprise and showed that his judgment in such things as who he was and how he stood with others was off the mark. The same might be said for his run-in with General Adams. Because Adams had no great reputation as a lawyer and was probably guilty of fraud, Lincoln thought his well-tested powers of invective could gain him victory at law and at the polls, but his dual-purpose campaign proved an embarrassing failure. That he was not a likely suitor where the genteel young ladies of Springfield were concerned he believed from the start, and he had come to expect failure in his relations with women of refinement. But here, too, he would prove to be mistaken.

Chapter 7

CAMPAIGN AND
COURTSHIP

I N JANUARY 1838, nine months after moving to Springfield, Lincoln was invited to deliver an address before the Young Men's Lyceum, an organization founded a few years earlier to provide a forum for aspiring young speakers and politicians.[1] Because he later became a great political leader, Lincoln's address, "The Perpetuation of Our Political Institutions," is often treated as a revealing statement of his incipient political philosophy, and psychobiographers have found it replete with clues to Lincoln's Napoleonic ego and towering aspirations. But these ways of approaching the Lyceum address need qualification. While the speech is certainly an indicative instance of self-presentation, with presumably much to tell us about the twenty-eight-year-old speaker, it is very much a product of its time and place. Reading it out of its historical context has the effect of obscuring what Lincoln himself intended it to represent.

A student of the lyceum activity in Lincoln's Springfield has shed light on the matter by suggesting that the speech was "carefully crafted to impress his peers." Thomas F. Schwartz points out that Lincoln, a newcomer to Springfield, had been embroiled during the preceding months with James Adams in what became a bitterly partisan and public controversy. "Not wanting to arouse any further animosity, he needed to select a nonpartisan topic that appealed to the interests of his audience, while allowing him an opportunity to demonstrate his knowledge and oratorical ability."[2] By looking into the history of the lyceum movement in Springfield generally and the Young Men's Lyceum and its activities, Schwartz is able to show that Lincoln, rather than choose a novel or original subject for his maiden lyceum appearance, opted for one that was already familiar.[3]

A further point to be made about the Lyceum address is that it clearly aimed at putting on display Lincoln's command of the accepted oratorical manner and techniques, as is evident in such a passage as this: "They were a forest of giant oaks; but the all-resistless hurricane has swept over them, and left only, here and there, a lonely trunk, despoiled of its verdure, shorn of its foliage; unshading and unshaded, to murmur in a few more gentle breezes, and to combat with its mutilated limbs, a few more ruder storms, then to sink, and be no more."[4] This kind of forced and mannered oratory would lose its appeal for Lincoln, but he employed it at the Young Men's Lyceum in 1838 to show his audience that he could do it. Understood as a rehearsal of familiar, nonpartisan themes in the hackneyed oratorical style of the day, Lincoln's speech comes across as much less provocative and more conventional than it might otherwise appear to modern readers.

The most striking (though hardly original) aspect of the Lyceum speech is undoubtedly Lincoln's contention that the only danger to American political institutions lies from within. "It cannot come from abroad. If destruction be our lot, we must ourselves be its author and finisher."[5] If people gradually lose their attachment to the government, he says, "men of sufficient talent and ambition will not be wanting to seize the opportunity, strike the blow, and overturn that fair fabric, which for the last half century, has been the fondest hope, of the lovers of freedom, throughout the world."[6] Since the experiment of democracy had succeeded, the ambition of such men cannot be gratified "in supporting and maintaining an edifice that has been erected by others" or even in acquiring "a seat in Congress, a gubernatorial or a presidential chair." "What!" asks Lincoln, "think you these places would satisfy an Alexander, a Caesar, or a Napoleon? Never! Towering genius disdains a beaten path. It seeks regions hitherto unexplored. . . . It thirsts and burns for distinction; and, if possible, it will have it, whether at the expense of emancipating slaves, or enslaving freemen."[7]

This passage has provoked much speculation as to what it reveals about Lincoln's latent conception of himself. James Hurt, for example, has observed that "Lincoln described the potential rebel in romantic, Byronic terms which reveal the figure's deep attraction for Lincoln himself."[8] Certainly the provocative reference to emancipating slaves triggers for posterity the question of whether Lincoln here, at some level, has himself in mind. Unfortunately, we can only speculate about that, but what we may say with confidence is that he does have Napoleon in mind and, further, that his "Byronic" conception of Napoleon was almost certainly colored by Byron's lengthy meditation on the Battle of Waterloo and Napoleon in Canto III of *Childe Harold's Pilgrimage*. Lincoln not only knew this famous passage but had a special affinity for it, as is clear from the testimony of his fellow circuit lawyer, Henry C. Whitney, who told of Lincoln's taking up Whitney's office copy of Byron in 1854 and reading several stanzas from this passage aloud. According to Whitney, "This poetry was very familiar to him evidently; he looked specifically for, and found it with no hesitation, and read it with a fluency that indicated that he had read oftentimes before."[9]

Byron's meditation at a tree on the Waterloo battlefield is set in the spring, a year after the battle, and Childe Harold muses on the meaning of the battle for the survivors:

> They mourn, but smile at length – and, smiling, mourn:
> The tree will wither long before it fall;
> The hull drives on, though mast and sail be torn;
> The roof-tree sinks, but moulders on the hall
> In massy hoariness; the ruined wall
> Stands when its wind-worn battlements are gone;
> The bars survive the captive they enthral;
> The day drags through though storms keep out the sun;
> And thus the heart will break, yet brokenly live on:[10]

This perspective on what passes and what endures is similar to that in "Oh why should the spirit of mortal be proud!" which, beginning in the 1840s, became Lincoln's favorite and most frequently quoted poem.[11] Striking a somber note, the poet moves on to the prime mover of the event, Napoleon himself.

> There sunk the greatest, nor the worst of men,
> Whose Spirit, antithetically mixed,
> One moment of the mightiest, and again
> On little objects with like firmness fixed;
> Extreme in all things! hadst thou been betwixt,
> Thy throne had still been thine, or never been;
> For Daring made thy rise as fall. . . .[12]

Napoleon's virtues are his faults, and the poet implies that what brought him up also brought him down. "Extreme in all things!"

Whitney told this story several times, remembering different stanzas in the third canto of *Childe Harold* as the starting point for the 1854 office reading, but he was consistent about the culminating stanza of the passage, the forty-fifth:

> He who ascends to mountain-tops, shall find
> The loftiest peaks most wrapt in clouds and snow;
> He who surpasses or subdues mankind,
> Must look down on the hate of those below.
> Though high *above* the Sun of Glory glow,
> And far *beneath* the Earth and Ocean spread,
> *Round* him are icy rocks, and loudly blow
> Contending tempests on his naked head,
> And thus reward the toils which to those summits led.[13]

The image of Lincoln reciting these lines has great resonance for any retrospective view of him as president, when he had reached the peak of his ambition and had to contend with hatred and tempests as the reward for his toils. But this is strictly after the fact. His reading this passage for Whitney in 1854 surely had a different import. It probably evidenced a long-standing fascination with Bryon's portrait of the most conspicuous example of ambition and "greatness" in his own time. For the young man in 1838 working up his Lyceum speech, we cannot be sure how the passage was apprehended or what it meant, but the forbidding tone of futility and despair makes Napoleon something of a pathetic figure and an unlikely model for Lincoln's dreams of glory.

❧

LINCOLN'S LOVE of poetry was shared in some measure by the companionable group of young Springfield men that gravitated to him. James H. Matheny remembered that "about 1837–8 & 9 a parcel of young men in this City formed a Kind of Poetical Society" and that Lincoln contributed some poems, one of which was the seduction poem cited in the previous chapter.[14] William H. Herndon was also a member of this group. Having been unceremoniously removed from Illinois College by his father because of his warm sympathy for the abolitionism of his teachers, Herndon went to work in Speed's store and lived for a time with Lincoln and Speed on the second floor. According to Herndon, "The young men who congregated about the store formed a society for the encouragement of debate and literary efforts. Sometimes we would meet in a lawyer's office and often in Speed's room. Besides the debates, poems and other original productions were read. Unfortunately we ruled out the ladies."[15]

The atmosphere in the store, which Herndon called Lincoln's "headquarters," was apparently very congenial. "The store had a large fireplace in the rear, and around it the lights of the town collected every evening."[16] But when the subject turned to politics, the congeniality of these "lights" disappeared. In the late fall of 1839, the politically active young men of both parties were gearing up for the presidential race of the coming year, and sharp differences were unavoidable. "The disputants waxed warm and acrimonious as the discussion proceeded," Herndon wrote. "Douglas, I recollect, was leading on the Democratic side. He had already learned the art of dodging in debate, but still he was subtle, fiery, and impetuous. . . . At last, with great vehemence, he sprang up and abruptly made a challenge to those who differed with him to discuss the whole matter publicly, remarking that, 'This store is no place to talk politics.' "[17]

This was the origin of a memorable "tournament" of public debate that took place in November and December 1839, in which Whig orators alternated speeches with Democrats, debating questions of national policy. Lincoln was the second Whig speaker to appear on the opening night of the debates, and his success was evident from the grudging admiration expressed in the Democratic *Illinois State Register*. Still, it found excuses for the Democratic champion Stephen A. Douglas, who had been sandwiched between two Whig speakers, and it admonished Lincoln for his manner. "His argument was truly ingenious. He has however, a sort of assumed clownishness in his manner which does not become him, and which does not truly belong to him. It is assumed – assumed for effect. Mr. L. will sometimes make his language correspond with this clownish manner, and he can thus frequently raise a loud laugh among his Whig hearers, but this entire game of buffoonery convinces the mind of no man, and is utterly lost on the majority of his audience."[18] The *Register*'s uncharacteristic acknowledgment that Lincoln scored well against Douglas on Wednesday, November 19, the opening night of the debates, may merely have been a calculated way of emphasizing his failure to answer Douglas effectively the following evening. "Mr. Lincoln of Wednesday night was not the Mr. Lincoln of Tuesday. He could only meet the arguments of Mr. Douglas by relating stale anecdotes and old stories, and left the stump literally whipped off of it, even in the estimation of his own friends."[19]

Later in the week, Lincoln's friend Edward D. Baker took his turn for the Whigs and provoked an angry response from the audience that threatened to get out of hand. The brother of the editor of the *Register* told Herndon that he had precipitated the excitement by his protest against Baker's remarks: "Baker Said this – 'Wherever there is a land office there is a paper to defend the Corruptions of office.' This was a personal attack on my Bro Geo Webber.: I was in the Court House and in my anger I cried 'Pull him down.' "[20] Herndon, who was in the crowd, described the ensuing commotion that was capped by the dramatic appearance of Lincoln, who descended on the scene, deus ex machina, through a trapdoor in the ceiling.

> Just then a long pair of legs were seen dangling from the aperture above, and instantly the figure of Lincoln dropped on the platform. Motioning with his hands for silence and not succeeding, he seized a stone water-pitcher standing near by, threatening to break it over the head of the first man who laid hands on Baker. "Hold on, gentlemen," he shouted, "this is the land of free speech. Mr. Baker has a right to speak and ought to be heard. I am here to protect him, and no man shall take him from this stand if I can prevent it." His interference had the desired effect. Quiet was soon restored, and the valiant Baker was allowed to proceed.[21]

Baker's speech and the predicament it got him into exemplify the difficulty of observing the fine line between the political and the personal. This is a perennial difficulty in American politics and one that Lincoln himself faced often during these years.

Having failed to measure up to Douglas on his second time out was apparently a source of real chagrin for Lincoln. His friend Joseph Gillespie remembered that "He was conscious of his failure and I never saw any man so much distressed He begged to be permitted to try it again and was reluctantly indulged and in the next effort he transcended our highest expectations."[22] In this appearance, the last for the Whigs and occurring on the day after Christmas, Lincoln drew a very meager crowd. And though he professed mortification that so few people were present, his speech was considered so great a success that it was subsequently published in pamphlet form as a campaign document. Unlike his Lyceum address, which was on a familiar oratorical theme, Lincoln's speech in December 1839 focused on a hot political topic, the sub-treasury, a depository for government funds newly proposed by the Democrats. To judge from its reception, the speech was considered extremely effective. Lincoln's arguments were hard-hitting and tightly targeted, using the close reasoning that became his trademark. Although the body of his speech was crafted in disciplined prose, he allowed himself a florid and expansive peroration that outdid the rhetoric even of the Lyceum address: "If ever I feel the soul within me elevate and expand to those dimensions not wholly unworthy of its Almighty Architect, it is when I contemplate the cause of my country, deserted by all the world beside, and I standing up boldly and alone and hurling defiance at her victorious oppressors. Here, without contemplating consequences, before High Heaven, and in the face of the world, I swear eternal fidelity to the just cause, as I deem it, of the land of my life, my liberty and my love."[23]

This abrupt shift from specific, carefully argued objections to a scheme for depositing government revenues to a highly emotional pledge of loyalty to one's country seems incongruous and overwrought to modern readers, and we know that Lincoln moved away from this flamboyant mode in the years that followed. But we are also aware that this kind of language and self-presentation belonged to the oratorical conventions of the day and they produced a very favorable effect on Lincoln's audience. In a word, the peroration of the sub-treasury speech must be understood in its context, and nothing was more important in this respect than the upcoming presidential campaign.

The Whig party was desperate to win the presidency. In their frustration, the Whigs had begun to picture the long twelve-year rule of the Democrats under Andrew Jackson and Martin Van Buren as an intolerable stifling of their liberties. The Whigs' anxiety was so great that Democrats were pictured not just as adversaries but as oppressors, and the fate of freedom and democracy was viewed as seriously at risk. In this fevered perspective, the object for the Whigs became not merely victory at the polls but the political salvation of the Republic.

Largely for this reason, the campaign of 1840 was unlike any other before or since. The frenzied efforts of the Whigs to gain success at all costs reflected the pressure created by that desperation. From their determined search for the means of victory came many innovations that have since become campaign standards: slogans, placards, emblems, political advertisements, floats, rallies, and campaign hats.[24] In nominating William Henry Harrison instead of Henry Clay, the Whigs deliberately passed over their leading statesman and chose a superannuated military hero who had, conveniently, no real political track record. Adopting no campaign platform, they ran an energetic and largely expedient campaign that would be labeled in our own time pure hype. Even their leading theme was improvised on the fly. An opposition newspaper had sniped in March that "upon condition of his receiving a pension of $2,000 and a barrel of cider, General Harrison would no doubt consent to withdraw his pretensions, and spend his days in a log cabin on the banks of the Ohio."[25] The Whigs quickly embraced the insult, and the "Log Cabin and Hard Cider" campaign was born. Log cabins were erected as campaign headquarters all across the country, and drinking hard cider became a ritual act of Whig solidarity with the common man, not to mention its beneficial effects as a source of political enthusiasm at party rallies. Thus, as Albert J. Beveridge observed, "the campaign became a volcanic eruption of volatile and unintelligent sentimentalism. Harrison was the poor man's friend, the farmer's champion, the log cabin and hard-cider candidate; Van Buren, an aristocrat who ate his meals from gold plates and drank his champagne from crystal goblets."[26] The loud Democratic protests of such unadulterated hoopla were utterly unavailing, and the result has been called "the rowdiest, noisiest presidential campaign in the history of the country."[27]

Abraham Lincoln, as a member of the Whig party's central committee, played a leading role in organizing and directing the statewide effort. He appears to have been the principal author of a detailed plan for getting out the vote at maximum Whig strength, and he took the lead in writing and publishing a campaign newspaper, *The Old Soldier.*[28] Though the Whigs were a minority party in Illinois, by the opening of the campaign in January 1840 Lincoln was uncharacteristically optimistic and upbeat. To his partner, Congressman John T. Stuart, Lincoln wrote: "The nomination of Harrison takes first rate. You know I am never sanguine; but I believe we will carry the state. The chance for doing so, appears to me 25 percent better than it did for you to beat Douglass. A great many of the grocery sort of Van Buren men, as formerly, are out for Harrison. Our Irish Blacksmith Gregory, is for Harrison. I believe I may say, that all our friends think the chance of carrying the state, verry good."[29] Here it is clear that Lincoln's optimism was linked to the proven appeal of Harrison for "the grocery sort" (men who hang out in saloons) and Irish immigrants, two groups that usually shied away from the Whigs (who were perceived as aristocratic) and voted with the Democrats.

Lincoln's enthusiasm at the prospect of winning the 1840 presidential campaign and bringing the Whigs into power seems to have taken possession of him, and he betrayed no sign of having been tempered by concerns of conscience. There were, in fact, Whigs who had misgivings about characterizing the Democrats in power as out-and-out oppressors and conducting a campaign of sheer expediency that justified anything and everything in terms of victory. For example, Lincoln's friend James C. Conkling poked fun at speeches (such as Lincoln's subtreasury speech) that depicted "in the most glowing colors that awful and horrid state of oppression under which we exist and by which we are just permitted to breathe and describ[ed] that paradisaical happiness, peace and contentment we shall enjoy under the influence of reform."[30] Another Whig, Albert T. Bledsoe, claimed many years later to have disputed the morality of the cynical "Log Cabin and Hard Cider" campaign with Lincoln at the time.

One who witnessed the Presidential campaign of that ever memorable year would have supposed that the whole world had run mad, and rushed into the wild contest on the sublime issues, that log cabins are the best of all buildings, hard-cider the most delicious of all drinks, and coon-skins the finest of all furs. In no age or country, perhaps, since the dawn of civilization was humbuggery exhibited in more gigantic and grotesque forms than in the Harrison campaign of 1840. We then beheld the great mass-meeting at Springfield; log-cabins, barrels of hard-cider, coons, and coon-skins were everywhere visible, amid great crowds of shouting, singing, hurrahing and haranguing "friends of the people." It seemed as if Pandemonium had been let loose upon earth. Reason was everywhere reeling in the storm, and madness ruled the masses. Oh, how sad! We then saw with sorrow, and predicted with confidence, the ruin of the country. But Mr. Lincoln was merry. He entered into the very soul of the contest with a glee which seemed perfectly assured of "the glad success." Hence, when we ventured to express our intense mortification that the Whig Party, which had claimed a monopoly of all the intelligence and decency of the country, should descend to the use of such means, Mr. Lincoln replied: "It is all right; *we must fight the devil with fire; we must beat the Democrats, or the country will be ruined.*"[31]

Bledsoe wrote from the point of view of an embittered southerner who believed that the Civil War had been a perversion of justice and the American Constitution. Consequently, his opinion of Lincoln, who had once been his friend and associate both in politics and at the bar, was deeply jaundiced, and he obviously focused on the 1840 campaign for the purpose of showing Lincoln in the act of opting for expediency and victory over principle. Nonetheless, his portrayal of Lincoln's attitude toward the campaign is not at odds with the facts and circumstances as one is able to discern them. Certainly the surviving anecdotes depict a lively form of political combat that favored ridicule over reason, partisanship over principle, and sheer spectacle over all. That Lincoln's performance was no exception is suggested by the anecdotes about him that can be traced to this campaign.

One story sounds like legend, but its placement in the 1840 election makes it of interest. It concerns Lincoln's encounter with some of his old friends from New Salem days, most of whom were Democrats. A. S. Kirk told Herndon:

> In 1840 Mr Lincoln was a Candidate for the legislature. He went out to Mr Kyles store [west of Springfield] in Sangamon Co. to make a speech and did so. After he was done making the Speech the boys – some of his old acquaintants – democrats, Said to Lincoln – "See here Lincoln, if you can throw this Cannon ball further than we Can, We'll vote for you" Lincoln picked up the large Cannon ball – felt it – swung it around – and around and said "Well, boys if thats all I have to do I'll get your votes" and then he swung it, the Cannon ball, around and around and gave it a good pitch or throw: the Cannon ball thrown by Lincoln went Some four or Six feet further than any one Could throw it.[32]

One senses here the situation of a "rising man" being confronted by those he is rising above. As in legend, he makes believers (and voters) out of them by an unequivocal proof of "superiority."

A more revealing story involves Lincoln's successful stratagem to lure the fast-rising Stephen A. Douglas into a political trap. Finding a reference in a biography of the Democratic candidate for president, Martin Van Buren, that they thought Douglas would dispute, Lincoln and his friend William Fithian procured a letter from Van Buren confirming it, then sprang their trap. James H. Matheny described the resulting encounter to Herndon: "Says he was present, he thinks in the Market house in 1840 and heard a debate between Douglas & Lincoln – the subject Martin Van Buren. Lincoln had asserted that Van had voted for Negro Suffrage under certain limitations. Douglas denied it. Lincoln then read from Hollands life of Van Buren. Douglas said it was a forgery. Lincoln drew Fithians letter from Van Buren on Douglas. Douglas got mad – Snatched up the book and Slung it into the crowd –

saying d—n such a book."[33] Here Lincoln and his partner have used the platform to stage a scene in which Douglas is forced to play an unwanted role. This theatrical stratagem worked flawlessly and was doubly productive, for it brought out an embarrassing fact about Van Buren – that he voted for limited Negro suffrage – and perhaps best of all, it caused Douglas to acknowledge it as an embarrassment. Carried out like a prank, this connivance shows that Lincoln was not limited to spontaneous and spur-of-the-moment ploys but used cunning and stealth.

Forethought and preparation figure in another anecdote recalled from the 1840 campaign. In the town of Albion, Lincoln, as a presidential elector for Harrison, was scheduled to debate his counterpart on the Van Buren ticket, Isaac Walker. While Walker no longer lived in Albion, Lincoln was concerned about the advantage the hometown boy might have as a returning prodigal, so he devised a strategy to offset it. The story of how Lincoln appeared at the log schoolhouse the day of the debate seeking to borrow a copy of Byron's works was told by Gibson William Harris, one of the pupils, who later clerked in Lincoln's law office. The appearance of the politician in the classroom provoked the interest of Harris and other students, who subsequently attended the debate. "His style of speaking even then was remarkably direct and forcible," Harris recalled. Speaking first, Lincoln began by citing a passage from one of the dark, brooding poems of Byron he had been reading, *Lara*:

> He, their unhoped but unforgotten lord,
> The long self-exiled chieftain is restored;
> There be bright faces in the busy hall,
> Bowls on the board, and banners on the wall.
> He comes at last, in sudden loneliness,
> And whence they know not, why they need not guess;
> They more might marvel, when the greetings o'er,
> Not that he came, but why he came not before. . . .

"In vain," wrote Harris, "did Mr. Walker's rejoinder ring the changes on auld lang syne. Lincoln's sallies on 'why came not before' had taken the wind out of his opponent's sails completely."[34]

Another surviving anecdote concerns Lincoln's less gentle put-down of a Democratic politician, Colonel E. D. ("Dick") Taylor, whom Herndon described as "a showy, bombastic man, with a weakness for fine clothes and other personal adornments."[35] Matheny remembered that once, in the midst of a speech by Taylor in which he railed against the "aristocracy" of the Whigs, Lincoln managed to reach out and jerk open Taylor's vest; "it unbuttoned and out fell Dick['s] ruffle shirt like a pile of Entrails." Tumbling out with the shirt was a gold watch on a chain bedecked with many seals. "This was too much for the good People – Democrat & Whig alike – and they burst forth in a furious & uproarious laughter."[36]

When it came Lincoln's turn to speak, Ninian W. Edwards remembered that Lincoln responded:

> whilst Col. Taylor had his stores over the county, and was riding in a fine carriage, wore his kid gloves and had a gold headed cane, he was a poor boy hired on a flat boat at eight dollars a month, and had only one pair of breeches and they were of buckskin now said he if you know the nature of buckskin when wet and dried by the sun they would shrink and mine kept shrinking until they left for several inches my legs bare between the top of my Socks and the lower part of my breeches – and whilst I was growing taller they were becoming shorter: and so much tighter, that they left a blue streak around my leg which you can see to this day – If you call this aristocracy I plead guilty to the charge.[37]

If, as Matheny and Herndon recalled, Colonel Taylor was deeply pained by Lincoln's treatment of him, his mortification probably did not compare with that felt by Lincoln's most celebrated victim, Jesse B. Thomas, Jr. Thomas was a well-connected young lawyer and politician, a few years older than Lincoln. His uncle had been a U.S. senator, and his father-in-law was an Illinois Supreme Court judge and prominent Democrat. Thomas was supposed to be a Whig, but perhaps in deference to his celebrated father-in-law, he sometimes took sides with the Democrats, which probably helped put him at odds with Abraham Lincoln.[38] He doubtless disapproved of the "Log Cabin and Hard Cider" campaign, and he seems to have called Lincoln and his associates to task in a speech on July 20 for a political dirty trick – namely, putting it out that he was the author of an anonymous troublemaking letter that they had written themselves.[39] In an encounter that came to be known in Springfield as "the skinning of Thomas," Lincoln replied by attacking his opponent unmercifully. According to Herndon, "He imitated Thomas in gesture and voice, at times caricaturing his walk and the very motion of his body. Thomas, like everybody else, had some peculiarities of expression and gesture, and these Lincoln succeeded in rendering more prominent than ever. The crowd yelled and cheered as he continued. Encouraged by these demonstrations, the ludicrous features of the speaker's performance gave way to intense and scathing ridicule."[40] Lincoln's relentless assault had a devastating effect on his adversary, a former circuit judge, reducing him to tears and forcing him to flee the platform.[41]

Lincoln had a long history of making fun of his antagonists, but this penchant for stinging invective of a cruelly personal sort had been largely confined to written material. On the platform he was up to the rough-and-tumble of political dispute and could give as well as take. He could be tough on his opponents, but he had no reputation of being a bully or of resorting unduly to blatant personal abuse on the platform, and he had on some occasions played the role of quieting the boisterous passions of others. Exactly why Lincoln, on this occasion, pulled out all the stops and grossly breached the line between the political and the personal remains unclear. It may well have been partly due to the all-out, no-holds-barred spirit of the 1840 campaign, but breach it he certainly did.

Most of those Herndon interviewed concerning this incident remembered only the tenor of Lincoln's speech, that it was "terrible" in its denunciation and that Lincoln showed no mercy.[42] Twenty years later, according to one informant, Lincoln's treatment of Thomas was "still spoken of by those who heard it as awfully severe."[43] But strangely enough, the most detailed recollection of the speech by an eyewitness did not represent it as underhanded or unfair. Though he was writing as a sharp critic of Abraham Lincoln's shortcomings as a man and politician, Albert T. Bledsoe, who was Jesse B. Thomas's law partner at the time, did not emphasize Lincoln's recklessness or cruelty. Here is his account in full:

> We well remember, we shall never forget, his reply to Judge Thomas, [subsequently] of the Supreme Court of Illinois, who, in a public address, had attacked "the Long Nine" of which body Mr. Lincoln was the most distinguished member. Mr. Lincoln did not hear the speech, being absent at the time of its delivery; but he was sent for, informed of its contents, and made his appearance as Judge Thomas was about to conclude and take his seat. He rose to reply. The excitement of the crowd was intense. Mr. Lincoln's effort was absolutely overwhelming and withering. He had not proceeded far, indeed, before Judge Thomas began to blubber like a baby, and left the assembly. Yet there was nothing of the *orator*, as that word is usually

understood, either in the manner or the language of the speech. His manner was easy, natural, and self-possessed, and his language was simple, direct, and plain Anglo-Saxon English, delivered in a conversational, rather than an oratorical, style and tone. But every word was a real "rail-splitter."

He began by saying, that he was a humble member of "the Long Nine," so that he could not swell himself up to the great dimensions of his learned and eloquent adversary. The effort to do so would, he feared, be attended with the fate of the frog in the fable, which tried to swell itself to the size of the ox. But he could do this – he could just prick a few pin-holes in his adversary, and let him down to his natural size.

He then began to apply his pin. He described, with minute accuracy, the political career of Judge Thomas, and his various somersaults. He told how it was, and under what circumstances, a new light had struck the learned Judge, and with what wonderful agility he went right over. The Judge could not long stand Mr. Lincoln's pin. On the contrary, as we have already said, he began to blubber like a baby, and withdrew from the assembly. He cried all the rest of the day. He came to our office for sympathy, and we should have sincerely pitied the poor fellow, if every feeling of compassion had not been swallowed up in contempt.[44]

Bledsoe shows little sympathy for the hapless Thomas, and it may be significant that their partnership was dissolved less than a month after this event.[45] One can only assume that he saw merit in Lincoln's branding Thomas as a political turncoat, something that Lincoln showed in the George Forquer–lightning rod incident that he knew how to do to good effect.

The aftermath of the incident is instructive. The *Illinois State Register* not unexpectedly characterized Lincoln's action as a "rude assault" and concluded: "It is just to say that many of our Whig citizens are among the foremost and loudest in condemning the conduct of Mr. Lincoln. He has fallen into the ditch which he dug for his neighbor."[46] That Lincoln went too far is implicitly acknowledged in almost every account except Bledsoe's, and Herndon wrote that "the whole thing was so unlike Lincoln, it was not soon forgotten either by his friends or enemies." Lincoln himself apparently concluded that he had done wrong. "I heard him afterwards say that the recollection of his conduct that evening filled him with the deepest chagrin," Herndon wrote. "He felt that he had gone too far, and to rid his good-nature of a load, hunted up Thomas and made ample apology."[47]

It is possible to see this apology as evidence of calculation on Lincoln's part, rather than sincerity, and to conclude that he repented of his behavior only when he saw that most people disapproved. This is Bledsoe's theory of Lincoln's character generally (though not in this instance), that his behavior was governed by a "thirst for distinction," which took the form of an unprincipled pursuit of popularity. It would be a mistake to dismiss such considerations, for Lincoln was undoubtedly ambitious and was still very much involved in the process of defining himself. But neither can one ignore the fact that those who knew Lincoln well believed that he was naturally tenderhearted and that, in the words of David Davis, he "could bear no malice" and sincerely regretted what he had done.[48]

His future law partner, Stephen T. Logan, thought he had set out to do even worse. Lincoln, he told Nicolay, "was always very independent and had generally a very good nature. Though he had at times, when he was roused, a very high temper. He controlled it then in a general way, though it would break out sometimes – and at those times it didn't take much to make him whip a man. He wanted to whip Judge Jesse Thomas here once in a canvass for an election."[49] What Logan's testimony points up here is that though Lincoln may have wanted to whip Thomas, he ridiculed him instead. Public ridicule was, after all, closely akin to getting whipped, something that Lincoln was well aware of. Earlier in the year Stephen A. Douglas had taken exception to something printed about him in the *Sangamo Journal* and tried to cane the editor, Simeon Francis, on the streets of Springfield. Lincoln made light of this encounter in a letter to his law partner Stuart: "Yesterday Douglas, having chosen to consider himself insulted by something in the 'Journal,' undertook to cane Francis in the street. Francis caught him by the hair and jammed him back against a market-cart, where the matter ended by Francis being pulled away from him. The whole affair was so ludicrous that Francis and everybody else (Douglas excepted) have been laughing about it ever since."[50]

Joshua Speed remembered another incident from the campaign of 1840 that shows the same impulse toward violence. Speed's recollection had to do with Lincoln's reaction to a rumor that a Democrat, Reuben Radford, who controlled a gang of railroad workers, was keeping the Whigs from voting at one of the polling places. "Lincoln jumped up and went down to see what was the Matter and to see fair play." This may have been the time that Herndon remembered Lincoln's seizing an ax handle from a hardware store before advancing on the scene.[51]

"Radford was angry – Said much to Lincoln. Lincoln – said 'Radford you will spoil & blow if you live much longer.'" Speed recalled that "Lincoln wanted to hit Radford, but Could get no chance to do so. Lincoln said 'I intended to Knock him down & go away and leave him a-Kicking.'"[52] He wanted to, but he didn't.

–ᴓ

IN TRYING to pinpoint the time of Lincoln's emergence as a man of consequence, both in his own estimation and in the eyes of his public, Herndon put his finger on the year 1840. Coaching the prospective biographer Ward Hill Lamon, he wrote in his inimitable style: "From the facts before me Mr Lincoln as Early as 1830 be[g]an to dream of destiny –. I think it grew & developed & bloom[ed] with beauty &c in the year *1840 Exactly*. Mr Lincoln on that year was appointed general Elector from the State –. Mr Lincoln told me that his ideas of something – burst on him in 1840."[53] This is the kind of statement that makes scholars suspicious of Herndon, for he begins by saying that he has studied the facts and come to a conclusion, which he then clinches by saying Lincoln told him as much. But this conclusion has a plausibility that does not depend on Herndon. The year 1840, which was given over almost entirely to the Harrison campaign, was clearly pivotal for Lincoln. At its outset he was still, as his law student, Milton Hay, put it, "outranked" by such men as Stuart, Logan, John J. Hardin, Edward D. Baker, and Orville H. Browning. "At that time . . . he was so to speak just emerging above the horizon."[54] His acceptance into Springfield society had been established in 1839. It had been marked, in the first instance, by his being selected a trustee of the town; in December his name had appeared in connection with a cotillion for the elite of the city and assembled legislators. The unfolding of the election year showed Lincoln coming to the fore in a dramatic political contest, gaining statewide visibility as a party spokesman, and being elected to the Illinois legislature for a fourth consecutive term. If there was a point at which the ambitious young man who was "never sanguine" had reason to glimpse the kind of future he had dreamed about as a possible reality, 1840 was a likely time.

Lincoln was part of the so-called Springfield Junto, the small group of dedicated Whigs who devised party strategy and fought the Democrats in the newspapers. His talents as a polemicist were well known even before he had come to Springfield, although it is hard to identify the actual pieces he wrote with certainty. But there is no doubt that he had come to prominence by this time as a stump speaker. When the Junto fell out of favor with party rank and file in March, Lincoln was apprehensive that he would not be renominated, but he discovered that his abilities could not be dispensed with. He wrote his law partner about the results of the local nominating convention: "Ninian [Edwards] was verry much hurt at not being nominated; but he has become tolerably well reconciled. I was much, verry much, wounded myself at his being left out. The fact is, the country delegates made the nominations as they pleased; and they pleased to make them all from the country, except Baker & me, whom they supposed necessary to make stump speeches."[55] The nominating convention was a new and still controversial institution, and one can sense here that Lincoln, the country boy who had made it into the power circle of the party, now had misgivings about the rank and file from the country making the party's decisions.

Although Lincoln spent much of the year of 1840 making stump speeches, no texts of these extemporaneous speeches survive, and almost all accounts are both biased and brief. Here is a report from the *Sangamo Journal*, Lincoln's own paper, of a speech at the court town of Tremont on May 2.

> Immediately after dinner, the large Court House was filled to overflowing, and the debate was opened by Mr. Lincoln, who after some general and appropriate remarks concerning the design and object of all Governments, drew a vivid picture of our prosperous and happy condition previous to the time of the war which was waged against the U.S. Bank, the constitutionality, as well as the great utility of which he vindicated in a most triumphant manner. He next turned his attention to the Sub-Treasury, the hideous deformity and injurious effects of which were exposed in a masterly style. He then reviewed the political course of Mr. Van Buren, and especially his votes in the New York Convention in allowing Free Negroes the right of suffrage, and his Janus-faced policy in relation to the war. In this part of his speech Mr. Lincoln was particularly felicitous, and the frequent and spontaneous bursts of applause from the People, gave evidence that their hearts were with him. He related many highly amusing anecdotes which convulsed the house with laughter; and concluded his eloquent address with a successful vindication of the civil and military reputation of the Hero of Tippecanoe.[56]

The reader of the sub-treasury speech will find much of the territory Lincoln covered in his speech at Tremont familiar, and the reference to Van Buren's vote for Negro suffrage indicates that this story, which worked so well against Douglas, had found its way into his repertoire. There were relatively few blacks in Illinois at the time, and while the general populace clearly did not want slavery, most did not want blacks either, much less blacks with voting rights. This meant one could score against one's opponents by showing that they favored giving blacks the vote. Not until he was president did Lincoln come to advocate such things himself, and in 1840 he delighted in exposing Van Buren's little-known liberality toward free blacks as a political sin.

Because political meetings and speeches were reported by an aggressively partisan press, it is almost impossible to find contemporary appraisals of Lincoln's abilities as a stump speaker that are unbiased. The Democratic papers usually reported his speeches as pathetic failures; the Whig papers characterized the same speeches as rousing triumphs. Perhaps the closest one can come is a Democratic reporter's account of an appearance in Mount Vernon, in which he specifies the qualities that are needed for success on the stump. "Mr. Lincoln," the reporter admitted, was "listened to with attention; possessing much urbanity and suavity of manner, he is well calculated for a public debater; as he seldom loses his temper, and always replies jocosely and in good humor, — the evident marks of disapprobation which greet many of his assertions, do not discompose him, and he is therefore hard to foil."[57] "Urbanity and suavity of manner" must, of course, be understood in comparative terms, but the fact that this reporter allowed such a description is indicative of the progress Lincoln was making. Keeping his temper, as we have seen, was something Lincoln worked at, whereas deflecting opponent's sallies with humor may have come much more naturally. And self-confidence and self-control were surely the keys to keeping his composure when under fire.

The great hallmark of Lincoln's stump speaking was already the "amusing anecdotes which convulsed the house with laughter." He took full advantage of the fact that political rallies were, for his audiences, a species of entertainment, occasions at which the responsibilities of citizenship could be discharged while having a good time. In this such rallies are often compared to the religious camp meetings of the time, which combined the attributes of an emotional prayer meeting and a picnic. At the monster rally the Whigs staged in Springfield in June, which featured a spectacular parade and a barbecue for fifteen thousand people, speechmaking predominated, and the orators unleashed a "flood of eloquence" on a seemingly insatiable audience. Lincoln's contribution was later recalled by an eyewitness:

> Mr. Lincoln stood in a wagon, from which he addressed the mass of people that surrounded it. . . . At times he discussed the questions of the time in a logical way, but much time was devoted to telling stories to illustrate some phase of his argument, though more often the telling of these stories was resorted to for the purpose of rendering his opponents ridiculous. . . . One story he told . . . was not one it would be seemly to publish; but rendered, as it was, in his inimitable way, it contained nothing that was offensive to refined taste.[58]

One reason Lincoln here conformed his racy stories to the requirements of refined taste was that an important new element had been added to the Whig campaign rallies of 1840 – the ladies. Women were almost universally denied the vote at that time and generally did not participate in political meetings, nor was it ordinarily thought proper to do so. Political events were often boisterous and, especially in places like central Illinois, could easily produce stories and language unsuitable for mixed company, to say nothing of the constant threat of physical violence. But something remarkable happened in 1840 that was a dramatic departure from previous campaigns: women turned out in droves to support the Whigs and their candidate, Old Tippecanoe.

The sudden outpouring of female support for William Henry Harrison and his party was by no means confined to Illinois. The most detailed study of the 1840 campaign shows that women of all sections, from Maine to the southern states, arose in support of the Whigs. Robert Gray Gunderson reports that "While most activities were limited to 'smiles and songs and encouragement,' some women entered into the contest with a vigor quite remarkable for the era of *Godey's Lady's Book*. Lucy Kenney took up her pen in behalf of Harrison and produced one of the first political pamphlets ever written by an American woman: *The Strongest of All Government Is That Which Is Most Free, An Address to the People of the United States*."[59] Out in Illinois, some women went so far as to hold political meetings and make speeches. In Vandalia a female orator was reported in the *Sangamo Journal* as saying: "When the war whoop on our prairies was the infant's lullaby, our mothers reposed in security for Harrison was their protector. We would indeed be traitors to our sex if our bosoms did not thrill at his name."[60]

To the astonishment of the Democrats, these women recruits to the Whig cause were more than mere embellishments; they were active. "They attended conventions, rode in floats, and 'by their charms promoted the election.' Chivalrous Whig managers published invitations 'To the Ladies,' who responded by accompanying their men to Harrison meetings."[61] And they sang. Singing was a regular feature of this rousing campaign, and the women joined in enthusiastically. The most famous song of the campaign contained a verse that celebrated their contribution:

> The beautiful girls, God bless their souls, souls, souls,
> The country through
> Will all, to a man, do all they can
> For Tippecanoe and Tyler too.

This was the last verse, and it put a new spin on the chorus:

> For Tippecanoe and Tyler too,
> For Tippecanoe and Tyler too,
> And with them we will beat little Van;
> Van, Van is a used up man,
> And with them we will beat little Van.[62]

The Democrats, of course, professed to find the public participation of women in politics an unseemly and offensive spectacle, but it was obvious that it had a decided effect and contributed significantly to the Whig party's enthusiasm and momentum. Sent out by the Democrats to campaign for Van Buren, Vice President Richard Johnson, himself a war hero and former officer under Harrison, affected to be greatly shocked at what he found on the hustings. "I am sorry to say that I have seen ladies too joining in with [Whigs] and wearing ribands across their breast with two names printed on them." Johnson's own notorious behavior of living in sin with a black woman did not deter him from pointedly regretting that "ministers of the Gospel and men professing morals are not only looking on with indifference, [but] are actually joining in to carry on their abominations."[63]

The tinge of sexuality conveyed by Johnson's reference to the impropriety of women wearing campaign ribands across their breasts is hardly incidental. Whig and Democrat alike could not have failed to recognize that latent sexuality was part of the volatile mixture that was responsible for the exuberance and high spirits that prevailed in the Harrison campaign. As Gunderson puts it, "their mere presence contributed a new and alluring component to politics."[64] Contemporary accounts of the lively demonstrations that characterized the Whig efforts spoke repeatedly and pointedly of "graceful forms," "exquisitely moulded arms, and delicate hands raised aloft, waving Harrison banners," and of "balconies and windows . . . filled with women, well dressed, with bright eyes and bounding bosoms, waving handkerchiefs, exhibiting flags and garlands, and casting bouquets of flowers upon us."[65] The women, one must assume, were in varying degrees aware of the situation. In this context the ultimate political message was sent by the Tennessee women who would have nothing to do with Democratic men and wore sashes that proclaimed "Whig husbands or none."[66]

ONE OF THE WOMEN swept up in the Whig campaign in Springfield, Illinois, and who may have heard Lincoln deliver his speech to the monster rally in June, was a twenty-one-year-old native of Lexington, Kentucky, Mary Todd. In Springfield on an extended visit to her eldest sister, Elizabeth Todd Edwards, she had been so keenly interested in politics that a family member described her as having been, at age fourteen, "a violent little Whig."[67] In the social center and gathering place that was her sister's home in Springfield, she was surrounded by Whig politicians. Her brother-in-law, Ninian W. Edwards, was serving in the state legislature, as was a prominent cousin, John J. Hardin of Jacksonville. Another cousin, Stephen T. Logan, had twice been elected circuit judge. Her first cousin, John T. Stuart, represented the Springfield district in the U.S. Congress, and during the course of the energetic campaign of 1840, she would be courted by his law partner, Abraham Lincoln.

Mary Todd seems to have arrived in Springfield late in 1839. Well-born and well educated, she was confident and outgoing, and she soon made a strong impression. It was probably at one of her sister's social affairs that Lincoln first met this beguiling visitor. Mary had a high opinion of herself and a sharp tongue, and like Lincoln, she had a love for center stage. She quickly stood out among the fashionable young belles of Springfield, and eligible bachelors soon took note, for as a friend remembered, she was "capable of making herself quite attractive to young gentlemen."[68]

One of her first big social events in Springfield would have been the cotillion party given in December during the first session of the state legislature to be held in Springfield. Lincoln was one of the managers of the cotillion, and his name appeared, along with several others, on a mock-chivalric invitation to an absent favorite, Eliza Browning, the wife of the Whig legislator from Quincy, and the recipient of Lincoln's April Fool letter. Lincoln probably had a hand in writing the light-hearted invitation that referred to Mrs. Browning as "your *Honoress*," but the letter that accompanied the invitation was written by Hardin and contained the best line. Referring to the difficulty of finding lodging in the little town during the legislative session, Hardin gallantly offered "to give you the privilege of hanging on a peg in my closet, whenever it may suit your convenience."[69]

Lincoln's role in this social byplay suggests that he was becoming somewhat more comfortable with Springfield's social scene than he had been in 1837. A tradition that he told Mary Todd on this occasion that he wanted to dance with her "in the worst way," however, seems doubtful. Herndon, who recalled taking a turn around the floor with Mary Todd about this time, scoffed at the idea that Lincoln could dance – "What Lincoln dance? Could a sparrow imitate an eagle" – and there is little evidence to indicate that he was wrong.[70] Nonetheless, Elizabeth Todd Edwards thought Lincoln was attracted to her sister from the first. "He was charmed with Mary's wit and fascinated with her quick sagacity – her will – her nature – and Culture – I have hap-pened in the room where they were sitting often & often and Mary led the conversation – Lincoln would listen & gaze on her as if drawn by some Superior power, irresistably So: he listened – never Scarcely Said a word."[71]

Though markedly different in obvious ways – in education, family background, upbringing – Lincoln and the young Mary Todd had more in common than is usually granted. For one thing, both were fond of reciting poetry. A cousin testified that "Mary's love for poetry, which she was forever reciting, was the cause of many a jest among her friends. Page after page of classic poetry she could recite and liked nothing better."[72] And both were ardent Whigs. Mary had known Lincoln's "beau ideal of a statesman," Henry Clay, from childhood and knew him as a family friend, a circumstance that could not have failed to impress the young politician. She was also ambitious. Her sister Elizabeth later insisted that even before coming to Springfield, Mary had declared her intention of marrying a future president of the United States. She told Herndon: "Mary was quick, lively, gay – frivalous it may be, Social and loved glitter Show & pomp & power. She was an Extremely Ambitious woman and in Ky often & often Contended that She was destined to be the wife of some future President – Said it in my presence in Springfield and Said it in Earnest."73

Elizabeth Edwards admitted that she and her husband at first encouraged this budding interest. Though she regarded Lincoln as having social liabilities and being somewhat standoffish – "a cold Man – had no affection – was not Social – was abstracted – thoughtful" – still, Edwards told Herndon, she "Knew he was a rising Man and nothing Else modifying this, desired Mary at first to Marry L."74 Lincoln's courtship of Mary Todd, thus encouraged by his conspicuous status as "a rising man," exactly coincided with the 1840 political campaign. Elizabeth Edwards testified that "Mr Lincoln Commenced Seeing Mary about 1839 & 4[0] – the winter of 1839 & 40,"75 just as the campaign was taking off. By the time of the presidential election in November, Lincoln and Mary Todd were romantically involved. That the campaign had something to do with their getting together seems inescapable, particularly in view of what happened to their love affair as soon as the election was over: it collapsed. The story of what happened in this strange courtship – how it developed and how it faltered and fell apart – is difficult to piece together, for there are few clues and virtually no direct testimony. As a result, it has been little understood, and most of what has been written about its inception and development is not only largely speculative but largely mistaken.

If Abraham Lincoln and Mary Todd fell in love during the memorable Harrison campaign, if the courtship of Springfield's most famous couple was one of its many colorful episodes, why did no one recall it? The answer seems to be that no one knew about it. Though this at first appears bizarre, there is a reasonably good explanation, the key to which is chronology. During the time when Lincoln and Mary were getting acquainted, the period described by Elizabeth Edwards, Lincoln was anchored in Springfield. In December 1839 and the first few months of 1840, he was first occupied with the legislature, then the Illinois Supreme Court, and then the Sangamon Circuit Court. At the same time, he was busy organizing the Whigs across the state by correspondence and starting up the campaign newspaper, *The Old Soldier*. With the coming of spring, he began to make speaking trips to other localities, often combining these with legal business and court appearances. For the period between the first of April and the election in November, he was gone from Springfield well over half the time, some eighteen to nineteen weeks.[76]

Lincoln was not the only party to this budding romance who traveled. Mary left Springfield for an extended visit to relatives in Columbia, Missouri, sometime in June and did not return until September.[77] A letter written from Columbia in July to her bosom friend, Mercy Ann Levering, betrays no sign of a Springfield love affair, let alone an engagement, though there are some intriguing details. She wrote: "Every week since I left Springfield, have had the felicity of receiving various numbers of their interesting papers, Old Soldiers, Journals & even the *Hickory Club*, has crossed my vision. This latter, rather astonished your friend, *there* I had deemed myself forgotten."[78] This says that someone in Springfield is sending her the Harrison campaign paper (*The Old Soldier*), the Whig paper (*Sangamo Journal*), and, much to her surprise, someone is also sending the Van Buren campaign paper (*Old Hickory*). Mary confesses surprise at having been remembered by the sender of the Democratic paper, possibly a reference to Stephen A. Douglas, who was said to be interested in her.[79] What she mentions next has often been thought to be a reference to Douglas's frequent debating opponent, Abraham Lincoln. "When I mention *some letters*, I have received since leaving S— you will be somewhat surprised, as I *must confess* they were entirely *unlooked for*. this is *between ourselves*, my dearest, but of this more anon; every day I am convinced this is a stranger world we live in, the *past* as the future is to me a mystery."[80] If this refers to unexpected letters (or content) from Lincoln, as seems possible, it is the only contemporary reference to their burgeoning romance.

A family tradition that Mary, while in Missouri, was actually visited by Lincoln is rather conclusively ruled out by the existing evidence of his whereabouts that summer, but he almost certainly was thinking of her. He had himself been away from Springfield for two weeks in April and nearly all of May, so that if he continued to be fascinated by Mary, her departure in June would have been cause for keen regret. Biographers have assumed that Lincoln and Mary were courting by this time, but there is no evidence of any sort of overt courtship between them prior to the Missouri visit, and Mary's letter in July to Mercy Levering, who knew Mary's Springfield life intimately, indicates only that something surprising, private, and of potential interest has been introduced by the unexpected letters. She *does* mention that she and her cousin

Ann are involved in a social whirl, with "many beaux 'dancing atten-dance' on us," and that a certain young lawyer, a grandson of Patrick Henry, "cannot brook the mention of my return." But Mary appears to mention this admirer for the purpose of making the point that however ostentatiously eligible he might appear, he won't do: "I love him not, & my hand will never be given, where my heart is not." She also makes a point of confessing to Mercy that "my beaux have *always* been *hard bargains.*"[81]

If Mary had returned to Springfield eleven days after writing this letter, she would have arrived just in time for the state and local elec-tions on August 3. A candidate for his fourth term in the Illinois legisla-ture, Lincoln was used to leading his party at the polls, but this time he came in fifth, just high enough to retain his seat. Being on the road and heavily involved in a statewide campaign as a Harrison elector may well have compromised his local effort. To judge from Mary's letter and her circumstances, she could hardly have gotten to Springfield any sooner, but the evidence of another contemporary letter indicates that she actu-ally arrived much later. Writing to the same Mercy Ann Levering on September 21, Mercy's devoted suitor, James C. Conkling, spoke of Mary Todd, "who has just returned from Missouri."[82] Even if he was speaking loosely, Mary probably arrived well after the first of Sep-tember, which meant that she missed seeing Abraham Lincoln, who had taken off on an extended speaking trip on August 18.

The import of all this attention to chronology is that Lincoln and Mary did not see each other from sometime in June until he returned briefly to Springfield from his speaking excursion, probably in late Sep-tember, and then for no more than a few days. Mary's July letter to Mercy Levering, which discussed the attention she was getting in Mis-souri but said nothing about a Springfield romance, effectively rules out a serious attachment or engagement before that time. Conkling's letter on September 21 talked about Mary Todd at some length because of Mercy's interest in her. He had first seen her "on a Saturday evening at the Journal Office where some fifteen or twenty ladies were collected together to listen to the Tippecanoe Singing Club."[83] Conkling gos-siped about other friends of Mercy's who were getting married and even described a wedding he attended with Mary Todd, but he said nothing about any attachment to Lincoln. In this letter Conkling described Mary as "the very creature of excitement you know and never enjoys herself more than when in society and surrounded by a company of merry friends," but writing again in late October, he reported that "she did not appear as merry and joyous as usual. It appeared she looked around for former friends and asked 'Where are they?'" The upshot is reasonably clear: if Lincoln and Mary were romantically involved by late October, their friends were unaware of it.

Nonetheless, the basis for a romance had probably already been laid. With local elections over and the national campaign moving into its climactic phase, the Whigs had decided to send a pair of speakers – Secretary of State A. P. Field and Abraham Lincoln – to canvass the southern part of the state, the region known locally as Egypt. The man who knew Abraham Lincoln best during this period, Joshua F. Speed, told Herndon that Lincoln had initiated the affair with Mary Todd by correspondence on his speaking tour. Herndon's notes on his interview read: "In 1840 Lincoln went into the Southern part of the State as Elector Canvasser debator Speaker – Here first wrote his *Mary* – She darted after him – wrote him."[84] Except for Elizabeth Edwards's testimony about Lincoln's early fascination with Mary's wit and conversation, which presumably refers to the time when they first met, Speed's is the only authoritative testimony about the inception of this elusive love affair. It suggests that being on the road and constantly stimulated by the provocative participation of women at political rallies prompted Lincoln to think of Mary, a passionate Whig and active campaigner. She confessed to Mercy Levering in December that during the campaign she had become "quite a *politician*, rather an unladylike profession, yet at such a *crisis*, whose heart could remain untouched while the energies of all were in question?"[85]

Lincoln seems to have returned from speaking in Egypt in late September, but his known whereabouts in the weeks following indicate that he could have been in Springfield only a few days before joining the circuit to represent the clients of Stuart & Lincoln.[86] Thereafter his court appearances and stump speaking kept him far afield for another six weeks, and he did not return until several days after the presidential election on November 2. The implications of all this time spent on the road electioneering are all too clear. If he had managed to spark a love affair with Mary Todd by mail during the summer or early fall, Lincoln could have spent no more than a few days in her company. And very soon after his return to Springfield – within days, in fact – he decided he had made a mistake.

~~

WHAT CAUSED this sudden change of heart? Though this has been a matter of wide speculation in Lincoln biography, seen in the light of the events just outlined, it is probably less mysterious than it has appeared. In the first place, it should not be too surprising that a romance conceived and nourished by correspondence might falter when the would-be lovers come face-to-face. Since they had spent almost no time in each other's presence as lovers, there would be the inevitable problems of how to address each other, how familiar to be, and how, in general, to behave. Particularly if one's idea of what a person is like has been the product of one's own imagination, the reality is bound to be different.

And Mary apparently *was* different from the woman Lincoln had become acquainted with in the early months of 1840 – physically different. Conkling's letter of September 21, which announced her return from Missouri, slyly makes fun of her increase in size. "Verily, I believe the further West a young lady goes the better her health becomes. If she comes here she is sure to grow – if she visits Missouri she will soon grow out of our recollection and if she should visit the Rocky Mountains I know not what would become of her. Miss Todd certainly does improve astonishingly and soon bids fair to rival Mrs. Glenn if she does not exceed old Father Lambert."[87] That Mary herself was concerned about her weight is evidenced in her next letter to Mercy Levering, in which she confessed: "I still am the same ruddy *pineknot*, only not quite as great an exuberance of flesh, as it once was my lot to contend with, although quite a sufficiency."[88] Lincoln, who had once expressed interest in courting an absent woman who turned out to be "a fair match for Falstaff," must have experienced something like déjà vu.

Joshua Speed told Herndon that the cause of Lincoln's falling out of love with Mary was another woman, Matilda Edwards. "Lincoln – seeing an other girl – & finding he did not love [Mary] wrote a leter saying he did not love her."[89] Having gotten the affair started by letter some weeks earlier, Lincoln apparently hoped to end it the same way. But Speed says he told Lincoln this was a mistake: "Words are forgotten – Misunderstood – passed by – not noticed in a private Conversation – but once put your words in writing and they Stand as a living & eternal Monument against you."[90] Besides, it was cowardly to break off in this way, Speed implied, and he persuaded Lincoln to tell

Mary in person. Herndon's telegraphic notes on the story as told by Speed read: "Went to see 'Mary' – told her that he did not love her – She rose – and Said 'The deciever shall be decieved wo is me.'; alluding to a young man She fooled – Lincoln drew her down on his Knee – Kissed her – & parted – He going one way & She an other."[91] Back in their room, Speed pronounced the sympathetic kiss "a bad lick," because it effectively canceled the intended breakup, but allowed "it cannot now be helped."[92]

Mary's reaction, as recalled by Speed, suggests two things. The first is that in blaming herself for losing Lincoln's love, she was probably thinking of her well-attested flirtations with other men, Stephen A. Douglas in particular, which were apparently intended to make Lincoln jealous and more attentive (the deceiver is deceived). The second is that at least in this interview, Lincoln had not mentioned the true reason for his change of heart, Matilda Edwards. Matilda was the strikingly beautiful eighteen-year-old daughter of an eminent Illinois Whig, Cyrus Edwards of Alton.[93] Lincoln may have met her when he spoke at Alton in April, but she does not seem to have figured in this story until she arrived in Springfield with her father about a week or so after Lincoln had returned to town.[94] Lincoln could not have missed her arrival, for she lodged at the home of her cousin, Ninian W. Edwards, living under the same roof and possibly sleeping in the same bed as Mary Todd. In her first letter home, Matilda noted that Joseph Gillespie, her father's protégé and traveling companion, had "found a second Caroline in Miss Mary Todd. She is a very lovely and sprightly girl."[95] This serves as a reminder that as of November 30, however things stood privately between them, Mary Todd was not publicly engaged to Abraham Lincoln but was free to entertain the attentions of another man.

Assuming that Lincoln and Mary Todd had some kind of relationship in mid-November 1840, what was it? If they were engaged to be married, there is no contemporary evidence of it. Speed's story points to a love affair conceived in the mind of an absent campaigner that quickly unraveled when he came home, with no mention of an engagement. But his version maintains that Lincoln's first attempt to get out of the relationship was a failure because of Mary's self-reproach and Lincoln's tenderheartedness. According to Speed, there was a second encounter somewhat later on with far more dramatic results. Herndon's notes on this part of his interview with Speed read as follows: "Lincoln did love Miss Edwards – 'Mary' saw it – told Lincoln the reason of his change of mind – heart & soul – released him – Lincoln went crazy – had to remove razors from his room – take away all knives and other such dangerous things – &c – it was terrible – was during the Special session of the Ills Legislature in 1840."[96]

What could have happened to cause Lincoln, the "rising man" who was beginning to achieve real status and recognition, suddenly to become, in the eyes of his roommate, mentally unhinged and possibly suicidal? Here again, we have very little to go on, but chronology provides some clues. If Speed's account is correct, Lincoln's first attempt to break up with Mary came when he saw another woman, presumably Matilda Edwards, and realized he did not love Mary. This would have been sometime after the middle of November, when Matilda arrived, only a few days after his return to Springfield. The second, more shattering encounter occurred during the special sessions of the legislature, which ran from November 23 to December 5. If Speed remembered this detail correctly, both meetings must have occurred within a period of about three weeks.

If we look for reasons for stress in Lincoln's life at this juncture, they are not hard to find. He had put in a solid year of hard campaigning, in which he assumed a lion's share of his party's organizing, planning, writing, and speaking. He had been frequently on the road at a time when that meant traveling dirt roads on horseback, in all weathers, staying in overcrowded inns and hotels, sleeping several persons to a room, and eating wretched food. When he returned after the election, he had just finished a grueling stretch of nearly three months on the road, giving stump speeches to strange and sometime hostile crowds almost daily, while trying to make as many court dates and snag as many clients as he could. David Davis told Herndon that "Lincoln was around Every where discussing politics: . . . Douglas & Lincoln went in 1840 all around the Circuit with [Circuit Judge] Treat, & Spoke in the afternoon."[97] And while Harrison won the national election, Lincoln's strenuous effort to carry Illinois for the Whigs had failed by a painfully narrow margin. In short, arriving in Springfield in November 1840, Abraham Lincoln must have been physically and emotionally exhausted.

And he had to go right back to work. The Sangamon Circuit Court opened on November 9, a day or two after he arrived, and its sessions overlapped the beginning of the special session of the legislature two weeks later, when Lincoln was expected to lead the Whigs in the House of Representatives. The governor had called the special session – to be held two weeks before the start of the regular session – to deal with the problem of a dangerously accelerating state debt, caused by the improvident system of internal improvements that Lincoln and his fellow legislators had rashly put through in 1837. The reversal of these actions, which were bankrupting the state, must have caused Lincoln real pain and embarrassment, as did the Whigs' futile efforts to save the State Bank. It was in the service of this doomed cause that Lincoln committed an act of folly for which he suffered instant ridicule and humiliation, the memory of which pained him the rest of his life. This was his infamous leap out the window of the Second Presbyterian Church.

On the last day of the special session, as part of a desperate move to keep the members of the Democratic majority from passing an antibank measure by denying them a quorum, Whig members refused to appear at the church, which was serving as temporary quarters for the House of Representatives. Lincoln and two other Whig members attended to make sure that the ayes and nays were called and that the absence of a quorum was duly observed. This worked for a time, but to their astonishment, after they had demanded another roll call and been counted present, the tally showed that the sergeant at arms had managed to round up enough members to produce a quorum. Barred from absenting themselves by the doors, the panicked Whigs opened a window and scrambled out.[98] This, of course, availed them nothing as far as the quorum was concerned, for there were no Whigs left to demand another roll call, but its resounding effect was to make Lincoln a laughingstock. The *Illinois State Register* recorded the incident with particular relish:

> Mr. Lincoln, of Sangamon, who was present during the whole scene, and who appeared to enjoy the embarrassment of the House, suddenly looked very grave after the Speaker announced that a quorum was present. The conspiracy having failed, Mr. Lincoln, came under great excitement, and having attempted and failed to get out the door, very unceremoniously raised the window and jumped out, followed by one or two other members. This gymnastic performance of Mr. Lincoln and his flying brethren did not occur until after they had voted and consequently the House did not interfere with their extraordinary feat. We have not learned whether these flying members got hurt in their adventure, and we think it probable that at least one of them came off without damage, as it was noticed that his legs reached nearly from the window to the ground![99]

The humiliation of this inglorious escapade was painful and immediate. Coming as it did at a time of demonstrable stress, it seems the kind of event that could have been related – as either partial cause or effect – to the dramatic emotional breakdown that Speed described for Herndon: "Lincoln went crazy – had to remove razors from his room – take away all knives and other such dangerous things – &c – it was terrible." If this happened as and when Speed remembered it, the breakdown's debilitating effects were short-lived, for Lincoln continued to appear in the legislature during this period.

But if one can glimpse some of the extraordinary physical and emotional stress that Lincoln may have been subject to, what was it that triggered the "crazy spell," as it was called? Speed's brief account says only that Mary confronted Lincoln with the fact that he didn't love her but instead loved someone else, Matilda Edwards. "Lincoln did love Miss Edwards – 'Mary' saw it – told Lincoln the reason of his change of mind – heart & soul – released him." This sounds like the kind of encounter Lincoln was hoping for, with Mary saying, in effect, "I know you don't love me, and I know the reason, so don't feel obligated to me." Why would such a development cause Lincoln to go off the deep end?

Assuredly, Speed's cryptic account as reported by Herndon doesn't tell the whole story. Speed's version came from Lincoln, but Herndon collected other accounts that came through Mary. One of these was that of her brother-in-law Ninian W. Edwards: "Says – Sept 22d 1865 – That during Lincoln's Courtship with Miss Todd – afterwards Lincoln's wife – that he, Lincoln, fell in Love with [Matilda] Edwards . . . the Lincoln and Todd engagement was broken off in consequence of it – Miss Todd released Lincoln from the Contract, leaving Lincoln the privilege of renewing it . . . if he wished – Lincoln in his conflicts of duty – honor and his love went crazy as a *Loon*."[100] Edwards undoubtedly believed that there had been a formal engagement, a contract, that was broken because of Lincoln's falling in love with Matilda Edwards. The other account that came through Mary was that of her sister and Ninian's wife, Elizabeth, who had her own version of what happened. She told Herndon:

> Mr Lincoln loved Mary – he went Crazy in my own opinion – not because he loved Miss Edwards as Said, but because he wanted to marry and doubted his ability & Capacity to please and support a wife. Lincoln & Mary were Engaged – Every thing was ready & prepared for the marriage – Even to the Supper &c – . Mr L failed to meet his Engagement – Cause insanity. In his lunacy he declared he

hated Mary and loved Miss Edwds. This is true, yet it was not his real feelings. A Crazy man hates those he loves when at himself.[101]

Elizabeth Edwards believed not only that the couple was engaged but that in the winter of 1840–41 they came within an ace of being married. Herndon took this sensational testimony to mean that Lincoln's crazy spell resulted in Mary's being left at the altar by a defaulting bridegroom. There is little doubt that this is what Elizabeth Edwards intended, for she repeated her story independently for Herndon's collaborator, Jesse W. Weik. But no one else remembered this abortive wedding ceremony, and it now seems reasonably certain that she was mistaken.[102]

Herndon collected one other version of the story that purports to come through Lincoln, that of James H. Matheny. Herndon's notes on the interview with Matheny read: "That Lincoln often told him directly & indirectly that he was driven into the marriage – Said it was Concocted & planned by the Edwards family – : That Miss Todd – afterwards Mr's Lincoln told L. that he was in honor bound to marry her – : That Lincoln was crazy for a week or so – not knowing what to do – : That he loved Miss Matilda Edwards and went to see her and not Mrs Lincoln – Miss Todd."[103]

Much, if not all, of Matheny's information from Lincoln appears to have come after the affair and by way of justification. As Matheny's full testimony makes clear, Lincoln had a political motive for depicting his marriage in this light, for he was losing popularity with younger Whigs for having married into the Springfield aristocracy. But Herndon's interview with Matheny contains a potentially important piece of testimony that, if accurate, could help explain not only why Lincoln might have thought the Edwards family had maneuvered him into an unwanted situation but also why he subsequently went "crazy as a Loon." This is the recollection that Mary Todd told Lincoln "that he was in honor bound to marry her." The idea that he could be represented as having behaved dishonorably toward a woman was indeed the kind of emotional dynamite that could have blown Lincoln's mental composure.

∽

MARY'S FAMILY spoke of an "engagement," whereas Speed and Matheny did not.[104] This may reflect a difference in terminology, or it may point to a real disagreement between Lincoln and Mary Todd about the status of their relationship. The common element in their stories, besides his "crazy spell," is Matilda Edwards. All agree that Lincoln's feelings for her had something to do with the difficulty; this included Elizabeth Edwards, who thought Lincoln's saying he loved Matilda proved his lunacy. Herndon, who got married in the spring of 1840 and moved out of the store, was not himself close to this situation and obtained virtually all his information from others. He was at first persuaded by the testimony about Matilda Edwards, but after years of brooding over the question, he realized that he had to choose between this story and that of Elizabeth Edwards. Herndon eventually decided that Edwards could not be mistaken about a matter that so nearly concerned her, an ill-judged decision that has damaged his reputation as a biographer.

In trying to identify a date on which Lincoln might have failed to appear for his own wedding, Herndon hit upon a telling reference occurring in a later letter from Lincoln to Speed to "that fatal first of Jany. '41." Though Lincoln biographers have long abandoned Elizabeth Edwards's improbable story of an abortive wedding ceremony, they have clung to Herndon's theory that something decisive happened on that day in Lincoln's life. The context of the letter, as we shall see, makes it appear that Lincoln may well have been referring to something that happened on that date to Speed, but most biographers have calculated that the "fatal first" must have been the day when a Lincoln-Todd engagement was broken or, as the editors of the *Collected Works* phrase it, when "Lincoln asked to be released from his engagement to Mary Todd."[105] Perhaps so, but there is no testimony or other compelling evidence to this effect.

Speed, who was closer to Lincoln than anyone else during this period, said the relationship was ruptured three to four weeks earlier, during the special session of the legislature. Moreover, he told Herndon that after the break "Lincoln kept his promises and did not go to see her for months,"[106] casting doubt on speculation that Lincoln asked for his release on January 1, 1841. Competing claims are hard to adjudicate in the absence of evidence, but as it happens, there is a contemporary document that bears on this issue, a letter written from Springfield about the middle of December 1840 conveying news of the social circle to which our principals belonged. It was written by Mary Todd.

Almost as if written in anticipation of our curiosity, Mary's letter to

Mercy Ann Levering in Baltimore talks about all the things we are interested in: Lincoln, Speed, who is being attentive to whom, who is engaged and about to commit "the crime of matrimony," and even an appraisal of the new girl, Matilda Edwards. Here is the passage in Mary's letter that introduces her:

> Mr Edwards has a cousin from Alton spending the winter with us, a most interesting young lady, her fascinations, have drawn a concourse of beaux & company round us, occasionally, I *feel as Miss Whitney* [unidentified], we have too much of such useless commodities, you know it takes some time for habit to render us familiar with what we are not greatly accustomed to – Could you step in upon us some evenings in these "western wilds," you would be astonished at the change, *time* has wrought on the hill, I would my Dearest, you now were with us, be assured your name is most frequently mentioned in our circle, *words of mine* are not necessary to assure you of the loss I have sustained in your society, on my return from Missouri, my time passed most heavily, I feel quite made up, in my present companion, a congenial spirit I assure you. I know you would be pleased with Matilda Edwards, a lovelier girl I never saw. *Mr Speed's* ever changing heart I suspect is about offering *its young* affections at her shrine, with some others, there is considerable acquisition in our society of *marriagable gentlemen*, unfortunately only "birds of passage." *Mr Webb*, a widower of modest merit, last winter is our *principal lion*, dances attendance very frequently, we expect a very gay winter, . . .[107]

When she announces Matilda's presence, Mary acknowledges that this had "drawn a concourse of beaux & company round us," implying that this cast her in an unaccustomed role that she hadn't gotten used to. Before returning to the interesting subject she has raised – Matilda's attracting a "concourse of beaux" – she writes of how much she misses her old friend Mercy. In reintroducing the visitor, Mary gives Matilda her due as a "congenial spirit" and beautiful girl and then mentions Joshua Speed as one of the concourse of beaux. Speed was presumably Matilda's most notable suitor because of his reputation for an "ever changing heart," but Mary specifies that there were "some others." According to Herndon's informants, Abraham Lincoln was one of these.

This passage concludes with a very clear statement of who among the *"marriagable gentlemen"* is paying Mary the most attention. Edwin ("Bat") Webb, a widower and a Whig legislator, is her *"principal lion,"* and he comes to see her often or, as she puts it, "dances attendance very frequently." What about Lincoln, who, according to most biographers, was at this time either engaged or very nearly engaged to the writer of this letter? He is mentioned by name twice, though it is far from clear what the first reference means. Characterizing the way things have changed since Mercy was in Springfield, Mary writes: "Speed's 'grey suit' has gone the way of *all flesh*, an interesting suit of *Harrison blues* have replaced his *sober livery*, Lincoln's, *lincoln green* have gone to dust, Mr Webb sports a *mourning p[in]* by way of reminding us *damsels*, that we *'cannot come it.'* "[108] The other reference to Lincoln concerns an excursion that is in preparation: "we have a pleasant jaunt in contemplation, to Jacksonville, next week there to spend a day or two, Mr Hardin & Browning are our leaders the van brought up by Miss E[dwards] my humble self, Webb, Lincoln & two or three others whom you know not, we are watching the clouds most anxiously trusting it may snow, so we may have a sleigh ride – Will it not be pleasant?"[109] The leaders of this proposed jaunt, Hardin and Browning, were married, and Webb, as Mary has indicated, could be expected to be "dancing attendance" on her.

Herndon and others have suggested that Mary's courtship strategy was to play one suitor off against another, and that may well be what her reported speech to Lincoln about the deceiver's being deceived was all about. She protested in a letter to Mercy Levering six months later that in spite of the impression she had given in her letters, she was not interested in Webb, who was nearly twenty years older, and that she then "deeply regretted" the impression his pursuit of her had on others, probably meaning Lincoln. So it is possible that the situation described in this letter is one in which she is trying to attract Lincoln's attention or make him jealous by pretending to enjoy the attentions of Webb. But it does not seem possible to read this letter as consistent with an existing but unacknowledged engagement. If there was an engagement between Lincoln and Mary Todd, it must have been either before or after this letter of mid-December 1840.

Most Lincoln biographers have taken the position that Abraham and Mary had been actively courting much of the year and were at this point already engaged, but if forced to make this choice, most would probably place the supposed engagement later rather than earlier. And for understandable reasons. In spite of the fact that Speed said the relationship was ruptured earlier, his testimony to this effect has been largely overlooked and seems, in fact, at odds with other evidence. There is, in the first instance, Lincoln's eye-catching reference to "that fatal first of

Jany. '41." There is also clear evidence, for example, that Lincoln became so afflicted by what he called "hypochondriaism" during that month that he was unable to attend the legislature for more than a week. This episode was identified by witnesses on the scene as the result, in the words of Lyman Trumbull, of his "love affairs which some of his friends feared had well-nigh unsettled his mental faculties."[110] Moreover, the well-documented January episode has readily absorbed the vivid testimony about a "crazy spell," the incident that Speed believed happened several weeks earlier and was but the prelude to the January breakdown.

So what does it matter whether there was an actual engagement or not, whether the couple broke up in early December or early January, and whether there were two episodes of mental aberration or one? Actually, it matters a great deal. The standard account of this courtship has Lincoln and Mary actively courting over the course of the year and becoming engaged sometime before year's end.[111] Then, on January 1, 1841, something happened that resulted in their engagement's being broken. Most biographers follow Elizabeth Edwards's view that Lincoln lost his nerve, that he "doubted his ability & Capacity to please and support a wife." As a result of backing out of this engagement, Lincoln slowly sank into a deep depression in January 1841 from which he only gradually emerged.

Consider how this contrasts with the story presented here thus far: Lincoln found himself attracted to the vivacious visitor from Kentucky but didn't know how to approach her. After they had become acquainted, either he was on the road campaigning or she was away visiting relatives, so he finally approached her by mail in the late summer or early fall, and she responded eagerly. With Lincoln constantly on the road, they had at most a few days together before his return in November, at which point he almost immediately decided to break it off. The cause of this change of heart was nominally Lincoln's interest in another woman, Matilda Edwards, but Mary apparently told him that backing out under these circumstances was dishonorable. This charge plunged him into a brief but violent despair in late November or early December, an outburst that Speed feared was suicidal. Lincoln thereafter avoided calling on Mary, but a complicating factor appeared when it developed that Speed, Lincoln's guide and confidant, was also in love with Matilda Edwards and went so far as to propose. All of this made a shambles of Lincoln's emotional life and caused his slide into the deep depression of mid-January.

These are two very different stories, but what really matters is that they have markedly different implications for the emerging character of Abraham Lincoln. One is about a man in love who has found the right woman but whose doubts get the better of him. The other is about a man who discovers too late that his fascination with a "creature of excitement" was superficial, but whose connection to her has somehow become entangled with his personal honor. The conventional story has been abandoned here, not because the other story is more complex and more interesting, as it undoubtedly is, but because of the evidence. The conventional view of the courtship is not supported by contemporary documents, such as Mary's own letters and those of her friends; it pays no heed to what Lincoln's closest friend and confidant, Joshua Speed, said about the origin and timing of the affair; and it also ignores the clear and consistent testimony of those closest to the principals that Lincoln said at the time that he did not love Mary but loved Matilda Edwards instead.[112]

❧

AFTER HIS NOMINATION to the presidency in 1860, Lincoln received a letter from a woman to whom he replied: "Your kind congratulatory letter, of August, was received in due course – and should have been answered sooner. The truth is I have never corresponded much with ladies; and hence I postpone writing letters to them, as a business which I do not understand."[113] Though he was probably not thinking about the letter he wrote to Mary Todd in 1840 that started all the trouble, what he wrote in 1860 suggests that his experience in this line had been limited and not happy. Certainly he must have been bewildered in 1840 to find that his epistolary expressions of romantic interest in Mary Todd, which he soon found were misplaced, could have entangled him so tightly in the long, drawn-out affair that his friend Jesse K. Dubois later christened the Mary Todd "embrigglement."[114]

One element in the equation was surely Mary's volatile personality and temperament. Lincoln had known Mary only from seeing her on social occasions, where as a newcomer she was putting her most charming foot forward. He could hardly have been aware that she had what her Springfield acquaintances would later recognize as a violent temper.[115] Her family did not so much deny this quality as present it in a more positive light. Of her behavior during this period her sister Elizabeth wrote: "She was also impulsive and made no attempt to conceal her feelings; indeed, it would have been an impossibility had she desired to do so, for her face was an index to every passing emotion. Without desiring to wound, she occasionally indulged in sarcastic, witty remarks, that cut like a damascus blade, but there was no malice behind them."[116] A young woman who could wound by words without intending to was presumably even more dangerous when angry and aroused.

Lincoln had proved himself a strong, resilient man with a thick skin and the ability to retain his self-composure in the face of difficulty. But, as we have seen, he also had deep and tender feelings and an uncertain sense of his own identity and social standing, and he could not always control his emotions. Mary's angry charge that he was behaving dishonorably must have found his vulnerable spot like a heat-seeking missile. His brother-in-law pinpointed the crux of the problem when he told Herndon: "Lincoln in his conflicts of duty – honor and his love went as crazy as a *Loon*."[117] Mary admitted to the biographer Josiah Holland that during their courtship she had "trespassed, many times & oft, upon his great tenderness & amiability of character."[118] Had she been a man, he would have known how to respond: he could have ridiculed her in public, planted a malicious piece about her in the newspaper, or knocked her down and left her a-kicking. But women were a special problem for him, and this incident is a prime case in point. How to comport oneself with women on a regular basis was difficulty enough; how to deal with the turbulent emotions of a courtship in crisis an even greater challenge; but how to defend one's honor against a woman scorned was too much for him.

Chapter 8

THE MARY TODD
"EMBRIGGLEMENT"

WRITING HOME to his son in Alton, State Senator Cyrus
Edwards, in Springfield attending the state legislature,
reported a social outing in progress: "Your Sister [Matilda]
started with Miss Todd for Jacksonville on Thursday morning under
the protection of Mr Hardin, accompanied by Gillespie, Lincoln,
Webb and Brown of Vermilion. They will return on Monday. We miss
them very much."[1] This was the excursion that Mary Todd was looking
forward to in her December 1840 letter to Mercy Ann Levering, an
excursion that seemed to anticipate a pairing not only of herself and her
"principal lion," Edwin ("Bat") Webb, but of Senator Edwards's
daughter, Matilda, and Abraham Lincoln. The senator's letter is dated
only "Decr. 1840," but the evidence of Lincoln's known whereabouts
shows that this absence from Springfield could have occurred only over
the Christmas holiday, between Thursday, December 24, and Tuesday,
December 29, when Lincoln was back on the floor of the legislature. It
is possible that the entire party returned from Jacksonville intact, but as
Edwards's letter was not postmarked until Tuesday, December 29, it is
also possible that the women stayed over and that the Monday on
which they were expected was the following one, January 4. Thus, Lincoln and Mary Todd could not have had a confrontation of any kind on
"that fatal first of Jany. 41" if he was in Springfield and she was still in
Jacksonville.[2]

Lincoln's taking part in a social outing and his regular appearance on
the floor of the legislature suggest that he was functioning perfectly well

in December 1840. But his friend Speed recalled that this was about the time Lincoln became sufficiently concerned about his health to write a letter to a famous Cincinnati physician. Responding to William H. Herndon's lecture on Lincoln and Ann Rutledge and the deep and lasting effect it supposedly had on him, Speed told Herndon that he knew nothing of that affair but recalled: "Lincoln wrote a letter (a long one which he read to me) to Dr [Daniel] Drake of Cincinnatti discriptive of his case. Its date would be in Decer 40 or early in January 41. – I think that he must have informed Dr D of his early love for Miss Rutledge – as there was a part of the letter which he would not read."[3] Speed's identification of what was in the letter that Lincoln would not let him see is, of course, highly speculative, but it is worth noting that in retrospect, he readily associated what he *did* hear with Lincoln's reported state of mind following the death of Ann Rutledge.

Except for Lincoln's allusion fifteen months later to "that fatal first of Jany. 41," there is no evidence of anything unusual happening in Lincoln's life on January 1. Herndon took this reference to mean that the aborted wedding ceremony that Elizabeth Edwards described must have happened on this date, but she seems to have confused this with another occasion.[4] Lincoln's allusion may very well relate to something of moment in the life of his friend Joshua Speed, who sold out his interest in James Bell & Co. to Charles Hurst, who also lived over the store with Lincoln and Speed. Speed told Herndon, "I sold out to Hurst 1 Jany 1841. and came to Ky in the spring," but there is no indication that he and Lincoln experienced an immediate change in living quarters.[5] If Speed had already decided to go back to Kentucky when he sold out, this would indeed have affected Lincoln, but since there is also strong evidence that Speed and Lincoln were at this time in love with the same woman, it seems likely that his feelings, already in considerable turmoil, were mixed.

Lincoln attended the legislature as usual, but soon after the first of the year he began to show signs of losing control. On January 8, the clever man whose shrewd use of humor and self-deprecation made him such an effective speaker on the floor of the House lashed out in uncharacteristic anger and had to be called to order by the Speaker. Taunted by a slighting reference to "that jumping scrape" (the leap from the church window), "Mr. Lincoln said that as to jumping, he should jump when he pleased and no one should hinder him."[6] He tried to regain his composure a day or so later by replying to the same antagonist in a more characteristic vein. Picturing himself as the longest of the "Long Nine," Lincoln was reported as saying: "I desire to say to my friend from Monroe (Mr. Bissell) that if any woman, old or young, ever thought there was any peculiar charm in this distinguished specimen of number 9, I have, as yet, been so unfortunate as not to have discovered it."[7] A few days later, as a result of his ill-fortuned relations with women, he was sunk too deeply in depression to attend the legislature at all.

Dr. Anson Henry, the man whose candidacy Lincoln was attempting to advance in the luckless contest with James Adams, ministered to his despondent friend, who was confined for about a week.[8] Herndon assumed that the "crazy spell" Speed had described, when Lincoln appeared suicidal, was part of this same well-documented episode, but the testimony indicates otherwise. Ida M. Tarbell interviewed one of Lincoln's fellow legislators, H. W. Thornton, many years later, and he told her: "Mr Lincoln boarded at W*m* Butlers near to Dr. Henry's where I boarded – The missing days from Jan. 12*th* to 19*th* Mr Lincoln spent several hours each day at Dr. Henry's (his physicians Drs. Henry & Merryman) a part of these days I remained with Mr Lincoln[.] His most intimate friends had no fears of his injuring himself[.] He was very sad and melancholly, but being subject to these spells, nothing serious apprehended."[9] Another close friend who claimed to be an observer of Lincoln's condition painted a somewhat different picture. Orville H. Browning told John G. Nicolay that he also lived at the Butlers' and that for about a week Lincoln "was so much affected as to talk incoherently, and to be delirious to the extent of not knowing what he was doing," but he said nothing about Lincoln's being suicidal and indicated that the "his derange[ment] lasted only about a week or such a matter."[10] Browning's summary judgment of the incident was succinct: "I think that Mr. Lincoln's aberration of mind resulted entirely from the situation he thus got himself into – he was engaged to Miss Todd, and in love with Miss Edwards, and his conscience troubled him dreadfully for the supposed injustice he had done, and the supposed violation of his word which he had committed."[11]

The wife of William Butler, who cooked and laundered for Lincoln before he was married, apparently helped care for him at this time and was therefore presumably knowledgeable about his condition.[12] She told her sister, Sarah Rickard, that she had asked Lincoln directly about his despondency. Sarah subsequently told a reporter:

Mr Lincoln did not seem to recover, and my sister, who had watched him closely, decided that he had something on his mind. At last she decided upon a plan of action, and one day went into Mr. Lincoln's room, closed the door, and walking over to the bed, said: "Now, Abraham, what is the matter? Tell me all about it."

And he did. Suffering under the thought that he had treated Mary badly, knowing that she loved him and that he did not love her, Mr. Lincoln was wearing his very life away in an agony of remorse. He made no excuse for breaking with Mary, but said, sadly, to my sister: "Mrs. Butler, it would just kill me to marry Mary Todd."[13]

That his debility was connected to his unfortunate "love affairs," as Lyman Trumbull put it, was apparently common gossip in Springfield and was treated as considerably less than tragic by some of his friends. The women of the John J. Hardin family, who had entertained Lincoln and his friends over Christmas at Jacksonville, came to Springfield for socializing in early January. Upon returning home on January 16, Hardin's younger sister, Netty, wrote back to her brother: "We have been very much distressed, on Mr Lincolns account; hearing he had two Cat fits, and a Duck fit since we left. Is it true? Do let us hear soon."[14] Hardin apparently reassured his family about the condition of his friend, for his wife, Sarah, wrote him on January 26: "I am glad to hear Lincoln has got over his cat fits[.] we have concluded it was a very unsatfactory way of terminating his romance[.] he ought to have died or gone crazy[.] we are very much dissapointed[.] indeed Jane Goudy has made him the hero of a tale but she say[s] it will never do for him to get well."[15]

Although he apparently resumed his attendance of the legislature on January 19,[16] the melancholy and emaciated Lincoln had become an object of pity as well as humor among his associates. On January 20, he wrote his partner John T. Stuart a brief letter to urge the appointment of Dr. Henry as the Springfield postmaster. "I have, within the last few days, been making a most discreditable exhibition of myself in the way of hypochondriaism and thereby got an impression that Dr. Henry is necessary to my existence."[17] Three days later he confessed in a letter to Stuart: "I am now the most miserable man living. If what I feel were equally distributed to the whole human family, there would not be one cheerful face on the earth. Whether I shall ever be better I can not tell; I awfully forebode I shall not. To remain as I am is impossible; I must die or be better, it appears to me."[18]

Reminiscences of incidents like this are admittedly not nearly so authoritative as contemporary evidence, such as Lincoln's own letters. Fortunately, two other contemporary accounts of Lincoln's condition in January 1841 have survived. One is a straightforward account in a letter to Kentucky, in which a relative of James Bell responds to a query about the eye-catching romance of two former Kentuckians – the upstart politician, Abraham Lincoln, and the aristocratic belle, Mary Todd. Jane D. Bell wrote her correspondent:

> Miss Todd is flourishing largely. She has a great many Beaus.
> You ask me how she and Mr. Lincoln are getting along. Poor fellow, he is in rather a bad way. Just at present though he is on the mend now as he was out on Monday for the first time for a month dying with love they say. The Doctors say he came within an inch of being a perfect lunatic for life. He was perfectly crazy for some time, not able to attend to his business at all. They say he don't look like the same person. It seems he had addressed Mary Todd and she accepted him and they had been engaged some time when a Miss Edwards of Alton came here, and he fell desperately in love with her and found he was not so much attached to Mary as he thought. He says if he had it in his power he would not have one feature in her face altered, he thinks she is so perfect (that is, Miss E.) He and Mr. Speed have spent the most of their time at Edwards this winter and Lincoln could never bear to leave Miss Edward's side in company. Some of his friends thought he was acting very wrong and very imprudently and told him so and he went crazy on the strength of it so the story goes and that is all I know . . . [torn off] No one but Speed . . . [torn off][19]

The letter shows that the Lincoln-Todd affair had, by this time, become the subject of keen interest even back in Kentucky. Jane Bell does not claim to know the facts and repeats only what she has heard, but she did have connections to Speed, and her information seems to come from that quarter. Like the Hardins, Mrs. Bell cannot suppress her mild amusement at Lincoln's bizarre behavior. Neither could James C. Conkling, who on January 24 wrote at length on the subject to his sweetheart, Mercy Ann Levering, in Baltimore.

> Last evening I spent upon the Hill [*the site of the Edwards and Levering homes*]. Mrs. L. informed me she had lately written you and had given you some particulars about Abraham, Joshua and Jacob. [*Mrs. Lawrason Levering writing about Lincoln, Speed, and Conkling (Jacob Faithful)*] Poor L! how are the mighty fallen! He was confined about a week, but though he now appears again he is reduced and emaciated in appearance and seems scarcely to possess strength enough to

speak above a whisper. His case at present is truly deplorable but what prospect there may be for ultimate relief I cannot pretend to say I doubt not but he can declare "That loving is a painful thrill, And not to love more painful still" but would not like to intimate that he has experienced "That surely 'tis the worst of pain To love and not be loved again."

And Joshua too is about to leave. I know not what dreadful blow may be inflicted upon the interests of our State by his departure.[20]

Had not Mrs. Levering already written Mercy with "some particulars about Abraham, Joshua, and Jacob," Conkling's letter might have drawn a clearer and more straightforward picture of Lincoln's predicament. But the obscure verse he quotes tell us that it involves the discovery on Lincoln's part that loving can be a "painful thrill," and not loving can prove "more painful still." This surely fits the situation Lincoln found himself in with Mary Todd. The part about the worst pain – that it comes from love that is not reciprocated – aptly describes his situation with Matilda Edwards.

⤙

IT BECOMES increasingly clear that Lincoln's debility was directly related to what he and others perceived as his obligations to Mary Todd. But uncertainties abound. Was he engaged to her? And if so, why could he not honorably change his mind and break the engagement if he no longer wanted to marry her? Had Mary released him? Is it reasonable to suppose that she was holding him to a proposal even while entertaining the attentions of other men such as Bat Webb, and all the time "flourishing largely" on the social scene? There is evidence that the situation was genuinely confused, at least in the minds of observers. A member of the family, the wife of Ninian W. Edwards's brother Benjamin, remembered that particular winter because her house was across from the Second Presbyterian Church at the only time it was the temporary home of the House of Representatives. "I heard a rumor of an engagement between Mr. Lincoln and Mary Todd, yet I considered it one of those unfounded reports always floating in society, for I really thought Mr. Douglas was more assiduous in his attentions than Mr. Lincoln."[21] Like her sister-in-law Elizabeth Edwards, she was entertaining young women who had come to town for the social scene associated with the meeting of the legislature: "our house seemed the favorite rendezvous for all these young girls, who often tried to tease Mary about her 'tall beau.' She bore their jokes and teasings good naturedly but would give them no satisfaction, neither affirming nor denying the report of her engagement to Mr. Lincoln."[22]

If Mrs. Benjamin S. Edwards remembered this correctly, Mary contributed to the confusion by refusing, at least in this instance, to affirm the engagement or deny it. Her elder sister acknowledged to Herndon that the situation for Mary became awkward. "The world had it that Mr L backed out. and this placed Mary in a peculiar Situation & to set herself right and to free Mr Lincoln's mind She wrote a letter to Mr L Stating that She would release him from his Engagements."[23] A release is mentioned by several well-placed informants, but it makes little sense as a private communication, particularly if its purpose was to clear the air publicly. But it would make enormous sense if it had been done to free Lincoln formally from an obligation that was contributing to his unshakable "hypochondriaism."

We know that memory often distorts, but the fact that a certain memory is demonstrably distorted need not mean that it is based on nothing or that it is useless. A example of how distorted memory may still be useful presents itself in pair of anecdotes, neither of which can be accurate but which combine nonetheless to suggest that Mary's release of Lincoln came through the offices of Dr. Anson Henry. In a fanciful story about her courtship that Mary told her White House confidante, Elizabeth Keckley, Henry comes to plead for a despairing Lincoln, and Mary ends his suffering by sending word that she will marry him.[24] This didn't happen, but it is interesting that Mary puts Henry in the story. That Henry played a part in securing a release would accord with what Lincoln himself wrote to Stuart about the doctor's services in his behalf, and it may be what Elizabeth Edwards meant, in part, when she told Herndon, "Doct. Henry who admired and loved Mr. Lincoln had much to do in getting Mary and Lincoln together again."[25] The other anecdote is even stranger. After Lincoln and Mary Todd were married, a young relative of Lincoln's named Harriet Hanks came to Springfield to go to school and live in the Lincoln household. Years later she repeated a story that she had heard at that time from Mary. Jesse W. Weik's notes of his interview with her read: "Mrs L. was engaged to Sen Douglas but she broke off engagement – she became sick – Douglas did not want to release her but her bro in law Dr Wallace who was treating her told Douglas he must give her up."[26] There is virtually no possibility that such a story about Mary Todd and Stephen A. Douglas could be true, for no evidence comes even close to supporting so dramatic an episode. But it does appear possible that it could represent, for whatever reason, an inverted account of what happened in January 1841 with Lincoln and Mary Todd: Lincoln became ill, and the indispensable physician, Dr. Henry, convinced Mary to write him a letter of release.

Lincoln's return to the legislature after a week's incapacity was a struggle, as his own letters amply show. "Pardon me for not writing more," his letter to Stuart on January 20 concluded, "I have not sufficient composure to write a long letter."[27] His letter of three days later, in which he said he "must die or be better," concluded by giving Stuart leave to recommend him for a government post abroad because, he said, "I fear I shall be unable to attend to any business here, and a change of scene might help me."[28] Though he continued to attend the legislative proceedings, his somber mood and bearing greatly reduced his effectiveness, and in the most heated issue – the Democrats' brazen packing of the Supreme Court – he apparently took no part in the debates at all, a circumstance that may have been decisive in the narrow Whig defeat.[29] In the remaining weeks of the session he had so little impact that some of his friends remembered him as hardly participating at all.[30]

The legislature finished its work and adjourned on March 1. A few days later, James Conkling reported news of Springfield's social scene to Mercy Ann Levering.

> The Legislature have dispersed. Whether any persons regret it I cannot pretend to say. Miss Todd and her cousin Miss Edwards seemed to form the grand centre of attraction. Swarms of strangers who had little else to engage their attention hovered around them, to catch a *passing smile*. By the way, I do not think they were received, with even ordinary attention, if they did not obtain a *broad grin* or an *obstreporous laugh*. And L. poor hapless simple swain who loved most true but was not loved again – I suppose he will now endeavor to drown his cares among the intricacies and perplexities of the law.[31]

Mary Todd, in tandem with her housemate Matilda Edwards, had apparently enjoyed a triumphant season. They had so dominated the social scene when the Hardin family visited in January as to discourage their rivals; Sarah Hardin reported to her husband the attitude of an eligible but disappointed young lady as follows: "she has come to the conclusion that it would not break her heart if Mary and Matilda was to marry them all."[32]

Lincoln, by contrast, put in the most anguished season of his young life. His natural resiliency failed him, and he found it very hard to recover his spirits. Two recollections of his condition at this period portray his affliction at different levels. Turner R. King, who had recently come to Springfield, told Herndon: "In March 1841 I used to see Mr. Lincoln – hanging about – moody – silent & &c. The question in his mind was [']Have I incurred any obligation to marry that woman'. He wanted to dodge if he could."[33] The break with Mary Todd had taken place, but Lincoln was dogged by the feeling that he was still under an obligation to her. In this light his lingering malaise seems a clouded question of ethics or perhaps a tarnished sense of personal honor. But Speed remembered something that pointed to a more profound crisis. He suggested that the misfortunes of that fateful winter had such a devastating effect on Lincoln's spirits that he was losing the will to live. It may have been about this time – Speed wasn't certain – that Lincoln wrote a poem on suicide and had it published in the *Sangamo Journal.*[34] Speed says he told Lincoln frankly "in his deepest gloom" that he must rally himself or die.[35] Lincoln, who had written the same sentiment to Stuart, responded by saying that he was not afraid of death and was "more than willing," but what held him back was "that he had done nothing to make any human being remember that he had lived."[36] This incident was clearly marked in Lincoln's own view of his life, for he reminded Speed of this exchange years later in the White House, when he had finally done something that he hoped would be remembered, the Emancipation Proclamation. What is remarkable is that in the spring of 1841 Lincoln's reasons for living had virtually been reduced to a single consideration – what his own generation would have called his "thirst for distinction."

-ð-

LINCOLN'S FRIEND of long standing, Orville H. Browning, eluded Herndon, but he gave a long interview to Lincoln's secretary and biographer, John G. Nicolay, in 1875. Nicolay and John Hay decided not to use the story of Lincoln's complicated "love affairs" in their massive biography because of Robert Todd Lincoln's distaste for including anything about his mother or sensitive episodes in his father's early life.

Nicolay's interview was thus unknown to subsequent Lincoln biographers until it was discovered a few years ago, with a valuable cache of other unknown interviews, by Lincoln scholar Michael Burlingame. In his interview Browning spoke to Nicolay at considerable length about the matter at hand. Not only was he a close friend at the time, a fellow Whig legislator, but he lodged at the Butlers', where Lincoln boarded, and he claimed to have spent a good deal of time talking the matter over with Mary Todd. "She was a girl of much vivacity in conversation," he told Nicolay, "but was subject to similar spells of mental depression as Mr. L. As we used familiarly to state it she was always 'either in the garret or cellar.' She had taken a fancy to Mr. Lincoln and I always thought she did most of the courting until they became engaged."[37]

Browning's account seems to shed light on a vexing question – namely, why, apart from a normal wish to do the right thing, Lincoln felt himself so oppressed by his obligation to Mary Todd.

> In those times I was at Mr. Edwards' a great deal, and Miss Todd used to sit down with me, and talk to me sometimes till midnight, about this affair of hers with Mr. Lincoln. In these conversations I think it came out, that Mr. Lincoln had perhaps on one occasion told Miss Todd that he loved Matilda Edwards, and no doubt his conscience was greatly worked up by the supposed pain and injury which this avowal had inflicted upon her.
>
> I always doubted whether, had circumstances left him entirely free to act upon his own impulses, he would have voluntarily made proposals of marriage to Miss Todd. There is no doubt of her exceeding anxiety to marry him. She made no concealment that she had very bitter feelings towards her rival Matilda Edwards.
>
> Miss Todd was thoroughly in earnest [in] her endeavours to get Mr. Lincoln, while on the other hand Miss Edwards was something of a coquette. . . . I always thought then and have thought ever since that in her affair with Mr. Lincoln, Mary Todd did most of the courting.[38]

Browning was here speaking circumspectly at a time when Mary Todd Lincoln was still alive, but if he was right about Mary's eagerness and determination to marry Lincoln, it helps explain why Lincoln felt so harried and plagued by the situation. The letter of release spoken of by Elizabeth Edwards may have brought Lincoln temporary relief, but every indication, including his later testimony, points to his continued anguish over Mary's disappointed feelings and state of mind, for which he blamed himself. In describing his understanding of the release,

Mary's brother-in-law, Ninian W. Edwards, implied that it was deliberately open-ended: "Miss Todd released Lincoln from the Contract, leaving Lincoln the privilege of renewing it . . . if he wished."[39] His wife was even more explicit about the terms of the release. She said that "though [Mary] had released him in the letter Spoken of – yet She Said that She would hold the question an open one – that is that She had not Changed her mind, but felt as always."[40] If the release was indeed cast in this way, it would have been like exchanging a contract to purchase for an option, and the intended effect would hardly have been lost on Lincoln.

Mary Todd seems to have had strong feelings for Abraham Lincoln. The problem was that her behavior, then as well as later, did not always look like true affection or love. By all accounts, she carried on gaily during the winter months, flirting and accepting the attentions of other men, giving her friends the impression that she was serious about at least one of these, and generally maintaining the image of the belle of the ball. A long letter written in June to Mercy Ann Levering shows this situation very well.

"The last two or three months have been of *interminable* length," she begins, "after my gay companions of last winter departed, I was left much to the solitude of my own thoughts, and some *lingering regrets* over the past, which time can alone overshadow with its healing balm." Some of these regrets come out a little later on with the mention of Bat Webb, who had been "dancing attendance" as Mary's "principal lion."

> in your last, you appeared impressed with the prevalent idea that we were *dearer* to each other than friends, the idea was neither new nor strange, dear Merce, the knowing world have coupled our names together for months past, merely through the folly & belief of *another*, who strangely imagined we were attached to each other, in your friendly & confiding ear allow me to whisper that my *heart can never be his*, I have deeply *regretted that his constant visits, attentions* && should have given room for remarks, which were to me unpleasant, there being a slight difference of some eighteen or twenty summers in our years, would preclude the possibility of congeneality of feeling, without which I should never feel justifiable in resigning my happiness into the safekeeping of another, even should that other be far too worthy for me, with his two *sweet little objections*.[41]

So much for Webb, though apparently not even Mary's closest friends could tell from her outward behavior toward him that she was not interested in matrimony. Her reference to "the folly & belief of *another*" may well refer to Lincoln, though it could also refer to someone who had been speculating on Mary's attachment to Webb. Another regret was the loss of excitement. "We had such a continual round of company, gayety && last winter, that after their departure the monotony of the place was almost unbearable," and she admitted that she has finally "become habituated to quiet." After giving news of Mercy's beau, James Conkling, she mentioned receiving letters from Joshua Speed in Kentucky. And then this: "*His* worthy friend [presumably Lincoln], deems me unworthy of notice, as I have not met *him* in the gay world for months, with the usual comfort of misery, imagine that others were as seldom gladdened by his presence as my humble self, yet I would that the case were different, that he would once more resume his Station in Society, that 'Richard should be himself again,' much, much happiness would it afford me."[42]

Mary's way of expressing herself in her letters, while frequently incisive and witty, is often problematic. Her sentences can be fragmentary and elliptical, while her punctuation is consistently inconsistent. Because of these problems, the passage above about Lincoln is difficult to interpret. Assuming that the phrase "for months" marks the end of a sentence, what follows seems to mean something like this: "As misery is said to love company, I comfort myself by imagining that other people have been just as infrequently gladdened by his presence as I have been." The final line of the passage – "much, much happiness would it afford me" – is almost universally taken as clear evidence of the kind of thing that Browning said she confessed to him in their midnight talks: that she wanted Lincoln back. She did not confess this to Mercy, but then she had never admitted to her friend that she and Lincoln were ever romantically involved. But if she had her heart secretly set on getting Lincoln back, why, near the end of this letter, did she offer a teasing suggestion of a new interest? Noting that Douglas has been elevated to a judgeship (as part of the packing of the Illinois Supreme Court), she refers to his having been a former admirer of Mercy, who was now engaged to Conkling. "Now that your fortune is made, I feel much disposed in your absence, to lay in my *claims*, as he is talented & agreeable & sometimes *countenances* me." If this is a letter of one who is pining away for Lincoln, the pining is well disguised. But disguised it may well be. Though she affects great intimacy with Mercy in these letters, our perspective enables us to see that she actually played her cards very close to the vest.

⊸

AN INTRIGUING aspect of this unfolding story is the role played by Joshua Speed. We know from his testimony and Lincoln's own letters that Speed acted as Lincoln's confidant and adviser in the affair with Mary Todd. Speed wrote Herndon in 1866: "In the winter of 40 & 41, [Lincoln] was very unhappy about his engagement to his wife – Not being entirely satisfied that his *heart* was going with this hand. How much he suffered then on that account none know so well as myself. He disclosed his whole heart to me."[43] This was claiming a great deal, considering how notoriously reticent and secretive Lincoln was to become about personal matters, but after reading Lincoln's letters and hearing Speed's testimony, Herndon accepted the claim. "Lincoln loved this man more than any one dead or living; and it may truthfully be said that Lincoln 'poured out his whole soul['] to Speed in his love scrapes with Miss Todd."[44]

Their letters show that Lincoln and Speed regarded themselves not only as close friends but as something like soul mates, psychologically and temperamentally very much in tune. Like Lincoln, Speed combined a keen mind with a conspicuous streak of poetic tenderness. A family historian wrote: "He had a vein of sentiment in his nature which made him fond of flowers and poetry, which his active business never eradicated. Evidences of this are found in his letters and lectures, and his friends recall how often it was manifested in his conversation."[45] Speed returned to Kentucky in late spring of 1841 and showed his solicitude for Lincoln when writing back to William Butler in Springfield: "I am glad to hear from Mrs Butler that Lincoln is on the mend. Say to him that I have had but one attack since I left Springfield and that was on the river as I came here."[46] Hypochondriaism, or the "hypo," as they called an attack of anxiety or depression, was apparently an affliction common to both men. A year later, when Speed was having severe withdrawal pangs about his own engagement, Lincoln demonstrated his solicitude by writing him a series of encouraging letters: "You know my desire to befriend you is everlasting – that I will never cease, while I know how to do any thing."[47]

If the evidence of Lincoln's pursuit of Matilda Edwards is too abundant and well informed to be explained away, the testimony of several well-connected witnesses depicts Speed as another of Matilda's suitors during that fateful winter, and the question naturally arises: were these intimate friends rivals for the hand of the same woman?[48] This would seem to be too colorful a circumstance to have escaped notice and comment, but no testimony to this effect is known. James C. Conkling came close in his letter to Mercy Ann Levering, when he seemed to link the news of Lincoln's debility in January to the imminent departure of Speed. Elizabeth Todd Edwards certainly implied a connection between Speed's being turned down and his departure: "Mr. Speed came [to the Edwards home] to see Miss Matilda Edwards – left & went to Ky – Miss Edwards staying."[49] But Conkling's linking of the two friends may have come about not so much because they had been in active competition as because they had suffered the same fate, a common failure to gain the affections of Matilda Edwards.

Like many things we would like to know about the past, the nature of Lincoln and Speed's rivalry over Matilda Edwards is unavailable to us, at least at present. Speed said nothing about the matter in known documents, and this, of course, could mean that the rivalry amounted to nothing. It is worth noting that Lincoln shows no hesitancy a year later in calling attention to Speed's courtships. Writing to disabuse his friend of the notion that he may not love the woman he is engaged to, Lincoln asks: "How came you to court her? Was it because you thought she desired it; and that you had given her reason to expect it? If it was for that, why did not the same reason make you court Ann Todd, and at least twenty others of whom you can think, & to whom it would apply with greater force than to *her*?"[50] Whatever form the rivalry took, it is one of the blank places in the jigsaw puzzle for which the pieces are lost.

The most likely explanation would seem to be that neither man was seriously considered by Matilda Edwards. If Conkling's letters depict the effect of Lincoln's admittedly more complex failure with Matilda, a long letter Speed wrote to his younger sister in March apparently recorded the effect of his own lack of success. In it he confessed that he was melancholy and told why: "I endeavor to persuade myself that there is more pleasure in pursuit of any object, than there is in its possession. This general rule I wish *now* most particularly to apply to women. I have been most anxiously in pursuit of one – and from all present appearances, if my philosophy be true I am to be most enviably felicitous, for I may have as much of the anticipation and pursuit as I please, but the possession I can hardly ever hope to realize."[51] Speed also confessed that his reasons for staying in Illinois were disappearing. "There is nothing here but some of the very cleverest fellows that God ever made – the truest friends and warmest hearts – that is worth living in this country for."[52] This is hardly the language of one who has reservations about his closest friend. The strong survival of their friendship, and especially Lincoln's extraordinary solicitude for Speed the following year, make it clear that no discernible or lasting ill effects resulted from their being in love with the same woman. If anything, their common failure seems to have made them closer.

⌐

SPEED RETURNED to Kentucky. As he indicated to his sister Eliza in March, financial conditions in Illinois had become unpromising for a young entrepreneur like himself. In addition, his father had died the previous year, and his mother wanted him to return and take charge of the family affairs.[53] In the meantime, Lincoln slowly regained his composure and his ability to function. A letter to Stuart in Washington began, "You see by this that I am neither dead nor quite crazy yet."[54] Near the end of the legislative session, in response to a speaker telling a story at his expense, Lincoln convulsed the House of Representatives with laughter at one of his own stories, the hilarity of which must have been in the telling.[55] By mutual consent, the firm of Stuart and Lincoln dissolved, and Lincoln became the junior partner of the most knowledgeable practitioner at the Springfield bar, Stephen T. Logan.

In June, Lincoln was drawn into a strange case that looked for a time like murder most foul, agitating the whole town of Springfield and generating a lynch mob type of frenzy at the supposed evil that had been perpetrated. In a letter to Speed, Lincoln described the energetic search for the corpus delicti: "Away the People swept like a herd of buffaloes, and cut down Hickoxes mill dam *nolens volens*, to draw the water out of the pond; and then went up and down, and down and up the creek, fishing and raking, and ducking and diving for two days, and after all, no dead body found."[56] But in spite of the direct testimony of one of the suspects that the missing man had been murdered by the other two, a doctor was produced by the defense (which included Abraham Lincoln) and testified that the alleged victim was alive and unwell in Warren County. As Lincoln noted to Speed, the collective disappointment was crushing.

When the doctor's story was first made public, it was amusing to scan and contemplate the countenances, and hear the remarks of those who had been actively engaged in the search for the dead body. Some looked quizical, some melancholly, and some furiously angry. Porter, who had been very active, swore he always knew the man was not dead, and that *he* had not stirred an inch to hunt for him; Langford, who had taken the lead in cutting down Hickoxes mill dam, and wanted to hang Hickox for objecting, looked most awfully wobegone; he seemed the *"wictim of hunrequited haffection"* as represented in the comic almanic we used to laugh over; and Hart, the little drayman that hauled Molly home once, said it was too *damned* bad, to have so much trouble, and no hanging after all.[57]

The humor in this letter is an interesting gauge of Lincoln's morale, which was surely on the rise. Not only did he see the humor in the situation, but he saw it with the shrewd eye of a satirist. The deft depictions of Porter, Langford, and Hart are worthy of a Mark Twain. Interesting, too, are the comic references to "unrequited affection" and to "Molly," a nickname for Mary Todd. The incident involving the drayman Ellis Hart had been celebrated in verse by Lincoln's friend, Dr. Elias H. Merryman, after Mary had defied convention by hitching a ride home through muddy streets on a dray, a rough conveyance used for hauling freight.

> Up flew windows, out popped heads,
> To see this Lady gay
> In silken cloak and feathers white
>   A riding on a dray.
> At length arrived at Edwards' gate
> Hart backed the usual way
> And taking out the iron pin
>   He rolled her off the dray.[58]

The reference to the almanac, where the lovelorn figure is rendered comic by the surefire device of giving him a foreign accent, suggests that Lincoln at least was regaining something of his former perspective on life.

One's sense that this is the case is perhaps reinforced by Lincoln's use of the legal Latin phrase *nolens volens*, "whether willing or unwilling." Knowledge of Latin was the hallmark of an educated person in Lincoln's day, and he was keenly aware that this was something he lacked. In an autobiographical statement in 1859, he wrote of his Indiana boyhood, "If a straggler supposed to understand latin, happened to sojourn in the neighborhood, he was looked upon as a wizzard. There was absolutely nothing to excite ambition for education."[59] Though in later years he would take a stab at Latin grammar while riding the circuit, he always avoided the pretense of knowing Latin and seemed to believe that more than anything else, this void was what made his education, to use his word, "defective."[60] One can make too much of his seemingly casual dropping of a Latin phrase used frequently in court, but there was something in the meaning of that compact phrase that was a deep reflection of the outlook on life that had been taking shape in his mind since childhood and that the untoward events of the past year had only confirmed. Success was predicated on survival, and this meant learning to cope with what comes, *nolens volens*, "whether willing or unwilling."

At the end of the summer of 1841, Lincoln followed Speed to Kentucky and stayed several weeks. At Farmington, the Speed family home near Louisville, Lincoln found a remarkable building and a houseful of congenial company. Farmington was imposing by the standards of the day, and its handsome design was said to have come from the hand of Thomas Jefferson. It was by far the grandest and most spacious house Lincoln had ever lived in. Speed's sisters took a special fancy to Lincoln and engaged him in playful high jinks. In a letter to Mary Speed after his return home, Lincoln bantered her about their having been "cronies" and referred to "shutting you up in a room to prevent your committing an assault and battery upon me."[61] Speed's mother, Lucy Fry Speed, whose family had been neighbors of Jefferson's in Virginia, took a kindly interest in her visitor and presented him with something expressly aimed at helping him cope with his "blues," an Oxford Bible.[62] When he felt like changing the scene, Lincoln went into town and talked with Speed's older brother James, a lawyer, and read books from his library. "I saw him daily," wrote James many years later, "he sat in my office, read my books, and talked with me about his life, his reading, his studies, his aspirations."[63] Months later, Lincoln wrote: "I am living upon the remembrance of the delicious dishes of peaches and cream we used to have" at Farmington.[64] The change of scene and the warm hospitality seem clearly to have checked Lincoln's despondency and given his spirits a new direction.

But while Lincoln's spirits gradually improved in the hospitable company of Speed's family, Joshua, who was presumably himself somewhat on the mend, suffered an unexpected emotional ambush: he fell madly in love. During Lincoln's stay, he courted and promptly proposed to a beautiful young woman named Fanny Henning.[65] A family tradition has it that Lincoln helped bring this about by distracting Fanny's guardian uncle with political talk so that Speed could get Fanny alone to propose.[66] No sooner had Speed declared himself than he almost immediately began to have doubts and second thoughts. This marked the beginning of a long process in which the roles the two friends had been playing for months became oddly reversed, for it now fell to Lincoln to offer counsel and support. Speed returned to Illinois with Lincoln in September to finish up his business affairs, and his anxieties about whether he was doing the right thing only increased. Lincoln's own anxieties, on the other hand, continued to diminish.[67]

Upon Speed's return to Kentucky in January 1842, Lincoln wrote a remarkable series of letters, both before and after Speed's wedding in February, aimed at bolstering the bridegroom's resolve. In giving Herndon copies, Speed offered to explain the circumstances. "In the summer of 1841, I became engaged to my wife. He [Lincoln] was here on a visit when I courted her. And strange to say something of the same feeling which I regarded as so foolish in him took possession of me – and kept me very unhappy from the time of my engagement until I was married. This will explain the deep interest he manifested in his letters on my account."[68]

"Deep interest" hardly does justice to the obsessive concern for Speed's emotional welfare that is manifest in Lincoln's letters. The first was written even before Speed's departure for Kentucky.

> Feeling, as you know I do, the deepest solicitude for the success of the enterprize you are engaged in, I adopt this as the last method I can invent to aid you, in case (which God forbid) you shall need any aid. I do not place what I am going to say on paper, because I can say it any better in that way than I could by word of mouth; but because, were I to say it orrally, before we part, most likely you would forget it at the verry time when it might do you some good. As I think it reasonable that you will feel verry badly some time between this and the final consummation of your purpose, it is intended that you shall read this just at such a time.[69]

This letter begins on a note of deep sympathetic feeling, but its burden is highly analytical and exemplifies the logical organization of a legal brief.

> Why I say it is reasonable that you will feel verry badly yet, is, because of *three special causes*, added to the *general one* which I shall mention.

The general cause is, that you are *naturally of a nervous tempera-ment*; and this I say from what I have seen of you personally, and what you have told me concerning your mother at various times, and concerning your brother William at the time his wife died.

The first special cause is, *your exposure to bad weather* on your journey, which my experience clearly proves to be verry severe on defective nerves.

The second is, *the absence of all business and conversation of friends,* which might divert your mind, and give it occasional rest from that *intensity* of thought, which will some times wear the sweetest idea thread-bare and turn it to the bitterness of death.

The third is, *the rapid and near approach of that crisis on which all your thoughts and feelings concentrate.*[70]

If the concern with general and special causes is analytic, the sub-stance is surprisingly clinical, with Lincoln going into Speed's tempera-ment, his hereditary endowments, his environmental circumstances, and mental tendencies. What is of particular interest here is that Lin-coln presumably knows so much about Speed's emotional vulnerabilities precisely because they bear a strong relationship to his own. "If, on the contrary, you shall, as I expect you will at some time, be agonized and distressed, let me, who have some reason to speak with judgment on such a subject, beseech you, to ascribe it to the causes I have mentioned; and not to some false and ruinous suggestion of the Devil."[71] Lincoln goes on to emphasize that these causes are not universal: "*The particular causes,* to a greater or less extent, perhaps do apply in all cases; but the *general one,* nervous debility, which is the key and conductor of all the particular ones, and without which *they* would be utterly harmless, though it *does* pertain to you, *does not* pertain to one in a thousand. It is out of this, that the painful difference between you and the mass of the world springs."[72] If Lincoln is here speaking, as he implies, from per-sonal experience and in the belief that he and Speed are very much alike, this letter represents a rare instance of self-analysis and even self-revelation.

His experience tells him that "nervous debility" is the general cause of the depressed feelings that skew judgment and inhibit action. Par-ticular causes, however, can and do contribute to the overall effect, and he mentions three that he presumably knows at first hand. The first is bad weather, "which my experience clearly proves to be verry severe on defective nerves." It has been pointed out that his serious debility the previous January coincided with a severe cold spell.[73] The second is "*the absence of all business and conversation of friends,* which might divert your mind, and give it occasional rest from that *intensity* of thought," a pointedly Byronic consideration that harks back to a passage in Byron's *Childe Harold* that Lincoln had called Speed's attention to: "The blight of Life – the Demon Thought."[74] Here Lincoln himself waxes poetic and speaks in a distinctly Byronic mode of that "which will some times wear the sweetest idea thread-bare and turn it to the bitterness of death."

The third particular cause is *"the rapid and near approach of that crisis on which all your thoughts and feelings concentrate."* It is possible that this, too, reflects Lincoln's experience of the previous year. Elizabeth Edwards was certain that Lincoln had once stood her sister Mary up by failing to appear at a ceremonious occasion, which she remembered as his own wedding. This is confirmed only by ambiguous evidence and was denied by her own husband and members of her family circle.[75] But John J. Hardin's younger sister, Martinette, also remembered vividly an occasion where Lincoln was expected, and humiliated Mary Todd by not appearing.[76]

The second part of this letter is often quoted for its closely reasoned refutation of what Lincoln judged to be "the painful point" with Speed: "the apprehension that you do not love her as you should." Speed feared that he had "reasoned" himself into a false position, but Lincoln replies, "What do you mean by that? Was it not that you found yourself unable to *reason* yourself *out of* it?" Lincoln shows that Speed's own actions in courting Fanny Henning were in response to the heart, not the head. "Say candidly, were not those heavenly *black eyes*, the whole basis of all your early *reasoning* on the subject?"[77] As with the first part of the letter, it is tempting to see in this part a reflection of Lincoln's own predicament of the previous year, when he suffered from the apprehension that he did not love Mary Todd as he should. This, in fact, is the way Speed seemed to represent the situation, when he wrote Herndon that "something of the same feeling which I regarded as so foolish in him took possession of me." It is, of course, by no means clear how closely Lincoln intended these parallels to apply, but he did claim to speak not only from a keen knowledge of Speed's temperament but from his own experience.

⤙

IN SPEED'S FIRST letter back to Lincoln from Kentucky, written on January 25, his alarm took an unexpected turn. Whereas he had been apprehensive about his own love for Fanny, or lack of it, he was now apprehensive about her health and her life. Lincoln's reply is almost triumphant.

> You well know that I do not feel my own sorrows much more keenly than I do yours, when I know of them; and yet I assure you I was not much hurt by what you wrote me of your excessively bad feeling at the time you wrote. Not that I am less capable of sympathising with you now than ever; not that I am less your friend than ever, but because I hope and believe, that your present anxiety and distress about *her* health and *her* life, must and will forever banish those horid doubts, which I know you sometimes felt, as to the truth of your affection for her."[78]

Again Lincoln alludes to his own experience of the previous year: "Why Speed, if you did not love her, although you might not wish her death, you would most calmly be resigned to it. Perhaps this point is no longer a question with you, and my pertenacious dwelling upon it, is a rude intrusion upon your feelings. If so, you must pardon me. You know the Hell I have suffered on that point, and how tender I am upon it. You know I do not mean wrong."[79]

Lincoln's "pertenacious dwelling" was upon the question of whether Speed, in spite of his doubts and apprehensions, really loved Fanny. This, then, was the point upon which Lincoln says he has suffered and was still tender, the question of whether his own doubts and apprehensions (presumably about Mary Todd) were genuine and should have been heeded. Despite a perfect opportunity to do so, he does not insist that the cases are the same and that he was foolish or wrong to yield to his own misgivings. He only offers his hellish experience and its lingering effect as evidence that he does not mean to do Speed wrong.

The next two lines may be connected to this theme or they may be incidental news notes, but the juxtaposition is intriguing. The first is this: "I have been quite clear of hypo since you left, – even better than I was along in the fall." The "hypo," of course refers to the depressed spirits to which their mutual "nervous debility" makes them especially susceptible. Writing of "the Hell I have suffered" may simply have conjured up thoughts of his continued relief, or it may just be an obvious thing to report to a fellow sufferer and sympathizer.

The line that follows is even more intriguing. "I have seen Sarah but once. She seemed verry cheerful, and so, I said nothing to her about what we spoke of." When Speed provided copies of these letters to

Herndon, he requested that references to Sarah be removed wherever they occurred.[80] There is little doubt that these refer to Sarah Rickard, the younger sister of William Butler's wife, who was then a girl of nearly seventeen.[81] Both Speed and Lincoln would have seen a lot of her at their friend Butler's, where she was a frequent visitor. Why her cheerfulness should have affected Lincoln's speaking to her on a subject he had discussed with Speed is unknown, as is the reason that Speed wanted her name erased from Lincoln's letters when they were published. Sarah told Herndon that Lincoln had taken her out and even proposed marriage to her in a lighthearted way, but she did not try to make it into a love affair. "Mr. Lincoln did Propose marriage to me in the winter of 1840 and 41, as was his costom he brings quotations from the Bible how [know?] but Sarah will become Abrahams wife. My reasons for refusing his Proposal was that I was young only 16 years old and had not thought much about matrimony. I had the highest Regard for Mr Lincoln and he seemed allmost like an older Brother being as It were one of my Sisters family."[82] But one of Herndon's informants claimed that "it was currently reported in 38–40 that Lincoln Courted *Sarah* Rickard – that she flung him high & dry."[83] These reports suggest some kind of involvement between Lincoln and Sarah Rickard, but Lincoln's cryptic reference to her does not sound much like a report on a romance in progress.

Speed's letters to Lincoln do not survive, but he sent another on February 1. Lincoln's reply is strikingly intense with concern for the fate of his friend, who, though already married, Lincoln thinks may still be in danger.

> Yours of the 1st. Inst. came to hand three or four days ago. When this shall reach you, you will have been Fanny's husband several days. You know my desire to befriend you is everlasting – that I will never cease, while I know how to do any thing.
> But you will always hereafter, be on ground that I have never ocupied, and consequently, if advice were needed, I might advise wrong.
> I do fondly hope, however, that you will never again need any comfort from abroad. But should I be mistaken in this – should excessive pleasure still be accompanied with painful counterpart at times, still let me urge you, as I have ever done, to remember in the dep[t]h of even the agony of despondency, that verry shortly you are to feel well again. I am now fully convinced, that you love her as ardently as you are capable of loving. Your ever being happy in her presence, and your intense anxiety about her health, if there were

nothing else, would place this beyond all dispute in my mind. I incline to think it probable, that your nerves will fail you occasionally for a while; but once you get them fairly graded now, that trouble is over forever.[84]

Though he warned that he had not occupied the ground Speed was then on, this was not speculation but still very much the voice of experience: remember that "the agony of despondency" will soon pass; even though you are past the crisis and reasonably happy, it is probable that "your nerves will fail you occasionally for a while." He even offered advice to forestall the recurrence of anxiety. "I think if I were you, in case my mind were not exactly right, I would avoid being *idle*; I would immediately engage in some business, or go to making preparations for it, which would be the same thing."[85]

Although Lincoln knew that Speed, by the time he received this letter, would have endured the dreaded culmination of his ordeal – marital union – it was composed in anticipation of the event. The opening of his next letter shows how intensely involved emotionally Lincoln had become in Speed's situation, which climaxed with the wedding ceremony on February 15. "I received yours of the 12th. written the day you went down to William's place, some days since; but delayed answering it, till I should receive the promised one, of the 16th., which came last night. I opened the latter, with intense anxiety and trepidation – so much, that although it turned out better than I expected, I have hardly yet, at the distance of ten hours, become calm."[86]

This is empathy, or fellow feeling, in a rare degree. That Speed's marriage was recognized and treated as an emotional crisis by both men is revealing, but that Lincoln should experience it as his own sheds light on the sources of his own discomfiture.

> I tell you, Speed [Lincoln's letter continues], our *forebodings*, for which you and I are rather peculiar, are all the worst sort of nonsense. I fancied, from the time I received your letter of *saturday*, that the one of *wednesday* was never to come; and yet it *did* come, and what is more, it is perfectly clear, both from it's *tone* and *handwriting*, that you were much *happier*, or, if you think the term preferable, *less miserable*, when you wrote *it*, than when you wrote the last one before. You had so obviously improved, at the verry time I so much feared, you would have grown worse.[87]

In the light of actual events, one's fears seem somehow ridiculous, a reflection that suggests the folly of living by fears and forebodings.

For Lincoln and Speed, the quintessential fear comes to focus with women, and Lincoln went on to point out why. "Again; you say you much fear that the Elysium of which you have dreamed so much, is never to be realized. Well, if it shall not, I dare swear, it will not be the fault of her who is now your wife. I now have no doubt that it is the peculiar misfortune of both you and me, to dream dreams of Elysium far exceeding all that any thing earthly can realize. Far short of your dreams as you may be, no woman could do more to realize them, than that same black eyed Fanny."[88] That the real should fall short of the ideal is not the tragedy or cruel misfortune that it often is in Byron, nor should it cause one to undervalue the real. The fault is in the idealizing impulse, in dreaming dreams that produce the false expectations of Elysium. This being the case, the remedy is clear: embrace the reality. Although somewhat awkward to apply in the case of Speed and Fanny, Lincoln drives home his message by reaching back to his childhood for an appropriate homily: "My old Father used to have a saying that 'If you make a bad bargain, *hug* it the tighter.' "[89]

⁓

LINCOLN's consciousness that he had involved himself in Speed's ordeal to an extraordinary degree is indicated by a separate letter that he included for Fanny's consumption: "I write another letter enclosing this, which you can show her, if she desires it. I do this, because, she would think strangely perhaps should you tell her that you receive no letters from me; or, telling her you do, should refuse to let her see them."[90] The tenor of the letter for Fanny's consumption is useful in gauging the difference between his own heightened feelings and those of a normal well-wisher. "Yours of the 16th. Inst. announcing that Miss Fanny and you are 'no more twain but one flesh,' reached me this morning. I have no way of telling how much happiness I wish you both; tho' I believe you both can conceive it. I feel som[e] what jealous of both of you now; you will be so exclusively concerned for one another, that I shall be forgotten entirely."[91] This is a far cry from "I opened [the letter announcing your marriage] with intense anxiety and trepidation – so much, that although it turned out better than I expected, I have hardly yet, at the distance of ten hours, become calm."[92]

A month later Speed wrote to say that all was well, and Lincoln's letter of response betrays a telling succession of emotions: happiness, relief, and chagrin.

It can not be told, how it now thrills me with joy, to hear you say you are *"far happier than you ever expected to be."* That much I know is enough. I know you too well to suppose your expectations were not, at least sometimes, extravagant; and if the reality exceeds them all, I say, enough dear Lord. I am not going beyond the truth, when I tell you, that the short space it took me to read your last letter, gave me more pleasure, than the total sum of all I have enjoyed since that fatal first of Jany. '41. Since then, it seems to me, I should have been entirely happy, but for the never-absent idea, that there is *one* still unhappy whom I have contributed to make so. That still kills my soul. I can not but reproach myself, for even wishing to be happy while she is otherwise.[93]

This letter, with its reference to "that fatal first of Jany. '41," was the source of Herndon's original speculation that it named the date of Lincoln's "crazy spell" and broken engagement with Mary Todd, a theory that virtually every subsequent biographer has embraced and one that cannot be entirely discounted. But read in the context of Lincoln's previous letters, to say nothing of this one, the remark about the fatal first of January would appear to refer primarily to something momentous in *Speed's* life, rather than Lincoln's.[94] This suggestion is reinforced a few sentences later, when Lincoln refers again to Sarah Rickard. "One thing I can tell you which I know you will be glad to hear; and that is, that I have seen Sarah, and scrutinized her feelings as well as I could, and am fully convinced, she is far happier now, than she has been for the last fifteen months past."[95] Fifteen months before the date of this letter is almost precisely January 1, 1841, and whatever happened then is represented as something in which Speed and Sarah are closely concerned. Not only is Speed concerned, but Lincoln is sure he will take comfort in knowing that Sarah is "far happier now" than she had been.

What prompts biographers to connect the "fatal first" to something momentous in Lincoln's life, of course, is what immediately follows, the lament about one lingering source of misery. More than one commentator has noted that this marks an abrupt turning point in the letter and, indeed, in the entire series of letters on Speed's situation.[96] Whereas Lincoln has been playing the role of counselor to Speed's troubled soul, with scarcely any mention of his personal affairs, it is precisely at this point that the polarity is reversed and Lincoln's own troubles reemerge. And what he says about them leaves little doubt that he is referring to his inextinguishable guilt over his treatment of Mary Todd. "Since then [receiving Speed's letter], it seems to me, I should have been entirely happy, but for the never-absent idea, that there is *one* still unhappy whom I have contributed to make so. That still kills my soul."

The force of this statement commands attention. It suggests that in Lincoln's speaking incessantly for months only of Speed's troubles, his own have been, if submerged, never far from the surface, "never absent." It more than suggests that the guilt he feels has effectively poisoned whatever happiness comes his way. Except for his gratification at Speed's success, almost the only evidence of any personal happiness is an enigmatic postscript to his February 13 letter: "P.S. I have been quite a man ever since you left."[97] If this refers to a successful interaction with a woman, sexual or otherwise, his later confession suggests that his guilt would not let him enjoy it.

With Speed's crisis behind him, the pace of the correspondence slackened, but the newly rejuvenated Speed, seeing that Lincoln's anxieties had resurfaced, now resumed the role of counselor. On July 4 Lincoln wrote a revealing reply that, in response to some frank advice on Speed's part, takes the analysis of his "never absent" feeling to a much deeper level.

> As to my having been displeased with your advice, surely you know better than that. I know you do; and therefore I will not labour to convince you. True, that subject is painfull to me; but it is not your silence, or the silence of all the world that can make me forget it. I acknowledge the correctness of your advice too; but before I resolve to do the one thing or the other, I must regain my confidence in my own ability to keep my resolves when they are made. In that ability, you know, I once prided myself as the only, or at least the chief, gem of my character; that gem I lost – how, and when, you too well know. I have not yet regained it; and until I do, I can not trust myself in any matter of much importance.[98]

It is not just what he has done to Mary, whom he refers to later in the letter as "our friend here," that concerns him. He could remedy that by proposing, which is probably what Speed has advised him to do. But reflection on his case has shown Lincoln a more general and more consequential casualty of this affair: the ability to stick to his decisions once he has made them. This realization produced a devastating loss of self-confidence, which is all the more devastating because this very ability was once the proudest mark of his character. Not being able to trust himself in a "matter of much importance" may help explain, if indeed it is not a veiled reference to, Lincoln's decision not to run for reelection to a fifth term in the legislature. The election was only a few weeks away, and Lincoln's absence from the hustings was his first in ten years of sustained political activity.

Speed's letter had evidently tried to lift his friend's spirits by giving Lincoln credit for his own happiness. Lincoln's response is properly read as an extension of the self-analysis just offered, for it exposes the fatalistic underpinnings of his constitutional outlook and frame of mind.

> You make a kind of acknowledgement of your obligations to me for your present happiness. I am much pleased with that acknowledgement; but a thousand times more am I pleased to know, that you enjoy a degree of happiness, worthy of an acknowledgement. The truth is, I am not sure there was any merit, with me, in the part I took in your difficulty; I was drawn to it as by fate; if I would, I could not have done less than I did. I always was superstitious; and as part of my superstition, I believe God made me one of the instruments of bringing your Fanny and you together, which union, I have no doubt He had fore-ordained. Whatever he designs, he will do for *me* yet. "Stand *still* and see the salvation of the Lord" is my text just now.[99]

Here is the true fatalist and the true fatalist's dilemma: if what I did was fated to be, it was not really my doing. And as a fatalist, he saw clearly the implications of this line of reasoning for his own predicament: what has been foreordained for me is, *nolens volens*, what is going to happen.

❧

LINCOLN'S FATALISM, which he frankly labeled superstition, was, from the earliest time, part of who he was. It was presumably an out-growth of the Calvinistic religious worldview in which he was raised. He rebelled against its doctrines of orthodox Christian belief, but he retained, as part of his way of apprehending the world and human events, the fatalistic premise at its core: that man does not control his own destiny. Lincoln's essential fatalism is abundantly evident in his life and writings and was well attested by those who knew him best. His wife summed up for Herndon her husband's basic outlook in one of his sayings: "Mr Lincolns maxim and philosophy was – 'What is to be will be and no cares of ours can arrest the decree.' "[100] Herndon agreed that this was a frequent saying of his law partner but remembered it as concluding that "no prayers of ours can reverse the decree."[101] He also remembered, as did others, that Lincoln frequently quoted

Shakespeare's Hamlet: "There's a divinity that shapes our ends, / Rough-hew them how we will."[102] Joseph Gillespie, whose detailed and highly analytical letters to Herndon contain many perceptive remarks on Lincoln's intellect, testified that Lincoln was very much aware of the constitutional nature of his fatalism and the moral dilemma that such a view presented: "Mr Lincoln told me once that he could not avoid believing in predestination although he considered it a very unprofitable field of speculation because it was hard to reconcile that belief with responsibility for ones act."[103]

As this remark suggests, Lincoln's fatalism did not preclude a belief in moral responsibility, even though he could not give a satisfactory explanation of how these two things could be reconciled. Among the fundamentalist hoosiers Lincoln grew up with, there were those who carried their Calvinism to the point of objecting to moral reform efforts, such as temperance, but Lincoln was never one of these. In 1842, though he himself had no taste for alcohol and drank little, he joined the surging temperance movement and lent his powers as a speaker to the Washingtonians, the national temperance organization that was then enjoying an enormous vogue across the country. Such was his stature as a speaker that he was invited to give the principal address on the birthday of George Washington, for whom the organization was named.

"You will see by the last Sangamo Journal," Lincoln wrote to Speed in his letter of March 27, "that I made a Temperance speech on the 22. of Feb. which I claim that Fanny and you shall read as an act of charity to me; for I can not learn that any body else has read it, or is likely to. Fortunately, it is not very long and I shall deem it a sufficient compliance with my request, if one of you listens while the other reads it."[104] The temperance address delivered before the Springfield Washington Temperance Society has earned an important place in Lincoln's early writings for the light it sheds on his developing sense of how change can be effected. Lincoln here comes down decisively on the side of persuasion, as opposed to coercion or compulsion, an aspect of his thought with enduring consequences.

The opening of the address insists that the conspicuous success enjoyed by the Washingtonians "is doubtless owing to rational causes; and if we would have it to continue, we shall do well to enquire what those causes are."[105] Though it can be construed as ironic in a fatalist, this is Lincoln's basic approach to problems that lend themselves to analysis: the assumption that there are causes involved that are at once rational and intelligible. The success of the Washingtonians is presented as comparative; it is great when judged by the comparative lack of success of earlier reformers. The problem has been that previous champions of the temperance cause "have been Preachers, Lawyers, and hired agents. Between these and the mass of mankind, there is a want of *approachability*, if the term be admissible, partially at least, fatal to their success. They are supposed to have no sympathy of feeling or interest, with those persons whom it is their object to convince and persuade."[106] These reformers engaged in "too much denunciation against dram sellers and dram drinkers," something Lincoln regards as "both impolitic and unjust. It was impolitic, because, it is not much in the nature of man to be driven to any thing; still less to be driven about that which is exclusively his own business; and least of all, where such driving is to be submitted to, at the expense of pecuniary interest, or burning appetite."[107]

To expect people who are denounced not to respond in kind, Lincoln argued, adapting one of his familiar maxims, "was to expect a reversal of human nature, which is God's decree, and never can be reversed. When the conduct of men is designed to be influenced, *persuasion*, kind, unassuming persuasion, should ever be adopted."[108] It is thus, in this formulation, not the totality of human actions that is "God's decree" but irreversible human nature, a view that would appear to leave wiggle room for a fatalist. "Such is man, and so must he be understood by those who would lead him, even to his own best interest."[109]

The core membership of the Washingtonians was composed not of self-righteous teetotalers but of reformed drunkards, who obviously came at the problem not by way of creed or precept but from personal experience. They are, Lincoln says approvingly, "practical philanthropists."[110] They realize, in spite of what some people profess, that "moral influence" is indeed a "powerful engine." He illustrates this in a waggish Lincolnian way by arguing that what keeps men from coming to church wearing their wives' bonnets is mere fashion, which is simply one form of "the influence that other people's actions have [on our own] actions."[111]

Like the Lyceum address of 1838, Lincoln's temperance speech ends with an emphasis on rationality as the solution to society's problems. "Reason," he urged at the Lyceum, "cold calculating, unimpassioned reason, must furnish all the materials for our future support and defence."[112] To the Washingtonians four years later he declared: "Happy day, when, all appetites controled, all passions subdued, all matters subjected, *mind,* all conquering *mind,* shall live and move the monarch of the world. Glorious consummation! Hail fall of Fury! Reign of Reason, all hail!"[113] This hardly sounds like fatalism, but there is a commonality of sentiment in these two pronouncements that points to the futility of passion and the importance of subduing one's appetites. This is the burden of his fatalistic maxim: "What is to be will be and no cares of ours can arrest the decree."[114] Whether he spoke of "cares" or "prayers," the point is much the same: the best way to deal with difficulty is to avoid emotionalism and cultivate self-control.

The temperance address of February 1842, which was delivered at the height of Lincoln's involvement with Speed's marital crisis, fairly resonates with personal significance. It reflects the color and direction of Lincoln's thinking about human affairs in general, as well as the more pointed and personal questions of moral responsibility that had been plaguing him for more than a year. The strong identification with the Washingtonians, not in spite of but *because* of their being reformed drunkards, represents an empathy born of experience. Like himself in the humiliating throes of mental debility, the suffering alcoholics need understanding and support, but no one can effect their rescue and rehabilitation but themselves. The Romanticism of the age, such as that reflected in the Byronic poems he was reading, explored the haunted chasms of the self, but Lincoln was learning the perils of self-indulgence and the value of self-control.

⤙

HERNDON EMPHASIZED the damage Lincoln's speech and its stance did to his popularity among "professing Christians," who were offended at his criticism of those who ostracized drunkards on religious grounds.[115] The Democrats were sure that popularity was precisely what Lincoln was after. Their paper asked: "does any rational man believe for a moment that Abraham Lincoln, B. S. Clement and Edward D. Baker have joined the Washingtonian Society from any other than political motives. Would they have joined it if it had been exceedingly unpopular?"[116] It is possible that both these views are applicable, for the temperance address also bristles with implications for politics. It strongly implies that the rank and file need not be in thrall to their leaders, self-appointed or otherwise. Perhaps the clearest admonition for political action is found in the related preference for the carrot over the stick. "It is an old and true maxim, that a 'drop of honey catches more flies than a gallon of gall.' So with men. If you would win a man to your cause, *first* convince him that you are his sincere friend."[117]

Lincoln had, in 1840, been seen by himself and others as a "rising man," someone in the process of establishing himself as an organizer and leader, one of the lawgivers of his party. Whereas the energetic Hard Cider campaign witnessed his unambiguous ascendancy, the events of late 1840 and early 1841 seriously disrupted this process. When his party needed him in the hard fight over the makeup of the Illinois Supreme Court in January and February 1841, he was of little help. By the summer of 1842, though still a member of the Springfield Junto, he was no longer on the Whig ticket for the state legislature,[118] or, as he phrased it to a correspondent, he was "off the track."[119] The extent to which this was a personal decision is not altogether clear, and none of his biographers has inquired very seriously into the matter. The few clues that exist suggest that he chose not to run for reelection, but with no indication why. Springfield's Democratic paper said in March, "Mr. Lincoln, perhaps, will not accept the nomination, though urged by Baker, who thinks Mr. Lincoln's influence in the Legislature would elect Baker, U.S. Senator."[120] He may have been positioning himself for a crack at the congressional seat occupied by John T. Stuart, who would not seek reelection. To Joshua Speed he confessed in his letter of July 4 that he was not yet capable of decisive action because he still doubted his ability "to keep [his] resolves when they are made." In personal affairs, this clearly meant that he was not ready to renew his courtship of Mary Todd. In politics, it may have meant that he was simply undecided about his next move.

The scriptural admonition with which Lincoln punctuated the personal part of his letter to Speed – "Stand *still* and see the salvation of the Lord" – is a further clue to his state of mind. It was offered in the context of his being an active agent for good in Speed's affair, to which he demurs on fatalistic grounds: "I always was superstitious; and as part of my superstition, I believe God made me one of the instruments of bringing your Fanny and you together, which union, I have no doubt He had foreordained. Whatever he designs, he will do for *me* yet. 'Stand *still* and see the salvation of the Lord' is my text just now."[121] The biblical passage from which this is taken is a prophetic promise to the badly outnumbered forces of Jehoshaphat that they will prevail against their enemies simply by appearing at the battleground and having faith in the outcome. "Ye shall not need to fight in this battle: set yourselves, stand ye still, and see the salvation of the Lord with you, O Judah and Jerusalem."[122] This comes to pass when the enemies of Jehoshaphat destroy each other. The larger meaning of the biblical quotation Lincoln invoked thus had to do with knowing when to act and when it was more advantageous to "stand still." If this was a lesson being learned in the crucible of his ordeal, it would prove a valuable one indeed.

Chapter 9

HONOR

LINCOLN'S BIOGRAPHERS are generally agreed that he secretly resumed his courtship of Mary Todd in the summer of 1842 under the auspices of their mutual friend, Mrs. Simeon Francis. It was in these secret meetings at the Francis home, they say, that he became involved in the joint project of Mary and her friend Julia Jayne to make public sport of the Democratic state auditor, James Shields. This took the form of a series of pseudonymous letters that appeared during August and September in the pages of the *Sangamo Journal*, letters purporting to come from a place called the Lost Townships and from the pen of a farm woman named Rebecca. Drawn into the fun by the two young women, Lincoln is supposed to have contributed one of the most hilarious and insulting letters and, when the angry auditor demanded the name of the author, gallantly instructed the editor to attribute all the letters to himself. This, in essence, is presumed to be the background for one of the "scrapes" Lincoln most regretted, his near duel with James Shields.[1]

But it almost certainly didn't happen that way. While some of the elements in this colorful story derive from credible testimony, the story itself will not stand close scrutiny. In the first place, the biographers' chronology of this incident is entirely presumptive. In spite of the easy assumption of informants and biographers alike, there is no direct evidence that Lincoln and Mary were meeting before the dueling affair, which climaxed on September 22, while there is strong evidence that their reconciliation was effected later.[2] Moreover, there are clear indications that Julia Jayne and Mary Todd contributed nothing to the satiri-cal Lost Townships series before Shields had already demanded the name of the offending author, an objection entirely fatal to Lincoln's supposed act of gallantry.

Nonetheless, the episode was a highly dramatic one with important long-range consequences for Abraham Lincoln. It started off inno-cently enough with a piece he composed for the *Sangamo Journal*, written, as he stoutly insisted, strictly for "political effect." He had been writing editorial matter and political pieces for years, and according to William H. Herndon, "Whatever he wrote or had written, went into the editorial page [of the *Sangamo Journal*] without question."[3] The opportunity Lincoln responded to was a seemingly irresistible one. The Democratic state officers had been forced, by the impending collapse of the State Bank and the depressed value of its currency, to order a refusal to accept such currency in payment of state taxes. This was seen, in the words of one commentator, as "the peak of perfidy – the State refusing to honor the currency of its own institution."[4] In this situation, it fell to the state auditor, James Shields, to announce and enforce this vastly unpopular measure. For the Whigs, this was an unlooked-for political windfall. Never mind that the ravaging of the state's finances was prin-cipally caused by the internal improvements system that Lincoln and his friends had championed and helped to push through five years ear-lier. The ruling Democrats had been forced to invoke painfully unpopu-lar measures, and the Whigs were out to make the most of it.

The currency crisis was not disclosed until after the state elections in early August, but political observers could clearly see it coming. The first of the Lost Townships letters was dated August 10 and appeared in the *Sangamo Journal* on August 19. The letter resembles an earlier one purporting to come from the fictitious Lost Townships and has all the earmarks of a newspaper editor's attempt to fill out his columns with something at once political and amusing.[5] Rebecca, the supposed author, quotes extensively from her farmer husband, Jonathan, who quotes Andrew Jackson to his neighbors. The tone is mildly political without being an out-and-out partisan polemic. The pace is leisurely, the English is reasonably standard, and while there is whimsy, there is not much humor. The state's financial problems are discussed, but the nearest the letter comes to an indictment of state officials is this: "We heard a few days ago, by a traveller from Quincy, that the Governor was going to send instructions to collectors, not to take anything but gold and silver for taxes."[6] As there is no mention of the auditor, the likelihood that this letter was written by Julia Jayne and Mary Todd for sport at the expense of James Shields is virtually nil.

The second Lost Townships letter, the one written by Lincoln, is entirely different. Dated August 27, the day after Shields's order to refuse State Bank currency for taxes was issued, it takes out after the auditor with a vengeance. What made the situation so perfect for Lincoln, who was by this time an old hand at pseudonymous satire, was that his victim, though genial and generally well liked, was a vain and therefore vulnerable man. A native of Ireland and a staunch Democrat, Shields was a handsome bachelor who was thought to pride himself on his fancied attractiveness to women. Shields was thus doubly susceptible to satiric treatment. As Herndon observed, "Blind to his own defects, and very pronounced in support of every act of the Democratic party, he made himself the target for all the bitterness and ridicule of the day."[7] Lincoln's letter gave him both barrels.

Unlike the first letter, in which Rebecca expresses herself for the most part in standard English, Lincoln's is rendered entirely in comic dialect. Though addressed in personal terms to "Mr. Printer," much of the letter consists of a reported dialogue between the fictitious farm wife Rebecca and a neighbor named Jeff. After a brief introduction, it opens with Rebecca calling on her neighbors to inquire about their new baby.

> "How are you Jeff," says I, – he sorter started when he heard me, for he hadn't seen me before. "Why," says he, "I'm mad as the devil, aunt Becca."
> "What about," says I, "aint its hair the right color? None of that nonsense, Jeff – there aint an honester woman in the Lost Township than –"
> "Than who?" says he, "what mischief are you about?"[8]

The object of Jeff's anger is, of course, not his wife's behavior but the proclamation that State Bank currency would not be accepted for taxes. Though basically sympathetic, Aunt Becca decides to use this occasion for some fun. "I saw Jeff was in a good tune for saying some ill-natured things, and so I tho't I would just argue a little on the contrary side, and make him rant a spell if I could."[9]

This sets the stage for the political points Lincoln wants to score against Shields and the Democrats. The justification for refusing to accept state paper, as Aunt Becca repeats with a straight face, is that, quoting the official announcement, *"there will be danger of loss"* if it isn't done. But Jeff insists that the only loss at issue is the loss to the Democratic state officeholders, the issuers of the proclamation, who would have to take their salaries in depreciated state paper. It is enough to make a minister swear, says Jeff, "to have tax to pay in silver, for nothing only that [Governor] Ford may get his two thousand a year, and Shields his twenty four hundred a year, and [State Treasurer] Carpenter his sixteen hundred a year, and all without 'danger of loss' by taking it in State paper."[10]

Lincoln next deftly puts the knife in by referring to a clerk in Shields's office named Wash who had embezzled state funds: "Wash, I 'spose, actually lost fifteen hundred dollars out of the three thousand that two of these 'officers of State' let him steal from the Treasury, by being compelled to take it in State paper." He then gives it an ingenious twist by having Jeff wonder if these state officers are going to insist that the depreciated value of the stolen state paper be made up in silver for the benefit of the thief.

Jeff concludes that Shields is lying about the situation and that he is doing so because he is not a true Democrat but a Whig. The charge of being a liar would ordinarily be considered fighting words, though their political context here would probably suffice to mitigate or defuse the injury. Political insults were part of the game, so long as they didn't descend to the personal. Jeff tells Rebecca an anecdote that is supposed to demonstrate that Shields is a Whig and not a Democrat:

> I seed him when I was down in Springfield last winter. They had a sort of a gatherin there one night, among the grandees, they called a fair. All the galls about town was there, and the handsome widows, and married women, finickin about, trying to look like galls, tied as tight in the middle, and puffed out at both ends like bundles of fodder that hadn't been stacked yet, but wanted stackin pretty bad. And then they had tables all round the house kivered over with baby caps, and pin-cushions, and ten thousand such little nick-nacks, trying to sell 'em to the fellows that were bowin and scrapin and kungeerin about 'em. They wouldn't let no democrats in, for fear they'd disgust the ladies, or scare the little galls, or dirty the floor.[11]

It is here that Lincoln's satire crosses the line. His political point has been made: that Shields's proclamation is so offensive and unacceptable that loyal Democrats will conclude he must be a Whig. It was an old trick, but Lincoln's saucy dialect and animated characterization brought it to life and made it effective. That he was enjoying himself is evidenced by the racy metaphor about married women in tight clothing, which is both comic and suggestive but which, for this time and place, certainly transgressed the boundaries of propriety and good taste. But what immediately followed veered off from the political and took dead aim at the personal.

> I looked in at the window, and there was this same fellow Shields floatin about on the air, without heft or earthly substance, just like a lock of cat-fur where cats had been fightin.
> He was paying his money to this one and that one, and tother one, and sufferin great loss because it wasn't silver instead of State paper; and the sweet distress he seemed to be in, – his very features, in the exstatic agony of his soul, spoke audibly and distinctly – "Dear girls, *it is distressing,* but I cannot marry you all. Too well I know how much you suffer; but do, *do* remember, it is not my fault that I am so handsome and *so* interesting."[12]

The references to "great loss" and "State paper" are political, but the gratuitous sarcasm of "the exstatic agony of his soul" is doubly offensive. Not just personal, this passage is not even masked in dialect, so that the presence of the pseudonymous satirist behind the words is clearly, if briefly, revealed.

This letter appeared in the *Sangamo Journal* on September 2, and Shields, according to his friend Dr. John D. Whiteside, lost no time in demanding that the editor reveal the name of its author.[13] Shields sending a friend to demand the name of the author was surely red-hot news among Springfield Whigs, quickly becoming the object of gossip and speculation in the circle of which Mary Todd and her friends were a part. That he had made his inquiry by September 8 is shown by the content of another letter signed "Rebecca" that appeared the next day in the *Sangamo Journal.* "Why, when I found out that it was the man what Jeff seed down to the fair, that had demanded the author of my letters, threatnin to to [*sic*] take personal satisfaction of the writer, I was so skart that I tho't I should quill-wheel right where I was."[14] For personal satisfaction, Rebecca offers in this letter to let him squeeze her hand, an allusion to a charge from the previous letter that Shields was notorious for squeezing young ladies' hands. "If this should not answer, there is one thing more that I would do rather than get a lickin," she writes, and that is to marry Shields. "I know he's a fightin man, and would rather fight than eat; but isn't marrying better than fightin, though it does sometimes run into it?"[15]

This letter is not nearly so clever in its handling of Rebecca's dialect and distinctive tone of voice as the one Lincoln admitted writing. In making Rebecca a widow (she had been married the previous week), it expediently changes the fictional equation, probably in preparation for her remarriage the following week. This letter may indeed have been composed by Julia Jayne, possibly in collaboration with Mary Todd. But since its subject is Shields demanding the name of the author, and since Mary and Julia had not written either of the first two letters, it seems clear that Shields must have taken offense *before* their involvement. Mary claimed only to have written the verses that appeared the following week on September 16, announcing the nuptials of Rebecca and her challenger. They began:

> Ye jews-harps awake! the A[uditor]'s won –
> Rebecca, the widow, has gained Erin's son,
> The pride of the north from the emerald isle
> Has been woo'd and won by a woman's sweet smile.[16]

In reminiscing about these events many years later, Mary told a correspondent, "Shields was always, a subject of mirth, his impulsiveness & drolleries were irresistible. On one occasion, he made himself, so conspicuous, that I committed his follies, to rhyme & some person, looking over the silly verses – carried them off and had them published in the daily paper of the place."[17] Her belief that the verses had caused Lincoln to be challenged is on a par with many of the other details she includes that are demonstrably wrong, but there seems little reason for doubting that she wrote the verses.[18]

But if Mary made no claim to have written anything but the verses, there are reasons for thinking that Julia Jayne was actively involved and that she may have written or participated in the writing of the September 8 letter. Authoritative informants suggest that she was indeed somehow involved in this affair. Her husband, Lyman Trumbull, told Jesse W. Weik, "It is my impression that Miss Todd and Miss Jayne had something to do in writing the poetry published in the Illinois Journal, at which Gen'l Shields took offence, but I cannot give you particulars."¹⁹ Julia's younger brother William, who became a good friend of Lincoln's in later years, claimed to have delivered the poem to the newspaper. He told Herndon: "When I was a boy *Mrs* Lincoln and *Mrs* Trumbull, both girls at that time got me to drop the Satiracle poetry against Shields – Gen Jas Shields – which in part caused the challeng by Shields."²⁰ William Butler, who was close to Lincoln and played a role in the duel, told John G. Nicolay that Julia (who was still living) did *all* the writing, and he went on to speculate about how Lincoln got involved. "They had a party at Edwards' and Shields squeezed Miss [Julia Jayne's] hand. (She was afterwards Mrs. [Lyman Trumbull]) [.] Miss [Jayne] took her revenge by writing the letters from the 'Lost Townships' and probably with Mary Todds connivance sent them to the editor of the Journal by Mr. Lincoln."²¹

Like most informants recalling the events years later, Butler embraced the theory that Lincoln took the blame for defamatory matter written by the two women. "The editor seeing the personal nature of the articles, asked Lincoln whom he should give as the author, in case he was called upon to furnish the name. The requirements of gallantry of course left Lincoln no alternative but to tell the editor that he would be personally responsible."²² But such theorizing seems in all cases to represent not firsthand knowledge but after-the-fact attempts to understand or rationalize the women's known involvement in Lincoln's "affair of honor." It is, of course, possible that Julia and/or Mary wrote the September 8 letter and that the editor consulted with Lincoln before publishing it, and it is also possible that Lincoln told him to ascribe the letter to himself. But there is a positive and powerful objection to this theory – namely, Lincoln's categorical denial, when challenged, that he had written anything in the series but the letter of September 2.

When one examines these stories closely, it is hard to make sense of them. What, if he really was concerned, was the editor worried about? The young women had nothing to fear from Shields, for even if their identity should be revealed, he could never challenge or chastise them. It would have been unmanly for Shields to complain, and he would almost certainly never have done so. By the gentlemen's code in effect, only the editor would be faulted, for giving out their names. Editors were frequently caught in the middle in these situations, and in this case Lincoln's telling the editor to give his own name as the author might be regarded as an act of protection for his friend Simeon Frances. But if this were the case, in denying his authorship to Shields, Lincoln would have betrayed his friend as well as the two women, a circumstance that could scarcely have gone unremarked at the time.

⁓

AS WITH MANY dramatic incidents, the affair of the Lost Townships letters clearly inspired speculation. From certain agreed-upon facts – that Lincoln and Mary had met secretly at the Francis home, that Mary and Julia wrote one or more of the Lost Township pieces, that Shields had demanded the name of the author, and that Shields had then challenged Lincoln – a story eventually emerged. Even though all these elements rest on reasonably reliable evidence, the story itself went awry. In order to create stories from facts, one must make assumptions, but assumptions can be treacherous, and they have a way of circling back on themselves. Perhaps the key assumption that caused observers to go astray in the Shields affair was this: that Lincoln and the two young women must have been in league in writing the Lost Townships letters. Why should we assume this to have been true? Because Lincoln, who wrote one of the letters, was secretly courting Mary, who was involved in the writing of another. How do we know he was secretly courting Mary at this time? Because he was mixed up with her in the writing of the Lost Townships letters. This line of inference, of course, won't wash, for it is a patently circular argument: it assumes what it attempts to prove.

Unwarranted assumptions have a way of begetting their like. An instance of this kind of reasoning appears in the *Collected Works*, where the editors report that a certain document in Lincoln's hand was gotten up at this very time as a kind of courtship offering. "It is laced together with pink ribbon tied in a bow at the top, as it was prepared for Mary Todd on the day when her satiric contribution to the Rebecca letters was published in the *Sangamo Journal*."[23] The document, certified by the clerk of the County Commissioners Court on September 9, 1842, proves to be a tally of candidates and votes received in Lincoln's first three races for the state legislature, showing that after finishing eighth in the 1832 election (the top four being elected), Lincoln had the second-highest total of any candidate in 1834 and the highest total in 1836. "It is difficult to avoid the conjecture," write the editors, "that Lincoln produced this prosaic but obviously sentimental document as a result of his meetings with Mary at the home of Simeon Francis during the letter-writing episode."[24]

But it is difficult to avoid such a conjecture only if one assumes that the document was created at the time the vote tallies were certified by the clerk. What is much more difficult, if we are to accept this document as a courtship gesture in September 1842, is why the proud politician, anxious to impress his female collaborator, should make no mention of the second half of his political career: his successive reelection to office in 1838 and 1840. The editors of Lincoln's *Collected Works* seem to have been misled by the great Lincoln biographer, Albert J. Beveridge, who overlooked the fact that the electoral tally was incomplete.[25] The assumption that Lincoln created this incomplete record of his electoral accomplishments for presentation to Mary Todd in September 1842 defies belief. What recommends it to the editors of the *Collected Works* is a further assumption about the significance of the certification date, which rests on additional assumptions about Lincoln's collaboration with Mary Todd in the Lost Townships letters. Unfortunately, none of these assumptions, which promiscuously feed on and reinforce one another, is borne out by the evidence.

What helps keep us on track in the Shields affair, as this instance shows, is close attention to chronology. Unless we can be sure that Lincoln and Mary Todd's meetings at the Francis house were going on as early as August, we cannot confirm a conspiracy. In like manner, unless we can be sure that Shields sent his inquiry to the editor *after* the two women's contribution appeared in the newspaper and not before, we can hardly assign them a role in writing the satire that precipitated the challenge. Neither of these conditions, as it turns out, can be affirmed. Strong evidence (to be introduced later) indicates that Lincoln and Mary did not resume their courtship until after the duel, and we have already seen that Shields's demand to know the name of the author was far more likely to have been the cause than the effect of the women's involvement.

Shields eventually challenged Lincoln to a duel, but not before a certain amount of time had passed, another circumstance that works to cloud the chronology. Lincoln's letter, the first to mention Shields by name, appeared on Friday, September 2, and Shields apparently had Dr. John Whiteside demand the name of the author without delay. But knowing that a challenge would need time to be played out, Shields first went to Quincy to attend to urgent state business. Whiteside, who would serve as his second, wrote: "An offensive article in relation to Mr. Shields appeared in the *Sangamo Journal* of the 2d of September last; and, on demanding the author, Mr. Lincoln was given up by the editor. Mr. Shields, previous to this demand, made arrangements to go to Quincy on public business; and before his return Mr. Lincoln had left for Tremont to attend the court, with the intention, as we learned, of remaining on the circuit several weeks."[26] Lincoln does not seem to have left Springfield until September 15, and Shields must have just missed him, for he and Whiteside took off for Tremont the next day.

This sequencing of events tells us a great deal. First, the second letter attacking Shields personally, possibly written by Julia Jayne herself or in collaboration with Mary Todd, appeared (on September 9) while Shields was out of town. If he didn't arrive back in Springfield until September 16 and immediately left for Tremont, he probably would not have had time to have Whiteside again demand the name of the writer and no doubt merely assumed it was another of Lincoln's productions.[27] (He may also have seen Mary Todd's satirical verses, which were published on the day he left.) This would account for his reference to "articles of the most personal nature" in the note he had Whiteside deliver the next morning in Tremont to Abraham Lincoln.

> A. Lincoln, Esq.
> I regret that my absence on public business compelled me to postpone a matter of private consideration a little longer than I could have desired. It will only be necessary, however, to account for it by informing you that I have been to Quincy on business that would not admit of delay. I will now state briefly the reasons of my troubling you with this communication, the disagreeable nature of which I regret – as I had hoped to avoid any difficulty with any one in Springfield, while residing there, by endeavoring to conduct myself in such a way amongst both my political friends and opponents, as to escape the necessity of any. Whilst thus abstaining from giving provocation, I have become the object of slander, vituperation and personal abuse, which were I capable of submitting to, I would prove myself worthy of the whole of it.

Especially for modern readers who find dueling a barbarous form of conduct inconsistent with reputable behavior, Shields's last sentence is worth noting. For someone like Shields, who considered that he carefully avoided giving offense, letting a public insult pass without notice was tantamount to acknowledging that he was cowardly. His note continued:

In two or three of the last numbers of the Sangamo Journal, articles of the most personal nature and calculated to degrade me, have made their appearance. On enquiring I was informed by the editor of that paper, through the medium of my friend, Gen. White-side, that you are the author of those articles. This information satisfies me that I have become by some means or other, the object of your secret hostility. I will not take the trouble of enquiring into the reason of all this, but I will take the liberty of requiring a full, positive and absolute retraction of all offensive allusions used by you in these communications, in relation to my private character and standing as a man, as an apology for the insults conveyed in them.

This may prevent consequences which no one will regret more than myself. Your ob't serv't,

Jas. Shields[28]

This may have put Lincoln in mind of a passage from Thomas Moore's life of Lord Byron, which told of his lordship's receiving a menacing letter from a Colonel Grenville on the subject of what the poet had written about him in a satirical work. Byron refused to reply until the letter had been toned down, something that Moore, as his designated friend, promptly arranged with Grenville's friend.[29] Like Byron, Lincoln saw at once that Shields had overplayed his hand. He had assumed things that weren't true, such as Lincoln's authorship of letters written by others, and he had demanded a retraction of things for which Lincoln was not responsible. In these circumstances, Shields presumably had no business speaking ominously of consequences.[30] When Whiteside called for Lincoln's response later in the day, he was handed the following reply:

Jas. Shields, Esq.

Your note of to-day was handed me by Gen. Whiteside. In that note you say you have been informed, through the medium of the editor of the Journal, that I am the author of certain articles in that paper which you deem personally abusive of you; and without stopping to enquire whether I really am the author, or to point out what is offensive in them, you demand an unqualified retraction of all that is offensive; and then proceed to hint at consequences.

Now, sir, there is in this so much of assumption of facts, and so much of menace as to consequences, that I cannot submit to answer that note any further than I have, and to add, that the consequences to which I suppose you allude, would be matter of as great regret to me as it possibly could to you. Respectfully,

A. Lincoln[31]

Lincoln's gifts as an adversary, his ability to find and seize an advantage under pressure, are here conspicuously on display. Shields, in apparent acknowledgment of Lincoln's objections, wrote again the same evening, taking care to specify more accurately which article the editor had actually attributed to Lincoln.

> A. Lincoln, Esq.
> In reply to my note of this date [September 17], you intimate that I assume facts, and menace consequences, and that you cannot submit to answer it further. As now, sir, you desire it, I will be a little more particular. The editor of the Sangamo Journal gave me to understand that you are the author of an article which appeared I think in that paper of 2d Sept. inst, headed the Lost Townships, and signed Rebecca or Becca. I would therefore take the liberty of asking, whether you are the author of said article or any other over the same signature, which has appeared in any of the late numbers of that page. If so, I repeat my request of an absolute retraction of all offensive allusion contained therein in relation to my private character and standing. If you are not the author of any of the articles, your denial will be sufficient. I will say further, it is not my intention to menace, but to do myself justice. Your ob't serv't,
> Jas. Shields[32]

This note was not delivered to Lincoln until two days later, and although he permitted himself to read it, he then returned it, telling Whiteside "that there could be no further negotiation between them until the first note was withdrawn."[33] This was a kind of chess game in which Lincoln was shrewdly maintaining the upper hand by careful adherence to form and turning Shields's demand for a retraction against him by insisting upon one of his own. Having lost time and moral momentum, Shields finally issued a challenge.

❧

IN THE CLASS of society that Lincoln was born into, fighting was commonplace, and it could be very rough. If you hooked up with the wrong antagonist, you could easily lose an eye or an ear in what everyone considered a fair fight. More "respectable" classes may have considered this rowdy and disreputable behavior, but even they frequently offered to settle their differences by an appeal to force. This usually meant a fistfight, but what kind of combat would ensue on such occasions was often in doubt, so that what was required was a certain readiness to defend one's honor. Lincoln was once reported as responding to just such a menacing personal attack on the floor of the legislature. Denying that he had intended a motion as a personal reflection on his two accusers, who threatened to hold him "responsible," he was reported as saying that "he was glad he had made it; the hydra was exposed; and all the talk about settling this matter at another tribunal, he had no objection to, if gentlemen insisted on it. He was always ready, and never shrunk from responsibility."[34] This kind of response, which characterized Lincoln's public demeanor, was regarded as manly and was universally admired.

With the self-consciously aristocratic classes with whom Lincoln was more and more associated, fighting was more formalized and less frequent. But because of the very real consequences of dueling, it could be fatal. Although it would be extraordinary in late-twentieth-century America for someone to think that he must put his life at risk over an insult, such as being called a liar, in the era of the Founding Fathers and the first half of the nineteenth century, it was frequently the case. The code of honor had very clear rules and procedures, and as Lincoln rose in society, he had more to do with people who considered themselves bound by this code. At the same time, appealing to the code was a way for someone like Shields – an aspiring, self-made immigrant – to assert his aristocratic pretensions.

Whereas the code of honor presumably established what a gentleman might say or not say about another gentleman, Lincoln seems to have operated on the basis of what he called the "set-off." By "set-off" he meant a fair reply to something offered by someone else. In 1837 he claimed in print that his slander on James Adams's patriotism in the Sampson's Ghost letters was not serious but only a set-off: "Gen. Adams himself, in reply to the Sampson's Ghost story, was the first man that raised the cry of toryism, and it was only by way of set-off, and never in seriousness, that it was bandied back at him."[35] Here the claim of set-off has all the earmarks of a blatant rationalization, but not all examples are of this sort. During the heat of the 1840 campaign, Lincoln exchanged political salvos and then letters with a political antagonist, William G. Anderson. In his letter he denied being "the aggressor" in the incident and wrote: "You say my 'words imported insult.' I meant them as a fair set-off to your own statements, and not otherwise; and in that light alone I now wish you to understand them."[36] Without our knowing what was said on either side, it is difficult to adjudicate this exchange, but Lincoln here seems to acknowledge that what he said, if unprovoked, could be interpreted as an insult. His claim is that it was prompted by, and was no more insulting than, what Anderson had said about him.

This would seem to point to a crucial distinction in the kind of political combat Lincoln considered himself involved in. Whereas the traditional code of honor made certain kinds of remarks out of bounds, in Lincoln's arena one might answer in kind, if provoked. The problem for Lincoln was precisely that some of his satiric thrusts against Shields had been not only personal but wholly unprovoked. He had been writing these pseudonymous pieces for years and had probably been guilty of crossing the line frequently. The *Register* had complained in exasperation over a similar kind of attack a few years earlier. "Our object is now to tell the editor of the Journal that he acts unfairly in licensing his unknown correspondence, to use the weapons of personal abuse against us. We are cut off from all reply in such a case. We know not the accuser and cannot reply to him. The advantage is all on his side, and if he be a man and a 'gentleman,' he must know this is so."[37]

The rule appealed to here was nonpartisan and no doubt broadly approved: personal abuse at the hands of unknown assailants was both unmanly and ungentlemanly. That is, it was not only cowardly but doubly discreditable to anyone presumed to be a "gentleman," a status that implied not only privilege but principled behavior. As a rising man in Springfield in the 1840s, Abraham Lincoln was unavoidably faced with the question of whether or not he was, or was capable of behaving as, a "gentleman." Men from conspicuously aristocratic backgrounds would probably be reluctant to challenge someone like Lincoln, for it was an outright acknowledgment of peer status. But lampooning someone as sensitive about his gentlemanly status as the egotistic Irishman, James Shields, was another matter. It meant that once found out, Lincoln would have to decide how far he was willing to carry his own gentlemanly pretensions. Like most people of the time, he was against dueling, itself against the law in Illinois. But the code of honor had considerable force, and a formal challenge was no trifling matter, especially for a politician.

~

IF LINCOLN had misgivings about accepting Shields's challenge, they were apparently not evident to observers. He promptly named Dr. Merryman as his "friend," or second, the person designated in a formal duel to act for the principal in the necessary negotiations. Ostensibly charged with arranging the terms and conditions of the prospective duel, in practice the seconds principally aimed at resolving the difficulty peacefully and avoiding an actual fight. Merryman, who, like his counterpart, Whiteside, published his version of events in the Springfield newspaper, implied that he enlisted in the affair because of his knowledge of the protocols of dueling, the infamous code duello. "I knew Mr. Lincoln, was wholly unpracticed both as to the diplomacy and weapons commonly employed in similar affairs; and I felt it my duty, as a friend, to be with him, and, so far as in my power, to prevent any advantage being taken of him as to either his honor or his life."[38]

At their initial meeting the two seconds pledged themselves to work for a peaceful resolution of difficulties and proceeded to occupy the same buggy for part of the trip back to Springfield. But circumstances conspired against them, and they bungled their peacemaking effort. Arriving in Springfield late Monday evening, Lincoln's associates discovered that the duel was already widely known, and they heard rumors of an imminent arrest. Without consulting Whiteside, they made plans to dictate the terms of the duel – weapons, time, and place – and flee the city the next day. Whiteside's plan was apparently to get Governor Thomas Ford and the powerful Democratic leader General W. L. D. Ewing to talk the ungovernable Shields out of the duel,[39] but before he could put it into action, Whiteside learned from Merryman on Tuesday that Lincoln had written out the terms and departed for Jacksonville. The incredulous Whiteside could neither agree to terms nor negotiate further under these conditions, nor could he consult his principal, who was still on his way back to Springfield with a lame horse. As a protest, he withdrew his pledge to Merryman, but he agreed to advise Shields of what had happened and to meet Lincoln's party in Missouri on Thursday, the appointed day.

The terms that he refused to accept had been written out by Lincoln the night before and were prefaced with instructions for Merryman as to how far Lincoln was willing to go in adjusting the quarrel.

In case Whitesides shall signify a wish to adjust this affair without further difficulty, let him know that if the present papers be withdrawn, & a note from Mr. Shields asking to know if I am the author of the articles of which he complains, and asking that I shall make him gentlemanly satisfaction, if I am the author, and this without menace, or dictation as to what that satisfaction shall be, a pledge is made, that the following answer shall be given –

"I did write the 'Lost Township' letter which appeared in the Journal of the 2nd. Inst. but had no participation, in any form, in any other article alluding to you. I wrote that, wholly for political effect. I had no intention of injuring your personal or private character, or standing as a man or a gentleman; and I did not then think, and do not now think that that article could produce or has produced that effect against you, and had I anticipated such an effect I would have forborne to write it. And I will add, that your conduct towards me, so far as I knew, had always been gentlemanly; and that I had no personal pique against you, and no cause for any."[40]

When Merryman suggested this approach at their meeting, Whiteside reportedly told him "it was useless to talk of an adjustment, if it could only be effected by the withdrawal of Mr. Shields' paper, for such withdrawal Mr. Shields would never consent to."[41]

Because they had to take circuitous routes – Lincoln's party by way of Jacksonville to procure weapons, Shields's by way of Hillsborough to pick up General Ewing – both parties had to travel hard to make it by Thursday to Alton, seventy miles away. Lincoln now was assisted by three friends: Merryman, William Butler, and Albert T. Bledsoe; Shields was assisted by Whiteside, Dr. Thomas M. Hope, and Ewing. The parties, accompanied by what was described in the Alton newspaper as "large numbers of our fellow-citizens,"[42] proceeded to an island in the Mississippi River that was in the state of Missouri.

Once on the ground, with no "adjustment" in sight, Lincoln's terms now came into play. They were:

1st. Weapons – Cavalry broad swords of the largest size, precisely equal in all respects – and such as now used by the cavalry company at Jacksonville.

2nd. Position – A plank ten feet long, & from nine to twelve inches broad to be firmly fixed on edge, on the ground, as the line between us which neither is to pass his foot over upon forfeit of his life. Next a line drawn on the ground on either side of said plank & parallel with it, each at the distance of the whole length of the sword and three feet additional from the plank; and the passing of his own such line by either party during the fight shall be deemed a surrender of the contest.[43]

Nothing could demonstrate more clearly the truth of the observation of a contemporary authority on dueling that the challenged party – in having the selection of the place, distance, time, and weapons – "has thus, by a choice designed to be least dangerous to himself, and most hazardous to his opponent, possessed an advantage."[44]

Shields was a man of about ordinary size, and while he had had military training and was no stranger to the use of a sword, he was, by these terms, seriously outclassed. The cavalry broadsword was large and heavy; it was often double-edged and designed not for artful swordplay, but for slashing. To wield it effectively required considerable arm strength and technique. But Lincoln's terms added a consideration that favored him even further. The battleground was restricted to two enclosed boxes, separated by a plank and bounded by a parallel line that was the sword's length plus three feet away. Because the combatant could not leave his box, the advantage went, all else being equal, to the man with the greatest reach. Not only was Abraham Lincoln abnormally tall, but a notable feature of his physique was his disproportionately long arms.[45]

It is tempting to see Lincoln's sense of humor at work in these specifications, especially in the blatant manner in which they work to his advantage. Likewise in the penalties for overstepping the boundaries: death for passing over the plank and "surrender of the contest" for transgressing the back line, as if duels could be decided by a foot fault.[46] But the humor here is more likely a function of hindsight. All indications are that Lincoln took his situation seriously and crafted his terms deliberately as a means of avoiding defeat. Usher Linder said that he asked Lincoln soon after the incident why he had selected broadswords and that Lincoln replied: "To tell you the truth, Linder, I did not want to kill Shields, and felt sure that I could disarm him, having had about a month to learn the broadsword exercise; and furthermore, I didn't want the d—d fellow to kill me, which I rather think he would have done if we had selected pistols."[47]

Although most affairs of honor were settled long before reaching the dueling field, Lincoln and Shields were both determined to see it through. Merryman reported that when he first arrived in Tremont, he asked Lincoln what he proposed to do. "He stated that he was wholly opposed to duelling, and would do anything to avoid it that might not degrade him in the estimation of himself and friends; but, if such degradation or a fight were the only alternatives, he would fight."[48] The difference between them was that Lincoln was willing to have the quarrel "adjusted" whereas Shields, as his friends soon discovered, was not.

John J. Hardin, a leading Whig, was one of those who hurried to the scene to help effect a reconciliation and, in partnership with Revel W. English, a Democrat, offered to submit the case to impartial judges. To this end they drafted a formal note on the scene to Merryman and Whiteside that concluded: "Let the whole difficulty be submitted to four or more gentlemen, to be selected by ourselves, who shall consider the affair, and report thereupon for your consideration."[49] Though this plan was ultimately not followed, it produced some progress, and Shields's friends, without his knowledge, eventually declared his offending note withdrawn. At this, by prior agreement, Lincoln's friends conveyed their principal's admission that he did write the September 2 letter "solely for political effect" and his denial that he intended to injure "the personal or private character or standing of Mr. Shields as a gentleman or a man."[50] With this, support for Shields apparently collapsed. According to Whiteside, "This was all done without the knowledge or consent of Mr. Shields, and he refused to accede to it, until Dr. Hope, General Ewing, and myself declared the apology sufficient, and that we could not sustain him in going further."[51] This ended the duel, for though Shields would apparently have preferred to fight, his friends had effectively declared it unnecessary. His honor, in other words, was no longer in need of vindication.

Shields was not the only one who hoped for a more dramatic conclusion to this contest, for it is apparent from several accounts that William Butler was deeply disappointed in the outcome. He had, at the beginning of the affair, driven his buggy all night with Dr. Merryman to get to Tremont before Shields and Whiteside and warn Lincoln, pointedly bringing along a pair of dueling pistols. His eagerness to have a fight is indicated by the suggestion he made to Lincoln for the trip from Tremont back to Springfield: "You ride in the buggy with Whitesides, and I will get into the buggy with Shields, and I will propose to Shields that we all stop in the prairie on our way down and 'settle the matter' (i e have the duel then and there.)."[52] When a fight was finally in prospect, he regarded the efforts to stop it as rank interference. He told John G. Nicolay, "All hands went down there, crossed over to the island, cleared a spot of ground, set up the boards and the duel was about to proceed, when Hardin and English interfered and stopped it."[53] Nicolay's notes continue: "Butler says he does not know how the matter was arranged – that he had become disgusted with the whole proceeding and was sitting on a log about thirty feet away expecting to see a bloody fight, when much to his astonishment the whole affair came to an end – the seconds suddenly stepping between the combatants and taking their swords from them."[54]

Thus ended Lincoln's one and only affair of honor. To modern readers it has all the trappings of comic opera, but we miss an important point if we do not recognize that the combatants were in deadly earnest, that they were willing to risk their lives for something presumably more important: their honor. It is clear from the example of Shields and his friends that honor in this sense is something that goes beyond personal integrity or self-respect. It crucially involves and is largely determined by the expectations of one's friends. Particularly for politicians, who depended for their viability on their supporters, honor in this sense was indispensable.

⟿

JOHN J. HARDIN was a year younger than Abraham Lincoln and one of the ablest and most admired men of Lincoln's immediate world. The son of a distinguished Kentuckian who had been briefly a U.S. senator, Hardin was a graduate of Transylvania College who came to Illinois the same year Lincoln did, 1830, and settled in Jacksonville. Hardin served in the Black Hawk War when Lincoln did, but unlike Lincoln, he possessed a knowledge of military matters and played a leading role in the expedition. His recognized ability as a military leader was to make him a prominent participant in several important actions of the Illinois state militia. He preceded Lincoln to the bar by several years but followed him in the state legislature, being elected three successive terms to the House of Representatives beginning in 1836. He was very much a leader. It was Hardin, not Lincoln, who would be elected to succeed John T. Stuart in Congress at the next election. Indeed, if Hardin had not been killed in the Mexican War in 1847, Lincoln's career in Illinois politics might have been very different.[55]

Hardin played a crucial role in resolving the difficulties between Shields and Lincoln and avoiding a duel. He was now to play an even more important part in Lincoln's life that has gone unrecognized by his biographers. Whereas Mrs. Simeon Francis has been given the credit for getting Lincoln and Mary Todd back together, it probably belongs to Hardin and his wife Sarah. Hardin was a cousin of Mary Todd's and had played host to the excursion party that traveled, at Christmastime 1840, to his home in Jacksonville. The Hardins may have had cause to remember this visit, for a remark in a January 1843 letter from John, then in Springfield, to his wife seems to refer to this occasion: "They are threatening to get up a party to go down on the Rail Road to

Jacksonville next Thursday or Friday. . . . As I have not forgotten two winters ago, I shall not ask any one, so do not trouble yourself lest I overrun you with company."[56] Whatever happened at Christmastime in 1840, the Hardins were apparently anxious not to have a repeat performance.

The Hardins thus knew all about the travails of Lincoln and Mary Todd. It was, after all, Hardin's sister, Martinette, who wrote her brother in January 1841 asking about the truth of reports reaching Jacksonville that Abraham Lincoln had had, as she put it, "two Cat fits, and a Duck fit."[57] Martinette was now eighteen and about to be married to another Kentuckian, Alexander McKee. The wedding took place five days after the Shields duel on September 27,[58] and there is good reason to believe that Lincoln and Mary Todd were there.[59]

As this is an unrecorded chapter in Lincoln's life, a review of the evidence is in order. To begin with, the bride herself testified that Lincoln was present. But she also implied that Shields was too, a circumstance that would scarcely have gone unremarked. Speaking of the duel more than fifty years later, Martinette told a reporter, "They returned to Springfield on the evening of my wedding, and brother brought them both up to the house. They did not have time to change their clothes, so they appeared as they were, to the astonishment of all our guests."[60] Mistaking Springfield for Jacksonville indicates that the reporter was confused, and this, together with other errors and doubtful points, suggests that the details of this account stand in particular need of confirmation.

No confirmation has been found for Shields's presence at the wedding, which seems very unlikely. He may, of course, have passed through Jacksonville on his way back to Springfield and been introduced. But for the presence of Lincoln and Mary Todd there is confirmation. First, there is the recollection of Sarah Rickard, whose name figures so mysteriously in Lincoln's letters to Speed. She admitted to Herndon the truth of what he had heard from other sources: that Lincoln had taken her out during this period and teasingly proposed marriage. It is clear from the Hardin letters of the period that Sarah Rickard was a close friend of Martinette's, which lends authority to her testimony about being at the wedding.[61] Describing the event to a reporter, Sarah said: "I sat next to Mr. Lincoln at the wedding dinner. He was going with me quite a good deal then. Mary Todd sat just across. Of course, rather than bring constraint upon the company, they spoke to each other, and that was the beginning of the reconciliation."[62] Sarah could have been mistaken or she could have been trying to insert herself in the life of a great man, but she specified the name of the bride, the place, and the occasion, all of which gives this report a strong ring of authenticity.

John and Sarah Hardin's role in getting Lincoln and Mary Todd back together may appear accidental but probably was not. Christopher C. Brown, the son-in-law of John T. Stuart, was reported as the source of an "absolutely true" story published in the 1890s to the effect that the Hardins had cleverly arranged a meeting at their home between Abraham and Mary that resulted in their reconciliation. His story is probably a more detailed and colorful version of one told by his mother-in-law, Mrs. John T. Stuart. In Brown's version, the Hardins arranged things so that all their visitors paired off and went for a ride except Mary Todd, who had no escort. Mary was thus sitting on the porch alone when Lincoln was ushered onto the scene. "And it was there their differences were arranged: and when the party returned, they thought they understood why Mary Todd had refused to go riding with them."[63]

Brown could not have been present, but his story is interesting even as family hearsay, particularly since Mary Todd was considered part of the family he had married into.[64] His mother-in-law's version is more sparsely recorded, but it has a compelling provenance. She claims to have heard this story from Mary Todd Lincoln herself, and only a few months after it happened. Ida Tarbell's notes of her interview with Mrs. Stuart read as follows:

> Mrs. L[incoln] told Mrs Stuart of the reconciliation afterwards. They had bought the house in 8th st[reet] but a child of the former occupant was so ill that the family could not leave at the time appointed and Mrs S. took Mr.[s.] L who had broken off at the Globe [the hotel the newlywed Lincolns were living in] – to her house to live for & in 3 weeks. Mrs L. then told her much of her former life. She said after she & Mr L broke off she was very sad. A friend at Jacksonville knowing the state of affairs had invited a number of Springfield young people down for a visit. The girls were at his house – one day the whole party was going out to ride – no one spoke to Mrs Lincoln (Miss Todd) about going. She saw the carriage arrive & from the chamber window watched them depart to her great chagrin & surprise. Suddenly Mr L drove up & asked for her. She went down & he

said he had come for her to join the party. She went & a reconciliation followed. The meetings were held clandestinly for a time
at the house of a friend & one day she announced to her sister
Mr[s.] E that she was going to be married.[65]

It may not be possible to form a clear picture of precisely how this
"chance" meeting was arranged, but it seems to add up to an unexpected
encounter whose dramatic possibilities were probably enhanced by the
connivance of the Hardins. If Hardin had persuaded Lincoln to come
home with him to Jacksonvile and stay on for the wedding, Mary's presence would hardly have been a surprise to Lincoln. But his appearance
could certainly have come as a surprise to her. And if he had been prevailed upon by his hosts to save her from an embarrassing situation, his
chivalry and her gratitude could well have reignited some of the attraction he once felt for her.

⤙

IF THESE STORIES point to the beginning of a fateful reconciliation in
Jacksonville between Lincoln and Mary Todd, it means that the events
leading up to the challenge, the near-duel with Shields, and the renewal
of the courtship happened in fairly rapid succession, a space of about
five weeks. In another five weeks, the reunited couple was to marry. But
it also means that the standard version of the way Lincoln's courtship of
Mary Todd is related to the duel is exactly backward. Rather than Lincoln's involving himself in the Lost Townships letters as part of a
friendly conspiracy with Mary and her friends, it was *his* letter that created the controversy by introducing Shields by name, while Mary and
Julia Jayne were the ones who joined the fun, though this apparently
had nothing to do with Lincoln. As we have seen, this version of events
affords no occasion for any gallantry on Lincoln's part, for he protected
no one.

Back in Springfield, the dueling spirit refused to die out. The two
participants who were most dissatisfied with the peaceful outcome of
the original affair – Shields and Butler – were soon at sword's point
themselves, or something like it. In a letter dated October 5, Lincoln
described the scene for his friend Joshua Speed:

> You have heard of my duel with Shields, and I have now to inform
> you that the duelling business still rages in this city. Day-before-
> yesterday Shields challenged Butler, who accepted, and proposed
> fight[t]ing next morning at sun-rising in Bob. Allen's meadow, one

hundred yards distance with rifles. To this, Whitesides, Shields'
second, said "No" because of the law. Thus ended, duel No. 2. Yesterday, Whitesides chose to consider himself insulted by Dr. Merryman, and so, sent him a kind of *quasi* challenge inviting him to meet
him at the planter's House in St. Louis on next friday to settle their
difficulty. Merryman made me his friend, and sent W. a note
enquiring to know if he meant his note as a challenge, and if so, that
he would, according to the law in such case made and provided, pre-
scribe the terms of the meeting.[66]

As can be imagined from this much of the account, the affair between
the former seconds, Whiteside and Merryman, degenerated into an
inconclusive wrangle about terms, and Lincoln concluded his report
with the observation "the town is in a ferment and a street fight some
what expected."[67]

But Lincoln informed Speed that his true purpose in writing was
really something else, something more important. The passage that follows probably holds a number of clues, if not the key, to Lincoln's
dilemma and its resolution.

> But I began this letter not for what I have been writing; but to say
> something on that subject which you know to be of such solicitude to
> me. The immense suffering you endured from the first days of Sep-
> tember till the middle of February you never tried to conceal from
> me, and I well understood. You have now been the husband of a
> lovely woman nearly eight months. That you are happier now than
> you were the day you married her I well know; for without, you
> would not be living. But I have your word for it too; and the
> returning elasticity of spirits which is manifested in your letters. But I
> want to ask a closer question – "Are you now in *feeling* as well as
> *judgement*, glad you are married as you are?" From any body but me,
> this would be an impudent question not to be tolerated; but I know
> you will pardon it in me. Please answer it quickly as I feel impatient
> to know.[68]

Lincoln here chose his words with care. He carefully prepared the context so as to define the case precisely. Speed had suffered for six months
and had now been "the husband of a lovely woman nearly eight months,"
clear indications that Lincoln was going back over the preceding events
with great deliberation. All signs point to a happy result, but Lincoln
wanted to ask a more penetrating and personal question. In so doing,
he carefully framed the query so that it applied only to the present, to
now. He then bracketed his question so that Speed could not equivocate

and was obliged to answer as to his present *feeling* as well as *judgment*. And, we should note, Lincoln stressed his impatience to know the answer.

The core of Lincoln's query comes down to the age-old distinction between the heart and the head. The phrasing would seem to be an indication that one side of his nature had reached a conclusion and that he was now consulting Speed in hopes of quelling or confirming his doubts as to the other. Whichever side we opt for would be a speculation, for it is by no means evident that he was drawn by one side or the other, his feeling or his judgment. The conventional view, which coincides with the romantic or sentimental one, presumes that Lincoln had been listening to his heart and wanted to know what his fellow sufferer, Speed, who had passed through a comparable ordeal, had to say for the head. In other words, it is usually assumed that Lincoln's feelings for Mary Todd had been reawakened or confirmed and that he wanted to check with Speed to see how wise his own decision to marry seemed in retrospect. But if we judge according to the available clues and by what we know about how Lincoln subsequently made important decisions, we may well arrive at a different conclusion.

When Speed had presumably raised this question with Lincoln some months earlier and advised him as to how to resolve his situation with regard to Mary Todd, Lincoln, in his reply of July 4, had pleaded the priority of a larger issue: "I acknowledge the correctness of your advice too; but before I resolve to do the one thing or the other, I must regain my confidence in my own ability to keep my resolves when they are made. In that ability, you know, I once prided myself as the only, or at least the chief, gem of my character; that gem I lost – how, and when, you too well know. I have not yet regained it; and until I do, I can not trust myself in any matter of much importance."[69] There seems little doubt that Lincoln was here referring to his decision to back out of his arrangement with Mary Todd, a decision that precipitated an emotional calamity. Lincoln's dilemma, as he saw it in the summer of 1842, was whether to stay the course he had elected and try to live down the guilty feelings that "killed his soul" or to reverse himself and expediently resume a courtship that had lost its appeal. The first alternative had the advantage of consistency, of reinstating the "gem" of his character and showing that he was capable of keeping his "resolves"; the second offered release from the tortured feelings of guilt and something like absolution from the dreaded imputation of dishonorable behavior.

William H. Herndon had no doubt that in choosing to propose marriage, Lincoln had made a calculated decision. In the chapter on "Lincoln and Mary Todd" he drafted for the use of his collaborator Jesse W. Weik, Herndon wrote: "Lincoln knew that he did not love the girl: he had promised to wed her: he knew what would eventually come of it and it was a conflict between sacrificing his *honor* and sacrificing his *domestic peace*: he chose the latter – saved his honor and threw away domestic happiness. Who but Lincoln would have done this?"[70] Herndon's judgment on this matter has often been questioned and discounted, particularly in light of his presumed bias against Mary Todd Lincoln. His conclusion here is, indeed, presumptive and after the fact, but he was far from the only person close to Lincoln to hold this opinion. Joshua Speed, whose view probably guided Herndon's, was not living in Springfield when Lincoln and Mary were reconciled and could say no more about it than "they got together somehow." But he did not hesitate to say definitely why Lincoln had decided to do what he did: "Lincoln Married her for honor – feeling his honor bound to her."[71]

James H. Matheny *was* in Springfield when Lincoln and Mary Todd got back together and was asked to be a groomsman at their wedding. He gave Herndon an account of his involvement in the quickly arranged marriage ceremony and his impressions of the entire episode. Herndon's notes on his interview with Matheny read as follows:

> Says – That Lincoln and himself in 1842 were very friendly – That Lincoln came to him one evening and Said – Jim – "I shall have to marry that girl." Matheny Says that on the Same Evening Mr & Mrs Lincoln were married – That Lincoln looked and acted as if he was going to the Slaughter – : That Lincoln often told him directly & indirectly that he was driven into the marriage – Said it was Concocted & planned by the Edwards family –: That Miss Todd – afterwards Mrs Lincoln told L. that he was in honor bound to marry her.[72]

As we have seen, Lincoln had a political motive for casting his situation in this light, for he was trying to persuade Matheny and his young Whig friends that he had not married into the Todd-Stuart-Edwards family in order to join the "aristocracy."[73] But there seems no reason to doubt that he actually said it.

Speed and Matheny were not the only close friends to use the phrase "honor bound" in describing Lincoln's predicament and his ultimate decision to marry. Orville H. Browning, whose testimony has only recently come to light, claimed to be conversant with these matters at first hand, as a result of close contact at the time with both parties. He told John G. Nicolay: "In this affair of his courtship, [Lincoln] undoubtedly felt that he had made [a mistake] in having engaged himself to Miss Todd. But having done so, he felt himself in honor bound to act in perfect good faith towards her – and that good faith compelled him to fulfill his engagment with her, if she persisted in claiming the fulfillment of his word." He added: "I always doubted whether, had circumstances left him entirely free to act upon his own impulses, he would have voluntarily made proposals of marriage to Miss Todd. There is no doubt of her exceeding anxiety to marry him."[74]

It is tempting to see, as the basis of all this talk about Lincoln's having considered himself "honor bound," his own language in the matter. If we accept this version of his motivation – that he felt "honor bound" to marry Mary Todd – then the crux of his problem was no longer whether Mary Todd was the right choice or whether "his heart was going with his hand," as Speed had characterized Lincoln's original dilemma. To judge from his letters and his behavior during this period, Lincoln had been suffering from a loss of confidence and the consequent loss of the "gem" of his character, his ability to keep his mind made up. His July 4 letter to Speed indicates an acute awareness that he needed to regain that confidence and that ability, not merely to resolve his situation with respect to Mary Todd or run for political office, but in order to redeem his own character and regain his self-respect.

The honor affair with Shields had come unexpectedly, provoked by the kind of loose ethical behavior that Lincoln had been practicing for a long time, but it came at a time of intense self-examination. In seeing the affair through to an "honorable" conclusion, Lincoln had not so much done the *right* thing – in fact, his participation embarrassed him all his life – as the *gritty* thing, the *determined* thing. He never wavered or waffled, and by this method he emerged with his honor intact. He must also have seen that Shields, to preserve his own honor, had had to give over his own strong feelings and yield to the judgment of his friends. Happening on to Mary Todd at the Hardins' wedding in the wake of so signal a conclusion of this ordeal may well have crystallized the lessons he had been learning all year and helped reveal the solution to his problem. What Lincoln had learned from the events of that eventful year was perhaps complicated, but it possibly exemplified his father's homely advice that he had tried out on Speed several months earlier about making a bad bargain.[75]

～

THE WEDDING of Abraham Lincoln and Mary Todd was performed on the same day it was announced, November 4, 1842. This was just one month to the day after Lincoln had written his anxious letter to Speed, and the marriage must have taken place soon after Speed's reply reached Springfield. After their reunion in Jacksonville the couple apparently continued to meet during October at the home of Simeon Francis.[76] That they should keep their meetings and their discussions of marriage secret was understandable, especially given the active opposition of Mary's sister and her husband, who, according to a member of the family, "thought Lincoln plebeian."[77] What was startling then – and is startling still – was the abruptness of the wedding announcement, by which even the closest friends and relatives were given only a few hours' notice. Matheny testified that he was asked by Lincoln to be a groomsman on the day of the wedding, and Mary broke the news to the sister with whom she was living no sooner. Elizabeth Edwards told Herndon: "The marriage of Mr L & Mary was quick & sudden – one or two hours notice."[78] When Elizabeth protested to her sister that this gave her no time to prepare and that she would have to send out for gingerbread, Mary is said to have replied, "Ginger bread [is] good enough for plebians."[79]

Whether or not the decision to marry reflected a spur-of-the-moment decision is impossible to determine, but it was a gesture calculated to convey a certain strength of purpose and, at the same time, to forestall any advisory comment or opposition. It seemed to anticipate questions and criticism and to say defiantly to all parties: "Don't bother to tell us what you think of the wisdom of this decision; it is already made, and you may take it or leave it."

The wedding at the Edwards house was small, and eyewitnesses disagreed about Lincoln's demeanor. Matheny's recollection that "Lincoln looked and acted as if he was going to the Slaughter" was countered by that of Mary's sister Frances Wallace, who said he "was cheerful as he ever had been, for all we could see."[80] What Lincoln himself was feeling is not on record, but Herndon and others have called attention to a story that persisted in the William Butler family. The Butler children remembered that on seeing their boarder putting on his best clothes and blacking his boots before the wedding, Speed Butler, then a small boy, asked Lincoln where he was going. He answered, "To hell, I reckon."[81] This wry remark made a strong impression on the Butler family, but its meaning for Lincoln himself was probably related to something he knew from Thomas Moore's life of Lord Byron. About the ending of the unfinished satire *Don Juan*, one of Lincoln's favorite poems in these years, Byron had written: "I had not quite fixed whether to make him end in Hell, or in an unhappy marriage, not knowing which would be the severest. The Spanish tradition says Hell: but it is probably only an Allegory of the other state."[82]

When Herndon tried to get John T. Stuart to talk about these matters, all he would say was that he thought "that the marriage of Lincoln to Miss Todd was a policy Match all around."[83] By "policy" he apparently meant that, on both sides, it was a course of action considered "expedient, prudent, or advantageous." Love, Stuart seemed to be saying, had very little to do with it. For Mary, it appears to have been the consummation of a long-standing wish. This is the implication of her family's and most other testimony, and she certainly had other suitors and bright prospects for other matches. But for Lincoln, whatever else it might have been, it was the culmination of a long and severe inner struggle. Deciding to reopen his courtship with the willful and aristocratic Mary Todd was a pivotal decision, and having seen it through to its ultimate conclusion apparently left Lincoln with a sense of numbed astonishment. Just a week after the ceremony he concluded a letter to a friend with the note, "Nothing new here, except my marrying, which to me, is a matter of profound wonder."[84]

Chapter 10

TRANSITIONS AND
TRANSFORMATION

As a "frontispiece" to his biography of Abraham Lincoln, William H. Herndon wanted to use a passage from Lord Byron that he described to his collaborator as "just the thing for Lincoln's life." The lines Herndon had in mind were from the poem Byron couldn't decide how to end, *Don Juan*:

> Between two worlds Life hovers like a star,
>   'Twixt Night and Morn, upon the horizon's verge.
> How little do we know that which we are!
> How less what we may be![1]

Whatever relevance to Lincoln's life as a whole Herndon may have seen in these lines, they resonate with significance for the period from 1831 to 1842. For these were years of a remarkable transformation, in which Lincoln found himself negotiating the distance between distinctly different worlds. The movement from youth to maturity was, of course, the natural and inevitable journey from innocence to experience, but in Lincoln's case this critical phase was overlaid by other transitions. The shift from country to village and from village to town constituted more than a progressive change of location. It marked conscious but troublesome transitions in social milieu, not merely in the kinds of people he associated with but in the ways his character and behavior were judged.

Rising in the world, which was apparently Lincoln's ambition from the start, seems to have meant a quest primarily for recognition or distinction, but it also implied movement upward in the social scale. As

Lincoln soon discovered, such a passage not only entailed vexing differences in manners and behavior; it also affected his sense of identity. Being in transition between different worlds during these years manifestly affected his sense of who he was and what he might become. As Byron's lines suggest, these are things to which such sojourners bring very little knowledge, so that the journey readily becomes a venture in self-discovery.

But the familiar legend that forcefully informs our sense of the young Lincoln's experience leaves most of this out of account. When we think about the young Lincoln, we tend to see his efforts to rise in the retrospective lens of his ultimate triumph. We know that he started out at the bottom and had to struggle upward, but it is easy to minimize or overlook his anxieties, for we also know how it all turned out. What is harder to grasp is the way things were or must have seemed to him at the time. Coming up as a young man, very much on his own and not able to count on many of the things that can assure or lead to a promising future, he struggled with anxiety and self-doubt. Sociable and full of fun with his fellows, he was often inwardly filled with a nameless sense of apprehension and even doom. Fixated on the future, Lincoln experienced a sense of foreboding about his own personal destiny that became at some point an almost palpable dread, a condition that was almost certainly heightened and intensified by his reading of Byron's darker poems. When we take into account his mental anguish and misgivings, his rise appears even more remarkable than the legend allows.

The kind of evidence that would presumably shed most light on such matters of self-definition is lacking. If Lincoln ever kept a diary or other record of his inner struggles to reflect on who he was and how he should comport himself, we know nothing of it. The kind of searching self-examination with which the young John Adams filled his diary, for example, is entirely absent. Nor do we have more than a few glimpses of such matters in the testimony of the people in whom he confided. Joshua Speed provided many clues and much useful information, but he withheld the substance of their most intimate discussions during the four years they were roommates, a particularly critical period for Lincoln.

What we have instead is the body of evidence featured in the foregoing chapters consisting of the reminiscences of his friends and acquaintances, augmented to some extent by his own writings and by a highly fragmentary contemporary record. Taking bearings on Lincoln's situation at any given time under these conditions is admittedly difficult, but charting some of the significant transitions in his experience between the years 1831 and 1842 affords perspective on the larger transformation, and it brings to focus certain themes that converge in the fateful events of the final year.

-⊸

IN THE WORLD that Abraham Lincoln grew up in, the foremost object of boyhood was to become a man. Attaining manhood entailed more than reaching a certain age; in practice it meant proving oneself physically in contests with other boys and eventually with other men. This worked itself out in all sorts of competitive games and contests, but the ultimate proof of manliness was physical courage and the willingness to meet others in combat, to fight. As a boy in Indiana, Lincoln was different from others in being studious, but he competed very successfully in sports and feats of strength, and he claimed superiority as a fighter. According to witnesses, when his stepbrother and proxy, John Johnston, got the worst of a fight in 1828, the nineteen-year-old Lincoln broke the rules and intervened. An acquaintance remembered: "Wm Grigsby was too much for Lincoln's man – Johnson. After they had fought a long time – and it having been agreed not to break the ring, Abe burst through, caught Grigsby – threw him off some feet – stood up and swore he was the big buck at the lick – [According to another witness, Lincoln at this point waved a whiskey bottle over his head.] After Abe did this – it being a general invitation for a general fight they all pitched in and had quite a general fight."[2]

Another former neighbor told Herndon about a sequel to this event that further suggests Lincoln's reputation as a fighter: "after the fite between Wm Grigsby and John D Johnson Abraham told Wm Grigsby that he had whiped Johnson but i can whip you but Wm told him that he did not dispute that but if he Lincoln would give he Grigsby a fair cance he would fite him he Lincoln wish to now how he wish to fite, Grigsby told Lincoln he would fite him a duel Lincoln told Grigsby that he Lincoln was not going to fool his life away with one Shot, So the mater stoped."[3] Fourteen years later Lincoln had risen far, but as a consequence, the matter of a challenge could not be stopped so simply.

When Lincoln appeared in New Salem at the age of twenty-two, he still excelled at games and tests of strength. "He could beat any of the

boys wrestling, or running a foot race, in pitching quoits or tossing a
copper, could ruin more liquor than all the boys of the town together,
and the dignity and impartiality with which he presided at a horse race
or fistfight, excited the admiration and won the praise of everybody that
was present and participated."[4] This was the recollection of Stephen A.
Douglas in his first debate with Lincoln in 1858, and except for the
deliberate zinger about drinking, which was false, this picture of Lincoln at New Salem is amply confirmed in the recollections of others.
What is also confirmed is that by the time he arrived at New Salem,
Lincoln had virtually given up fighting and had become something of a
peacemaker.

Giving up fighting may have been a way of distinguishing himself or
of avoiding the taint of rowdiness, but in the social world that Lincoln
belonged to, it was a singular decision. Fighting was the most dramatic
and unambiguous way to demonstrate manliness, which was serious
business. Lincoln could not have hoped to get ahead if his contemporaries had doubted or questioned his manliness, something that was
esteemed as a virtue and rewarded with reputation.[5] Indicative of how
and why Lincoln came to give up fighting is surely his decision at about
the same time to change his politics, which was strictly a man's game.
Though he was raised among people who were almost all strong supporters of Andrew Jackson, Lincoln, even before he reached voting age,
became an opponent of Jackson, apparently under the influence of the
anti-Jackson storekeeper he worked for in Indiana, William Jones.[6] His
cousin, Dennis Hanks, told Herndon that Lincoln "was till 20 years of
age a Jackson Democrat – turned whig – or whiggish about 1828–9 –
think Col Jones made him a whig – dont know it. . . . Abe as I said
before was originally a Democrat after the order of Jackson – so was his
father – so we all were – Abe turned whig in 1827–8."[7] Dennis later testified that Lincoln didn't change politics until after he came to Illinois
in 1830,[8] but the discrepancy hardly matters. In either case, Lincoln's
decisions to give up fighting and change political allegiance belong to
the same three-year period, 1828–31.

Too little has been made by Lincoln's biographers of this striking
political metamorphosis. The backwoods people Lincoln sprang from
took their politics seriously and tended to identify strongly with the
western war hero Andrew Jackson, who was for them the personifica-
tion of manliness in all its dominating and willful virility. Why Lincoln
should have chosen at the age of nineteen to stand up and oppose his

neighbors and even his own family on so volatile an issue is a complicated question to which there can be no simple answer.[9] One thing
about which we can be certain is that it required real courage, and this
suggests that one of the appeals of making so defiant a statement may
well have been its value as a dramatic assertion of manliness.

This is not to say that his anti-Jackson sentiments were merely expedient or otherwise insincere. There is every reason to think that in
deciding to oppose Jackson and take his political ideals from the likes of
John Quincy Adams and Henry Clay, Lincoln was assuming a position
that was congenial to his nature and in keeping with the view of human
affairs that was forming in his mind. If this meant opposing his father,
the change would probably have been all the more attractive. The point
here is that demonstrating the courage required to take such a stand was
a powerful and effective substitute for fighting in the necessary business
of asserting his manhood. According to one study of the culture in
which Lincoln was raised, these very political people carried the concept
of manliness "into the political realm by labeling candor – the moral
courage to speak one's opinions freely without fearing consequences –
as manly."[10] Especially if it were done fearlessly and well, political dis-
sent could be acknowledged as a mark of manliness and honor.

Settling in New Salem was not, for Lincoln, a change of political
climate. Like the hoosiers he lived among in Indiana, a very large proportion of the inhabitants of the New Salem area were also staunch fol-
lowers of Andrew Jackson. Being a politically aspiring young man
whose hero was Henry Clay put Lincoln at odds with most of his new
neighbors, and this was very likely a factor in his being challenged to
square off against Jack Armstrong soon after his arrival. As one of them
put it, "Lincoln was pretty stout, and the boys made it up to see what
there was in him."[11] In other words, they wanted to see if he was all talk.
Steadfastly refusing to "tussle and scuffle," Lincoln insisted on a more
rule-bound form of wrestling and then, following the match, successfully staved off an attempt to take advantage of and intimidate him.
What won the day for him was apparently his willingness to fight, if
necessary, and his refusal to lose his composure or back down. Thereafter he was known in the community as a peacemaker and did his
fighting in the political arena.

A story of his peacemaking offers an illuminating contrast with this
encounter. One of Bill Greene's brothers told Herndon the story of
another newcomer who resisted Armstrong's bullying:

Jack Armstrong & a man had a difficulty – Jack called him a liar – a
son of a bitch – coward – &c. &c the man backed up to a wood pile –
got a Stick – struck Jack a blow – felled him. Jack Armstrong was
as strong as 2 men. Jack wanted to whip the man badly. At last
they agreed to Compromise the Matter – Made Abe arbitrator – Abe
said – "Well Jack what did you say to the man" Jack repeated what he
had said – Lincoln then Said – Jack if you were a stranger in a strange
place as this man is, and you were called a d—d liar &c – What
would you do – Said Jack ["]hit by God." "Well then Jack." Said
Lincoln "this man has done no more to you than you would have
done to him."[12]

The newcomer's mistake of provoking Armstrong and then having
to hit him with a club in self-defense underscores the astuteness
of Lincoln's demeanor in his own contest with the Clary's Grove
champion.

While Lincoln's readiness to stand up for himself and his willingness
to intercede on behalf of his friends "to show fair play" were important
ingredients in his early success as a politician, it was also a success that
depended on his being perceived as sincere and open-handed in his
political arguments, as opposed to dissembling or hiding behind a false
mask of civility. One could hardly hope to gain credit for a manly display of candor if the audience suspected calculation or deceit. Lincoln's
famous reputation for fairness and honesty was in part rooted in his
political deportment. Yet his behavior in the political arena had a darker
side, one that trafficked in shadier and less reputable tactics and one
that his constituents were only dimly aware of, if at all: his newspaper
writings.

⁓

LINCOLN'S CAREER as a writer of anonymous and pseudonymous
articles in the rabidly partisan newspapers of his region is difficult to
trace, for while computer analysis of word patterns holds out the tanta-
lizing possibility of identifying authorship, we thus far lack adequate
means of distinguishing the actual pieces he wrote. That he wrote such
articles on political subjects from an early date is sufficiently affirmed by
those who were close to him. James H. Matheny, for example, testified
that Lincoln frequently sent articles to the *Sangamo Journal* before he
moved to Springfield. His testimony is compelling because Matheny
was well placed in the Springfield post office to observe the flow of con-
tributions and had an accurate means of identifying the sender. He told

Herndon: "I was deputy P. M. [postmaster] under Mitchell [in Spring-field] from 1832 to 35 say. – got to Know Lincoln's hand writing as such P. M – He Lincoln used to write Editorials as far back as 1834 – or 5 for Francis – the Sangamon Journal – [I] took hundreds of such Editorials from Lincoln to the Journal office – Lincoln was P. M at that time because his letters were *franked*."[13] Observing the steady stream of letters sent postage-free from New Salem to the Whig paper in Springfield enabled Matheny to learn to recognize Lincoln's distinctive handwriting.

At least one of the pieces Lincoln sent to editor Simeon Francis during this early period was apparently sent back. In 1834, having just been elected to his first term in the Illinois House of Representatives, Lincoln wrote a letter to the *Journal* lampooning Peter Cartwright, the celebrated preacher living near New Salem, who combined frontier evangelism and Democratic politics. For Lincoln, Cartwright was a political adversary whose reputation and influence needed to be held in check. For Samuel Hill, the New Salem merchant whose store was Lincoln's political headquarters, Cartwright was a sworn personal enemy. Their combined hostility to Cartwright laid the basis for the composition of a recently discovered letter, the only known example of Lincoln's early brand of attack journalism.[14]

Cartwright had stirred up a furor in the summer of 1834, when it came out that a letter he had written to a Methodist periodical pointed to the need for common school teachers in Illinois and of the advantages of filling these places with young men "under the influence of our own church."[15] This sounded to the members of other denominations like a scheme to capture the budding common schools for the Methodists and prompted a Baptist editor to take strong exception through the medium of a circulated handbill, which demanded: "Is this not enough to make the parson hang his sham'd face, decline as a candidate for office, and hunt a place to hide himself from the free people of Sangamon County?"[16]

Cartwright responded with a letter to the editor of the *Sangamo Journal* dated August 24, 1834, which was headed "The Valley of the Mississippi, or the Moral Waste. NO. 1." His strategy was to associate his accusers with the type of easterner who patronized and belittled the people of the frontier West as living in a moral wasteland. "We have been represented as totally destitute of all kinds of Literature, without religion, immoral, intemperate, rude, uncultivated in our manners, denying the obligation of the Sabbath for civil or religious purposes, destitute of any Evangelical Preachers,"[17] Cartwright protested. Then these same people, he averred, try to insinuate themselves into the favor of the very westerners they abuse in order to solicit funds to support national societies.

> And after they have appealed to the best feelings of an uninformed and abused community and obtained their money for their national societies and agents, is it then right to slander and misrepresent them? Does it not come with an ill grace from these very sectarian *national agents*, to cry "sectarianism," "sectarianism," "persecution," "persecution," when any other church opposes their monopolizing plan, and thinks the preferable way is, to carry on these benevolent societies by the churches in their individual or denominational capacity?[18]

Cartwright was a formidable and truculent adversary who could not be physically intimidated, and he ended his letter with a taunt: "And if any Editor or individual thinks proper to reply to these hasty remarks, I wish to come out in a tangible form, and with a proper name, and in some future number I may give some further remarks on the subject."[19]

Enter Abraham Lincoln. Elected to office for the first time only a few weeks earlier, he may have been feeling his political oats, for he composed a blistering response that flatly accused "Uncle Peter" of rank hypocrisy, of deliberate duplicity, and of using of his position as a minister of the gospel for financial and political advantage. As one of the New Salem residents who told Herndon about this incident put it, "it used the old man very Ruff[;] it was a hard one."[20] This bare-knuckled abuse of its subject is apparently what caused Simeon Francis, the editor of the *Sangamo Journal*, to refuse to publish it, but the letter eventually was printed by Lincoln's friend Francis Arenz in his newspaper, the *Beardstown Chronicle*.[21]

Lincoln may have been recruited to write this attack by Hill, who hated Peter Cartwright, for it was signed "Samuel Hill" when it appeared, and editor Arenz specified that "It is inserted by request and paid for as an advertisement."[22] But two reliable witnesses remembered independently that Lincoln was known to be the writer, and there is little doubt that it bears his stamp. Lincoln's attack is based on a presumed discrepancy between the positions taken by Cartwright in his letter to the Methodist periodical, the *Christian Advocate*, and that of his "Moral Waste" letter to the *Journal*. In the former, according to

Lincoln, he referred to the Illinois country as "this land of moral desolation," while in the latter he professed to be offended by writers and preachers who took this very line. Whereas Cartwright's letters had been aimed at the preachers who came out West and bewailed the character of the people and at the same time made money off them, Lincoln's strategy was to show that Cartwright was himself one of these.

> Again he says, "Is it not evident to all informed observers that the devil might get all the poor ignorant heathens in this Valley if they did not get the money." To this I incline to answer yes. I believe the people in this country are in some degree priest ridden. I also believe, and if I am not badly mistaken "all informed observers" will concur in the belief that Peter Cartwright bestrides, more than any four men in the northwestern part of the State.
>   He has one of the largest and best improved farms in Sangamon county, with other property in proportion. And how has he got it? Only by the contributions he has been able to levy upon and collect from a priest ridden church. It will not do to say he has earned it "by the sweat of his brow;" for although he may sometimes labor, all know that he spends the greater part of his time in preaching and electioneering.[23]

This is the tried-and-true debater's tactic of making your opponent his own accuser by showing that he is guilty of the very thing he rails against. Lincoln learned to use this device to perfection in the course of his career, but here it was landed as a very low blow indeed, for no fair-minded observer would class Peter Cartwright, a deeply committed pioneer preacher by any measure, with eastern interlopers interested mainly in exacting tribute. While some of his arguments were more legitimate and his rhetoric and humor quite effective, Lincoln's false slurs against Cartwright's character, which were knowing and deliberate, were the equivalent in public debate of Jack Armstrong's foul in the famous wrestling match.[24]

This comparison suggests both the attraction and the difficulty for Lincoln of engaging in this kind of attack. While by the standards of the time and place, he was reasonably fair and honorable in his public demeanor, he could and did resort to underhanded methods when writing for newspapers, where his identity was hidden from public view. His readers, like the spectators at the wrestling match with Armstrong, were basically partisan and did not usually protest irregular behavior that defied or bent the rules of fair play. On the contrary, they tended to take delight in any and all hits against their political opponents. The seductive appeal of demagogy is, of course, that meanspirited and unfair arguments do score points. Though neither honest nor honorable, they can and do have an effect. Thus, like Armstrong's "legging" of the boastful newcomer, Lincoln's demagogic newspaper writings earned him little or no censure from his friends.

His adversaries, particularly those receiving the brunt of his attacks, complained bitterly, and their complaints were sometimes very near the bone. In 1839 the Democratic paper in Springfield aimed a stinging retort straight at Lincoln. "The writer is no doubt one of the Junto, whose members deliberate in secret, write in secret, and work in darkness – men who dare not let the light of day in upon their acts – who seek to rule a free people by their edicts passed in midnight secrecy. . . . The *mask* is on them in all their acts."[25] This must have struck home, for it was part of an article that correctly exposed a decision of the Junto to oppose the candidacy of Lincoln's old New Salem friend, Bowling Green, a measure that Lincoln denied but that was subsequently shown to be true.[26] Following the Sampson's Ghost series, which dealt in dubious charges and innuendo, James Adams finally flushed him out into the open in 1837, but Lincoln remained unrepentant. And in the rare instance when Jesse B. Thomas complained about Lincoln's dirty newspaper tricks from a public platform in 1840, he was rewarded with a "skinning" that was merciless in its ferocity.

The "skinning of Thomas" was the eruption of one of the most potent forces in Lincoln's personality, what Robert Bray has called "the power to hurt."[27] Though under control most of the time, Lincoln was capable of inflicting verbal punishment on his adversaries through ridicule and invective. While he had the physical attributes for the role, he was not a bully. But, as we have seen, he was capable of hurtful and humiliating treatment when aroused. How well he controlled himself when writing anonymously or under a pseudonym is difficult to say, since so few of the multitude of pieces he is supposed to have written have been identified. But his Cartwright letter in 1834 and the Sampson's Ghost pieces in 1837 suggest that he could be abusive in pursuit of a partisan end and reckless about the truth. If, in fact, these examples and the Lost Townships letter are at all typical, the Lincoln of the newspaper columns had a far less savory and respectable character than his public persona.

In September 1842, James Shields had had enough and called Lincoln out. It has seemed to many of Lincoln's biographers that, with the

Shields affair, Lincoln learned his lesson, that finally and forcefully being called to account for his newspaper skulduggery over the Lost Townships letter made him see the error of his ways. This is an attractive thesis, but the story of Lincoln's ongoing struggle to find himself suggests that there probably was more to it. The Shields affair came at a time when Lincoln was concerned at least as much with his own inner self-image as with his public persona. His mental peace and stability had been badly disrupted by the charge that he had behaved dishonorably and by his painful and public inability to cope with it. The recurring thought that someone continued to suffer from his actions, as he confessed to Speed a few months earlier, still killed his soul and worked to deprive him of any personal happiness. What was needed, he implied, was some sort of deliverance, some decisive action to restore his lost self-confidence and self-esteem. At the personal and private level, it required decisions about how he was going to conduct himself and who he was going to be.

Robert Bray found the telling phrase "the power to hurt" in one of Lincoln's congressional speeches, but Lincoln's own source may well have been Shakespeare's famous Sonnet 94.

> They that have pow'r to hurt and will do none,
> That do not do the thing they most do show,
> Who, moving others, are themselves as stone,
> Unmoved, cold, and to temptation slow;
> They rightly do inherit heaven's graces
> And husband nature's riches from expense;
> They are the lords and owners of their faces,
> Others but stewards of their excellence.[28]

Shakespeare here calls attention to the self-evident superiority of those who have the power to hurt but choose to withhold it. In this perspective, to achieve the level of recognition and public admiration at which others become the stewards of one's own excellence, it is necessary not so much to use one's power to hurt as to master it. Such a realization as this may well have been dawning on the man who admitted to Shields: "I wrote that [article], wholly for political effect. I had no intention of injuring your personal or private character, or standing as a man or a gentleman; and I did not then think, and do not now think that that article could produce or has produced that effect against you, and had I anticipated such an effect I would have forborne to write it."[29]

If Lincoln was telling the truth when he wrote this, as opposed to merely smoothing over a reprehensible action, it possibly signaled the glimmering of a new realization or degree of understanding. He had been writing for "political effect" for several years with the clear intention of ridiculing and harassing his opponents, presumably taking great delight in their discomfort, but he may not have given serious thought to whether this was manly behavior. Pseudonymous attacks had a long history in political journalism, but in being covert and unforthright, they smacked of the devious and the underhanded, and as such were difficult to square with the kind of manliness recognized in more sophisticated society, which valued self-discipline and measured expression. This was perhaps a troubling question to one who was just then brooding over his own "personal or private character" and his own "standing as a man." But even more worrisome may have been the question of whether such behavior could accord with the status of a gentleman.

Until very recently the term "gentleman" had always been reserved for the favored few, and although it was rapidly coming to be used as an honorific for any decent and respectable male citizen, it still carried something of its former meaning. This was especially true when it was employed in such a context as Lincoln's apology (or explanation) to Shields. In this sense the term "gentleman" still marked a great divide in male society, a divide that the hoosier Lincoln and the Irish immigrant Shields were deeply conscious of having recently crossed. Proving that they had crossed it was in large part what was at issue, and it was almost the sole reason they eventually found themselves involved not in a fist-fight but in a challenge and choice of weapons. Receiving a challenge from someone who had obviously been injured and was determined to fight with lethal weapons could not help making an impression. Lincoln may, for the first time, have seen or understood "honor" and honorable behavior as all-important, as necessary, as a matter of life and death.

The power to hurt, whose dimensions and implications Lincoln was perhaps beginning to fathom in the fall of 1842, was curiously offset in his nature by something like its obverse, an inability to ignore the helpless. Mary Owens had noted a few years earlier that in spite of his lack of breeding and his social inadequacies, he was by no means insensitive in all respects. "In many things," she told Herndon, "he was sensi-

tive almost to a fault."[30] She illustrated her point with a story she remembered Lincoln telling her. "He told me of an incident; that he was crossing a prairie one day, and saw before him a hog mired down, to use his own language; he was rather fixed up and he resolved that he would pass on without looking towards the shoat, after he had gone by, he said, the feeling was eresistable and he had to look back, and the poor thing seemed to say so wistfully – *There now! my last hope is gone;* that he deliberately got down and relieved it from its difficulty."[31]

In isolation this story would be a curiosity, but the number and consistency of such stories in testimony about the young Lincoln make them hard to ignore. In Indiana, when his playmates caught and tortured a terrapin, one remembered that "Lincoln would Chide us – tell us it was wrong."[32] His stepsister remembered something similar and told Herndon that "Abe preached against Cruelty to animals, Contending that an ants life was to it, as sweet as ours to us."[33] One of his first essays was apparently on cruelty to animals.[34] His friend Speed told of an incident in which Lincoln left a party of men traveling together on horseback to relieve the distress of two small birds that had been blown from their nest by a storm. When his friends laughed at him for wasting his time hunting the nest from which the birds had fallen, Lincoln reportedly replied: "Gentlemen, you may laugh, but I could not have slept well to-night, if I had not saved those birds. Their cries would have rung in my ears."[35]

Though a number of these stories involve animals, they also make it clear that his peculiar solicitude extended to fellow human beings in pitiable circumstances. As a boy in Indiana he was reported to have carried home a drunken man who was in danger of freezing to death.[36] Near the beginning of our period, while serving in the Black Hawk War against the Indians in 1832, the twenty-three-year-old Lincoln reportedly interceded in dramatic and courageous fashion to save the life of an Indian who had wandered into camp. According to one of the company, the elderly Indian "delivered himself up, showing us an old paper written by Lewis Cass, Stating that the Indian was a good & true man Many of the men of the Army said 'we have come out to fight the Indians and by God we intend to do so.' " Lincoln, who was captain of his company, came between the Indian and the men who were intent on killing him, and ordered them not to harm him. Called a coward for thus taking the Indian's part, he reportedly challenged any man who thought him cowardly to test him. Lincoln prevailed, and the Indian went free. Greene told Herndon, "This is the first time or amongst the first times I ever saw Mr Lincoln aroused. He was unusually kind, pleasant – good humored, taking any & all things. But this was too much for Lincoln."[37]

At the end of our period, on his way to Alton to meet James Shields on the dueling ground in September 1842, Lincoln was observed along the road by an old acquaintance, the Rev. George J. Barrett, helping a family in difficulty. Barrett told Herndon:

> he was Coming from the South going North when he met Mr. Lincoln in 18— to his duel ground – Several men were with him – just as we met we came to a man who had mired down in the mud – couldn't get out. Lincoln was about to stop when one of his Company – "Now Lincoln don't make a d—d fool of yourself – Come – Come along –" Lincoln didn't pay no attention to what the man said – got off his horse – L took my horse & his own & tied them to the strangers waggon by ropes – Straps & strings – pulled the man with his family – When we got through scarcely any man Could have told what or who we were.[38]

The picture that emerges from such strikingly consonant stories is that of someone who, from an early age, was remarkably tenderhearted in the presence of suffering and helplessness. When he was not able to be helpful in such situations, he seems to have experienced great anguish, as in the well-known story of the slaves he saw on a boat in the Ohio River. Writing of this experience in a letter to Speed's sister, Lincoln described the pitiable condition of twelve chained slaves who had been sold down the river and "were strung together precisely like so many fish upon a trot-line."[39] Years later he reminded Speed, who had been with him on the boat, that the sight of those slaves "was a continual torment to me" and that similar sights were something "which has, and continually exercises, the power of making me miserable." Northerners who felt as he did but could not interfere out of loyalty to the Constitution were forced, Lincoln said, to "crucify their feelings."[40]

The hallmark of these stories is not merely a willingness but a positive need, a compulsion to respond and be helpful in desperate situations. What stands out and makes these stories memorable is not simply Lincoln's kindness; it is his selflessness, his unhesitating disregard of his own comfort and convenience. All the more remarkable is that he responded to the plight of animals as readily as he responded to people.[41] That this was in response to something deeply embedded in his makeup is suggested by the fact that in these situations he ignored the commonsense reactions of his companions, risked his standing with his peers, and disregarded the pressures of the urgent business at hand, such as his impending duel with Shields. It is difficult not to see this distinctive trait as akin to the emotional vulnerability that first became evident in his reaction to the death of Ann Rutledge.

Attending to this aspect of the young Lincoln's emotional makeup or character helps bring into focus an easily overlooked but crucial element in his entanglement with Mary Todd. Upon seeing the beautiful Matilda Edwards in Springfield in November 1840, Lincoln realized that his newly declared interest in Mary Todd was transient and that he did not love her. Persuaded by Speed to tell her so to her face, he pleaded his case successfully; she made no objection and only blamed herself. Had he been able to keep his cool, he would have been off the hook and free to pursue Matilda. But according to Speed, in reproaching herself, Mary had wept, and Lincoln had instinctively taken pity on her, comforting and kissing her. He may not even have realized what he had done (or undone) by this impulsive act until Speed explained the situation to him afterward, calling it "a bad lick." But by then it was too late. This realization was surely part of the emotional anguish that took possession of him a short time later, when according to Speed, Mary confronted him with his continued and apparently undisguised attraction for Matilda Edwards. Nor could Lincoln later free himself by force of will from a sense of responsibility for Mary's continued unhappiness. Some sixteen months after the breakup, in the midst of his sympathetic elation at Speed's good fortune in marriage, he confessed that the recurring thought of Mary's grief "still kills my soul."

These distinctive tendencies were clearly a deeply rooted part of Lincoln's nature, and when one tries to understand the ways in which they affected his development, they seem curiously related to his fatalism. In explaining his actions, he was quick to admit that there were forces at work over which he had little or no control. Of his extraordinary solicitude regarding Speed's courtship and marriage, he had told his friend, "I never had the power to withhold my sympathy from you." When Speed tried to give him credit for getting him through his marriage ordeal, Lincoln had replied: "The truth is, I am not sure there was any merit, with me, in the part I took in your difficulty; I was drawn to it as by fate; if I would, I could not have done less than I did."[42] In the explanation that Speed remembered Lincoln's giving for saving the two small birds, as well as Mary Owens's story about his helping the pig out of the mire, a similar note was sounded: Lincoln felt compelled to act as he did. This suggests that he understood what others regarded as his voluntary acts of sympathy or compassion as the result of a force acting upon *him*, not the other way around.

This is presumably why, as he groped for perspective and direction in the summer of 1842, he told Speed that he was pursuing a waiting game: "I always was superstitious; and as part of my superstition, I believe God made me one of the instruments of bringing your Fanny and you together, which union, I have no doubt He had fore-ordained. Whatever he designs, he will do for *me* yet. 'Stand *still* and see the salvation of the Lord' is my text just now."[43] Fewer than three months later he was challenged to a duel.

-☙

LINCOLN'S SUPERSTITION, which he frankly acknowledged to Speed and others, made him fatalistic, but it was not a fatalism that implied the total futility of human effort or human will. This was the view, for example, of Orville H. Browning, who described for John G. Nicolay the character of Lincoln's beliefs. "According to my observation Mr. Lincoln had a tolerably strong vein of superstition in his nature. I think he all his life more or less believed in presentiments. I have no doubt that this feeling had a most powerful influence in prompting him to make efforts for self improvement." Browning was not here referring to Lincoln's famous forebodings as president but to his keen sense of his own destiny when Browning first knew him as a young man. "I have no doubt that even in his early days he had a strong conviction that he was born for better things than then seemed likely or even possible." It was true, Browning acknowledged, that Lincoln was "always a most ambitious man." But his ambition was "to fit himself properly for what he considered some important predestined labor or work . . . , that he was destined for something nobler than he was for the time engaged in."[44]

Michael Burlingame has documented in great detail the manifold indications of Lincoln's ambition.[45] From his boyhood onward it was evident to those who knew him that he was earnestly in quest of distinction. By the time he reached Springfield in 1837 he was well on his way, recognized even by the aristocratic Elizabeth Edwards as "a rising man."[46] Lincoln's emotional dilemmas at this period were clearly compounded by his urgent desire to advance himself, for he told Speed, when his spirits hit bottom in the winter of 1840–41, that he was not afraid of death and "more than willing" to die except "that he had done nothing to make any human being remember that he had lived."[47] By the summer of 1842 he had brought himself back from the brink. If Browning's insight was well founded, Lincoln's presentiment that he had a noble destiny to fulfill was a core belief, perhaps the thing that most animated his existence. In this light his remark to Speed about standing still and waiting to see what God had in store for him may suggest not so much a man without will as someone who thought himself very much at a crossroads: he was waiting for an indication as to which way he should go.

It may seem strange that the man who had shocked his closest friends by his scornful rejection of Christian beliefs a few years earlier should address an intimate in these terms. In fact, this invocation of the Bible has led some to surmise that his beliefs were latently more Christian and orthodox than his friends supposed, but the testimony about Lincoln's profession of his religious beliefs traces the outline of yet another transition. The evidence for the young Lincoln's outspoken "infidelity" in New Salem – his deliberate disparagement of orthodox Christianity – is reasonably clear. As Herndon summarized it, "being natural skeptics, and being bold, brave men, [Lincoln and his associates] uttered their thoughts freely. They declared that Jesus was an illegitimate child. . . . These men could not conceive it possible that three could be in one, nor one in three Gods; *they could not believe that the Father ruined one of his own lovely children*."[48] This youthful plain speaking was never disputed by those who knew him, and even the Springfield citizens who sought to claim him for Christianity after his death were careful to specify that they were not talking about his early life.[49] As for his basic religious beliefs, Herndon and others were certain that at least until he entered the presidency, these never changed.[50] What did change during this early period, and changed dramatically, was the way he presented and expressed himself on religious matters.

The simplest way to describe this transition is to say that he learned discretion. Certainly James H. Matheny, who reported the shocking things Lincoln said when he first came to Springfield, saw it in these terms. He told Herndon: "as he grew older he grew more discrete – didn't talk much before Strangers about his religion . . . he held them off from policy."[51] But simply learning discretion does not do justice to the evidence, which suggests a much more complicated state of affairs.

Consider the testimony of Albert T. Bledsoe. Bledsoe was known as a person of enormous integrity, but he was also, at the time of writing his recollections of Lincoln in 1873, an embittered southerner, who regarded his former Springfield friend and political associate as a self-seeking and unprincipled politician who, in engineering the defeat of the Confederacy, had wantonly destroyed a noble and entirely legitimate nation. Bledsoe's occasion for writing was the appearance of Ward Hill Lamon's biography of Lincoln, which was ghostwritten by Chauncey F. Black and based largely on the testimony of Herndon's informants. Far from writing as an apologist, the politically antagonistic Black used and even featured the most shocking and, to his mainly Christian audience, most damning testimony about Lincoln's "infidelity." Bledsoe reacted strongly to this part of the biography, not only because he was an ordained minister and devout Christian but because he felt outrage at what he regarded as the duplicity that had been practiced on him during his ten-year acquaintance with Lincoln, which began in 1839.

> From our various conversations with [Lincoln] on the subject of religion, we had supposed that we had some adequate idea of his religious sentiments, but Colonel Lamon's work has dispelled this illusion. He never gave us to understand, it is true, that he entertained a belief in the being of God, or in a moral government of the world, much less in the truth of Christianity. But he always seemed to deplore his want of faith as a very great infelicity, from which he would be glad to be delivered; and all this was uttered with an air of such apparent modesty, that his gloom and despair, seeming to border on a state of insanity, awakened in our minds no other feeling than one of deep compassion.[52]

Bledsoe's testimony suggests that by 1839 Lincoln was representing his unbelief, at least with certain people, as a misfortune, thereby neutralizing a potential liability. Bledsoe assumed that Lincoln had simply been duplicitous in this representation of his religious posture, but this may have been too harsh and categorical a conclusion. Joshua Speed dropped an intriguing clue in something he told Herndon about Lincoln's reading during the years they lived together. "No course of reading ever was chalked out – He read law History, Browns Philosophy or Paley – Burns Byron Milton or Shakespeare – The news papers of the day."[53] Thomas Browne and William Paley cut no figure in the twentieth century, but their defenses of Christianity were highly regarded and widely read in Lincoln's day, and Speed's recollection that Lincoln read them during this period is evidence that he at least took the issue seriously. Dutifully reading the leading apologists without effect might be done mainly to impress, but it need not involve duplicity. Speed himself, whose religious stance paralleled Lincoln's in many ways, seems to have adopted the posture described by Bledsoe and maintained it most of his life.[54] Lord Byron, whose poetry Speed implied he introduced to Lincoln, could have served the two admirers as a model, for Byron's biographer, Thomas Moore, noted that pious people were attracted to "the spectacle of a great mind, like that of Byron, labouring in the eclipse of skepticism" and that this caused people to view "his fate with mournful sympathy."[55]

Nonetheless, the issue that Bledsoe raised of Lincoln's duplicitous behavior deserves consideration. In his race for Congress against Peter Cartwright in 1846, Lincoln issued a handbill to answer the charge that he was "an open scoffer at Christianity." He could have denied this outright if, as seems certain, he had long since given up scoffing openly on the subject, but he went a good deal further.

> That I am not a member of any Christian Church, is true; but I have never denied the truth of the Scriptures; and I have never spoken with intentional disrespect of religion in general, or of any denomination of Christians in particular. It is true that in early life I was inclined to believe in what I understand is called the "Doctrine of Necessity" – that is, that the human mind is impelled to action, or held in rest by some power, over which the mind itself has no control; and I have sometimes (with one, two or three, but never publicly) tried to maintain this opinion in argument. The habit of arguing thus however, I have, entirely left off for more than five years.[56]

If what Lincoln's friends told Herndon about his ridicule of the Bible and Christian doctrine during his New Salem and early Springfield years was true, this statement was misleading, at best, and only the narrowest construction could save it from being considered outright misrepresentation. If he "never denied the truth of the Scriptures" as a whole, he seems to have denied, through ridicule, the truth of many things contained in the Scriptures, such as eternal punishment and the virgin birth. And if he never spoke "with intentional disrespect of religion in general, or of any denomination of Christians in particular," he had spoken often with intentional disrespect of certain basic Christian beliefs. Admitting that he maintained the "Doctrine of Necessity," of course, was no admission at all, as he well knew, for this was an issue that perfectly respectable Christians wrangled over endlessly. As a denial, the handbill's text is more apparent than real, but it is notable as an example of Lincoln's artful ability to sidestep an issue.[57]

Another possible indication of the transition in Lincoln's representation of his religious beliefs is Matheny's own contention, which Herndon was inclined to believe, that Lincoln "played a sharp game" with the Springfield religious community at the height of his political fame. According to Matheny, Lincoln sought to neutralize politically damaging charges of infidelity in the 1850s by appearing to offer himself as an earnest candidate for conversion.[58] How valid this reading of events might have been, of course, is difficult to determine. There was at least one Springfield clergyman, the Reverend James Smith, who thought he had made considerable headway with Lincoln in that direction.[59] And though Herndon strongly resisted it, there is good evidence for thinking that Lincoln led Newton Bateman to believe in 1860 that he was something of a secret Christian.[60]

This skein of testimony about Lincoln's religious views over a thirty-year period is offered principally for its overall trajectory, which helps place the developments between 1831 and 1842 in perspective. What it suggests is that Lincoln was quite possibly doing more than merely learning to be discreet about his unorthodox and unpopular religious beliefs. By studying the Christian apologists and depicting himself as an unfortunate victim of unbelief, he was learning how to neutralize negative political effects by means of a highly manipulative form of self-presentation.

❦

SELF-PRESENTATION is, of course, not necessarily deception. Deciding how to present oneself to others is an unavoidable part of social interaction, and the diversity of our dealings with others requires, to some extent, a variety of faces. We naturally vary the face to fit the person or situation we are dealing with, whether sibling or parent, spouse or lover, customer or employer, enemy or friend. The point is that the self or persona that we present in each of these different situations amounts to a role, a dramatic invention tailored to the situation as we understand it. Disguising his religious views, or construing them in a more favorable light, became necessary for an ambitious and rising man who needed the good opinion of the public to succeed. The extent to which ambitious men are deliberately deceptive and willing to dissemble in order to advance is often a fascinating part of their stories, but it becomes a matter of even greater interest in a man whose reputation for honesty is a premier American legend.

It is well to remember that while Lincoln was popular and well liked from the time he arrived in New Salem and made friends readily, he was faced with the task of trying to win favor politically with a constituency that in one important consideration was at odds with him. The political issues of the day were admittedly largely local, but being an anti-Jackson man in a pro-Jackson community in 1832 was no asset. In his overlong letter announcing his initial candidacy, Lincoln stressed his knowledge of waterways and how these vital arteries might be improved, his support for usury laws and education, and his earnest ambition "of being truly esteemed of my fellow men." He rounded it off with a self-effacing personal appeal: "I was born and have ever remained in the most humble walks of life," a theme he was said to have reiterated in his first public speech, when he reportedly referred to himself as "humble Abraham Lincoln."[61]

We saw in an earlier chapter how this letter and way of presenting himself contrasted with the one he published four years later, which avoided substantive issues and began: "In your paper of last Saturday, I see a communication over the signature of 'Many Voters,' in which the candidates who are announced in the Journal, are called upon to 'show their hands.' Agreed. Here's mine!"[62] Unlike the first letter, which ended by almost conceding defeat, this letter has a jaunty tone that suggests a self-assured candidate looking forward to reelection. In the same contest, in the lightning-rod speech that Speed remembered so well, he boasted that though desirous of distinction, he would prefer death to the dishonorable behavior of his opponent. But upon his winning and assuming a position in the leadership of his party or faction, life became more complicated.

One of the things Lincoln's New Salem backers expected of him was to help get their neighborhood set off as a new county, but this proved difficult and had to wait on the resolution of the fight to bring the state capital to Springfield. In the midst of this process, Lincoln moved to Springfield and, in the view of some of his old neighbors, reneged on his obligations to those who first elected him. In his old age Uncle Johnny Potter responded to a reporter's question about the nickname Honest Abe.

I think . . . the most of us had more confidence in Abe's smartness than in his honesty. When Abe ran for the legislature, the time he was elected, Ned Potter and Hugh Armstrong had a pledge from him that he would try to get us cut off and made into a new county. You know this used to be a part of Sangamon. The division was the big question. We elected Abe on the Whig ticket, although the Democrats had the majority. Well, he put our petition in his pocket and didn't do anything for us. That is the way I recollect it. Afterward they cut us off and made this Menard county. Folks felt pretty sore about the way Lincoln did. He never came back here to live, but settled in Springfield and practiced law.[63]

Lincoln had actually presented a petition for a new county in his first term in the legislature, and he did eventually help with the setting off of the new county of Menard from Sangamon County. But it didn't come about until 1839, by which time he was clearly looking out for the interests of Springfield.[64] The creation of new counties proved so rancorous and divisive that Lincoln's former neighbors were not the only ones who felt betrayed. His benefactor William Butler, at whose table he took his meals, sent a scorching letter to Lincoln in Vandalia that apparently accused his friend of selling out. Lincoln's cool-headed reply says much about his ability to deal with hotheads but also about the seriousness with which he regarded any suggestion of duplicity where his friends were concerned.

You were in an ill-humor when you wrote that letter, and, no doubt intended that I should be thrown into one also; which, however, I respectfully decline being done. All you have said about our having been bought up by Taylor, Wright, Turley, enemies &c I *know you would not say, seriously, in your moments of reflection*; and therefore I do not think it worth while to attempt *seriously* to prove the contrary to you. I only now say, that I am willing to pledge myself in black and white to cut my own throat from ear to ear, if, when I meet you, you shall *seriously* say, that you believe me capable of betraying my friends for any price.[65]

Lincoln was learning that politics, in being highly competitive and adversarial and in being dependent on deal making and compromise, could be a minefield, defying even the best intentions to walk a straight line. A letter to Butler a week later, explaining some of the circumstances behind their difficulty, suggests the nature of the problem. "When I wrote to Frink & Murphy that I would go for their county, I only meant that I would go for giving them a county as against Springfield & the old county; and it never occurred to me that I was pledging myself to one party of the new-county men against another, for I did not then know they were divided into parties. When I consented for the lines to approach Springfield nearer than the petition asked, I really thought I was confering a favour upon the new-county."[66]

It would be naive not to question just how accurate these protestations were and to what extent they constituted, at least in part, a rationalization of some fast footwork in a highly charged and complicated proceeding. Delivering on your promises can be more difficult than it seems, particularly if you have made too many of them or have made commitments that turn out to be incompatible. In such circumstances the line between duplicity and diplomacy can readily become nonexistent. The result of thus revising and qualifying his position, as Lincoln seems to have done, was bound to be regarded as a species of double-dealing, and there is little doubt that his opponents regarded him as one of those described by Governor Ford as "dexterous jugglers."[67]

One can get the impression from the legend that surrounds Abraham Lincoln that it must have been his long record of upright dealing as a lawyer and politician that gained him the famous title of "Honest Abe," but this was not the case. "Honest Abe" was apparently a sobriquet earned in his New Salem days as a nonaligned and disinterested judge of horse races.[68] He seems nonetheless to have had, early and late, a general and plausible reputation for truthfulness and fair dealing. What probably impressed his friends and neighbors even more was his remarkable lack of cupidity. Living in a place populated largely by people attracted by the chance to acquire land and make money, Lincoln exhibited a lack of interest in acquiring wealth that was truly rare. Thus he could not be bought or bribed, but as his political opponents knew well, he was not a saint.

Herndon affirmed his partner's basic honesty and that he was "justly and rightfully entitled to the appellation – 'Honest Abe,' " but he also pointed out in a public lecture that Lincoln "was not always – to all persons & at all times *absolutely* Honest."[69] Herndon was saying no more than that Lincoln was human, that what was true of every other person was true of him. But he also knew that it was folly to deny that Lincoln could be slippery and that he could, particularly where partisan politics was concerned, dissemble and deceive. Albert T. Bledsoe admitted that Lincoln was "honest and truthful in all the ordinary affairs of life," but he insisted that "Mr. Lincoln was no stickler for truth in contests before the people for political office and power. On the contrary, he entertained the opinion, that 'all is fair in politics.' It was one of his favorite maxims, that 'we must fight the devil with fire'; that is, with his own weapons."[70]

It is tempting to see Lincoln's tendencies in this regard as merely the expediencies of being a politician and a lawyer. Party politicians have to pretend, or make themselves believe, that the policies and proposals of their opponents are either evil or ill advised and that their own are virtuous and unfailingly superior. In much the same way, lawyers are expected to fight just as hard for the guilty and the culpable as they would for the blameless and the wronged. But things are rarely so simple. Operating on one standard in the ordinary affairs of life and on another in politics offers obvious opportunities for a confusion, if not a conflict, of interests. But while Lincoln was known as a narrowly partisan politician, who seemingly had little difficulty in seeing only the worst in the other party's measures and only the best in his own, his experience as a lawyer was apparently somewhat different. Particularly in the early part of his career, Lincoln was said by some of those who knew him best to be notably ineffective when his client was obviously in the wrong. As Lincoln's second law partner, Stephen T. Logan, put it, Lincoln "had this one peculiarity: he couldn't fight in a bad case."[71] Lincoln's longtime friend Samuel C. Parks concurred: "at the bar when he thought he was wrong he was the weakest lawyer I ever saw."[72] His overall record of success as a lawyer suggests that this could not have remained generally true, but his ineffectiveness in certain cases must have been sufficiently evident to account for such testimony by close friends.[73] This prompts the intriguing question of whether this peculiar vulnerability might somehow be related to his behavior toward the helpless.

What might be called the Bledsoe view of Lincoln's character and career – that he was an unprincipled seeker after success with a quenchless thirst for distinction – can be amply countered and qualified by the evidence, but it would be a mistake to dismiss it out of hand. This is because, though negative and one-sided, it is based on valid perceptions of things that must be taken into account. Bledsoe's description of an unnamed transgression by Lincoln is a good example. "One of the meanest things which we ever knew Mr. Lincoln to do (or, indeed, any man), was the result of envy, which, considering the circumstances of the case, was ineffably base. He soon repented of it, however, as a *blunder*, if not as a crime, and bore the rebuke it called down on his head *so meekly*, that it was forgiven, and, in effect, forgotten. It was certainly at variance with the outward habit of his life, and was, therefore, supposed to be inconsistent with the usual state of his soul."[74] In the perspective of Lamon's biography and his own view of Lincoln's conduct as a national politician and president, Bledsoe concluded that he and his Springfield friends had been wrong to forgive Lincoln, who had only done the expedient thing by feigning contrition to regain the good opinion of his peers.

Without adopting Bledsoe's conclusions, one can see from this anecdote what is evident in other ways: that Lincoln's character in these years was far from settled and that he was still struggling to determine how he should conduct himself, what was honorable, and what was necessary for success. For Lincoln was unquestionably ambitious; his deepest feelings about the meaning of his own life did appear to be connected to his quest for distinction, and even in this formative stage of his career he was learning how to temporize, to back and fill, and to manipulate his image. In later years he was definitely something of a hairsplitter, a master of deflecting or sidestepping a charge that was substantially true. These are not the things for which he was to be most remembered by posterity or on which his greatness was to depend, but they were undoubtedly tools for political survival and advancement.

❧

THE GREATEST and most consequential transition for Lincoln in this period came to focus in his ill-starred courtship of Mary Todd. Over the course of these years, the young man whose standing and reputation had begun to soar saw his career hit a dramatic and unexpected snag. The natural attributes that were superbly suited for dealing with public, political, and intellectual matters in a male-dominated world were unavailing in this crisis, which took place in a realm that was private, personal, and emotional, and that crucially involved women. Inexorably, his emotional vulnerabilities came into play as the crisis deepened. Among the casualties of this traumatic development were his mental stability, his ability to function as a political leader, and his self-confidence. The end of our period is, in fact, defined by the point at which he took decisive steps to retrieve these very things, but we gain perspective by going back to the beginning.

The Abraham Lincoln who arrived at New Salem in 1831 was easy-going, good-natured, and open-handed, and these qualities made him immediately popular with his new neighbors. Unprepossessing to look at because of his homely face and gawky appearance, he surprised his new acquaintances by his wit and intelligence. His direct and self-assured manner is reflected in the story of his first meeting with Cole-man Smoot, who told Herndon:

> I had heard Abe Lincoln Spoken of very frequently and was very anx-ious to See him and I presume he had often heard my name Spoken and had expressed a desire to See me also. one day when I was at New Salem I went into the Store in which he was then acting as Clerk and some one Calling me by name Lincoln Came forward and Says is that Smoot I remarked to him that was my name he then remarked that he was very much disappointed as he had Expected to See an old Propst of a fellow ["a man of very Singular looks"] I told him I was Equally disappointed with himself for I Expected to See a good looking Man.[75]

If he was on easy terms with men, his relations with women were another story. Preferring the company of older, married women, he was reluctant, if not unable, to translate his cordiality and manly assets into the conventions of courtship. Earthy stories, his most potent social instruments, were completely off-limits, for one thing, and he suffered from a disinclination or inability to market himself as a romantic com-modity. In turning his commiseration with a seemingly rejected Ann Rutledge into a secret courtship, he very nearly succeeded in achieving marriage and a highly desirable mate without having to play the awk-ward and unwanted role of swain in public. But she died, and he tem-porarily lost his emotional balance. His disastrous courtship of Mary Owens a year later showed how awkward and uncertain this otherwise self-confident young man could be. He acknowledged that he didn't know how to comport himself with women, something that Mary Owens's testimony and his own letters roundly confirm. In completely misjudging the situation and compounding this by persisting in a pro-posal he did not really mean, he ended, as he painfully admitted in his letter to Eliza Browning, by making a fool out of himself.

In seeking his way in Springfield society, Lincoln found himself socially awkward and uncomfortable. The self-presentation that worked to perfection in New Salem and served him well in the legislature at Vandalia had, in the more socially charged and sophisticated arena of

Springfield, definite limitations. Reforming the way he talked was an accepted form of self-improvement, even in the country, and as such it constituted no threat to his identity. Though gaining command of the language in a way that would serve him in any venue, he could readily back into the hoosier dialect in which he had been raised, depending on the situation. If anything, the hoosierisms and country expressions added savor to his more sophisticated mode of discourse. But perhaps because it presented a more direct challenge to his own self-image, to polish his manners and play the gallant was problematical, if not beyond him. His inability to accept and conform to the protocols of refined behavior surely contributed to Speed's judgment that Lincoln "could act no part but his own."76 This inability did not, however, impede his progress as a successful politician, so long as he steered clear of entanglements with women.

The clumsiness and ineptitude of the Mary Owens affair, from which he apparently learned little, foreshadowed the calamity of the Mary Todd "embrigglement." Once again he plunged into an ill-advised courtship that he quickly regretted, but instead of coming up against another woman for whom he was "deficient in those little links which make up the great chain of womans happiness,"77 he had the misfortune to arouse the implacable feelings of a sharp-tongued and willful woman who wanted to marry him. Being entangled with such a woman while in love with another was a predicament that would have tested the mettle of an adept lothario, but Lincoln, in this situation, was a warrior without weapons. To make things worse, his best friend set his cap for the very woman Lincoln fancied himself in love with, and both were unsuccessful. An effective party leader in politics and a proven wheeler-dealer in the legislature, Lincoln found himself without resources to deal with the emotional crisis that ensued. It was a role he simply did not know how to play, and it nearly did him in.

With his public persona in shambles, the fast-rising political leader now became something of a woebegone. "Poor L! how are the mighty fallen!"78 wrote a member of his circle. Freeing himself from the "hypo" took months, and it seemed to lift only when Speed became engaged and, following Lincoln's example, almost immediately regretted it. Helping his friend through his crisis of confidence helped Lincoln to better understand his own condition, at least with respect to some of its contributing causes. He was brought to realize that some of his hopes and expectations, like Speed's, were unrealistic. As he told Speed, "it is the peculiar misfortune of both you and me, to dream dreams of Elysium far exceeding all that any thing earthly can realize."[79] This might be called the Byronic condition, and it may help explain why Speed told Herndon, rather cryptically, that Lincoln "Forsook Byron."[80]

While Lincoln's empathetic immersion in Speed's engagement ordeal proved therapeutic, it was a temporary diversion, and its conclusion left him without a sense of direction. In trying to get himself back on track in the summer of 1842, Lincoln seems to have decided that he had two problems. The first was that no matter how well other things went in his life, the recurring thought of Mary's unhappiness triggered uncontrollable feelings of guilt. These irrepressible feelings had the power to deprive him of all satisfaction and must have been very much akin to his spontaneous feelings for the helpless. His second problem was that he had lost and desperately needed to regain the "gem" of his character, the ability to stick unflinchingly to his own resolutions. If the first was largely incidental, almost like an accident or bad luck, the second problem involved a rent in his character. It seems likely from what he wrote to Speed on July 4 – "before I resolve to do the one thing or the other, I must regain my confidence in my ability to keep my resolves when they are made" – that he couldn't bring himself to deal with the first problem until he had solved the second. That is, he couldn't make an important decision until he was convinced that he could stick by it.

There was seemingly only one remedy for the first problem, and Speed probably told him what it was: to marry Mary Todd. "I acknowledge the correctness of your advice," Lincoln had responded, but he pleaded the necessity of first retrieving the lost gem of his character. Something was holding him back. The sticking point may have been that marrying Mary meant going back on his decision not to do so, a decision that squared with his feelings but that had cost him dearly. ("You know the Hell I have suffered on that point," he once reminded Speed.[81]) The dramatic events that would occur in rapid succession shortly thereafter – the Lost Townships letter, the Shields challenge, the near-duel, his reconciliation with Mary, and the hasty marriage – clearly worked to bring about a solution to the first problem. Mary got her wish at last, and the killing weight of guilt was lifted from what Lincoln had insisted was his soul. But it seems equally clear that these same events brought the resolution of the second problem as well.

In retrospect, it would seem that Lincoln's decision to marry in the fall of 1842 was not impulsive but carefully considered, perhaps even cal-culating, and ultimately wise. His irresistible inner promptings, such as his feelings of guilt about Mary, were coming from a deep, nonnego-tiable part of his nature and were telling him who and what he was. So was his obsessive need to regain his ability to keep his commitments. Somehow the two had become part of the same package, and it was imperative that he deal with them, for both his identity and his ability to function were in the balance. What was needed to solve his personal dilemmas was the same thing that was needed to rehabilitate his public persona: decisive action. He had responded decisively in the Shields affair, but that was in reaction to something that had been thrust upon him. He had been forced to learn that rising is not without risks. Wanting to be esteemed by your peers means having to defend your honor. If he had performed honorably, it was still a "scrape," a tawdry episode in which he could take little lasting pride.

His marriage to Mary Todd satisfactorily resolved all these problems, and it did so in dramatically decisive fashion. In yielding to his feelings of guilt, he affirmed something important in his identity that had often proved an embarrassment and a hindrance in the past. As Joshua Speed pointed out, Lincoln's vulnerability to helplessness and suffering in early life was the seed which blossomed and bore fruit when as presi-dent he rose above the bitterness and hatred of civil war and set an example of pity and compassion.[82] Perhaps more important was the recovery of his self-confidence. In deciding to reverse himself and honor his original commitment, which Mary had understood as a promise to marry her, he was opting for the discipline of his father's hard rule: "If you make a bad bargain, *hug* it the tighter."[83] But this too, would have enormous consequences.

⁓

AFTER HIS MARRIAGE, Lincoln's life changed. He positioned himself for the nomination of his party to Congress, only to discover that some of his political supporters thought his marriage into the Todd-Stuart-Logan clan meant he had deserted the rank and file for the aristocrats. Defending himself, he wrote to a supporter in Menard County: "It would astonish if not amuse, the older citizens of your County who twelve years ago knew me a strange, friendless, uneducated, penniless boy, working on a flat boat – at ten dollars per month to learn that I have been put down here as the candidate of pride, wealth, and aristocratic family distinction."[84] He protested to his groomsman, James H. Matheny, that this was a false perception. Matheny told Herndon that "after Lincoln was Married that Lincoln took him – Matheny to the woods and there and then Said in reference to L's marriage *in the Aristocracy* – 'Jim – I am now and always shall be the same Abe Lincoln that I always was.' "[85]

But he was not the same old Abraham Lincoln in several important respects. He had a better understanding of himself, for one thing. This is shown by the fact that he thereafter got control of or got beyond the causes of his "scrapes," the series of misadventures that had plagued and embarrassed him, such as the discreditable harangue with James Adams, the ill-fated leap from the church window, or his near-duel with Shields. Moreover, the debilitating episodes of the "hypo" did not recur. In his personal demeanor he gradually became more guarded and reserved, and more self-absorbed. While he was increasingly more melancholy in his appearance and behavior, he exercised a tighter control on his emotions. And while he continued to be friendly and sociable in his dealings with people generally, he would never again be on intimate terms with anyone of the kind that he had known with Joshua Speed.

By marrying, Lincoln put the vexing business of courtship behind him, and if he didn't exactly rid himself of woman trouble, he at least permanently reduced the number of troublesome women in his life to one. Mary proved a doting wife and mother, but his abstracted ways and what some would have called their differences in background and training frequently provoked her blazing temper and sharp tongue. If he married, in part, to pacify his feelings and sense of honor, he gained one kind of peace at the price of another. But the most important part of his decision to marry may have been that it was irrevocable. In committing himself to a bargain, however painful or difficult to honor, he proved something to himself and anyone who cared to notice.

From this time on Lincoln became known for his resolution. One whose acquaintance with him began a few years later reported, "I don't believe he could be made to give up anything on which he set his mind. He never got excited and never stormed around, but he was resolute."[86] This did not, of course, mean he was intractable. He was obliging to others and not reputed to be particularly stubborn or willful. Nonetheless, in matters of consequence, especially where he had committed himself, he was notably determined. Judge David Davis said, "When he formed his opinions he was firm."[87] Lincoln himself was fully aware of the significance of this development, for he told a young man who wrote him about entering the law: "Always bear in mind that your own resolution to succeed, is more important than any other one thing."[88] The woman he married, who often pressured him to do things he did not want to do, allowed that there were definite limits in this regard. He was, she said, "a terribly firm man when he set his foot down – none of us – no man nor woman Could rule him after he had made up his mind." She even described for Herndon the way he looked when he had made up his mind: "I could tell when Mr. Lincoln had decided any thing: he was cheerful at first – then he pressed – or compressed his lips tightly – firmly[.] When these thing[s] showed themselves to me I fashioned myself and So all others had to do sooner or later – and the world found it out."[89]

For Lincoln personally, restoring the gem of his character was an all-important development. Something he had taken for granted had somehow, in the disorienting confusion of an emotional ordeal, been lost. Trying to live without it proved as agonizing and difficult as trying to get it back. But his efforts and perseverance eventually had more than merely personal consequences. As his wife observed, the world found out about Lincoln's hard-won resolution, for his rock-solid ability to keep his resolves once they were made would undergrid his performance as president. And that would make all the difference.

Notes

Introduction

1. John L. Scripps to William H. Herndon (hereafter cited as WHH), June 24, 1865, in Douglas L. Wilson and Rodney O. Davis, eds., *Herndon's Informants: Letters, Interviews, and Statements About Abraham Lincoln* (Urbana: University of Illinois Press, 1997), 57; hereafter cited as *Herndon's Informants*.
2. See John Hill's story in the *Menard Axis*, February 15, 1862, reprinted in *Herndon's Informants*, 24–25.
3. James Hurt, *Writing Illinois: The Prairie, Lincoln, and Chicago* (Urbana: University of Illinois Press, 1992), 48.
4. William H. Herndon and Jesse W. Weik, *Herndon's Life of Lincoln*, ed. Paul M. Angle (Cleveland: World Publishing, 1949 [1930]), 353; hereafter cited as *Herndon's Life of Lincoln*.
5. J. G. Randall, Appendix: "Sifting the Ann Rutledge Evidence," *Lincoln the President: Springfield to Gettysburg*, 2 vols. (New York: Dodd, Mead, 1945), 2:325.
6. David Herbert Donald, *Lincoln* (New York: Simon & Schuster, 1995), 609.
7. Joshua F. Speed to WHH, December 6, 1866, *Herndon's Informants*, 498.
8. Don E. Fehrenbacher, *Lincoln in Text and Context: Collected Essays* (Stanford: Stanford University Press, 1987), 281. More recently, Fehrenbacher and his wife have completed their monumental compilation of remarks attributed to Lincoln, which constitutes a major contribution to Lincoln scholarship. See Don E. and Virginia Fehrenbacher, eds., *Recollected Words of Abraham Lincoln* (Stanford: Stanford University Press, 1996).
9. An unmarked and undated newspaper clipping in the file collected by the Lincoln Museum at Fort Wayne, Indiana, later transferred to the John Hay Library at Brown University, reports this as AL speaking to former Governor Dennison of Ohio.
10. For Davis's Indianapolis speech, see Rufus Rockwell Wilson, ed., *Intimate Memories of Lincoln* (Elmira, N.Y.: Primavera Press, 1945), 68–71. For his interviews with WHH, see *Herndon's Informants*, 347, 484, 529.
11. David Donald, *Lincoln's Herndon: A Biography* (New York: Da Capo, 1989 [1948]), 347.
12. Quoted in Benjamin P. Thomas, *Portrait for Posterity: Lincoln and His Biographers* (New Brunswick: Rutgers University Press, 1947), 250.
13. See, for example, the testimony of John T. Stuart (WHH interview), December 20, 1866, *Herndon's Informants*, 519.
14. *Herndon's Life of Lincoln*, xxxvii–xxxviii.
15. WHH to Ward Hill Lamon, March 6, 1870, Lamon Papers, Huntington

Library; printed in Emanuel Hertz, ed., *The Hidden Lincoln: From the Letters and Papers of William H. Herndon* (New York: Viking Press, 1938), 73–74.

16. To the examples of Donald and Beveridge, given above, may be added that of Paul M. Angle, "Editor's Preface," *Herndon's Life of Lincoln*: "Herndon was certainly not a liar. Surpassing even his devotion to Lincoln was his passion for truth. Never, knowingly, would he distort a fact" (xxxviii).

17. *Herndon's Life of Lincoln*, xi.

18. For example, in a manuscript titled "Lincoln in Ky," WHH gave the date of this incident as 1846 (Herndon-Weik Collection, HW3804-50, Library of Congress).

19. One of the few exceptions is Mary Todd Lincoln's testimony in which she reduced her own age by five years. Herndon's informant letters and interviews with information about Abraham Lincoln (hereafter cited as AL) are collected in *Herndon's Informants*.

Chapter 1

1. John T. Stuart (Howard interview), [May 1860], Abraham Lincoln Papers, Library of Congress; hereafter cited as ALP. This interview is included in David C. Mearns, ed., *The Lincoln Papers*, 2 vols. (Garden City: Doubleday, 1948), 1:159. Working from Howard's manuscript, Mearns transcribed "striking" as "sticking," and by one of the anomalies of handwriting, both are plausible readings. I follow the transcription of John G. Nicolay, who made a copy for the use of his partner in biography, John Hay, as the more likely word for this context, but a good case can also be made for "sticking." Nicolay's copy is in the John Hay Papers, Brown University Library. I am grateful to Michael Burlingame for pointing me to this source.

2. Stuart (Howard interview), [May 1860], ALP. This interview, one of two with Stuart, is not printed in *The Lincoln Papers*, almost certainly for the reason that the editor, Mearns, couldn't read it. The ink is extremely faded, and in many places the words are illegible. I have reconstructed the text by comparing the original with the copy made in the nineteenth century by John G. Nicolay (see note 1 above).

3. Stuart (Howard interview), [May 1860], ALP.

4. For the ways in which the Clarys, Armstrongs, Greenes, and Potters are interrelated, see Ralph Shearer Rowland and Star Wilson Rowland, *Clary Genealogy: Four Early American Lines and Related Families* (Sterling, Va.: Ralph and Star Rowland, 1980).

5. Royal Clary (Howard interview), [May 1860], ALP. Mearns, *The Lincoln Papers*, 1:156, transcribes the word "bravery" as "bearing," a reading that the manuscript will support. But as with the Stuart testimony cited above, the manuscript will also support a reading of "bravery," which is the way John G. Nicolay transcribed it (see note 1 above). Either word would fit my general argument here, but I follow Nicolay's reading as the more likely language for both the informant and the occasion.

6. Howard originally wrote: "I am sorry that you bet the money, not that I

believe there is a man on earth that can throw Lincoln threw Armstrong first fall dogfall second &" (ALP).

7. William G. Greene (Howard interview), [May 1860], ALP; printed in Mearns, *The Lincoln Papers*, 1:154.

8. W. D. Howells, *Life of Abraham Lincoln* (Bloomington: Indiana University Press, 1960 [1860]), 34–35.

9. Ibid., 35.

10. J. Q. Howard, *The Life of Abraham Lincoln: With Extracts from His Speeches* (Columbus: Follet, Foster, 1860), 18–19.

11. "Autobiography for John L. Scripps," [c. June 1860], Roy P. Basler et al., eds., *The Collected Works of Abraham Lincoln*, 8 vols. (New Brunswick: Rutgers University Press, 1953), 1:65; hereafter cited as *Collected Works*.

12. Erastus Wright to Josiah Holland, July 10, 1865, Josiah G. Holland Papers, New York Public Library; Mentor Graham (Howard interview), Mearns, *The Lincoln Papers*, 1:155.

13. James Short to WHH, July 7, 1865, in Douglas L. Wilson and Rodney O. Davis, eds., *Herndon's Informants: Letters, Interviews, and Statements About Abraham Lincoln* (Urbana: University of Illinois Press, 1997), 73–74; hereafter cited as *Herndon's Informants*.

14. Stuart (Howard interview), ALP.

15. Thomas P. Reep, *Lincoln at New Salem* (n.p.: The Old Salem Lincoln League, 1927), 98.

16. James Short to WHH, July 7, 1865, *Herndon's Informants*, 73.

17. Reep, *Lincoln at New Salem*, 33.

18. L. M. Greene and R. B. Rutledge. John M. Rutledge mentions Offutt as betting but says nothing about Clary.

19. L. M. Greene to WHH, July 30, 1865, *Herndon's Informants*, 80.

20. T. G. Onstot, *Pioneers of Menard and Mason Counties* (Forest City, Ill.: T. G. Onstot, 1902 [rpt. 1986]), 72.

21. R. B. Rutledge to WHH, [c. November 1, 1866], *Herndon's Informants*, 386.

22. A. H. Chapman (WHH interview), [1865–66], *Herndon's Informants*, 439.

23. Russell Godbey told WHH: "When a fight was on hand Abe would Sy to me – Lets go and break up the Row with a laugh & we generally did it –." *Herndon's Informants*, 450.

24. Levi Beardsley, *Reminiscences* (New York: Charles Vinten, 1852), 34.

25. Jennie Holliman, *American Sports (1785–1835)* (Durham: Seeman Press, 1931), 149.

26. Usher F. Linder, *Reminiscences of the Early Bench and Bar of Illinois* (Chicago: Chicago Legal News Co., 1879), 38.

27. Holliman, *American Sports*, 150.

28. Linder, *Reminiscences*, 39.

29. WHH to Truman Bartlett, September 25, 1887, in Emanuel Hertz, ed., *The Hidden Lincoln: From the Letters and Papers of William H. Herndon* (New York: Viking Press, 1938), 204.

30. John Hanks to Jesse W. Weik, June 12, 1887, *Herndon's Informants*, 615. Hanks actually gives Nancy Lincoln's height as six feet in another part of the same letter. Herndon told Weik: "The reputation of Mrs. Lincoln is that she was a

bold, reckless, daredevil kind of a woman, stepping to the very verge of propriety." WHH to Jesse W. Weik, January 19, 1886, Hertz, *The Hidden Lincoln*, 138–39.

31. Henry McHenry (WHH interview), October 10, 1866, *Herndon's Informants*, 369.

32. Walter Armstrong, *Wrestling*, in *The Badminton Library of Sports and Pastimes*, ed. The Duke of Beaufort, asst. Alfred E. T. Watson (London: Longmans, Green, 1889), 213.

33. James Gourley (WHH interview), [1865–66], *Herndon's Informants*, 451.

34. William Miller? in *Herndon's Informants*, 363. I am grateful to Donald Sayenga for information about early American wrestling and suggestions about the kind of hold employed in Lincoln's match with Armstrong.

35. Graeme Kent, *A Pictorial History of Wrestling* (London: Spring Books, 1968), 117.

36. Col. Risdon M. Moore, "Mr. Lincoln as a Wrestler," *Transactions of the Illinois State Historical Society for the Year 1904* (Springfield: Illinois State Historical Library, 1904), 434.

37. William G. Greene (Howard interview), ALP.

38. Judge James Harriott (WHH interview), [1865–66], *Herndon's Informants*, 703.

39. Royal Clary's testimony was given in 1860; Armstrong died in 1857.

40. Henry McHenry (WHH interview), [1865–66], *Herndon's Informants*, 369.

41. These are William G. Greene, Royal Clary, L. M. Greene, James Short, Henry Clark, R. B. Rutledge, John M. Rutledge, and John Potter.

42. R. B. Rutledge to WHH, [c. November 1, 1866], *Herndon's Informants*, 386.

43. John M. Rutledge to WHH, November 18, 1866, *Herndon's Informants*, 402.

44. Henry Clark (WHH interview), [1865–66], *Herndon's Informants*, 528.

45. Interview with Volney Hickox, "Lincoln at Home," *Illinois State Journal*, Springfield, Ill., October 15, 1874.

46. Hannah Armstrong (WHH interview), [1865–66], *Herndon's Informants*, 526.

47. Mentor Graham (WHH interview), October 10, 1866, *Herndon's Informants*, 370.

48. Walter B. Stevens, *A Reporter's Lincoln* (St. Louis: Missouri Historical Society, 1916), 7–8. I am grateful to Donald Sayenga for the suggestion that Potter may have here been talking about "points" rather than "joints."

49. R. B. Rutledge to WHH, [c. November 1, 1866], *Herndon's Informants*, 386.

50. J. G. Holland, *The Life of Abraham Lincoln* (Springfield, Mass.: Gurdon Bill, 1866), 45.

51. Ibid., 45.

52. Ward Hill Lamon, *The Life of Abraham Lincoln* (Boston: James R. Osgood, 1872), 93.

53. Isaac N. Arnold, *The Life of Abraham Lincoln* (Chicago: A. C. McClurg, 1887 [1884]), 32.

54. Ibid., 33.

55. J. G. Nicolay and John Hay, *Abraham Lincoln: A History*, 10 vols. (New York: Century, 1890), 1:80–81.

56. Ibid., 1:81.

57. WHH to J. G. Holland, May 26, 1865, Holland Papers, New York Public Library.

58. William H. Herndon and Jesse W. Weik, *Herndon's Life of Lincoln*, ed. Paul M. Angle (Cleveland: World Publishing, 1949 [1930]), 70.

59. Ida M. Tarbell, *The Life of Abraham Lincoln*, 2 vols. (New York: Lincoln Memorial Association, 1900), 1:64.

60. William E. Barton, *The Life of Abraham Lincoln*, 2 vols. (Indianapolis: Bobbs-Merrill, 1925), 1:164.

61. Carl Sandburg, *Abraham Lincoln: The Prairie Years*, 2 vols. (New York: Harcourt, Brace, 1926), 1:137.

62. Ibid.

63. Reprinted in Onstot, *Pioneers*, 81.

64. Reep, *Lincoln at New Salem*, 25.

65. Albert J. Beveridge, *Abraham Lincoln 1809–1858*, 2 vols. (Boston: Houghton Mifflin, 1928), 1:111.

66. Benjamin P. Thomas, *Lincoln's New Salem* (Chicago: Americana House, 1954 [1934]), 66n.

67. Benjamin P. Thomas, *Abraham Lincoln: A Biography* (New York: Alfred A. Knopf, 1952), 26. In his discussion of sources, Thomas suggests that he regarded the events described in Howells and uncorrected in the Samuel C. Parks copy, which Lincoln annotated, as authorized by Lincoln himself. "The discovery of a copy of William Dean Howells' campaign biography, *Life of Abraham Lincoln* (1860), corrected by Lincoln with marginal notations, enables us to treat many traditional incidents of his early life with certainty; for Lincoln's corrections are so meticulous that the book takes on the nature of an autobiography" (533). While many of the corrections in the Parks copy of Howells do indeed suggest meticulousness, this was, after all, a campaign biography, and Lincoln was correcting it as such. He wanted to rectify gross errors or misunderstandings, particularly ones with political implications, but there is no reason to suppose that his aim was to root out every minor error it contained. On the contrary, scholars have identified several obvious errors that he let stand, which he did for the equally obvious reason that they were not worth bothering about. Thus, "certainty" would seem to be much too strong a word for what Lincoln's corrections lend to Howells's narrative.

68. Armstrong, *Wrestling*, 204.

69. In addition to Lincoln's own description of this match (see note 36), see Joseph Gillespie to WHH, January 30, 1866; R. B. Rutledge to WHH, [c. November 1, 1866]; Royal Clary (WHH interview), [1865–66], *Herndon's Informants*, 186, 387, 373.

70. *Narrative of the Life of Frederick Douglass an American Slave*, ed. Benjamin Quarles (Cambridge: Harvard University Press, 1988), 104.

Chapter 2

1. AL to Martin Morris, March 26, 1843, Roy P. Basler et al., eds., *The Collected Works of Abraham Lincoln*, 8 vols. (New Brunswick: Rutgers University Press, 1953), 1:65; hereafter cited as *Collected Works*.

2. Quoted in Erastus Wright to Josiah G. Holland, July 10, 1865, Josiah G. Holland Papers, New York Public Library.

3. William Butler (Howard interview), [May 1860], in David C. Mearns, ed., *The Lincoln Papers,* 2 vols. (Garden City: Doubleday, 1948), 1:151.

4. Caleb Carman to WHH, November 30, 1866, in Douglas L. Wilson and Rodney O. Davis, eds., *Herndon's Informants: Letters, Interviews, and Statements About Abraham Lincoln* (Urbana: University of Illinois Press, 1997), 429; hereafter cited as *Herndon's Informants.*

5. See Caleb Carman (WHH interview), October 12, 1866, Carman to WHH, December 8, 1866, *Herndon's Informants,* 373, 504.

6. Caleb Carman to WHH, November 30, 1866, *Herndon's Informants,* 429.

7. Jason Duncan to WHH, [1866–67], *Herndon's Informants,* 539.

8. For Lincoln's stint as a hog drover, see George Close (Howard interview), [May 1860], in Mearns, *The Lincoln Papers,* 1:150.

9. John Hanks (WHH interview), [1865–66], *Herndon's Informants,* 455.

10. David Turnham (WHH interview), September 15, 1865, *Herndon's Informants,* 121.

11. Anna Caroline Gentry (WHH interview), September 17, 1865, *Herndon's Informants,* 131.

12. This list combines the testimony of Indiana informants and what Lincoln told John Scripps for his campaign biography. For the Indiana testimony, see Herndon's letters and interviews in *Herndon's Informants* and the interviews of William Fortune in Bess V. Ehrmann, *The Missing Chapter in the Life of Abraham Lincoln* (Chicago: Walter M. Hill, 1938), 75. John Locke Scripps, *Life of Abraham Lincoln,* ed. Roy P. Basler and Lloyd A. Dunlap (Bloomington: Indiana University Press, 1961), 35–36.

13. Scripps, *Life of Abraham Lincoln,* 36. There is also, of course, the possibility that the title was mentioned here for its political value.

14. Dilworth (Scripps, *Life of Abraham Lincoln,* 35), Pike and Barclay (Dennis F. Hanks to WHH, June 13, 1865, *Herndon's Informants,* 42), Scott (David Turnham to WHH, September 16, 1865, *Herndon's Informants,* 129).

15. A version of this expression turns up in the testimony of his cousins Dennis and John Hanks; his stepmother, Sarah Bush Lincoln; his stepsister Matilda Johnston Moore; his friends David Turnham and William Jones (by way of Dr. John Houghland), and A. H. Chapman. See *Herndon's Informants.*

16. This is an inference based on the testimony of his stepmother that he was a "Constant reader" of newspapers from 1827 to 1830 (WHH interview, September 8, 1865, *Herndon's Informants,* 107) and the suggestions of various Indiana informants that Lincoln worked for Jones in his store and was influenced by his anti-Jackson politics.

17. Sarah Bush Lincoln (WHH interview), September 8, 1865, *Herndon's Informants,* 107.

18. Ibid., 107. See William M. Thayer's, *The Pioneer Boy and How He Became President* (Boston: Walker, Wise, and Company, 1863), 130–31. Thayer claimed to have been given biographical material by the president himself, along with the "names and addresses of several of his early associates, reared with him in the wilderness, and of intimate friends in later life." (See William M. Thayer, *From Pioneer Home to the White House* (New York: Hurst, 1882,

[5]). Though very much a "rags to riches" genre book with fictionalized dialogue and pious moralizing, the scenes Thayer dramatized were apparently based on things related by his informants. See David C. Mearns, "Thayer's *The Pioneer Boy*: A Second and Harder Look," *The Library of Congress: Quarterly Journal of Current Acquisitions*, 3:13 (May 1956), 129–34). I am grateful to Michael Burlingame for information and helpful suggestions about Thayer.

19. Dennis F. Hanks (WHH interview), June 13, 1865, in Douglas L. Wilson and Rodney O. Davis, eds., *Herndon's Informants: Letters, Interviews, and Statements About Abraham Lincoln* (Urbana: University of Illinois Press, 1997), 41; hereafter cited as *Herndon's Informants*.

20. Sarah Bush Lincoln (WHH interview), September 8, 1865, *Herndon's Informants*, 107.

21. Some of his Indiana acquaintances did remember Lincoln reading at night, particularly when working away from home. See the testimony of Elizabeth Crawford (WHH interview) September 16, 1865, and Green Taylor (WHH interview), September 16, 1865, *Herndon's Informants*, 126, 130.

22. The best study of Lincoln and his father is John Y. Simon, *House Divided: Lincoln and His Father* (Fort Wayne: Louis A. Warren Library and Museum, 1987).

23. Quoted in Henry C. Whitney, *Life of Lincoln*, vol. 1, *Lincoln the Citizen*, ed. Marion Mills Miller (New York: Baker & Taylor, 1908), 75. Greene also reported his visit to Thomas Lincoln to Francis Fisher Browne, who published it in *The Every-Day Life of Abraham Lincoln*, ed. John Y. Simon (Lincoln: University of Nebraska Press, 1995 [1886]), 88.

24. John Romine (WHH interview), September 16, 1865, *Herndon's Informants*, 118.

25. Dennis F. Hanks (WHH interview), September 8, 1865, *Herndon's Informants*, 104.

26. Sarah Bush Lincoln (WHH interview), September 8, 1865, *Herndon's Informants*, 106–7.

27. Mathilda Johnston Moore (WHH interview), September 8, 1865, *Herndon's Informants*, 108.

28. Dennis F. Hanks (WHH interview), June 13, 1865, *Herndon's Informants*, 41.

29. Robert B. Rutledge to WHH, November 30, 1866, *Herndon's Informants*, 426.

30. Caleb Carman to WHH, December 8, 1866, *Herndon's Informants*, 504.

31. Mentor Graham (Howard interview), [May 1860], in Mearns, *The Lincoln Papers*, 1:156.

32. Russell Godbey (WHH interview), [1865–66], *Herndon's Informants*, 450.

33. William G. Greene (Howard interview), [May 1860], in Mearns, *The Lincoln Papers*, 1:154.

34. J. Rowan Herndon to WHH, August 16, 1865, *Herndon's Informants*, 92. From the testimony he elicited from his informants on Lincoln's reading posture, it seems clear that Herndon was intrigued by the topic. Because he knew his partner so well, he was probably not surprised that Lincoln is described as reading in all sorts of unusual positions, but almost never sitting in a chair. Lincoln's cousin, Harriet Chapman, said that even after his marriage, in his own home "his usual way of reading was lying down[.] in warm weather he Seemed to prefer the floor[.] he would turn a Chair down on the floor and put a pillow on it and lie thare for hours and read." Harriet Chapman to WHH, December 10, 1866, *Herndon's Informants*, 512.

35. Robert B. Rutledge to WHH, December 4, 1866, *Herndon's Informants*, 498.

36. Mentor Graham to WHH, July 15, 1865, *Herndon's Informants*, 76.

37. N. W. Branson to WHH, August 3, 1865, *Herndon's Informants*, 90.

38. Robert B. Rutledge to WHH, December 4, 1866, *Herndon's Informants*, 497.

39. Charles Maltby, *The Life and Public Services of Abraham Lincoln* (Stockton, Calif.: Daily Independent Steam Power Print, 1884), 27.

40. J. Rowan Herndon to WHH, August [16?], 1865, *Herndon's Informants*, 91. Herndon calls McNamar by the name he used when Herndon was living in New Salem: McNeil.

41. Dr. John Allen (Howard interview), [May 1860], in Mearns, *The Lincoln Papers*, 1:157.

42. Robert B. Rutledge to WHH, November 30, 1866, *Herndon's Informants*, 426.

43. J. Rowan Herndon to WHH, August [16?], 1865, *Herndon's Informants*, 92.

44. See WHH to Weik, October 21, 1885, in Emanuel Hertz, ed., *The Hidden Lincoln: From the Letters and Papers of William H. Herndon* (New York: Viking Press, 1938), 95.

45. Quoted by George Alfred Townsend, "Abraham Lincoln: A Talk with the Late President's Law Partner," *New York Tribune*, February 15, 1867; in Reinhard H. Luthin, *The Real Abraham Lincoln* (Englewood Cliffs, N.J.: Prentice-Hall, 1960), 22.

46. Herndon's marginal note on his 1887 interview with Graham's daughter, Elizabeth Herndon Bell, *Herndon's Informants*, 605.

47. Mentor Graham (Howard interview), [May 1860], in Mearns, *The Lincoln Papers*, 1:155.

48. Graham to WHH, May 29, 1865, *Herndon's Informants*, 10.

49. For reasons for thinking that Graham had meager learning, see Chapter 3, p. 94.

50. William G. Greene to WHH, June 7, 1865, *Herndon's Informants*, 26. Years later he told a reporter that the grammar he loaned Lincoln was Kirkham's. See the interview signed "N. A. J." and datelined Dallas, Texas, May 25, printed in the *Chicago Tribune*, June 7, 1891, p. 6.

51. Quoted, from an interview in the *Chicago Tribune*, in Wayne C. Temple, "Lincoln and the Burners at New Salem," *Lincoln Herald*, 67:2 (Summer 1965), 9.

52. Maltby, *The Life and Public Services of Abraham Lincoln*, 26–27.

53. Ibid., 30.

54. Ibid., 41.

55. Jason Duncan to WHH, [1866–67], *Herndon's Informants*, 539.

56. L. M. Greene to WHH, July 30, 1865, *Herndon's Informants*, 80.

57. *Collected Works*, 4:62.

58. Samuel Kirkham, *English Grammar in Familiar Lectures Accompanied by a Compendium; Embracing a New Systematick Order of Parsing a New System of Punctuation, Exercises in False Syntax, and a System of Philosophical Grammar in Notes: to Which Are Added an Appendix, and A Key to the Exercises; Designed for the Use of Schools and Private Learners* (Cincinnati: E. Morgan, 1838), 21. The edition that has been represented by the Rutledge family as coming from Lincoln bears an imprint of 1828.

59. Interview with Greene in the *The Weekly Inter Ocean* (Chicago) by G[eorge]

A. P[ierce], April 21, 1881. Clipping in the Nicolay and Hay Collection, Illinois State Historical Library.

60. Kirkham, *English Grammar*, 117.

61. William G. Greene (Howard interview), [May 1860], in Mearns, *The Lincoln Papers*, 1:152–53.

62. J. Rowan Herndon to WHH, July 3, 1865, *Herndon's Informants*, 69.

63. A. Y. Ellis (statement for WHH), January 23, 1866, *Herndon's Informants*, 174.

64. The most authoritative treatment of Lincoln's storytelling, clean and otherwise, is P. M. Zall, *Abe Lincoln Laughing: Humorous Anecdotes from Original Sources by and About Abraham Lincoln* (Berkeley: University of California Press, 1982). For a sampling of "improper" stories, see nos. 5, 110, 111, 191, 196, 197, 201.

65. See, for example, the story of Ethan Allen in A. Y. Ellis (statement for WHH), January 23, 1866, *Herndon's Informants*, 174. As AL is reported telling this story in 1860 (see *Herndon's Informants*, 437, 438), it seems doubtful that it dates from this period. In the same document the story of the Millerites must date no earlier than the 1840s.

66. A. Y. Ellis (statement for WHH), January 23, 1866, *Herndon's Informants*, 171.

67. Ibid., 173.

68. Dr. John Allen (Howard interview), in Mearns, *The Lincoln Papers*, 1:157–58.

69. William G. Greene to WHH, December 3, 1865, *Herndon's Informants*, 142.

70. Jason Duncan to WHH, [1866–67], *Herndon's Informants*, 540.

71. Robert B. Rutledge to WHH, [c. November 1, 1866], *Herndon's Informants*, 384.

72. Fern Nance Pond, *Intellectual New Salem in Lincoln's Day: An Address Delivered at Lincoln Memorial University, Harrogate, Tennessee, February 12, 1938* (Petersburg, Ill.: n. pub., 1938), 16.

73. Ibid., 16–17.

74. Hannah Armstrong (WHH interview), [1865–66], *Herndon's Informants*, 526.

75. John McNamar to WHH, November 25, 1866, *Herndon's Informants*, 420; see also his interview with Volney Hickox, "Lincoln at Home," *Illinois State Journal*, October 15, 1874.

76. For Kelso's arrival in New Salem in the summer of 1832, see Thomas P. Reep, *Lincoln at New Salem* (n.p.: Old Salem Lincoln League, 1927), 13.

77. James Short to WHH, July 7, 1865, *Herndon's Informants*, 74.

78. Note signed by Herndon on docketing of G. U. Miles to WHH, June 30, 1865, *Herndon's Informants*, 66.

79. Reep, *Lincoln at New Salem*, 54.

80. Hardin Bale (WHH interview), [1866], *Herndon's Informants*, 528.

81. Caleb Carman (WHH interview), October 12, 1866, *Herndon's Informants*, 374.

82. AL to James H. Hackett, August 17, 1863, *Collected Works*, 6:392.

83. James H. Matheny (WHH interview), November 1866, *Herndon's Informants*, 431.

84. AL to James H. Hackett, August 17, 1863, *Collected Works*, 6: 392.

85. Milton Hay in "Recollection of Lincoln: Three Letters of Intimate Friends," *Bulletin of the Abraham Lincoln Association*, 25 (December 1931), 7.

86. William G. Greene (Howard interview), [May 1860], in Mearns, *The Lincoln Papers*, 1:154.

87. Maltby, *The Life and Public Services of Abraham Lincoln*, 31.
88. See David Daiches, *Robert Burns* (London: G. Bell, 1952), 34–104.
89. John McNamar to WHH, November 25, 1866, *Herndon's Informants*, 421.
90. Milton Hay, in "Recollections of Lincoln: Three Letters of Intimate Friends," 8.
91. John McNamar to WHH, November 25, 1866, *Herndon's Informants*, 420.
92. J. Rowan Herndon to WHH, July 3, 1865, *Herndon's Informants*, 70.
93. William G. Greene to WHH, May 30, 1865, *Herndon's Informants*, 21.
94. William H. Herndon and Jesse W. Weik, *Herndon's Life of Lincoln*, ed. Paul M. Angle (Cleveland: World Publishing, 1949 [1930]), 102; hereafter cited as *Herndon's Life of Lincoln*.
95. See the discussion below at pp. 81–85.
96. James H. Matheny (WHH interview), [by March 2, 1870], *Herndon's Informants*, 577.
97. Ibid., May 3, 1866, 251.
98. Daiches, *Robert Burns*, 208.
99. Ibid., 209.
100. A. Y. Ellis (statement for WHH), January 23, 1866, *Herndon's Informants*, 172. See also Ellis to WHH, January 30, 1866, February 14, 1866, *Herndon's Informants*, 179, 210.
101. *Herndon's Life of Lincoln*, 355.
102. Philip S. Foner, ed., *The Complete Writings of Thomas Paine*, 2 vols. (New York: Citadel Press, 1945), 1:464.
103. Ibid.
104. Ibid.
105. Ibid.
106. Ibid., 1:466.
107. See WHH to Francis E. Abbot, February 18, 1870, published in *The Index*, 1 (April 2, 1870), 5–6; see also James H. Matheny (WHH interview), [by March 2, 1870], *Herndon's Informants*, 576.
108. Foner, *Complete Writings*, 1:470.
109. Constantin de Volney, *Volney's Ruins; or, Meditation on the Revolutions of Empires* (Boston: Charles Gaylord, 1833), 4.
110. Ibid., 25.
111. Ibid., 35.
112. Ibid., 51.
113. Ibid., 99–100.
114. Ibid., 99.
115. Isaac Cogdal (WHH interview), [1865–66], *Herndon's Informants*, 441. Herndon vouches, in the course of this interview, for Cogdal's claim to have discussed religion with Lincoln in his Springfield law office. Lincoln was said to have helped Cogdal with his law studies. See [R. D. Miller], *History of Mason and Menard Counties* (Chicago: O. L. Baskin, 1879), 749. For confirmation of Lincoln's unorthodox views on eternal punishments, compare the testimony of Jesse W. Fell: "On the inate depravity of Man, the character & office of the great head of the Church, the atonement, the infallibility of the written revelation, the performance of myricles, the nature & design

of present & future rewards & punishments, (as they are popularly called) and many other Subjects, he held opinions not only unsustained, but utterly at variance with what are usually taught in the Churches." Fell to W. H. Lamon, September 22, 1870, *Herndon's Informants*, 579. See also W. H. Hanna's interview with WHH: "Says that Since 1856 Mr Lincoln told him he was a Kind of universalist – That he never Could bring himself to the belief in Eternal punishment." *Herndon's Informants*, 458.

116. Mentor Graham to B. F. Irwin, March 17, 1874, cited in Reep, *Lincoln at New Salem*, 57.

117. Foner, *Complete Writings*, 1:497.

118. Hardin Bale to WHH, May 29, 1865, *Herndon's Informants*, 13.

119. WHH to Francis E. Abbot, February 18, 1870, *The Index*, 1 (April 2, 1870), 5.

120. John Hill to WHH, June 27, 1865, *Herndon's Informants*, 60–61.

121. Isaac Cogdal (WHH interview), [1865–66], *Herndon's Informants*, 441.

122. James H. Matheny (WHH interview), [by March 2, 1870], *Herndon's Informants*, 577.

123. Ibid., November 1866, 432.

124. Foner, *Complete Writings*, 1:547.

125. Ibid., 1:570.

126. WHH to Abbot, February 18, 1870, *The Index*, 5.

127. James H. Matheny (WHH interview), [1865–66], *Herndon's Informants*, 472.

128. Walter B. Stevens, *A Reporter's Lincoln* (St. Louis: Missouri Historical Society, 1916), 11–12.

129. For Mentor Graham's testimony, see above; for J. Rowan Herndon, see his letter to WHH, August 16, 1865, *Herndon's Informants*: "He frequently wusd the Bible" (92).

130. WHH to Abbot, February 18, 1870, *The Index*, 5.

131. See the printed version of the lecture Reed delivered in Springfield and elsewhere, "The Later Life and Religious Sentiments of Abraham Lincoln," *Scribner's Monthly* (July 1873), 333–43.

132. Stevens, *A Reporter's Lincoln*, 11.

133. Quoted in David Donald, *Lincoln's Herndon: A Biography* (New York: Da Capo Press, 1989 [1948]), 213.

134. *Herndon's Life of Lincoln*, 354.

Chapter 3

1. Statement for Jesse W. Fell, December 20, 1859, Roy P. Basler et al., eds., *The Collected Works of Abraham Lincoln*, 8 vols. (New Brunswick: Rutgers University Press, 1953), 3:511–12; hereafter cited as *Collected Works*.

2. William Wood (WHH interview), September 15, 1865, in Douglas L. Wilson and Rodney O. Davis, eds., *Herndon's Informants: Letters, Interviews, and Statements About Abraham Lincoln* (Urbana: University of Illinois Press, 1997), 124; hereafter cited as *Herndon's Informants*.

3. Thomas P. Reep, *Lincoln at New Salem* (n.p.: Old Salem Lincoln League, 1927), 98.

4. John Hanks (WHH interview), [1865–66], *Herndon's Informants*, 456.

5. John Hanks (WHH interview), June 13, 1865, *Herndon's Informants*, 44.

6. See Lincoln's description of being hired by Offutt and ensuing events in *Collected Works*, 4:63ff.

7. Jason Duncan to WHH, [1866–67], *Herndon's Informants*, 542.

8. John McNamar to WHH, June 4, 1866, *Herndon's Informants*, 259.

9. H. E. Dummer (WHH interview), [1865–66], *Herndon's Informants*, 442.

10. M. W. Delahay, "The Life and Character of Abraham Lincoln" [1870]. Huntington Library. A rare broadside of a lecture whose contents were later reprinted in Mark W. Delahay, *Abraham Lincoln* (New York: D. H. Newhall, 1939).

11. John Hanks (WHH interview), [1865–66] *Herndon's Informants*, 456.

12. "Communication to the People of Sangamon County," *Collected Works*, 1:6.

13. Reep, *Lincoln at New Salem*, 98.

14. Coleman Smoot to WHH, May 7, 1866, *Herndon's Informants*, 254.

15. A notice in the Vincennes, Indiana, *Western Sun & General Advertiser* a few years later indicates that Offutt had broken jail and was being sought by Sheriff John Purcell, who described his man as "very talkative and wishes to pass for a gentleman." December 27, 1834, 3:5. I am indebted to Mark L. Johnson of the Illinois Historic Sites Office for calling this notice to my attention.

16. According to H. E. Dummer (WHH interview), [1865–66], *Herndon's Informants*, 442.

17. J. Rowan Herndon to WHH, June 11, 1865, *Herndon's Informants*, 34.

18. Charles Maltby, *The Life and Public Services of Abraham Lincoln* (Stockton, Calif.: Daily Independent Steam Power Print, 1884), 30. For Lincoln's backing of Bogue, see Harry E. Pratt, *The Personal Finances of Abraham Lincoln* (Springfield, Ill.: Abraham Lincoln Association, 1943).

19. *Collected Works*, 4:64.

20. See Chapter 1, p. 19.

21. John T. Stuart (Howard interview), Abraham Lincoln Papers, Library of Congress (hereafter cited as ALP), collated with the copy made by John G. Nicolay. See Chapter One, note 1.

22. John T. Stuart (Nicolay interview), June 23, 1875, in Michael Burlingame, ed., *An Oral History of Abraham Lincoln: John G. Nicolay's Interviews and Essays* (Carbondale and Edwardsville: Southern Illinois University Press, 1996), 10.

23. *Collected Works*, 1:9.

24. James A. Herndon to WHH, May 29, 1865, *Herndon's Informants*, 16–17.

25. *Collected Works*, 4:64–65.

26. Caleb Carman (WHH interview), October 12, 1866, *Herndon's Informants*, 373.

27. Dennis F. Hanks to WHH, March 22, 1866, *Herndon's Informants*, 235.

28. *Collected Works*, 4:65.

29. See Chapter 5, p. 142.

30. These transactions are summarized in J. Rowan Herndon to WHH, October 28, 1866, *Herndon's Informants*, 378.

31. *Collected Works*, 4:65.

32. For the discovery of a new document that helps to clarify Lincoln's indebtedness, see Thomas F. Schwartz, "Lincoln's National Debt" (forthcoming). I

am grateful to Mr. Schwartz for permitting me to read an early draft of this paper.

33. Zarel C. Spears and Robert S. Barton, *Berry and Lincoln: Frontier Merchants: The Store That "Winked Out"* (New York: Stratford House, 1947), 15.

34. William G. Greene (Howard interview), [May 1860], ALP, in David C. Mearns, ed., *The Lincoln Papers*, 2 vols. (Garden City, N.Y.: Doubleday, 1948), 1:153. For Lincoln's storekeeping, see Benjamin P. Thomas, *Lincoln's New Salem* (Chicago: Americana House, 1961 [1934]), 88–92; for his indebtedness, see Pratt, *The Personal Finances of Abraham Lincoln*, 11–15. Also Spears and Barton, *Berry and Lincoln*.

35. *Collected Works*, 3:5–6.

36. Ibid., 3:16.

37. George Spears to WHH, November 3, 1866, *Herndon's Informants*, 393.

38. See the testimony of Parthena Hill, James McGrady Rutledge, Daniel Green Burner, and John Potter in Ida M. Tarbell, *The Early Life of Abraham Lincoln* (New York: S. S. McClure, 1896), 172–74.

39. James Davis (WHH interview), [1865–66], *Herndon's Informants*, 530.

40. Newspaper story quoting Mrs. Vienna Lyster, a daughter of Cameron, in Lincoln Scrapbook in Huntington Library, 151179 (vol. 3), 5.

41. Parthena Hill (WHH interview), [March 1887?], *Herndon's Informants*, 605. The decimal points, which are not in the source, have been added for clarity.

42. J. Rowan Herndon to WHH, May 28, 1865, *Herndon's Informants*, 7.

43. The shooting was reported in the *Sangamo Journal*, January 25, 1833.

44. Mentor Graham to WHH, May 29, 1865, *Herndon's Informants*, 10. That Lincoln boarded with Graham is confirmed by Caleb Carman in a letter to WHH, November 30, 1866, *Herndon's Informants*, 429. For Herndon's wife as Mentor Graham's sister, see Kunigunde Duncan and D. F. Nickols, *Mentor Graham: The Man Who Taught Lincoln* (Chicago: University of Chicago Press, 1944), 138.

45. Thomas F. Schwartz has located a document in the Illinois State Historical Library showing that the firm of Lincoln and Berry purchased merchandise from Beardstown merchants Knapp and Pogue on May 14, 1833. Whether Lincoln was still active in the firm is not known, but he was apparently liable for payment. I am grateful to Mr. Schwartz for sharing this information.

46. Reep, *Lincoln at New Salem*, 61.

47. *Collected Works*, 4:65.

48. Mentor Graham to WHH, May 29, 1865, *Herndon's Informants*, 10.

49. William G. Greene to WHH, June 7, 1865, *Herndon's Informants*, 26.

50. William G. Greene (Howard interview), in Mearns, *The Lincoln Papers*, 1:153.

51. David C. Mearns, " 'The Great Invention of the World': Mr. Lincoln and the Books He Read," in *Three Presidents and Their Books* (Urbana: University of Illinois Press, 1955), 57. James Short claimed the Greenes had no books.

52. See a memorandum in WHH's hand in the Herndon-Weik Collection (HW3745), Library of Congress.

53. John Hill to Ida M. Tarbell, February 6, 1896, Tarbell Papers, Allegheny College Library.

54. Statement for WHH, January 26, 1866, *Herndon's Informants*, 170.

55. Robert Gibson, *The Theory and Practice of Surveying; Containing All the*

Instructions Requisite for the Skilful Practice of This Art (New York: Evert Duycinck, 1814). Isaac N. Arnold reported in his biography that he owned a copy of this edition with Lincoln's name and handwriting in several places. *The Life of Abraham Lincoln* (Chicago: A. C. McClurg, 1887), 26n.

56. Elizabeth Herndon Bell (WHH interview), [March 1887?], *Herndon's Informants*, 606.
57. *Collected Works*, 1:21.
58. For the pay scale, see Thomas, *Lincoln's New Salem*, 103.
59. Henry McHenry (WHH interview), October 1866, *Herndon's Informants*, 534.
60. Robert L. Wilson to WHH, February 10, 1866, *Herndon's Informants*, 201.
61. Elizabeth Abell to WHH, February 15, 1867, *Herndon's Informants*, 557.
62. Russell Godbey (WHH interview), [1865–66], *Herndon's Informants*, 450. Lincoln's survey for Godbey is dated January 14, 1834. *Collected Works*, 1:20.
63. John B. Weber to WHH, November 5, 1866, *Herndon's Informants*, 396.
64. Ibid., 396.
65. Thomas Ford, *A History of Illinois from Its Commencement as a State in 1818 to 1847*, ed. Rodney O. Davis (Urbana and Chicago: University of Illinois Press, 1995), 123.
66. For a reproduction of Lincoln's plat of Huron, see *Collected Works*, 1:ff. 48.
67. See Thomas, *Lincoln's New Salem*, 112n. Lincoln's entry was in the north half of the northwest quarter of Section 3, Township 19 North, Range 7 West.
68. Peter Van Bergen (Nicolay interview), July 7, 1875, in Burlingame, *An Oral History of Abraham Lincoln*, 33.
69. William G. Greene to WHH, May 30, 1865, *Herndon's Informants*, 20. For a colorful sketch of Watkins, see Reep, *Lincoln at New Salem*, 122–24.
70. Robert L. Wilson to WHH, February 10, 1866, *Herndon's Informants*, 201.
71. Henry McHenry to WHH, May 29, 1865, *Herndon's Informants*, 15.
72. *Collected Works*, 4:65.
73. A. H. Chapman (statement for WHH), September 8, 1865, *Herndon's Informants*, 102. Chapman was the husband of Dennis F. Hanks's daughter, Harriet, and presumably got his information from the Hanks family and Lincoln's stepmother, Sarah Bush Lincoln.
74. Hardin Bale to WHH, May 29, 1865, *Herndon's Informants*, 13.
75. A. Y. Ellis (statement for WHH), January 23, 1866, *Herndon's Informants*, 170.
76. William G. Greene to WHH, May 30, 1865, *Herndon's Informants*, 20. See also Mentor Graham to WHH, May 29, 1865, ibid., 10.
77. See Ralph Shearer Rowland and Star Wilson Rowland, *Clary Genealogy – Four Early American Lines and Related Families* (Sterling, Va.: Ralph and Star Rowland, 1980), #927.
78. A. Y. Ellis to WHH, December 6, 1866, *Herndon's Informants*, 501.
79. Jason Duncan to WHH, [1866–67], *Herndon's Informants*, 540.
80. Ibid.
81. J. Rowan Herndon to WHH, July 3, 1865, *Herndon's Informants*, 69.
82. Jason Duncan to WHH, [1866–67], *Herndon's Informants*, 541.
83. Fern Nance Pond, ed., "The Memoirs of James McGrady Rutledge 1814–1899," *Journal of the Illinois State Historical Society*, 29 (April–January 1937–38), 84–85.
84. Robert L. Wilson to WHH, February 10, 1866, *Herndon's Informants*, 207.

85. Walter B. Stevens, *A Reporter's Lincoln* (St. Louis: Missouri Historical Society, 1916), 10.

86. Stephen T. Logan (Nicolay interview), July 6, 1875, in Burlingame, *Oral History of Abraham Lincoln*, 35.

87. Dennis F. Hanks (WHH interview), June 13, 1865, *Herndon's Informants*, 42.

88. William G. Greene to WHH, May 29, 1865, *Herndon's Informants*, 12.

89. Isaac Cogdal (WHH interview), [1865–66], *Herndon's Informants*, 440.

90. J. Rowan Herndon to WHH, May 28, 1865; Jason Duncan to WHH, [1866–67], *Herndon's Informants*, 90, 540.

91. J. Rowan Herndon to WHH, August 16, 1865; Duncan to WHH [1866–67], *Herndon's Informants*, 90, 540. See also Mentor Graham to WHH, May 29, 1865; L. M. Greene to WHH, July 30, 1865; Isaac Cogdal (WHH interview), [1865–66], *Herndon's Informants*, 8, 81, 440.

92. *Collected Works*, 4:65.

93. Ibid.

94. Henry McHenry (WHH interview), [October 1866], *Herndon's Informants*, 534.

95. Russell Godbey (WHH interview), [1865–66], *Herndon's Informants*, 450.

96. H. E. Dummer (WHH interview), [1865–66], *Herndon's Informants*, 442. For Dummer's education, see Paul M. Angle and Robert P. Howard, *One Hundred Fifty Years of Law* (Springfield, Ill.: Brown, Hay and Stephens, 1978), 12–13.

97. Henry McHenry (WHH interview) [October 1866], *Herndon's Informants*, 534.

98. R. B. Rutledge to WHH, November 30, 1866, *Herndon's Informants*, 426.

99. AL to John M. Brockman, September 25, 1860, *Collected Works*, 4:121.

100. *Collected Works*, 4:65.

101. See *Lincoln Day by Day: A Chronology 1809–1865*, ed. Earl Schenck Miers, 3 vols. (Washington: Lincoln Sesquicentennial Commission, 1960), vol. 1, ed. William E. Baringer, 1:49.

102. Henry McHenry to WHH, May 29, 1865, *Herndon's Informants*, 14. For what McHenry said on this subject as regards Lincoln's behavior after the death of Ann Rutledge, see 119–20.

103. Mentor Graham to WHH, May 29, 1865, *Herndon's Informants*, 11.

104. Henry McHenry to WHH, January 8, 1866; Isaac Cogdal (WHH interview), [1865–66], *Herndon's Informants*, 156, 441.

105. See *Lincoln Day by Day*, 1:50–56.

106. Francis Fisher Browne, *The Every-Day Life of Abraham Lincoln*, ed. John Y. Simon (Lincoln: University of Nebraska Press, 1995 [1886]), 88.

Chapter 4

1. Sarah Bush Lincoln (WHH interview), September 8, 1865, Douglas L. Wilson and Rodney O. Davis, eds., *Herndon's Informants: Letters, Interviews, and Statements About Abraham Lincoln* (Urbana: University of Illinois Press, 1997), 108; hereafter cited as *Herndon's Informants*.

2. Joseph C. Richardson (WHH interview), [September 14, 1865?]; David Turnham (WHH interview), September 15, 1865, *Herndon's Informants*, 120, 122.

3. Anna Caroline Gentry (WHH interview), September 17, 1865, *Herndon's Informants*, 131.

4. N. W. Branson to WHH, August 3, 1865, *Herndon's Informants*, 91. For Short as a ladies' man, see AL's reference to Short's "woman affair," Roy P. Basler et al., eds., *The Collected Works of Abraham Lincoln*, 8 vols. (New Brunswick: Rutgers University Press, 1953), 1:321; hereafter cited as *Collected Works*.

5. A. Y. Ellis (statement for WHH), January 23, 1866, *Herndon's Informants*, 170.

6. Elizabeth Herndon Bell (WHH interview), [March 1887?], *Herndon's Informants*, 606.

7. John Q. Spears (WHH interview), undated, *Herndon's Informants*, 705.

8. Caleb Carman (WHH interview), October 12, 1866, *Herndon's Informants*, 375.

9. James Taylor (WHH interview), [1865–66], *Herndon's Informants*, 482.

10. Hannah Armstrong (WHH interview), [1865–66], *Herndon's Informants*, 527.

11. J. Rowan Herndon to WHH, July 3, 1865, *Herndon's Informants*, 69.

12. Ibid., 69–70.

13. William Butler (Nicolay interview), June 13, 1875, Michael Burlingame, ed., *An Oral History of Abraham Lincoln: John G. Nicolay's Interviews and Essays* (Carbondale and Edwardsville: Southern Illinois University Press, 1996), 19.

14. Ibid.

15. Elizabeth Abell to WHH, February 5, 1867, *Herndon's Informants*, 557.

16. Johnson Gaines Greene (WHH interview), October 5, 1866, *Herndon's Informants*, 365.

17. William G. Greene (WHH interview), October 9, 1866, *Herndon's Informants*, 367–68.

18. Johnson Gaines Green (WHH interview), October 10, 1866, *Herndon's Informants*, 370.

19. John McNamar to WHH, November 25, 1866, *Herndon's Informants*, 421.

20. Lincoln Scrapbook, Huntington Library, 151179 (vol. 3), 5.

21. Thomas P. Reep, *Lincoln at New Salem* (n.p.: Old Salem Lincoln League, 1927), 48.

22. John Y. Simon, "Abraham Lincoln and Ann Rutledge," *Journal of the Abraham Lincoln Association*, 11 (1990), 15.

23. See Paul M. Angle, "Lincoln's First Love?" *Lincoln Centennial Association Bulletin*, 9 (December 1, 1927), 1–8; and J. G. Randall, Appendix: "Sifting the Ann Rutledge Evidence," *Lincoln the President: Springfield to Gettysburg*, 2 vols. (New York: Dodd, Mead, 1945), 2:321–42.

24. In addition to Simon, see Douglas L. Wilson, "Abraham Lincoln, Ann Rutledge, and the Evidence of Herndon's Informants," *Lincoln Before Washington: New Perspectives on the Illinois Years* (Urbana: University of Illinois Press, 1997), 74–98. The most detailed treatment of the subject is John Evangelist Walsh, *The Shadows Rise: Abraham Lincoln and the Ann Rutledge Legend* (Urbana: University of Illinois Press, 1993).

25. William G. Greene to WHH, May 30, 1865, *Herndon's Informants*, 21.

26. James Short to WHH, July 7, 1865, *Herndon's Informants*, 73.

27. Jason Duncan to WHH, [1866–67], *Herndon's Informants*, 541.

28. Duncan gives the date of his leaving New Salem as 1834 in his letter to

Herndon, but he was writing newspaper articles from Macomb in the fall of 1833 and winter of 1834. See the handful of surviving issues of *Beardstown Chronicle and Illinois Military Bounty Land Advertiser*, edited by Francis Arenz, in the Illinois State Historical Library.

29. Robert B. Rutledge to WHH, November 18, 1866, *Herndon's Informants*, 383.
30. Reep, *Lincoln at New Salem*, 49.
31. For the Rutledge family's understanding of the reasons behind McNamar's concealed identity and details of his sojourn, see Robert B. Rutledge to WHH, [c. November 1, 1866], *Herndon's Informants*, 383.
32. McNamar told WHH that AL had not yet returned from the Black Hawk War when he left Illinois and that on his way East he met soldiers on their way to the war. John McNamar to WHH, June 4, 1866, *Herndon's Informants*, 259.
33. Robert B. Rutledge to WHH, [c. November 1, 1866], *Herndon's Informants*, 383.
34. James Short to WHH, July 7, 1865, *Herndon's Informants*, 73.
35. Robert B. Rutledge to WHH, November 18, 1866, *Herndon's Informants*, 403.
36. Robert B. Rutledge to WHH, November 21, 1866, *Herndon's Informants*, 409.
37. See the postscript of David H. Rutledge's letter, dated July 27, 1835, reprinted in Walsh, *The Shadows Rise*, 47.
38. Quoted from the doctoral dissertation of Lorenzo D. Matheny (1836) in Milton H. Shutes, *Lincoln's Emotional Life* (Philadelphia: Dorrance, 1957), 45.
39. William H. Herndon and Jesse W. Weik, *Herndon's Life of Lincoln*, ed. Paul M. Angle (Cleveland: World Publishing, 1949 [1930]), 112. This was mild compared with the accent given the idea in WHH's 1866 lecture: "In her conflicts of honor, duty, love, promises, and womanly engagements – she was taken sick. She struggled, regretted, grieved, became nervous. She ate not, slept not, was taken sick of brain fever, became emaciated, and was fast sinking in the grave." From a reprinting of Herndon's lecture in *Lincoln and Ann Rutledge and the Pioneers of New Salem* (Herrin, Ill.: Trovillion Private Press, 1945), 40.
40. Esther Summers Bale (WHH interview), [October 1866], *Herndon's Informants*, 527.
41. Parthena Hill (WHH interview), [1865–66], *Herndon's Informants*, 604.
42. John Hill to Ida M. Tarbell, February 6, 1896, Tarbell Papers, Allegheny College Library.
43. Robert B. Rutledge to WHH, [c. November 1, 1866], *Herndon's Informants*, 383.
44. See Thompson Ware McNeely to WHH, November 12, 1866, *Herndon's Informants*, 397, for a generalized statement of what he heard older residents say about Lincoln's condition.
45. Angle, "Lincoln's First Love?" 7.
46. John Jones to Robert B. Rutledge, October 22, 1866, *Herndon's Informants*, 387.
47. Henry McHenry to WHH, January 8, 1866, *Herndon's Informants*, 156.
48. William G. Greene to WHH, May 30, 1865, *Herndon's Informants*, 21.
49. Elizabeth Abell to WHH, February 15, 1867, *Herndon's Informants*, 557.

50. Mentor Graham (WHH interview), April 2, 1866, *Herndon's Informants*, 243.

51. John Hill to Ida M. Tarbell, February 17, 1896, Tarbell Papers, Allegheny College Library. For confirmation of Samuel Hill's involvement, see Hardin Bale to WHH, May 29, 1865, *Herndon's Informants*, 13.

52. G. U. Miles to WHH, March 23, 1866, *Herndon's Informants*, 236. Note that two other witnesses, Mrs. William Rutledge and Parthena Hill, confirm Mrs. Green's testimony.

53. See WHH's parenthetical note in their second undated interview, *Herndon's Informants*, 441.

54. [R. D. Miller], *History of Mason and Menard Counties* (Chicago: O. L. Baskin, 1879), 749.

55. Isaac Cogdal (WHH interview), [1865–66], *Herndon's Informants*, 440.

56. Randall, "Sifting the Ann Rutledge Evidence," 335.

57. Isaac Cogdal (WHH interview), [1865–66], *Herndon's Informants*, 440.

58. Joshua F. Speed to WHH, November 30, 1866, *Herndon's Informants*, 431.

59. See Douglas L. Wilson, "Abraham Lincoln and the 'Spirit of Mortal,'" *Lincoln Before Washington: New Perspectives on the Illinois Years*, 133–48.

60. Joshua F. Speed wrote that Lincoln always referred this way to his mother. See *Reminiscences of Abraham Lincoln and Notes of a Visit to California: Two Lectures* (Louisville: John P. Morton, 1884), 19.

61. For a summary of evidence on these points, see William H. Townsend, *Lincoln and Liquor* (New York: Press of the Pioneers, 1934), 16, 26–27.

62. Green Taylor (WHH interview), September 16, 1865, *Herndon's Informants*, 130; the detail about the whiskey bottle comes from John Oskins.

63. Robert L. Wilson to WHH, February 10, 1866, *Herndon's Informants*, 205.

64. See, for example, the testimony of David Davis in *Herndon's Informants*, 348.

65. N. W. Branson to WHH, August 3, 1865, *Herndon's Informants*, 90.

66. See, for example, the testimony in *Herndon's Informants* of A. Y. Ellis (171), William G. Greene (142).

67. WHH to Jesse W. Weik, January 1891, Herndon-Weik Collection, Library of Congress; printed in Emanuel Hertz, ed., *The Hidden Lincoln: From the Letters and Papers of William H. Herndon* (New York: Viking Press, 1938), 259.

68. See Chapter 10, p. 300.

69. See WHH to Ward Hill Lamon, December 18, 1869, Huntington Library.

70. WHH to Jesse W. Weik, January 1891, Herndon-Weik Collection, Library of Congress; printed in Hertz, *The Hidden Lincoln*, 260.

71. See Jean H. Baker, *Mary Todd Lincoln* (New York: W. W. Norton, 1987), 88. Dr. Milton H. Shutes was convinced that syphiliophobia was "the probable cause of Lincoln's hypochondriasis." *Lincoln's Emotional Life*, 71.

72. L. M. Greene to WHH, May 3, 1866, *Herndon's Informants*, 250.

73. Johnson Gaines Greene (WHH interview), [1866], *Herndon's Informants*, 530.

74. B. R. Vineyard to Jesse W. Weik, March 14, 1887, *Herndon's Informants*, 608.

75. Esther Summers Bale (WHH interview), [1866], *Herndon's Informants*, 527. A fragmentary note to WHH, apparently from Mary Owens Vineyard and dated August 6, 1866, gives her height as five feet five inches and her weight as 150 pounds. See *Herndon's Informants*, 265.

76. Mentor Graham (WHH interview), April 2, 1866, *Herndon's Informants*, 243.

77. Johnson Gaines Greene (WHH interview), October 5, 1866; see also William G. Greene to WHH, January 23, 1866, *Herndon's Informants*, 364–65, 175.

78. Caleb Carman (WHH interview), October 12, 1866, *Herndon's Informants*, 374.

79. Ibid.

80. Walter B. Stevens, *A Reporter's Lincoln* (St. Louis: Missouri Historical Society, 1916), 10.

81. Fern Nance Pond, *Intellectual New Salem in Lincoln's Day: An Address Delivered at Lincoln Memorial University Harrogate, Tennessee, February 12, 1938* (Petersburg, Ill.: n. p., 1938), 12.

82. B. R. Vineyard to Jesse W. Weik, March 14, 1887, *Herndon's Informants*, 610.

83. O. H. Browning (Nicolay interview), June 17, 1875, Burlingame, *Oral History*, 3–4.

84. AL to Mrs. Orville H. Browning, April 1, 1838, *Collected Works*, 1:117.

85. Ibid., 1:118.

86. Ibid.

87. William G. Greene to WHH, January 23, 1866, *Herndon's Informants*, 175.

88. Mary Owens Vineyard to WHH, July 22, 1866, *Herndon's Informants*, 262.

89. See G. U. Miles to WHH, March 23, 1866, *Herndon's Informants*, 237.

90. Johnson Gaines Greene (WHH interview), [1866], *Herndon's Informants*, 530.

91. Ibid., 530–31.

92. Ibid., 531.

93. AL to Mary S. Owens, December 13, 1836, *Collected Works*, 1:54.

94. AL to Mary S. Owens, May 7, 1837, *Collected Works*, 1:78.

95. Ibid., 1:78.

96. Elizabeth Abell to WHH, January 13, 1867, *Herndon's Informants*, 544.

97. AL to Mrs. Orville H. Browning, April 1, 1838, *Collected Works*, 1:119.

98. AL to Mary S. Owens, August 16, 1837, *Collected Works*, 1:94.

99. AL to Mrs. Orville H. Browning, April 1, 1838, *Collected Works*, 1:119.

100. Orville H. Browning (Nicolay interview), June 17, 1875, Burlingame, *Oral History*, 4.

101. AL to Mrs. Orville H. Browning, April 1, 1838, *Collected Works*, 1:119.

102. Mary Owens Vineyard to WHH, July 22, 1866, *Herndon's Informants*, 262.

103. Ibid., May 23, 1866, 256.

104. Ibid., July 22, 1866, 263.

105. Lincoln refers to her as such in his letter to Mrs. Browning. See *Collected Works*, 1:118.

106. Mary Owens Vineyard to WHH, July 22, 1866, *Herndon's Informants*, 263.

107. L. M. Greene to WHH, July 30, 1865, *Herndon's Informants*, 81.

Chapter 5

1. WHH got this speech from his cousin James A. Herndon even before he began collecting materials for his biography and had it printed in the Springfield paper. See Douglas L. Wilson and Rodney O. Davis, eds., *Herndon's Informants: Letters, Interviews, and Statements About Abraham Lincoln* (Urbana: University of Illinois Press, 1997), 16–17; hereafter cited as *Herndon's Informants*.

2. J. Rowan Herndon to WHH, June 21, 1865, *Herndon's Informants*, 51.

3. James A. Herndon (WHH interview), [1865–66], *Herndon's Informants*, 460.

4. J. Rowan Herndon to WHH, June 21, 1865, *Herndon's Informants*, 51.

5. Stephen T. Logan (Nicolay interview), July 6, 1875, in Michael Burlingame, ed., *An Oral History of Abraham Lincoln: John G. Nicolay's Interviews and Essays* (Carbondale and Edwardsville: Southern Illinois University Press, 1996), 35.

6. Thomas Ford, *A History of Illinois from Its Commencement as a State in 1818 to 1847*, ed. Rodney O. Davis (Urbana: University of Illinois Press, 1995), 68.

7. Stephen T. Logan (Nicolay interview), July 6, 1875, Burlingame, *Oral History of Abraham Lincoln*, 35.

8. J. Rowan Herndon to WHH, May 28, 1865, *Herndon's Informants*, 7.

9. Henry McHenry (WHH interview), May 29, 1865, *Herndon's Informants*, 15.

10. Stephen T. Logan (Nicolay interview), July 6, 1875, Burlingame, *Oral History of Abraham Lincoln*, 35.

11. Jason Duncan to WHH, [1866–67], *Herndon's Informants*, 541.

12. John T. Stuart (Nicolay interview), June 23, 1875, Burlingame, *Oral History of Abraham Lincoln*, 10.

13. See the discussion in Chapter 10, p. 296–97.

14. William Butler (Nicolay interview), June 13, 1875, Burlingame, *Oral History of Abraham Lincoln*, 20.

15. John Hanks (WHH interview), [1865–66], *Herndon's Informants*, 456.

16. George Close (Howard interview), [May 1860], in David C. Mearns, ed., *The Lincoln Papers*, 2 vols. (Garden City, N.Y.: Doubleday, 1948), 1:150. The two candidates were John F. Posey and William L. D. Ewing, who were campaigning for the Illinois House of Representatives. See Edwin Davis, "Lincoln and Macon County, Illinois, 1830–1831," *Journal of the Illinois State Historical Society*, 25 (1932–33), 63–107.

17. William G. Greene to WHH, May 29, 1865, *Herndon's Informants*, 11.

18. "Communication to the People of Sangamo County," *Sangamo Journal*, March 15, 1832, in Roy P. Basler et al., eds., *The Collected Works of Abraham Lincoln*, 8 vols. (New Brunswick: Rutgers University Press, 1953), 1:6; hereafter cited as *Collected Works*.

19. John McNamar to WHH, June 4, 1866, *Herndon's Informants*, 259.

20. John T. Stuart (Nicolay interview), June 23, 1875, Burlingame, *Oral History of Abraham Lincoln*, 10–11.

21. William Butler (Nicolay interview), June 13, 1875, Burlingame, *Oral History of Abraham Lincoln*, 20.

22. Russell Godbey (WHH interview), [1865–66], *Herndon's Informants*, 450.

23. James H. Matheny (WHH interview), November 1866, *Herndon's Informants*, 432.

24. *Collected Works*, 4:65.

25. John Moore Fisk (WHH interview), February 18, 1887, *Herndon's Informants*, 715.

26. *Collected Works*, 4:65.

27. John T. Stuart (WHH interview), [1865–66], *Herndon's Informants*, 480.

28. Stephen T. Logan (Nicolay interview), July 6, 1875, Burlingame, *Oral History of Abraham Lincoln*, 36.

29. John T. Stuart (Nicolay interview), June 23, 1875, Burlingame, *Oral History of Abraham Lincoln*, 11–12.

30. Walter B. Stevens, *A Reporter's Lincoln* (St. Louis: Missouri Historical Society, 1916), 8.

31. John Hill to Ida M. Tarbell, February 6, 1896, Tarbell Papers, Allegheny College Library.

32. WHH to Ward Hill Lamon, February 25, 1870, Lamon Papers, Huntington Library, printed in Emanuel Hertz, ed., *The Hidden Lincoln: From the Letters and Papers of William H. Herndon* (New York: Viking Press, 1938), 64.

33. Thomas P. Reep, *Lincoln at New Salem* (n.p.: Old Salem Lincoln League, 1927), 29.

34. Robert L. Wilson to WHH, February 10, 1866, *Herndon's Informants*, 201–2.

35. J. Rowan Herndon to WHH, May 28, 1865, *Herndon's Informants*, 8. In sending this story to Francis F. Browne, WHH identified it as relating to the 1834 campaign. See Francis Fisher Browne, *The Every-Day Life of Abraham Lincoln: A Narrative and Descriptive Biography with Pen-Pictures and Personal Recollections by Those Who Knew Him* (Chicago: Browne & Howell, 1913), 48.

36. Coleman Smoot to WHH, May 7, 1866, *Herndon's Informants*, 254.

37. Joshua F. Speed, *Reminiscences of Abraham Lincoln and Notes of a Visit to California: Two Lectures* (Louisville: John P. Morton, 1884), 15.

38. Ibid., 15–16.

39. John T. Stuart (Nicolay interview), June 24, 1875, Burlingame, *Oral History of Abraham Lincoln*, 13.

40. Jesse K. Dubois (Nicolay interview), July 4, 1874, Burlingame, *Oral History of Abraham Lincoln*, 30.

41. *Collected Works*, 4:65.

42. John T. Stuart (WHH interview), [1865–66], *Herndon's Informants*, 481.

43. Willard L. King, *Lincoln's Manager: David Davis* (Cambridge, Mass.: Harvard University Press, 1960), 35. John J. Hardin in a letter to the Jacksonville *Patriot* as quoted in the *Illinois State Register*, Dec. 29, 1836, cited in Albert J. Beveridge, *Abraham Lincoln 1809–1858*, 2 vols. (Boston and New York: Houghton Mifflin Company, 1928), 1:198.

44. John T. Stuart (Nicolay interview), June 24, 1875, Burlingame, *Oral History of Abraham Lincoln*, 12–13.

45. *House Journal,* cited in William E. Baringer, *Lincoln's Vandalia: A Pioneer Portrait* (New Brunswick: Rutgers University Press, 1949), 57.

46. Paul Simon, *Lincoln's Preparation for Greatness: The Illinois Legislative Years* (Urbana: University of Illinois Press, 1971 [1965]), 35.

47. *Collected Works*, 1:48.

48. Ibid., 1:5.

49. Robert L. Wilson to WHH, February 10, 1866, *Herndon's Informants*, 202.

50. Ibid., 202–3.

51. James Gourley (WHH interview), [1865–66], *Herndon's Informants*, 451.

52. Ibid.

53. Robert L. Wilson to WHH, February 10, 1866, *Herndon's Informants*, 203.

54. Ibid., 203.

55. Reep, *Lincoln at New Salem*, 91.

56. Joshua F. Speed (statement for WHH), [1865–66], *Herndon's Informants*, 477–78.
57. Jesse K. Dubois (Nicolay interview), July 4, 1875, Burlingame, *Oral History of Abraham Lincoln*, 30.
58. Ford, *A History of Illinois*, 127.
59. Stephen T. Logan (Nicolay interview), July 6, 1875, Burlingame, *Oral History of Abraham Lincoln*, 36–37. Because this interview was for many years mistakenly believed to have been taken by William H. Herndon, Paul Simon, in his valuable study of Lincoln as a legislator, argued that its reliability was suspect. See Simon, *Lincoln's Preparation for Greatness*, 80. Michael Burlingame has shown conclusively that this interview was taken by John G. Nicolay.
60. Ford, *A History of Illinois*, 124. For a discussion of the internal improvements fever, see Simon, *Lincoln's Preparation for Greatness*, 48–54.
61. Usher F. Linder, *Reminiscences of the Early Bench and Bar of Illinois* (Chicago: Chicago Legal News Co., 1879), 61.
62. Stephen T. Logan (Nicolay interview), July 6, 1875, Burlingame, *Oral History of Abraham Lincoln*, 37.
63. Joshua F. Speed (WHH interview), [1865–66], *Herndon's Informants*, 476.
64. Ibid.
65. Peter Van Bergen (Nicolay interview), July 7, 1875, Burlingame, *Oral History of Abraham Lincoln*, 34.
66. William Butler (Nicolay interview), June 13, 1875, Burlingame, *Oral History of Abraham Lincoln*, 21.
67. For reasons to be skeptical about Linder's role, I am indebted to Rodney O. Davis.
68. Linder, *Reminiscences*, 58.
69. *Collected Works*, 1:61–69.
70. Jesse K. Dubois (Nicolay interview), July 4, 1875, Burlingame, *Oral History of Abraham Lincoln*, 30.
71. Ibid., 31.
72. For the identification of William Wilson, I am grateful to Rodney O. Davis.
73. Robert L. Wilson to WHH, February 10, 1866, *Herndon's Informants*, 204.
74. Ford, *A History of Illinois*, 57–58.
75. *Collected Works*, 1:75n. For an account of this issue, see Beveridge, *Abraham Lincoln 1809–1858*, 1:192–95; and Simon, *Lincoln's Preparation for Greatness*, 131–34.
76. *Collected Works*, 1:75.
77. Ibid., 1:74–75.
78. Linder, *Reminiscences*, 62.
79. Ibid.
80. Ibid.
81. Ibid., 63.
82. Ibid., 62–63.

Chapter 6

1. William Butler (Nicolay interview), 1875, in Michael Burlingame, ed., *An Oral History of Abraham Lincoln: John G. Nicolay's Interviews and Essays* (Car-

bondale and Edwardsville: Southern Illinois University Press, 1996), 22. It is possible that Butler's recollection does not relate to "the last winter" AL spent in Vandalia, for he goes on to say that AL had not yet finished his law studies and didn't have any prospects. Butler must be wrong in one of these details, and the account as given suggests that it more likely relates to 1837.

2. Joshua F. Speed, *Reminiscences of Abraham Lincoln and Notes of a Visit to California: Two Lectures* (Louisville: John P. Morton, 1884), 22.

3. Joshua F. Speed (statement for WHH), [1865–66], in Douglas L. Wilson and Rodney O. Davis, eds., *Herndon's Informants: Letters, Interviews, and Statements About Abraham Lincoln* (Urbana: University of Illinois Press, 1997), 590; hereafter cited as *Herndon's Informants*.

4. William Butler (Nicolay interview), 1875, Burlingame, *Oral History of Abraham Lincoln*, 23.

5. Speed, *Reminiscences*, 20–21.

6. For a detailed account of the James Adams affair, see Albert J. Beveridge, *Abraham Lincoln 1809–1858*, 2 vols. (Boston: Houghton Mifflin, 1928), 1:212–18.

7. "Second Reply to James Adams," *Sangamo Journal*, October 28, 1837, in Roy P. Basler et al., eds., *The Collected Works of Abraham Lincoln*, 8 vols. (New Brunswick: Rutgers University Press, 1953), 1:102; hereafter cited as *Collected Works*.

8. Lincoln's authorship of the Sampson's Ghost letters cannot be proved, and there is room for suspicion that Stuart or some other interested party may have had a hand in them. But the letters strongly appear to be a seamless part of the combative harassment of Adams that includes Lincoln's acknowledged handbill and signed public letters.

9. Rufus Rockwell Wilson, ed., *The Uncollected Works of Abraham Lincoln*, 2 vols. (Elmira, N.Y.: Primavera Press, 1947–48), 1:155. Because the Sampson's Ghost letters cannot be definitely confirmed as Lincoln's writing, they are not included in the *Collected Works* but may be consulted in Wilson.

10. Ibid., 1:157.

11. Ibid., 1:160.

12. "Reply to James Adams," *Sangamo Journal*, September 6, 1837, *Collected Works*, 1:96.

13. Wilson, *Uncollected Works*, 1:156.

14. Ibid., 1:158–59.

15. Ibid., 1:160.

16. "Handbill: The Case of the Heirs of Joseph Anderson vs James Adams," August 5, 1837, *Collected Works*, 1:89–93.

17. John T. Stuart (Nicolay interview), June 23, 1875, Burlingame, *Oral History of Abraham Lincoln*, 10.

18. "To the People of Sangamon County," *Collected Works*, 8:429. This incident seems to belong to the congressional election of 1836.

19. See Beveridge, *Abraham Lincoln*, 1:216.

20. Thomas F. Schwartz, "The Lincoln Handbill of 1837: A Rare Document's History," *Illinois Historical Journal*, 79 (Winter 1986), 274.

21. For signed letters, see "First Reply to James Adams," September 6, 1837, and "Second Reply to James Adams," October 18, 1837, *Collected Works*, 1:95–100,

101–6; for likely pseudonymous attacks by AL, see letters from "An Old Settler" in *Sangamo Journal*, September 30, October 7, and October 14, 1837.

22. AL to Mary S. Owens, May 7, 1837, *Collected Works*, 1:78.

23. P. K. McMinn, "Lincoln as Known to His Neighbors," *Saturday Evening
Post* (February 13, 1904). Clipping in Scrapbook 15, p. 61, Huntington Library.

24. AL to Mary S. Owens, May 7, 1837, *Collected Works*, 1:78.

25. Orville H. Browning (Nicolay interview), June 17, 1875, Burlingame, *Oral History of Abraham Lincoln*, 3–4. Browning was speaking of the time of their first
acquaintance in December 1836.

26. Frances Todd Wallace, quoted in a clipping from the *Chicago Times-Herald*,
August 25, 1895, 25; Tarbell Papers, Allegheny College Library.

27. Marietta Holdstock Brown, "A Romance of Lincoln," a newspaper clipping
is reprinted in "Martinette Hardin McKee Recalls Lincoln and Mary Todd,"
ed. Michael Burlingame, *Lincoln Herald*, 97:2 (Summer 1995), 72. Burlingame
reports the clipping has been attributed to "Indianapolis, Jan. 1896" by the
Lincoln Museum, Fort Wayne, Indiana.

28. Elizabeth Todd Edwards (WHH interview), [1865–66], *Herndon's Informants*, 443.

29. Walter B. Stevens, *A Reporter's Lincoln* (St. Louis: Missouri Historical Society, 1916), 8.

30. Quoted in Ruth P. Randall, *The Courtship of Mr. Lincoln* (Boston: Little,
Brown, 1957), 23.

31. Speed, *Reminiscences*, 34.

32. WHH to James H. Wilson, September 23, 1889, Herndon-Weik Collection,
Library of Congress.

33. James H. Matheny (WHH interview), [1865–66], *Herndon's Informants*, 470.

34. WHH to Jesse W. Weik, December 10, 1885, Emanuel Hertz, ed., *The
Hidden Lincoln: From the Letters and Papers of William H. Herndon* (New
York: Viking Press, 1938), 112.

35. WHH to Jesse W. Weik, January 5, 1889, *Herndon's Informants*, 719.

36. Charles B. Strozier calls this "a preposterous story" and suggests that it was "a
Lincoln joke that got lost in the translation." *Lincoln's Quest for Union: Public
and Private Meanings* (New York: Basic Books, 1982), 48. Neither this story
nor the one about the woman in Beardstown, both of which Herndon offered
seriously as authentic, is allowed by Strozier as evidence in opposition to his
theory that Lincoln was a virgin. Strozier argues that Lincoln and Speed both
suffered from a fear of intimacy, which is defined as "the capacity to commit
[oneself] to concrete affiliations and partnerships and to develop the ethical
strength to abide by such commitments." This seems to me a cogent argument and a valuable insight, but visiting prostitutes would seem not only
consistent with such a fear but possibly further evidence of it.

37. WHH to Jesse W. Weik, January 5, 1889, *Herndon's Informants*, 719.

38. John T. Stuart (WHH interview), [1865–66], *Herndon's Informants*, 481.

39. Ida M. Tarbell gives her informant as "Mrs. B. S. Edwards . . . the daughter-
in-law of Ninian Edwards," but that Mrs. Edwards, who *did* send letters
about her recollections of Lincoln to Tarbell, did *not* grow up in Springfield
and only arrived in 1839 as a married woman. Though Tarbell must have
mixed up her informants, there is no reason to doubt that the story is based
on real events. Tarbell Papers, Allegheny College Library.

40. James Gourley (WHH interview), [1865–66], *Herndon's Informants*, 451.

41. Milton Hay (Nicolay interview), July 4, 1875, Burlingame, *Oral History of Abraham Lincoln*, 27.

42. James H. Matheny (WHH interview), November 1866, *Herndon's Informants*, 432.

43. Ibid., [by March 2, 1870], 576.

44. Ibid., [1865–66], 472.

45. Ibid., [by March 2, 1870], 576.

46. John T. Stuart (WHH interview), [by March 2, 1870], *Herndon's Informants*, 576.

47. "Second reply to James Adams," October 18, 1837, *Collected Works*, 1:106.

48. James H. Matheny (WHH interview), November 1866, *Herndon's Informants*, 432.

49. Ibid., [by March 2, 1870], 576.

50. Jesse W. Weik, *The Real Lincoln* (Boston: Houghton Mifflin, 1922), 112.

51. William H. Herndon and Jesse W. Weik, *Herndon's Life of Lincoln*, ed. Paul M. Angle (Cleveland: World Publishing, 1949 [1930]), 473.

52. For a remarkably detailed chronological tracking of references to Lincoln's melancholy, see the chapter "Lincoln's Depressions" in Michael Burlingame, *The Inner World of Abraham Lincoln* (Urbana: University of Illinois Press, 1994), 92–122.

53. Robert L. Wilson to WHH, February 10, 1866, *Herndon's Informants*, 205.

54. James H. Matheny (WHH interview), November 1866, *Herndon's Informants*, 432.

55. Ibid., May 3, 1866, 251.

56. Speed, *Reminiscences*, 34.

57. John T. Stuart (WHH interview), [late June 1865], *Herndon's Informants*, 63.

58. *Herndon's Life of Lincoln*, 473.

59. WHH lecture, quoted in Weik, *The Real Lincoln*, 113.

60. WHH to Lamon, February 25, 1870, Lamon Papers, Huntington Library; printed in Hertz, *The Hidden Lincoln*, 68.

61. WHH to the editor of the *Religio-Philosophical Journal* (December 4, 1885), in Hertz, *The Hidden Lincoln*, 110.

62. Stevens, *A Reporter's Lincoln*, 11–12.

63. Joshua F. Speed to WHH, January 12, 1866, *Herndon's Informants*, 156. One of his New Salem friends, William G. Greene, thought Byron was one of AL's favorites. See William G. Greene to WHH, May 30 and November 27, 1865, *Herndon's Informants*, 21, 141.

64. *The Poetical Works of Lord Byron*, ed. Ernest Hartley Coleridge (New York: Scribner's, 1905), 146.

65. James H. Matheny (WHH interview), [1865–66], *Herndon's Informants*, 470.

66. *Poetical Works of Lord Byron*, 389.

67. Ibid., 387.

68. Ward Hill Lamon, *Recollections of Abraham Lincoln 1847–1865*, ed. Dorothy Lamon Teillard (Washington, D.C.: published by the Editor, 1911), 122.

69. *Poetical Works of Lord Byron*, 385.

70. WHH to Weik, February 21, 1891, Hertz, *The Hidden Lincoln*, 263. I have here retained WHH's observation but deleted his speculative psychological explanation.

Chapter 7

1. For basic information about the lyceum movement in Springfield, the Young Men's Lyceum, and the occasion of Lincoln's speech, see Thomas F. Schwartz, "The Springfield Lyceums and Lincoln's 1838 Speech," *Illinois Historical Journal*, 83 (Spring 1990), 45–49.
2. Ibid., 49. For a list of the principal psychobiographers who have magnified the significance of the Lyceum speech, see Schwartz's note at p. 45.
3. Ibid., 49.
4. Roy P. Basler et al., eds., *The Collected Works of Abraham Lincoln*, 8 vols. (New Brunswick: Rutgers University Press, 1953), 1:115; hereafter cited as *Collected Works*.
5. Ibid., 1:109.
6. Ibid., 1:111–12.
7. Ibid., 1:114.
8. James Hurt, "All the Living and the Dead: Lincoln's Imagery," *American Literature*, 52:3 (November 1980), 367.
9. Henry Clay Whitney, *Life on the Circuit with Lincoln*, ed., Paul M. Angle (Caldwell, Ida.: Caxton Printers, 1940), 148–49.
10. *Childe Harold's Pilgrimage*, canto 3:32, *The Poetical Works of Lord Byron*, ed. Ernest Hartley Coleridge (New York: Scribner's, 1905), 190.
11. See Douglas L. Wilson, "Abraham Lincoln and the 'Spirit of Mortal,'" *Lincoln Before Washington: New Perspectives on the Illinois Years* (Urbana: University of Illinois Press, 1997), 133–48.
12. *Childe Harold's Pilgrimage*, canto 3:36.1–7, 190.
13. Ibid., canto 3:45, 191. In addition to the account in *Life on the Circuit with Lincoln* (see above), Whitney reported this incident in 1866 and again in 1887. See H. C. Whitney to WHH, November 20, 1866, and August 23, 1887, in Douglas L. Wilson and Rodney O. Davis, eds., *Herndon's Informants: Letters, Interviews, and Statements About Abraham Lincoln* (Urbana: University of Illinois Press, 1997), 404, 632; hereafter cited as *Herndon's Informants*. In each of these three reports he gave a different stanza as Lincoln's beginning (34, 21, 32), but these are simply different points of departure for the same long passage.
14. See p. 182.
15. William H. Herndon and Jesse W. Weik, *Herndon's Life of Lincoln*, ed. Paul M. Angle (Cleveland: World Publishing, 1949 [1930]), 151.
16. Ibid., 150.
17. Ibid., 153–54.
18. *Illinois State Register*, November 23, 1839.
19. Ibid.
20. John W. Weber (WHH interview), [c. November 1, 1866], *Herndon's Informants*, 389.
21. Herndon and Weik, *Herndon's Life of Lincoln*, 158.
22. Joseph Gillespie to WHH, January 31, 1866, *Herndon's Informants*, 181. Gillespie remembers this as a speech in 1840, but the circumstances he describes point rather to the "tournament" of November and December 1839, which led up to the 1840 campaign.
23. *Collected Works*, 1:178–79.

24. *Encyclopedia of American History*, ed. Richard B. Morris (New York: Harper & Brothers, 1953), 183.

25. Ibid.

26. Albert J. Beveridge, *Abraham Lincoln 1809–1858*, 2 vols. (Boston: Houghton Mifflin, 1928), 1:271.

27. Paul M. Angle, *"Here I Have Lived": A History of Lincoln's Springfield 1821–1865* (New Brunswick: Rutgers University Press, 1950 [1935]), 110.

28. See "Lincoln's Plan of Campaign in 1840" in *Collected Works*, 1:180–81; "Campaign Circular from Whig Committee," *Collected Works*, 1:201–3; and "Communication to the Readers of *The Old Soldier*," *Collected Works*, 1:203–6.

29. AL to John T. Stuart, January 20, 1840, *Collected Works*, 1:184.

30. Quoted in Angle, *"Here I Have Lived*," 111n. The full extent of Conkling's description, with its details about "embezzlement and defalcation," suggests that he probably had Lincoln's sub-treasury speech specifically in mind.

31. From a review of Ward Hill Lamon's biography of AL in *The Southern Review* (1873), reprinted in Rufus Rockwell Wilson, ed., *Lincoln Among His Friends* (Caldwell, Ida.: Caxton Printers, 1942), 490.

32. A. S. Kirk (WHH interview), March 7, 1887, *Herndon's Informants*, 602–3.

33. James H. Matheny (WHH interview), [1865–66], *Herndon's Informants*, 471, referring to William M. Holland, *The Life and Political Opinions of Martin Van Buren, Vice President of the United States* (Hartford: Belknap & Hamersley, 1835).

34. Gibson William Harris, "My Recollections of Abraham Lincoln," *The Farm and Fireside* (December 1, 1904), 23. Harris has here patched together two passages from the opening of *Lara*, lines 3–6 and 43–46.

35. Herndon and Weik, *Herndon's Life of Lincoln*, 157.

36. James H. Matheny (WHH interview), [1865–66], *Herndon's Informants*, 471. This may have happened earlier, as Matheny dates it in 1836 or 1838, but he also represents this as Taylor's last attempt to stamp the Whigs as aristocrats. Ninian W. Edwards dates his story giving Lincoln's answer to the aristocracy argument in the campaign of 1840.

37. Ninian W. Edwards (WHH interview), [1865–66], *Herndon's Informants*, 447.

38. See [J. F. Snyder], "Jesse Burgess Thomas, Jr.," *Transactions of the Illinois State Historical Society for the Year 1904* (Springfield, 1904), 523–24.

39. For an account of this episode and the likelihood of Lincoln's actually having written the letters in question, see "Lincoln – Author of the Letters by 'A Conservative,' " *Bulletin of the Abraham Lincoln Association*, 50 (December 1937), 8–9; and Glenn H. Seymour, " 'Conservative' – Another Lincoln Pseudonym?" *Journal of the Illinois State Historical Society*, 29:2 (July 1936), 135–50.

40. Herndon and Weik, *Herndon's Life of Lincoln*, 159.

41. Herndon and Bledsoe report Thomas's tears; Bledsoe is the source for his flight from the platform.

42. David Davis (WHH interview), September 20, 1866, *Herndon's Informants*, 350.

43. Samuel C. Parks to WHH, March 25, 1866, *Herndon's Informants*, 239.

44. Bledsoe, *Lincoln Among His Friends*, 467–68.

45. Harry E. Pratt, "Albert Taylor Bledsoe: Critic of Lincoln," Illinois State Historical Society, *Transactions for the Year 1934* (n.p., n.d.), 159n.

46. Quoted in "Lincoln – Author of the Letters by 'A Conservative,' " 9.

47. Herndon and Weik, *Herndon's Life of Lincoln*, 159–60.

48. David Davis (WHH interview), September 20, 1866, *Herndon's Informants*, 350.

49. Stephen T. Logan (Nicolay interview), July 6, 1875, Michael Burlingame, ed., *An Oral History of Abraham Lincoln: John G. Nicolay's Interviews and Essays* (Carbondale and Edwardsville: Southern Illinois University Press, 1996), 36.

50. AL to John T. Stuart, March 1, 1840, *Collected Works*, 1:206.

51. Francis Fisher Browne, *The Every-Day Life of Abraham Lincoln*, ed. John Y. Simon (Lincoln: University of Nebraska Press, 1995 [1886]), 177.

52. Joshua F. Speed (WHH interview), [1865–66], *Herndon's Informants*, 475. Speed remembers this occurring in 1840, though his tying the event to the progress of the Northern Cross railroad may suggest an inconsistency.

53. WHH to Ward Hill Lamon, February 25, 1870, Lamon Papers, Huntington Library; printed in Emanuel Hertz, ed., *The Hidden Lincoln: From the Letters and Papers of William H. Herndon* (New York: Viking Press, 1938), 68.

54. Milton Hay (Nicolay interview), July 4, 1875, in Burlingame, *Oral History of Abraham Lincoln*, 28.

55. AL to John T. Stuart, March 26, 1840, *Collected Works*, 1:208. For his doubts about his own renomination, see AL to Stuart, March 1, 1840, *Collected Works*, 1:206.

56. *Collected Works*, 1:209–10.

57. Quoted in *Lincoln Day by Day: A Chronology 1809–1865*, ed. Earl Schenck Miers, 3 vols. (Washington: Lincoln Sesquicentennial Commission, 1960), vol. 1, ed. William E. Baringer, 144, from the *Illinois State Register*, October 16, 1840.

58. Judge John M. Scott, quoted in Ida M. Tarbell, *The Life of Abraham Lincoln*, 2 vols. (New York: Lincoln Memorial Association, 1900), 1:166–67.

59. Robert Gray Gunderson, *The Log-Cabin Campaign* (Lexington: University of Kentucky Press, 1957), 135–36. For a recent study that takes a closer look at Lucy Kenney and the participation of women in Virginia, see Elizabeth R. Varon, "Tippecanoe and Ladies Too: White Women and Party Politics in Antebellum Virginia," *Journal of American History*, 82:2 (September 1995), 494–521.

60. June 19, 1840, quoted in Gunderson, *The Log-Cabin Campaign*, 136.

61. Ibid., 137.

62. Ibid., 139.

63. Ibid., 245–46.

64. Ibid., 137.

65. Ibid., 138.

66. Ibid., 139.

67. Katherine Helm, *The True Story of Mary, Wife of Lincoln* (New York: Harper & Brothers, 1928), 41.

68. The date of Mary's arrival is not certain. She told Herndon: "I Came to Ills in 1837 – was in Illinois 3 Months – went to school two years after I Came to Illinois in Ky. I returned to Ills in 1839 or 40." See Mary Todd Lincoln (WHH interview), [September 1866], *Herndon's Informants*, 359. For her

attractiveness to young gentlemen, see William Jayne to WHH, August 17, 1887, *Herndon's Informants*, 624.

69. Both the invitation and Hardin's accompanying letter are in *Collected Works*, 1:156, 156n.

70. For the story that AL said he wanted to dance with Mary Todd "in the worst way" and her comment to her sister afterward that "he certainly did," see Helm, *The True Story of Mary, Wife of Lincoln*, 74. For Herndon's remark, see WHH to Isaac N. Arnold, October 24, 1883, printed in *A Letter from William H. Herndon to Isaac N. Arnold Relating to Abraham Lincoln, His Wife, and Their Life in Springfield* (n.p.: privately printed, 1937); original in Chicago Historical Society. For Herndon's story of dancing with Mary Todd, see Herndon and Weik, *Herndon's Life of Lincoln*, 166.

71. Elizabeth Todd Edwards (WHH interview), [1865–66], *Herndon's Informants*, 443.

72. Helm, *The True Story of Mary, Wife of Lincoln*, 32.

73. Elizabeth Todd Edwards (WHH interview), [1865–66], *Herndon's Informants*, 443. This paragraph on the affinities of AL and Mary Todd was written before the appearance of David Herbert Donald's fine biography, which makes essentially the same points. See *Lincoln* (New York: Simon & Schuster, 1995), 85.

74. Elizabeth Todd Edwards (WHH interview), [1865–66], *Herndon's Informants*, 443.

75. Ibid.

76. The best guide to Lincoln's whereabouts is *Lincoln Day by Day*, but the duration of his speaking trips is often hard to gauge very precisely. The count given here is thus an estimate.

77. The duration of Mary's visit is, like Lincoln's whereabouts, hard to gauge. The estimate of two to three months is based on the evidence of her letter to Mercy Ann Levering of July 23, 1840, from which she seems to have been in Columbia for more than a few weeks, and James C. Conkling's letter, cited below. Justin G. Turner and Linda Levitt Turner, *Mary Todd Lincoln: Her Life and Letters* (New York: Alfred A. Knopf, 1972), 14–19.

78. Ibid., 16.

79. See, for example, Herndon and Weik, *Herndon's Life of Lincoln*, 167.

80. Turner and Turner, *Mary Todd Lincoln: Her Life and Letters*, 16.

81. Ibid., 18.

82. James C. Conkling to Mercy Ann Levering, September 21, 1840, Carl Sandburg and Paul M. Angle, *Mary Lincoln: Wife and Widow* (New York: Harcourt, Brace, 1932), 172. For information on Levering and Conkling, see "A Story of the Early Days in Springfield – and a Poem," *Journal of the Illinois State Historical Society*, 16 (April–July 1923), 142–46.

83. Sandburg and Angle, *Mary Lincoln: Wife and Widow*, 171.

84. Joshua F. Speed (WHH interview), [1865–66], *Herndon's Informants*, 474.

85. Mary Todd to Mercy Ann Levering, December [15?], 1840, Turner and Turner, *Mary Todd Lincoln: Her Life and Letters*, 21.

86. According to *Lincoln Day by Day*, AL was "still stumping the lower part of state" on September 21 and by September 30 was appearing in court in the central part of the state at Tremont.

87. James C. Conkling to Mercy Ann Levering, September 21, 1840, Sandburg and Angle, *Mary Lincoln: Wife and Widow*, 172.
88. Mary Todd to Mercy Ann Levering, December [15?], 1840, Turner and Turner, *Mary Todd Lincoln: Her Life and Letters*, 22.
89. Joshua F. Speed (WHH interview), [1865–66], *Herndon's Informants*, 474–75.
90. Ibid., 476. For a discussion of the continuity of Speed's testimony, see Douglas L. Wilson, "Abraham Lincoln and 'That Fatal First of January,' " *Lincoln Before Washington*, 101–3.
91. Joshua F. Speed (WHH interview), [1865–66], Wilson and Davis, *Herndon's Informants*, 475.
92. Ibid., 476.
93. For details on Matilda Edwards, see H. O. Knerr, *Abraham Lincoln and Matilda Edwards* (Allentown, Pa.: n.p., n.d.) and J. Bennett Nolan, "Of a Tomb in the Reading Cemetery and the Long Shadow of Abraham Lincoln," *Pennsylvania History*, 19:3 (July 1952: pamphlet version).
94. This calculation is based on the Edwardses' having arrived in Springfield a week early for the legislative session, which began on November 23. For a description of the trip and Matilda's first impressions of Springfield, see the photostat of her November 30 letter to her brother Nelson in the Ruth Painter Randall Papers, Library of Congress, and in the Edwards Family Papers, Knox College Library, Galesburg, Ill.
95. Ibid.
96. Joshua F. Speed (WHH interview), [1865–66], *Herndon's Informants*, 475.
97. David Davis (WHH interview), September 19, 1866, *Herndon's Informants*, 347.
98. Joseph Gillespie, one of Lincoln's "flying brethren," who later became a highly respected judge, wrote out his own account of this incident for Herndon. See Gillespie to WHH, January 31, 1866, *Herndon's Informants*, 187–88.
99. *Illinois State Register*, December 12, 1840, quoted in Paul Simon, *Lincoln's Preparation for Greatness: The Illinois Legislative Years* (Urbana: University of Illinois Press, 1971 [1965]), 229.
100. Ninian W. Edwards (WHH interview), September 22, 1865, *Herndon's Informants*, 133.
101. Elizabeth Todd Edwards (WHH interview), [1865–66], *Herndon's Informants*, 443–44.
102. Even Elizabeth Edwards's husband admitted that his wife's version of the story was mistaken. See Douglas L. Wilson, "Abraham Lincoln and 'That Fatal First of January,' " *Lincoln Before Washington*, 127, n. 25. Note, however, that James H. Matheny, in his old age, told Jesse W. Weik that he had been asked to serve as a groomsman at the wedding that never came off. See Jesse W. Weik, *The Real Lincoln* (Boston: Houghton Mifflin, 1922), 60.
103. James H. Matheny (WHH interview), May 3, 1866, *Herndon's Informants*, 251.
104. Note, however, that Speed did refer to an engagement in other testimony. See Speed to WHH, November 30, 1866, *Herndon's Informants*, 430.
105. *Collected Works*, 1:228–29n.
106. Joshua F. Speed (WHH interview), [1865–66], *Herndon's Informants*, 476.
107. Turner and Turner, *Mary Todd Lincoln: Her Life and Letters*, 20.
108. Ibid., 20–21.

109. Ibid., 22.

110. Horace White, *Life of Lyman Trumbull* (New York: Houghton Mifflin, 1913), 427.

111. For example, Charles B. Strozier: "Lincoln courted [Mary] vigorously and successfully throughout 1839 and 1840." *Lincoln's Quest for Union: Public and Private Meanings* (New York: Basic Books, 1982), 38.

112. David Herbert Donald has recently declared that "those who blamed Matilda Edwards for the rupture seem to have their information from Mary Todd" and that "there is no credible evidence that Lincoln was in love with Matilda Edwards." *Lincoln* (New York: Simon & Schuster, 1995), 612n. The first part would seem to be clearly mistaken, for Speed, Matheny, Browning, Jane D. Bell (see below), and the members of Matilda's family were not solely dependent on Mary Todd for their information. The second part, having to do with the credibility of the evidence, each reader must judge for himself. As we shall see presently, Jane D. Bell was only reporting what she had heard contemporaneously from unnamed sources, but it is difficult to understand why Speed, Matheny, Browning, and the others should all lack credibility.

113. AL to Mrs. M. J. Green, September 22, 1860, *Collected Works*, 4:118.

114. Attributed to Lincoln's friend Jesse K. Dubois, in Milton Hay to John Hay, February 8, 1887, "Recollection of Lincoln: Three Letters of Intimate Friends," *Bulletin of the Abraham Lincoln Association*, 25 (December 1931), 9.

115. See, for example, the testimony of James Gourley, Jesse K. Dubois (*Herndon's Informants*, 453, 692), and Josiah P. Kent (Weik, *The Real Lincoln*, 126), all near neighbors of the Lincolns. Michael Burlingame has documented Mary Todd Lincoln's intemperate outbursts throughout the course of her marriage in *The Inner World of Abraham Lincoln* (Urbana: University of Illinois Press, 1994), 268–355.

116. Quoted in Walter B. Stevens, *A Reporter's Lincoln* (St. Louis: Missouri Historical Society, 1916), 75. This was part of a statement given to Stevens by Albert S. Edwards but is identified as coming from his mother, Elizabeth Todd Edwards, in Helm, *The True Story of Mary, Wife of Lincoln*, 55.

117. Ninian W. Edwards (WHH interview), September 22, 1865, *Herndon's Informants*, 133.

118. Mary Todd Lincoln to Josiah Holland, December 4, 1865, Turner and Turner, *Mary Todd Lincoln: Her Life and Letters*, 293. Not surprisingly, she told Holland that Lincoln had "entirely devoted himself to me, for two years before my marriage."

Chapter 8

1. Cyrus Edwards to Nelson G. Edwards, December [29?], 1840. Edwards Family Collection, Knox College Library. Stamped postmark: "Springfield / Dec 29." Postage: "12." Docketed: "Recd Jan 1841 / Ansd Feby 1st 1841 /Cyrus Edwards" and "Cyrus Edwards / 1840." The postmark is very faint, but under a microscope "Dec 29" can be clearly confirmed as the postmark date. For Lincoln's whereabouts, see *Lincoln Day by Day: A Chronology 1809–1865*, ed. Earl Schenck Miers, 3 vols. (Washington, D.C.: Lincoln Sesquicentennial Commission, 1960), vol. 1, ed. William E. Baringer.

2. Cyrus Edwards could have been writing on Saturday the twenty-sixth and meant that the party would be back in Springfield on Monday the twenty-eighth. But two circumstances strongly suggest that he may have been writing after the twenty-eighth and referring to an expected return of Matilda and Mary the following Monday, January 4. The first is his saying that the women are missed very much, which would be somewhat odd if they had been gone only two days. The other is that the letter was postmarked December 29 and, according to the recipient Nelson Edwards's docketing, was not received in Alton until January.

3. Joshua F. Speed to WHH, November 30, 1866, in Douglas L. Wilson and Rodney O. Davis, eds., *Herndon's Informants: Letters, Interviews, and Statements About Abraham Lincoln* (Urbana: University of Illinois Press, 1997), 431; hereafter cited as *Herndon's Informants*.

4. For the strong evidence collected by Ida M. Tarbell that no such ceremony took place, see Ida M. Tarbell, *The Life of Abraham Lincoln*, 2 vols. (New York: Lincoln Memorial Association, 1900), 1:174–80.

5. Joshua F. Speed to WHH, September 17, 1866, *Herndon's Informants*, 342. This is cited by Charles Strozier, *Lincoln's Quest for Union: Public and Private Meanings* (New York: Basic Books, 1982), 242n. He also cites a notice to this effect that appeared in the *Sangamo Journal* on January 8, 1841. Strozier assumes that the sale meant the end of Lincoln and Speed's sleeping arrangements, but there is no evidence for this. What we do know – that Hurst lived above the store with Speed and Lincoln before the sale – suggests the contrary. See William H. Herndon and Jesse W. Weik, *Herndon's Life of Lincoln*, ed. Paul M. Angle (Cleveland: World Publishing, 1949 [1930]), 150.

6. "Remarks in the Illinois Legislature," January 8, 1841, Roy P. Basler, et al., eds., *The Collected Works of Abraham Lincoln*, 8 vols. (New Brunswick: Rutgers University Press, 1953), 1:226; hereafter cited as *Collected Works*.

7. "Speech in Illinois Legislature Concerning Apportionment," [January 9, 1841?], *Collected Works*, 1:227–28.

8. At least one informant remembered that Mary Todd had turned down Lincoln's proposal of marriage and that "hur refusal to Comply actually Made Mr L. Sick and Consequently went to bed and no one was allowed to see him but his freind Josh Speed & his frend the *Doctor* I think Henry. And that strong Brandy was administered to him freely for about one Week" (A. Y. Ellis to WHH, written at the bottom of WHH's letter to Ellis of March 24, 1866, *Herndon's Informants*, 238).

9. H. W. Thornton to Ida M. Tarbell, December 21, 1895, Tarbell Papers, Allegheny College Library. Tarbell's rendering of this in her biography is slightly different (*The Life of Abraham Lincoln*, 1:180).

10. Orville H. Browning (Nicolay interview), June 17, 1875, Michael Burlingame, ed., *An Oral History of Abraham Lincoln: John G. Nicolay's Interviews and Essays* (Carbondale and Edwardsville: Southern Illinois University Press, 1996), 1–2.

11. Ibid., 1.

12. See Joshua F. Speed to William Butler, Louisville, May 18, 1841: "I am glad to hear from Mrs Butler that Lincoln is on the mend." Butler Papers, Chicago Historical Society.

13. Newspaper clipping apparently from the *St. Louis Globe-Democrat* in 1907,

datelined Kansas City, Missouri, February 9, by Nellie Crandal Sanford (Lincoln files, Illinois State Historical Library). This is an interview with Sarah Rickard Barret, aged eighty-two, and her husband, Richard F. Barret. Some of her recollections are clearly colored by accounts that appeared in published biographies, but much of what she relates seems clearly to be her own version of events. The conversation between her sister and AL is apparently unreported elsewhere.

14. Martinette Hardin to John J. Hardin, January 22, 1841, Chicago Historical Society. Martinette later married Alexander McKee; the labeling on her letter caused the editors of *Collected Works* (1:229n) to attribute these remarks to "Martin McKee."

15. Sarah Hardin to John J. Hardin, January 26, 1841, Chicago Historical Society. Jane Goudy wrote romances, and her brothers, who were printers, put some of them into print. See Douglas L. Wilson, "Abraham Lincoln and 'That Fatal First of January,'" *Lincoln Before Washington: New Perspectives on the Illinois Years* (Urbana: University of Illinois Press, 1997), 130n.

16. *Lincoln Day by Day*, 1:152.

17. *Collected Works*, 1:228.

18. Ibid., 1:229.

19. Jane D. Bell to Ann Bell of Danville, Kentucky, January 27, 1841. This text is taken from a copy of the letter supplied to Professor John B. Clark of Lincoln Memorial University by Mary B. E. (Mrs. Henry) Jackson, a relative of Jane D. Bell's, dated August 25, 1948, and in turn copied and supplied to Professor James G. Randall by R. Gerald McMurtry on November 7, 1950 (Randall Papers, Manuscript Division, Library of Congress). This text varies slightly from the extract printed in the *Lincoln Herald*, 50:4–51:1 (December 1948–February 1949), 47, which omits the final fragment.

20. James C. Conkling to Mercy Ann Levering, January 24, 1841, Carl Sandburg and Paul M. Angle, *Mary Lincoln: Wife and Widow* (New York: Harcourt, Brace, 1932), 178–79.

21. *Some Incidents in the Life of Mrs. Benj. S. Edwards*, ed. M[ary]. E[dwards]. R[aymond]. (n.p.: n.d.), 12–13. This rare piece of ephemera is in the Illinois State Historical Library.

22. Ibid., 13. For her part, Mrs. Benjamin S. Edwards doubted that Lincoln and Mary's really was a love affair, for she told Ida M. Tarbell, "He was deeply in love with Matilda Edwards." Mrs. Benjamin S. Edwards to Ida M. Tarbell, October 8, 1895, Tarbell Papers, Allegheny College Library.

23. Elizabeth Todd Edwards (WHH interview), [1865–66], *Herndon's Informants*, 444.

24. Elizabeth Keckley, *Behind the Scenes* (Buffalo: Stancil and Lee, 1931 [1868]), 233–34.

25. Elizabeth and Ninian W. Edwards (WHH interview), July 27, 1887, *Herndon's Informants*, 623.

26. Harriet Chapman (Weik interview), [1886–87], *Herndon's Informants*, 647.

27. AL to John T. Stuart, January 20, 1841, *Collected Works*, 1:228.

28. AL to John T. Stuart, January 23, 1841, ibid., 1:229–30.

29. See Paul Simon, *Lincoln's Preparation for Greatness: The Illinois Legislative Years* (Urbana: University of Illinois Press, 1971 [1965]), 247.

30. Speed recalled, "Though a member of the legislature he rarely attended its sessions." Joshua F. Speed, *Reminiscences of Abraham Lincoln and Notes of a Visit to California: Two Lectures* (Louisville: John P. Morton, 1884), 39. Lyman Trumbull remembered: "Mr. Lincoln took very little part in the legislation of that session." Horace White, *Life of Lyman Trumbull* (New York: Houghton Mifflin, 1913), 426.

31. James C. Conkling to Mercy Ann Levering, March 7, 1841, Sandburg and Angle, *Mary Lincoln: Wife and Widow*, 178–79.

32. Sarah Hardin to John J. Hardin, January 26, 1841, Chicago Historical Society.

33. Turner R. King (WHH interview), [1865–66], *Herndon's Informants*, 464.

34. Speed told Herndon about this poem in an interview in 1865 (*Herndon's Informants*, 30). When Herndon tried to pin down the date at which the poem was published, Speed was unsure: "My recollection is that the Poem on Suicide was written in the Spring of 1840. or Summer of 1841" (*Herndon's Informants*, 337). Herndon searched for the poem in the *Journal* but couldn't find it and suspected that Lincoln may have cut it out of the file copy (*Herndon's Life of Lincoln*, 172).

35. Speed, *Reminiscences of Abraham Lincoln*, 39.

36. Joshua F. Speed to WHH, February 7, 1866, *Herndon's Informants*, 197. I have here conflated two versions by Speed of the same story: the one he told Herndon and the one in his *Reminiscences of Abraham Lincoln*, 39.

37. Orville H. Browning (Nicolay interview), June 17, 1875, Burlingame, *Oral History of Abraham Lincoln*, 1.

38. Ibid., 2.

39. Ninian W. Edwards (WHH interview), September 22, 1865, *Herndon's Informants*, 133.

40. Elizabeth Todd Edwards (WHH interview), [1865–66], *Herndon's Informants*, 444.

41. Mary Todd to Mercy Levering, June 1841, in Justin G. Turner and Linda Levitt Turner, *Mary Todd Lincoln: Her Life and Letters* (New York: Alfred A. Knopf, 1972), 25, 26.

42. Ibid., 27.

43. Joshua F. Speed to WHH, November 30, 1866, *Herndon's Informants*, 430.

44. "Lincoln & Mary Todd," Herndon-Weik Collection, Library of Congress.

45. From the unsigned introduction to Speed's posthumously published lectures, Speed, *Reminiscences of Abraham Lincoln*, 5–6.

46. Joshua F. Speed to William Butler, May 18, 1841, Butler Papers, Chicago Historical Society.

47. AL to Joshua F. Speed, February 13, 1842, *Collected Works*, 1:269.

48. Those attesting to Speed's pursuit of Matilda Edwards include Mary Todd, Ninian W. Edwards, and Elizabeth Todd Edwards.

49. Elizabeth Todd Edwards (WHH interview), [1865–66], *Herndon's Informants*, 443.

50. AL to Joshua F. Speed, [January 3, 1842?], *Collected Works*, 1:266.

51. Joshua F. Speed to Eliza J. Speed, March 12, 1841, Speed Papers, Illinois State Historical Library.

52. Ibid.

53. See Mary Todd to Mercy Ann Levering, June 1841: "Mr Speed . . . has some

idea of deserting Illinois, his mother is anxious he should superintend her affairs." Turner and Turner, *Mary Todd Lincoln: Her Life and Letters*, 27.

54. AL to John T. Stuart, February 3, 1841, Roy P. Basler, ed., *The Collected Works of Abraham Lincoln: Supplement 1832–1865* (Westport, Conn.: Greenwood Press, 1974), 6.

55. See *Collected Works*, 1:243–44.

56. AL to Joshua F. Speed, June 19, 1841, *Collected Works*, 1:255.

57. Ibid., 1:257–58.

58. "A Story of the Early Days in Springfield – and a Poem," *Journal of the Illinois State Historical Society*, 16 (April–July 1923), 146.

59. AL to Jesse W. Fell, December 20, 1859, *Collected Works*, 3:511.

60. For AL's studying Latin grammar on the circuit, see David Davis (WHH interview), September 20, 1866, *Herndon's Informants*, 350. For his characterizing his education as "defective," see "Brief Autobiography," *Collected Works*, 2:459.

61. AL to Mary Speed, September 27, 1841, *Collected Works*, 1:259–60.

62. Ibid., 1:261.

63. Quoted in Albert J. Beveridge, *Abraham Lincoln 1809–1858*, 2 vols. (Boston: Houghton Mifflin, 1928), 1:320n.

64. AL to Mary Speed, September 27, 1841, *Collected Works*, 1:261.

65. For information about the remarkable Speed family, see Thomas Speed, *Records and Memorials of the Speed Family* (Louisville: Courier-Journal Job Printing, 1892).

66. See Robert L. Kincaid, *Joshua Fry Speed: Lincoln's Most Intimate Friend* (Harrogate, Tenn.: Lincoln Memorial University, 1943), 16.

67. See his remark to Speed in February that he is "clear of hypo since you left [January 1], – even better than I was along in the fall." AL to Joshua F. Speed, February 8, 1842, *Collected Works*, 1:268.

68. Joshua F. Speed to Herndon, November 30, 1866, *Herndon's Informants*, 430.

69. AL to Joshua F. Speed, [January 3, 1842?], *Collected Works*, 1:265.

70. Ibid.

71. Ibid.

72. Ibid., 1:265–66.

73. See William F. Petersen, *Lincoln-Douglas: The Weather as Destiny* (Springfield, Ill.: Charles C. Thomas, 1943), 74–79. According to the records Petersen cites, Lincoln's absence from the legislature in January 1841 coincided almost exactly with a cold spell in which the temperature plunged to twelve degrees below zero.

74. "To Inez," canto 1:ff. 84, *Childe Harold's Pilgrimage, The Poetical Works of Lord Byron*, ed. Ernest Hartley Coleridge (New York: Scribner's, 1905), 158. For Speed's testimony about AL and this poem, see *Herndon's Informants*, 30.

75. Ida M. Tarbell collected testimony that Ninian W. Edwards, the husband of Elizabeth Todd Edwards, was among the many family members who denied his wife's story of an abortive wedding ceremony involving Lincoln and Mary Todd (Tarbell, *Life of Abraham Lincoln*, 1:177).

76. "I will never forget the day that was to have been their wedding day. We all were there – the wedding supper was ready to serve. Mary went up to her room and I went with her to help her dress – she did look pretty – that's a

fact. We waited and waited, but Lincoln did not come. I thought Mary would go wild, she was so angry, then she was so mortified. I thought she would die when we heard the guests leaving the house, and the servants going about putting out the lights. Rising from the bed where she had thrown herself in all her bridal finery, with a tragic air, she bade me leave her, and to put out the lights and there Mary Todd fought out her battle alone." (Quoted in Marietta Holdstock Brown, "A Romance of Lincoln," newspaper clipping, reprinted in "Martinette Hardin McKee Recalls Lincoln and Mary Todd," ed. Michael Burlingame, *Lincoln Herald,* 97:2 (Summer 1995), 72.

Like Elizabeth Todd Edwards, she remembers this as an abortive wedding ceremony, but her recollection may have been colored by the account in Ward Hill Lamon's biography, which was based on Herndon's notes. It seems at least possible that both Martinette Hardin McKee and Elizabeth Todd Edwards could have been recollecting a party organized to announce an engagement at which, though Mary suffered, some or all of the guests remained unaware of the planned announcement that never was made.

77. AL to Joshua F. Speed, [January 3, 1842?], *Collected Works,* 1:266.
78. AL to Joshua F. Speed, February 3, 1842, *Collected Works,* 1:267.
79. Ibid., 1:268.
80. Joshua F. Speed to WHH, November 30, 1866, *Herndon's Informants,* 431.
81. For information on Sarah Rickard and her family, see John Carroll Power, *History of the Early Settlers of Sangamon County, Illinois* (Mount Vernon, Ind.: Windmill Publications, 1991 [1876]), 614, in which her birth is given as March 2, 1824.
82. Sarah Rickard Barret to WHH, August 3, 1888, *Herndon's Informants,* 664.
83. John Lightfoot (WHH interview), September 13, 1887, *Herndon's Informants,* 639.
84. AL to Joshua F. Speed, February 13, 1842, *Collected Works,* 1:269.
85. Ibid., 1:269–70.
86. AL to Joshua F. Speed, February 25, 1842, *Collected Works,* 1:280.
87. Ibid.
88. Ibid.
89. Ibid.
90. Ibid.
91. Ibid., 1:281.
92. Ibid., 1:280.
93. AL to Joshua F. Speed, March 27, 1842, *Collected Works,* 1:282.
94. For a discussion of this question, see Douglas L. Wilson, "Abraham Lincoln and 'That Fatal First of January,'" *Lincoln Before Washington: New Perspectives on the Illinois Years* (Urbana: University of Illinois Press, 1997), 99–132.
95. AL to Joshua F. Speed, March 27, 1842, *Collected Works,* 1:282.
96. Compare Benjamin Thomas, *Abraham Lincoln* (New York: Modern Library, 1968 [1952]), 89; Gary Lee Williams, "James and Joshua Speed: Lincoln's Kentucky Friends," Ph.D. Dissertation, Duke University, 1971 (University Microfilms), 30; and Wilson, "Abraham Lincoln and 'That Fatal First of January,'" *Lincoln Before Washington,* 121–25.
97. AL to Joshua F. Speed, February 13, 1842, *Collected Works,* 1:270.
98. AL to Joshua F. Speed, July 4, 1842, *Collected Works,* 1:288–89.

99. Ibid., 1:289.
100. Mary Todd Lincoln (WHH interview), [September 1866], *Herndon's Informants*, 358.
101. See the draft chapter for the Herndon-Weik biography in the Herndon-Weik Collection (HW4261), cited in *Herndon's Informants*, 358n.
102. Herndon and Weik, *Herndon's Life of Lincoln*, 352.
103. Joseph Gillespie to WHH, December 8, 1866, *Herndon's Informants*, 506.
104. AL to Speed, March 27, 1842, *Collected Works*, 1:282–83.
105. Ibid., "Temperance Address," 1:271.
106. Ibid., 1:272.
107. Ibid.
108. Ibid., 1:273.
109. Ibid., 1:272.
110. Ibid., 1:274.
111. Ibid., 1:277.
112. Ibid., "Address Before the Young Men's Lyceum," 1:115.
113. Ibid., "Temperance Address," 1:279.
114. Mary Todd Lincoln (WHH interview), [September 1866], *Herndon's Informants*, 358.
115. Herndon and Weik, *Herndon's Life of Lincoln*, 206.
116. *Illinois State Register*, March 11, 1843, quoted in *Lincoln Day by Day*, 1:179.
117. *Collected Works*, 1:273.
118. His name appears on a Whig circular dated July 2, 1842. *Collected Works*, 1:287–88.
119. AL to Frederick A. Thomas, April 21, 1842, *Collected Works*, 1:286.
120. *Illinois State Register*, March 25, 1842, quoted in *Lincoln Day by Day*, 179.
121. AL to Joshua F. Speed, July 4, 1842, *Collected Works*, 1:289.
122. II Chronicles 20:17, King James Version.

Chapter 9

1. WHH reported that this episode and the leap from the church window "were two things Mr. Lincoln always seemed willing to forget." He added: "During a visit which I made to the Eastern States in 1858, I was often asked for an account of the so-called duel; so often, in fact, that on my return home I told Mr. Lincoln of it. 'If all the good things I have ever done,' he said regretfully, 'are remembered as long and well as my scrape with Shields, it is plain I shall not soon be forgotten.'" William H. Herndon and Jesse W. Weik, *Herndon's Life of Lincoln*, ed. Paul M. Angle (Cleveland: World Publishing, 1949 [1930]), 183.
2. Herndon and Weik are responsible for the presumptive chronology, which has been universally followed, but they cite no evidence, and none has emerged.
3. Herndon and Weik, *Herndon's Life of Lincoln*, 179.
4. Roy P. Basler, ed., *Abraham Lincoln: His Speeches and Writings* (Cleveland: World Publishing, 1946), 154.
5. Previous Lost Townships letters, which are referred to at the opening of this one, had appeared in the *Journal* four years earlier as an amusing treatment of

the issue of setting off new counties. The editors of Lincoln's *Collected Works* note the stylistic similarities and the dates of the earlier letters. See Roy P. Basler et al., eds., *The Collected Works of Abraham Lincoln*, 8 vols. (New Brunswick: Rutgers University Press, 1953), I:291–92n; hereafter cited as *Collected Works*. Basler is also the author of the best study of the Lost Townships letters, and one must agree with him that *Journal* editor Simeon Francis is a likely candidate for the writer of the first and third letters, those dated August 10 and August 29. The latter is not discussed here (it appeared in the same issue of the *Journal* as the letter dated September 8), but it seems to be in the same style. See Basler, "The Authorship of the 'Rebecca' Letters," *The Abraham Lincoln Quarterly* (June 1942), 88.

6. *Sangamo Journal*, August 19, 1842.

7. Herndon and Weik, *Herndon's Life of Lincoln*, 184.

8. *Collected Works*, 1:292.

9. Ibid., 1:293.

10. Ibid., 1:294.

11. Ibid., 1:295.

12. Ibid., 1:295–96.

13. Whiteside's letter to the editor of *Sangamo Journal*, Herndon and Weik, *Herndon's Life of Lincoln*, 193. The name of the newspaper is mistakenly given as the *Sangamon Journal* throughout *Herndon's Life of Lincoln* but has been corrected in the citations that follow.

14. *Sangamo Journal*, September 9, 1842 (letter dated September 8).

15. Ibid.

16. Ibid., September 16, 1842. These verses are signed "Cathleen."

17. Mary Todd Lincoln to F. B. Carpenter, December 8, 1865, in Justin G. Turner and Linda Levitt Turner, *Mary Todd Lincoln: Her Life and Letters* (New York: Alfred A. Knopf, 1972), 298–99. See also her letter on the same subject two days earlier to Mary Jane Welles, ibid., 295–96.

18. Mary Todd Lincoln's accounts err substantially with regard to the time between the publication of the verses and the duel, the time between the duel and their marriage, and the distance to Tremont (stretching the 50 miles to 150 in one letter and 200 in another). Perhaps most revealingly, she misremembers or misrepresents their brief and long-broken engagement: "We were engaged & greatly attached to each other – two years before we were married." Ibid., 296.

19. Lyman Trumbull to Jesse W. Weik, April 17, 1895, from a copy in the Beveridge Papers, Box 411, Library of Congress.

20. William Jayne (WHH interview), August 15, 1866, in Douglas L. Wilson and Rodney O. Davis, eds., *Herndon's Informants: Letters, Interviews, and Statements About Abraham Lincoln* (Urbana: University of Illinois Press, 1997), 267; hereafter cited as *Herndon's Informants*.

21. William Butler (Nicolay interview), June 13, 1875, in Michael Burlingame, ed., *An Oral History of Abraham Lincoln: John G. Nicolay's Interviews and Essays* (Carbondale and Edwardsville: Southern Illinois University Press, 1996), 24.

22. Ibid.

23. *Collected Works*, 1:299n. The document itself is headed "Elections in Sang-

amon County Illinois, for State Representatives in the years 1832–1834 & 1836–" and appears on pp. 297–98.

24. Ibid., 1:299n.

25. See Albert J. Beveridge, *Abraham Lincoln 1809–1858*, 2 vols. (Boston: Houghton Mifflin, 1928), 1:343–44.

26. Whiteside's letter to the editor of the *Sangamo Journal*, quoted in Herndon and Weik, *Herndon's Life of Lincoln*, 193.

27. Whiteside referred in his account to "either of the articles which appeared in the *Journal*, headed 'Lost Townships,' and signed 'Rebecca,' " suggesting that he had in mind the one written by Lincoln and another one (ibid., 194).

28. Quoted in Merryman's letter to the editor of the *Sangamo Journal*, reprinted in *Collected Works*, 1:299–300n.

29. See Thomas Moore, *Letters and Journals of Lord Byron: With Notices of His Life*, 2 vols. (New York: J. & J. Harper, 1830–31), 1:256–57.

30. I am indebted to Joanne Freeman for help in sorting out the protocols of dueling that Shields and Lincoln were attempting to follow.

31. Quoted in Merryman's letter to the editor of the *Sangamo Journal*, reprinted in *Collected Works*, 1:299.

32. Ibid., 1:300n.

33. Whiteside's letter to the editor of the *Sangamo Journal*, in Herndon and Weik, *Herndon's Life of Lincoln*, 194.

34. *Collected Works*, 1:124–25.

35. Ibid., 1:100.

36. Ibid., 1:211. For other examples of AL's use of the term "set-off," see his letter to Eliza Browning, April 1, 1838: "all my powers of discovery were put to the rack, in search of perfections in her, which might be fairly set-off against her defects." *Collected Works*, 1:118. In a legal affidavit filed in behalf of Isaac Cogdal, petitioning for a new trial, March 7, 1840: "In order that no hardship may be imposed upon the plaintiffs by the granting of a new trial, the defendants propose to admit on the trial that their charges against him are correct, and only insist upon his payments and set offs." Rufus Rockwell Wilson, ed., *The Uncollected Works of Abraham Lincoln*, 2 vols. (Elmira: N.Y.: Primavera Press, 1947–48), 1:514. These are by no means perfect parallels, but they suggest the way in which the idea of a "set-off" had worked its way into AL's thinking.

37. *Illinois State Register*, November 9, 1839.

38. Merryman's letter to the editor of the *Sangamo Journal*, quoted in Herndon and Weik, *Herndon's Life of Lincoln*, 196.

39. Ibid., 201.

40. "Memorandum of Duel Instructions to Elias H. Merryman," *Collected Works*, 1:300–301.

41. Merryman's letter to the editor of the *Sangamo Journal*, quoted in Herndon and Weik, *Herndon's Life of Lincoln*, 200.

42. Editorial in the *Alton Telegraph*, September 24, 1842, quoted in Walter B. Stevens, *A Reporter's Lincoln* (St. Louis: Missouri Historical Society, 1916), 18.

43. "Memorandum of Duel Instructions to Elias H. Merryman," *Collected Works*, 1:301.

44. Lorenzo Sabine, *Notes on Duels and Duelling* (Boston: Crosby, Nichols, 1859), 29.

45. See the description of Robert L. Wilson: "his legs were long, feet large; arms long, longer than any man I ever knew, when standing Straiht, and letting his arms fall down his Sides, the points of his fingers would touch a point lower on his legs by nearly three inches than was usual with other persons." Wilson to WHH, February 1866, *Herndon's Informants,* 201.

46. Joanne Freeman provided the information that duels had been declared lost and the participants considered dishonored because, even for reasons that do not seem discreditable, they had not kept to their "mark."

47. Usher F. Linder, *Reminiscences of the Early Bench and Bar of Illinois* (Chicago: Chicago Legal News, 1879), 66–67.

48. Merryman's letter to the editor of the *Sangamo Journal,* quoted in Herndon and Weik, *Herndon's Life of Lincoln,* 196.

49. Ibid., 201.

50. Ibid.

51. Whiteside's letter to the editor of the *Sangamo Journal,* quoted in ibid., 195.

52. William Butler (Nicolay interview), June 1875, in Burlingame, *Oral History of Abraham Lincoln,* 25.

53. Ibid.

54. Ibid.

55. For information on John J. Hardin, see the article by Theodore C. Pease in the *Dictionary of American Biography,* 8:246. The Hardin family papers at the Chicago Historical Society are an important source of information on the activities of Lincoln's fellow Whigs. Hardin's letters to and from his wife, Sarah, constitute a unique historical treasure. I am grateful to family historian Frederick S. Sherman for information and enlightenment on this classic correspondence and notable American family.

56. John J. Hardin to Sarah Hardin, January 22, 1843, Hardin Papers, Chicago Historical Society.

57. Martinette Hardin to John J. Hardin, January 22, 1841, Hardin Papers, Chicago Historical Society.

58. The wedding date of September 27, 1842, is recorded in the marriage records of the town of Jacksonville.

59. *Lincoln Day by Day: A Chronology 1809–1865,* ed. Earl Schenck Miers, 3 vols. (Washington, D.C.: Lincoln Sesquicentennial Commission, 1960), vol. 1, ed. William E. Baringer, suggests that AL was in Bloomington attending court on September 28, the day after the wedding, which would largely preclude his being in Jacksonville the day before. But having to be in Springfield for the opening of U.S. District Court on October 1, AL would hardly have made such a laborious trip for a single court appearance (no other being recorded). In all likelihood, AL's Bloomington partner, Jesse Fell, appeared for their client. I am grateful to William Beard of the Lincoln Legal Papers project for pertinent information and helpful advice on this point.

60. Marietta Holdstock Brown, "A Romance of Lincoln," a newspaper clipping, is reprinted in "Martinette Hardin McKee Recalls Lincoln and Mary Todd," ed. Michael Burlingame, *Lincoln Herald,* 97:2 (Summer 1995), 72. Burlingame reports the clipping has been attributed to "Indianapolis, Jan. 1896" by the Lincoln Museum at Fort Wayne, Ind.

61. See, for example, Sarah E. Hardin to John J. Hardin, January 26 [1841], Hardin Papers, Chicago Historical Society.

62. From an interview with Sarah Rickard Barret and her husband, Richard F. Barret, reported by Nellie Crandall Sanford for the *St. Louis Globe-Democrat.* A clipping of this article, datelined Kansas City, Missouri, February 9, without heading or page number but dated in pencil 1907, is in the files of the Lincoln Collection, Illinois State Historical Library. In this account, Martinette's name is given as "Nellie," a mistake for her nickname, Nettie.

63. *Chicago Times-Herald,* September 8, 1895, 40. I am grateful to Michael Burlingame for transcriptions of the 1895 *Times-Herald* interviews.

64. Brown was born in 1834 and was living in Kentucky in 1842. See Wayne C. Temple, ed., *Lincoln as Seen by C. C. Brown* (Prairie Village, Kan.: Crabtree Press, 1963), 5.

65. Mrs. John T. Stuart (Tarbell interview), n.d., Tarbell Papers, Allegheny College Library. Tarbell's notes reflect her aural error in hearing the name "Hardin" as "Helden."

66. AL to Joshua F. Speed, October 5, 1842, *Collected Works,* 1:302–3.

67. Ibid., 1:303.

68. Ibid.

69. Ibid., July 4, 1842, 1:288–89.

70. "Lincoln and Mary Todd," Herndon-Weik Collection, Library of Congress.

71. Joshua F. Speed (WHH interview), *Herndon's Informants,* 475.

72. James H. Matheny (WHH interview), May 3, 1866, *Herndon's Informants,* 251.

73. This comes out in a later part of the same interview: "Matheny further Says that soon after the race – the political friendly race between Baker & Lincoln – which was in 1846 or 7 and after Lincoln was Married that Lincoln took him – Matheny to the woods and there and then Said in reference to L's marriage *in the Aristocracy* – 'Jim – I am now and always shall be the same Abe Lincoln that I always was –'" Lincoln Said this with great Emphasis – The cause of this was that in the Baker & Lincoln race it had been charged that L had married in the aristocracy – had marrid in the Edwards – Todd & Stuart family." *Herndon's Informants,* 251.

74. Orville H. Browning (Nicolay interview), June 17, 1875, Burlingame, *Oral History of Abraham Lincoln,* 2. The words "a mistake" do not appear in the manuscript and are presumed to have been inadvertently dropped.

75. See AL to Speed, February 25, 1842, *Collected Works,* 1:280.

76. There is abundant testimony that the couple met at the Francis home prior to the marriage. The present account differs from previous accounts on this point only in the matter of timing. The evidence presented here indicates that AL did not renew his courtship with Mary Todd until after the encounter in Jacksonville in late September, so the secret meetings at the Francis house so often referred to must have occurred thereafter.

77. Mrs. Benjamin S. Edwards (Tarbell interview), Tarbell Papers, Allegheny College Library.

78. Elizabeth Todd Edwards (WHH interview), [1865–66], *Herndon's Informants,* 444.

79. Mrs. Benjamin S. Edwards (Tarbell interview), Tarbell Papers, Allegheny College Library.

80. Frances Wallace (Tarbell interview), Tarbell Papers, Allegheny College Library.

81. Quoted in Beveridge, *Abraham Lincoln*, 1:355. For the variation Herndon collected, see Herndon and Weik, *Herndon's Life of Lincoln*, 180n. For Salome Butler's recollection, see Eugenia Jones Hunt, "My Personal Recollections of Abraham Lincoln and Mary Todd Lincoln," *Abraham Lincoln Quarterly*, 3 (March 1945), 238.

82. Thomas Moore, *Letters and Journals of Lord Byron: With Notices of His Life*, 2 vols. (New York: J. & J. Harper, 1830–31), 2:307. For Lincoln's affinity for *Don Juan*, see James H. Matheny (WHH interview), [1865–66], *Herndon's Informants*, 470. For Herndon's testimony through an unidentified informant that Lincoln often read their office copy of *Don Juan*, see David J. Harkness and R. Gerald McMurtry, eds., *Lincoln's Favorite Poets* (Knoxville: University of Tennessee Press, 1959), 40.

83. John T. Stuart (WHH interview), [1865–66], *Herndon's Informants*, 64.

84. AL to Samuel D. Marshall, November 11, 1842, *Collected Works*, 1:305.

Chapter 10

1. *Don Juan*, canto 15:99.1–4. Weik, who was in charge of compiling the manuscript in its final form, ignored several pleas by Herndon to use these lines. See WHH letters to Weik dated July 16, 1888, August 31, 1888, and February 5, 1889, Herndon-Weik Collection, Library of Congress.

2. Green Taylor (WHH interview), September 16, 1865, in Douglas L. Wilson and Rodney O. Davis, eds., *Herndon's Informants: Letters, Interviews, and Statements About Abraham Lincoln* (Urbana: University of Illinois Press, 1997), 130; hereafter cited as *Herndon's Informants*.

3. Nathaniel Grigsby to WHH, October 1865, *Herndon's Informants*, 140.

4. Roy P. Basler et al., eds., *The Collected Works of Abraham Lincoln*, 8 vols. (New Brunswick: Rutgers University Press, 1953), 3:6; hereafter cited as *Collected Works*.

5. See Nicole Etcheson, "Manliness and the Political Culture of the Old Northwest, 1790–1860," *Journal of the Early Republic*, 15 (Spring 1995), 59–77.

6. Nathaniel Grigsby convinced WHH that Jones was AL's "guide & teacher in Politics." Nathaniel Grigsby (WHH interview), September 16, 1865, *Herndon's Informants*, 127.

7. Dennis F. Hanks (WHH interview), September 8, 1865, *Herndon's Informants*, 103, 105.

8. See Dennis F. Hanks to WHH, March 12, 1866, and September 10, 1866, *Herndon's Informants*, 229, 337.

9. Although it seems likely that AL would have started out with the same political persuasion as his father, one well-placed witness believed AL's father was not a Democrat. See John Hanks (WHH interview), [1865–66], *Herndon's Informants*, 457.

10. Etcheson, "Manliness and the Political Culture of the Old Northwest," 67.

11. Walter B. Stevens, *A Reporter's Lincoln* (St. Louis: Missouri Historical Society, 1916), 7–8.

12. Johnson Gaines Greene (WHH interview), October 5, 1866, *Herndon's Informants*, 366.

13. James H. Matheny (WHH interview), November 1866, *Herndon's Informants*, 431.

14. For a full account of this incident and the evidence for Lincoln's authorship, see Douglas L. Wilson, "Abraham Lincoln Versus Peter Cartwright," in *Lincoln Before Washington: New Perspectives on the Illinois Years* (Urbana: University of Illinois Press, 1997), 55–73.

15. For a text of both Cartwright's and Lincoln's letters, as well as further details of the incident, see ibid.

16. *Rev. Peter Cartwright's Letter*. [Rock Spring, 1834]. See Cecil K. Byrd, *A Bibliography of Illinois Imprints 1814–58* (Chicago: University of Chicago Press, 1996), #245. For further information, see Wilson, "Abraham Lincoln Versus Peter Cartwright," *Lincoln Before Washington*, 72n.

17. Wilson, "Abraham Lincoln versus Peter Cartwright," *Lincoln Before Washington*, 61.

18. Ibid., 62.

19. Ibid., 62–63.

20. Caleb Carman to William H. Herndon, November 30, 1866, *Herndon's Informants*, 430.

21. *Beardstown Chronicle and Illinois Military Bounty Land Advertiser*, 2:19 (November 1, 1834), 1. The text is reprinted in Wilson, "Abraham Lincoln Versus Peter Cartwright," *Lincoln Before Washington*, 63–66.

22. *Beardstown Chronicle*, 4. For reasons for thinking that Lincoln, rather than Hill, was the writer of this letter, see Wilson, "Abraham Lincoln Versus Peter Cartwright," *Lincoln Before Washington*, 66–70.

23. *Beardstown Chronicle*, 1; reprinted in Wilson, "Abraham Lincoln Versus Peter Cartwright," *Lincoln Before Washington*, 64. Some textual anomalies have been corrected.

24. For a detailed critique of Lincoln's unfairness to Cartwright, see Robert Bray, " 'The Power to Hurt': Lincoln's Early Use of Satire and Invective," *Journal of the Abraham Lincoln Association*, 16:1 (Winter 1995), 43–51.

25. *Illinois State Register*, November 9, 1839, quoted in Albert J. Beveridge, *Abraham Lincoln 1809–1865*, 2 vols. (Boston: Houghton Mifflin, 1928), 1:304.

26. For an account of this episode, see Beveridge, *Abraham Lincoln*, 1:302–4.

27. Bray, " 'The Power to Hurt': Lincoln's Early Use of Satire and Invective."

28. *William Shakespeare: The Complete Works*, ed. Alfred Harbage (New York: Viking Press, 1984), 1468. Lincoln's use of the phrase "the power to hurt" is from "Speech in U.S. House of Representatives on the Presidential Question," July 27, 1848, *Collected Works*, 1:509.

29. "Memorandum of Duel Instructions to Elias H. Merryman," *Collected Works*, 1:300–1.

30. Mary Owens Vineyard to WHH, July 22, 1866, *Herndon's Informants*, 262.

31. Ibid., 262.

32. Nathaniel Grigsby (WHH interview), September 12, 1865, *Herndon's Informants*, 112.

33. Mathilda Johnston Moore (WHH interview), September 8, 1865, *Herndon's Informants*, 109.

34. Nathaniel Grigsby (WHH interview), September 12, 1865, *Herndon's Informants*, 112.

35. Joshua F. Speed, *Reminiscences of Abraham Lincoln and Notes on a Visit to California: Two Lectures* (Louisville: John P. Morton, 1884), 26.

36. John Hanks (WHH interview), June 13, 1865, *Herndon's Informants*, 45.

37. William G. Greene to WHH (interview), May 30, 1865, *Herndon's Informants*, 19.

38. Rev. George J. Barrett (WHH interview), [1865–66], *Herndon's Informants*, 436.

39. AL to Mary Speed, September 27, 1841, *Collected Works*, 1:260.

40. AL to Joshua F. Speed, August 24, 1855, *Collected Works*, 2:320.

41. For another animal story from the 1850s, see J. D. Wickizer to WHH, November 25, 1866, *Herndon's Informants*, 423–24.

42. AL to Joshua F. Speed, March 27, July 4, 1842, *Collected Works*, 1:282, 289.

43. AL to Joshua F. Speed, July 4, 1842, *Collected Works*, 1:289.

44. Orville H. Browning (Nicolay interview), June 17, 1875, in Michael Burlingame, ed., *An Oral History of Abraham Lincoln: John G. Nicolay's Interviews and Essays* (Carbondale and Edwardsville: Southern Illinois University Press, 1996), 6–7.

45. Michael Burlingame, *The Inner World of Abraham Lincoln* (Urbana: University of Illinois Press, 1994), 236–67.

46. Elizabeth Todd Edwards (WHH interview), [1865–66], *Herndon's Informants*, 443.

47. Joshua F. Speed to WHH, February 7, 1866, *Herndon's Informants*, 197. I have here conflated two versions by Speed of the same story: the one he told WHH and the one in his *Reminiscences of Abraham Lincoln*, 39.

48. WHH to Francis E. Abbot, February 18, 1870, in *The Index*, 1 (April 2, 1870), 5.

49. For example, see Rev. James Reed's public lecture, published as "The Later Life and Religious Sentiments of Abraham Lincoln," *Scribner's Monthly* (July 1873), 333–43.

50. For the testimony of a number of Lincoln's friends on this point, see William H. Herndon and Jesse W. Weik, *Herndon's Life of Lincoln*, ed. Paul M. Angle (Cleveland: World Publishing, 1949 [1930]), 356–60.

51. James H. Matheny (WHH interview), [by March 2, 1870], *Herndon's Informants*, 576.

52. Albert T. Bledsoe, review of W. H. Lamon's *Life of Abraham Lincoln* in *The Southern Review* (April 1873), reprinted in Rufus Rockwell Wilson, ed., *Lincoln Among His Friends: A Sheaf of Intimate Memories* (Caldwell, Ida.: Caxton Printers, 1942), 483–84.

53. Joshua F. Speed to WHH, December 6, 1866, *Herndon's Informants*, 498–99.

54. Speed reported that he told Lincoln in the White House, "If you have recovered from your skepticism, I am sorry to say that I have not." *Reminiscences of Abraham Lincoln*, 32.

55. Thomas Moore, *Letters and Journals of Lord Byron: With Notices of His Life*, 2 vols. (New York: J. & J. Harper, 1830–31), 1:254.

56. "Handbill Replying to Charges of Infidelity," July 31, 1846, *Collected Works*, 1:382.

57. It is also instructive for the terms in which he frames the issue of fatalism – "that the human mind is impelled to action, or held in rest by some power, over which the mind itself has no control" – and for its indication of the period at which he claims to have left off arguing about it.

58. James H. Matheny (WHH interview), March 6, 1870, *Herndon's Informants*, 577.

59. See Rev. James Smith to WHH, January 24, 1867, *Herndon's Informants*, 547–50.

60. See his testimony as quoted in J. G. Holland, *The Life of Abraham Lincoln* (Springfield, Mass.: Gurdon Bill, 1866), 236–41; and in Newton Bateman (WHH interview), [1865–66], and Newton Bateman to WHH, March 8, 1869, *Herndon's Informants*, 436, 572.

61. "Communication to the People of Sangamon County," March 9, 1832, *Collected Works*, 1:8–9; see A. Y. Ellis to WHH, January 23, 1866, *Herndon's Informants*, 171.

62. *Collected Works*, 1:48.

63. Stevens, *A Reporter's Lincoln*, 8.

64. See Harry E. Pratt, "Lincoln and the Division of Sangamon County," *Journal of the Illinois State Historical Society*, 47 (Winter 1954): 398–409.

65. AL to William Butler, January 26, 1839, *Collected Works*, 1:139.

66. AL to William Butler, February 1, 1839, *Collected Works*, 1:141.

67. Thomas Ford, *A History of Illinois from Its Commencement as a State in 1818 to 1847*, ed. Rodney O. Davis (Urbana and Chicago: University of Illinois Press, 1995), 127.

68. See the interview with William G. Greene: "He got the soubriquet of 'Honest Abe' by refusing to act as judge at horse races unless he was left free to decide the question fairly, and not according to the jockeying tactics then in vogue." *The Weekly Inter Ocean* (Chicago) April 21, 1881, by G. A. Pierce. Clipping in the Nicolay and Hay Collection, Illinois State Historical Library. I am grateful to Michael Burlingame for pointing out this source. See also Speed, *Reminiscences of Abraham Lincoln*, p. 20.

69. From WHH's first lecture on AL, "Analysis of the Character of Abraham Lincoln," *Abraham Lincoln Quarterly*, 1:7 (September 1941), 376.

70. Wilson, *Lincoln Among His Friends*, 489.

71. Burlingame, *Oral History of Abraham Lincoln*, 39.

72. Samuel C. Parks to WHH, March 25, 1866, *Herndon's Informants*, 238.

73. For further testimony evidencing AL's ineffectiveness, see the section "Law Practice" in the index of *Herndon's Informants*.

74. Wilson, *Lincoln Among His Friends*, 479.

75. Coleman Smoot to WHH, May 7, 1866, *Herndon's Informants*, 253–54.

76. Speed, *Reminiscences of Abraham Lincoln*, 34.

77. Mary O. Vineyard to WHH, May 23, 1866, *Herndon's Informants*, 256.

78. James C. Conkling to Mercy Levering, January 24, 1841, in Carl Sandburg and Paul M. Angle, *Mary Lincoln: Wife and Widow* (New York: Harcourt, Brace, 1932), 179.

79. AL to Joshua F. Speed, February 25, 1842, *Collected Works*, 1:280.

80. Joshua F. Speed (WHH interview), [1865], *Herndon's Informants*, 30.
81. AL to Joshua F. Speed, February 3, 1842, *Collected Works*, 1:268.
82. In telling a story of Lincoln's compassionate treatment of soldiers and their families, Speed observed that this was "the fruit of the flower we saw bloom in the incident of the birds" (*Reminiscences of Abraham Lincoln*, 28).
83. AL to Joshua F. Speed, February 25, 1842, *Collected Works*, 1:280.
84. AL to Martin S. Morris, March 20, 1843, *Collected Works*, 1:320.
85. James H. Matheny (WHH interview), May 3, 1866, *Herndon's Informants*, 251.
86. Dr. A. W. French, *Chicago Times-Herald* (Aug. 25, 1895), 25. I am indebted to Michael Burlingame for generously sharing transcriptions of the 1895 *Times-Herald* interviews.
87. David Davis (WHH interview), September 20, 1866, *Herndon's Informants*, 351.
88. AL to Isham Reavis, November 5, 1855, *Collected Works*, 2:327.
89. Mary Todd Lincoln (WHH interview), [September 1866], *Herndon's Informants*, 360, 358.

Acknowledgments

THIS BOOK owes its inception to Lydia Wills, who first suggested the possibility of a work based on the documents I was then helping to edit. Without her initiative and resourcefulness, the book would never have been launched. To my partner in the editorial project and many other ventures, Rodney O. Davis, it owes more than I can ever properly acknowledge. Without his coaching over the years and constant encouragement, this work would not have been attempted. The dedication names the person to whom I owe most of all and without whom the book could never have been completed.

Research is often thought to be a solitary endeavor, but those who engage in it know better. Research would be worthwhile if its only product were the delight of working with people who are willing to make one's dilemmas and difficulties their own. It is a privilege to acknowledge some of the libraries and other repositories this project has taken me to and some of the many people who have offered assistance. Knox College Library: Jeff Douglas, Irene Ponce, Carley Robison, Terry Wilson; Library of Congress: Clark Evans, James Gilreath, Oliver Orr, John R. Sellers, Mary Wolfskill; Illinois State Historical Library: Kim Bauer, Janice A. Petterchak, Cheryl Schnirring, Thomas F. Schwartz; Huntington Library: Virginia Renner, John Rhodehamel, Martin Ridge, Robert Skotheim, Paul M. Zall; Illinois Historical Survey: John Hoffman; Brown University Library: Jennifer Lee; Filson Club: James Holmberg; Massachusetts Historical Society: Peter Drummey; American Antiquarian Society: Marcus McCorrison; Lincoln Legal Papers:

Cullom Davis, William Beard; Lincoln Boyhood Home: Jerry Sanders; Chicago Historical Society: Archie Motley; Allegheny College Library: Margaret Moser, Connie Thorson.

For their willingness to discuss the problems of Lincoln research and interpretation and otherwise share their expertise, I am grateful to Gabor Boritt, Robert Bray, Roger Bridges, Richard N. Current, Robert Gray Gunderson, James T. Hickey, James Hurt, Robert W. Johannsen, George L. Painter, Merrill D. Peterson, John Y. Simon, Wayne C. Temple, C. E. Van Norman, Paul H. Verduin, John E. Walsh, and Garry Wills.

I am indebted to the several people who have been kind enough to read parts of this work in draft: Joseph J. Ellis, Joanne Freeman, Michael L. Johnson, David McCullough, Thomas F. Schwartz, and Richard S. Taylor. Rodney O. Davis and Terence A. Tanner, as only friends can do, went the whole hog. Michael Burlingame not only read and commented on the entire draft but generously shared the results of his own prodigious research.

It has been my good fortune during the course of this project to have been associated with two supportive institutions: Knox College and the Thomas Jefferson Memorial Foundation. The Knox College Faculty Research Fund was a perennial source of travel support, and the Huntington Library fellowship program provided two timely research grants. It is a special pleasure to acknowledge the generosity of John E. and Elaine Fellowes, whose endowed fund supports the scholarly and creative activities of the Knox College English department. It remains only to thank Jennifer Bernstein and Tina Bonnett, and to acknowledge the role of my editor at Alfred A. Knopf, Ashbel Green, for whose patience and support I am deeply grateful.

Index

Abbot, Francis, 81

Abell, Bennett, 61, 111, 130, 133

Abell, Elizabeth, 97, 111–12, 120; and AL's courtship of Mary Owens, 129–39

abolitionists, 165–6

Abraham Lincoln Association, 47

Adams, Gen. James: controversy with AL, 174–9, 186, 194, 195, 235, 277, 302

Adams, John, 294

Adams, John Quincy, 59, 297

Aesop's Fables, 55

Alexander, 196

Allen, Bob, 286

Allen, Dr. John, 61–2, 69, 71

Alley, Nelson, 95

Anderson, Joseph, 174, 175, 178

Anderson, Mary, 174

Anderson, Richard, 174

Anderson, William G., 277–8

Angle, Paul M., 12, 13, 114, 119, 326

Arenz, Francis, 128, 300

Armstrong, Duff, 31

Armstrong, Hannah, 33, 48, 71, 97, 111

Armstrong, Hugh, 149, 151, 314

Armstrong, Jack, 68, 111, 298, 328; wrestle with AL, 15, 19–51, 301–2

Armstrong, Jack (son), 35

Arnold, Isaac N., 39–40, 41, 42, 45, 50, 338

Baker, Edward D., 49, 174, 200, 210, 211, 262, 263

Baldwin, John, 91

Bale, Esther Summers (Mrs. Hardin), 118

Bale, Hardin, 72, 81, 82, 100

Barclay, James, *Dictionary*, 55

Barret, Richard F., 357, 365

Barret, Sarah Rickard, 357, 365; *see also* Rickard, Sarah

Barrett, Dr., 150–1

Barrett, Rev. George J., 306

Barton, William E., 43–4, 46

Basler, Roy P., 362

Bateman, Newton, 312

Beard, William, 364

Beardstown Canal, 99, 126, 127, 149, 154

Beardstown Chronicle, 300

Bell, Elizabeth Herndon, 96, 110, 332

Bell, James, 237

Bell, Jane D., 237, 355, 357

Benton, Sen. Thomas Hart, 144

Berry, William, 91–3

betting: on AL-Armstrong wrestle, 20, 23, 24, 34, 35, 36–7, 39; on AL-Thompson wrestle, 30

Beveridge, Albert J., 202; on Herndon's reliability, 12; biography of AL, 46–7, 273

Bible, 4, 55, 83, 309; AL's reading of, 73, 84; AL's critique of, 81–3

Bissell, William, 235

Black, Chauncey F., 38–9, 43, 44, 310

Black Hawk War, 6, 10, 19, 20, 29–30, 48–9, 66, 89–90, 91, 93, 100, 116, 142, 147, 152, 184, 283, 305

Blackstone, Sir William: AL's study of, 73, 104, 105, 107; *Commentaries on the Laws of England*, 104, 106

Blankenship, E. C., 91, 163

A Note About the Author

DOUGLAS L. WILSON was educated at Doane College and the University of Pennsylvania. He taught English and American literature from 1961 to 1994 at Knox College in Galesburg, Illinois, where he also served for many years as Director of the Library. Since 1994, he has been Saunders Director of the International Center for Jefferson Studies at Monticello in Charlottesville, Virginia, and Scholar in Residence at the University of Virginia. Wilson has written extensively on Thomas Jefferson and on the prepresidential life of Abraham Lincoln; his essays on these subjects have appeared in such periodicals as *The Atlantic Monthly, American Heritage, William & Mary Quarterly,* and *Civil War History.*

A Note on the Type

This book was set in a modern adaptation of a type designed by the first William Caslon (1692–1766). The Caslon face, an artistic, easily read type, has enjoyed over two centuries of popularity in our own country. It is of interest to note that the first copies of the Declaration of Independence and the first paper currency distributed to the citizens of the newborn nation were printed in this typeface.

Composed by Creative Graphics,
Allentown, Pennsylvania
Printed and bound by R. R. Donnelley & Sons,
Harrisonburg, Virginia
Designed by Anthea Lingeman